ADVENTURES
IN BIRD PROTECTION

An Autobiography by

THOMAS GILBERT PEARSON

President Emeritus of the National Association of Audubon Societies

With an introduction by

FRANK M. CHAPMAN

Curator of Ornithology, American Museum of Natural History

ILLUSTRATED

D. APPLETON-CENTURY COMPANY
INCORPORATED
NEW YORK   1937   LONDON

T. Gilbert Pearson

ADVENTURES IN
BIRD PROTECTION

TO

MY WIFE
ELSIE WEATHERLY PEARSON
Kindly critic, indulgent
friend and priceless co-worker

FOREWORD

THIS BOOK treats of many events in our Nation's history during that considerable span of years when men's thoughts were turning from the pioneer's attitude of destroying wild life to the present widespread desire for its preservation.

In these pages, also, there is told something of the experiences of a man who, working with the Audubon Society movement, was privileged to take some part in the struggles that have brought about this reformation.

T. G. P.

CONTENTS

CONTENTS

ILLUSTRATIONS

INTRODUCTION

IN THE YEAR 1901, William Dutcher, Chairman of the
Committee on Bird Protection of the American Ornithologists' Union, read a little book entitled *Stories of
Bird Life* by T. Gilbert Pearson, then teaching in the State
Normal and Industrial College at Greensboro, North Carolina. On December 17th of that year he wrote to its author
asking his aid in securing the passage of bird-protective laws
in North Carolina and in forming an Audubon Society in
that State.

Pearson's response is recorded in the following pages. It
marks the beginning of an association that opened new
horizons to him and was of inestimable importance to the
cause of bird conservation.

After three active, effective years in the South, Pearson was
called north by Mr. Dutcher for closer coöperation, and on
January 30, 1905, the National Association of Audubon Societies was organized with T. Gilbert Pearson as Secretary.
From that date forward Pearson was so closely associated with
the growth and work of this Association that the autobiography of one is virtually the history of the other. And, it may
be added, he has told his story without that emphasis on the
Ego which is the self-biographer's due. In it we find recorded
not only the growth of an individual, but the development
of public sentiment as it finds expression in law.

Then followed five extremely active years as Dutcher, who
was more or less confined by private business affairs, sent his
young aid here, there, and everywhere to interview individuals, attend conferences, make addresses before conventions,
or appear at legislative hearings. At the end of this time

Mr. Dutcher was removed by a tragic illness, and his protegé was left to carry on his work as the Executive Secretary and, later, President of the National Association.

Building on the foundation already laid by his predecessor, to the strength of which he pays just and generous tribute, Pearson, during the succeeding quarter of a century, erected a structure the proportions and endowment of which far exceed those of any other similar institution in the world. In addition, he has stimulated interest in organized bird protection in more than a score of foreign countries.

To an inherent love of birds and a born teacher's ease of presentation, Pearson added an eloquence that, for a man of Quaker parentage is apparently to be credited to his Southern environment. But whatever its origin, his trained gift of persuasive speech, whether addressed to lawbreakers, lawmakers, or potential patrons, has secured legal rights for Citizen Bird, placed the Audubon Society on a firm financial standing, and made Gilbert Pearson the leading bird conserver of his generation.

And in spite of his herein confessed inability to master the rules of English grammar, he has acquired such control over the English language that his readers will find themselves both beguiled and informed.

FRANK M. CHAPMAN

American Museum of Natural History

ADVENTURES IN
BIRD PROTECTION

ADVENTURES IN
BIRD PROTECTION

CHAPTER I

IN THE PINEY WOODS

THE BLAST of a locomotive sounded so loudly through the open pine woods that it must have echoed among the scattered live-oaks of Blue Pete Lake, a mile away. The train slowed and came to a grinding, jolting stop at Baukman's wood-rack. The fireman and a Negro brakeman began to throw split pine into the tender as the engineer lowered the spout of a wooden water-tank standing beside the track and connected its canvas nozzle with the engine.

I slid off my seat and hurried to the car door.

"Just a minute, Sonny," said the conductor. "We haven't come to Archer yet."

It had seemed to me that we never would get there. A thousand miles was a long way to travel by accommodation trains in 1882. It had taken us three days to make the journey.

In time, the engine, pulling its baggage-car and two day coaches, moved forward a few hundred yards, and we stepped out into the sand near a station the platform of which was used only for handling baggage and freight. Mr. William Lipsey, adorned with scanty whiskers and wearing a white suit, met us with a welcoming smile. We got into the surrey, Father, Mother, my sister Elizabeth, and I. Mr. Lipsey picked up the reins.

"The colored man will bring your baggage in the wagon," he said.

1

The town lay spread out all about us. Twelve or fifteen houses, stores and sheds could be seen scattered at irregular intervals. They had been built with no thought of orderly arrangement. A hog with her young pigs was lying in the road. She declined to move, so we drove around her. The loose sand was deep, and the horse walked slowly. The road passed between two fields enclosed by high rail fences. In each field was a house with chinaberry trees, a scuppernong-grape arbor, and some orange trees.

"These orange trees are just coming into bearing," Mr. Lipsey remarked pleasantly.

We entered the pine lands, where the trees were a hundred feet in height with the limbs mostly clustered near the top. There was no underbrush, and we could see for a great distance through the woods.

Soon we came to the Lipsey home. In the yard, flanked on both sides by newly planted orange-trees, grew bushes of crêpe myrtle and oleander and a single Spanish bayonet. We entered through the gate of the picket fence and approached the veranda where Mrs. Lipsey with her three children greeted us.

"Well, well, it is good to see some one from Indiana again," she said heartily. "Sit right down. I have some orange-juice all ready for you, but there is no ice in this country," she added, "although we have heard they are making it by steam some places."

"We have come to Florida to get away from ice," my father said. "I hope that I shall not see any more ice and slush."

"Not very likely, it's mostly sunshine and gentle breezes down here," said Mr. Lipsey. "As I wrote thee, it is the most wonderful country in the world. We are just now opening it up, and you have come at the right time to get in on the ground floor. There are only two other Northern families in this part of the country, although others will soon be coming. Land is cheap. Negro labor costs from forty to seventy-five cents a day, and everybody who plants orange trees now is going to be rich in ten years. Here are some new circulars just printed telling about the real-estate bargains in Alachua County.

"There, there, William," said his wife reprovingly, "the folks haven't got their things off yet and thee is already talking to them about orange-groves."

"It is very interesting to me," smiled Father. "I am glad to find out about the country. I have said good-by forever to the North, and, as Samuel said, 'Here I raise my Ebenezer.' "

The Lipsey boys were both barefoot, and I begged my mother to let me take off my shoes and stockings.

"January 21st is pretty early in the year to go without shoes," she said, "but this is Florida, and it certainly is warm."

I sat down and pulled off my new, brass-toed boots, then dashed down the steps and started across the lawn. The moment I stepped on the grass the bottoms of my feet seemed to be pricked in a hundred places, and with a howl I sat down, only to burst into louder shrieks as additional pains assailed me. Mr. Lipsey carried me to the veranda. He laid me face down and the families gathered around to render first aid. It was my initial experience with Florida sand spurs.

These are my memories of occurrences the day we reached Archer and the substance of some of the conversations that I recall.

My father arranged before long to purchase an area of woodland on which to build our home and start an orange-grove. Searching the neighborhood for a house in which to live for a time, he found that the only one available was built of logs. It had two large rooms, each with a fireplace, and a six-teen-foot covered dog-trot between. At the rear was a kitchen made of planks. My mother and sister were not pleased with living in what they called a "log cabin," and I heard Mother say to a neighbor that the only reason she had been willing to give up her comfortable home in Dublin, Indiana, was because the doctor told Father that he could no longer live in that climate.

I was delighted with the log house. It suggested Indians and bears. My father said that he guessed this was due to the pioneer blood in my veins and he told me that my Pearson ancestors had been pioneers ever since the first one came to this country and settled with William Penn at Philadelphia. When there came to be too many people in Pennsylvania to suit his descendants they migrated to North Carolina and afterward went West in covered wagons. My father as a little boy had lived in a log house in the Ohio wilderness, although I had been born in an Illinois town called Tuscola, where my family had lived for a short time.

It was not long before the sound of axes was echoing through the woods. Negroes, happy and glistening in the sunlight, were felling the towering long-leaf pines. There was no market for timber, so the logs were burned. At night I could see against the northern sky the dull red glow from the flaming log piles. My brother Charlie, who was twenty-six, had also come to Archer and he, too, was clearing away trees for an orange-grove.

In time our house was built and covered with shingles, riven with a frow from blocks of pine and finished with a drawing-knife. My father did the shingling, pulling up to the roof small groups of shingles I tied to the end of a rope. Acres of budded orange trees were set out and a few slender water-oaks were planted in the yard for shade trees. In the fields rows of corn, peanuts, upland rice and sweet potatoes began to appear. When my other sisters, Susan and Elfleda, arrived from Indiana, the Pearson family moved into the new house, odorous with yellow pine, and began a new life with high hopes of building its fortune.

Mr. Charles Bauknight, the chief citizen of the community, gave the use of his buggy shed for a neighborhood school.

Our teacher had all the pupils take part in a spelling-match every Friday afternoon. One day in my spelling book I noticed a strange combination of letters. There were two E's followed by an L. I asked the teacher if that was a word. "Yes," she said, "that is eel, a kind of fish." A few minutes later as the sixteen pupils stood in line along the wall she gave the word, "eel," and to a girl who could not spell it. The next tried, but failed, so did the third. The word was passed on down the line. I stood next to the foot of the class dancing with excitement until the teacher indicated that it was now my turn. Instantly I yelled, "E double L, E double L," and started running up the line. My exultation of spirit was brief, but the merriment of the class did not subside as quickly.

Several families from the mid-western states moved to Archer during the next two years. Nearly all of these were members of the Society of Friends and although they attended the Union services in the one church building of the community they longed for the Quaker services, to which they had been accustomed. At length it was decided to ask the White-water Quarterly Meeting of Friends at Richmond, Indiana, to authorize the establishment of a meeting here. This request was granted and at the first business-meeting only my father and mother could serve as clerks as they were the only adults in Archer who belonged to White-water Quarter. I also held a birthright membership and was rather proud of the fact.

So it came about that on April 5, 1884, there was established the first Monthly Meeting of Friends in Florida, about fifty grown people and children being present. My father helped haul logs to the saw-mill to have them cut into lumber, and he and other men donated their time to build a meeting-house in the construction of which the money expended probably did not exceed two hundred dollars. From that time on Sabbath School, First Day and Fourth

Day meetings were held regularly. All children had to study the Bible. I must have memorized a thousand texts of scripture.

Each winter some Friends minister would come from Indiana and hold "protracted meetings." Every night we would go to the meeting-house and hear impressive accounts of the folly of evil doing. Rallying hymns of a stirring nature would be sung by the congregation and those desiring to seek a better life were invited to come forward. Each day the neighborhood learned who had been converted the night before or what back-slider had been "redeemed." There was much concern felt for Miss Minnie Snavely, whose unwillingness to take the necessary spiritual step was generally attributed to her love for dancing, this sinful taste having been acquired before she came to live at Archer. At these meetings, also, many of the parents would wrestle in spirit in their efforts to acquire sanctification which was a second or higher experience not to be expected of most Christians.

There were four distinct groups of people in the neighborhood of Archer in those days. One consisted of the Bauknights, Flemings and Winecoffs, who had come from South Carolina. They were the most prosperous. They owned the stores, had nice homes, kept servants and were supposed to have money in the bank at Gainesville. Closely allied to them, in my mind, were certain planters—farmers their detractors called them. They had cultivated lands, china orange-groves and owned many cattle that roamed the pine lands and prairies. They seemed to live about Shell Pond, Micanopy, and in the Wacahoota region. Now and then they held a tournament on Priest Prairie where they ran their horses and with lances sought to catch a ring that was suspended from a cross-arm nailed to a pole. I was told that the men looked fine as they rode with bright sashes about their waists and long feathers in their hats, but that sometimes they got drunk after the tournament was over. A Quaker neighbor from Iowa, who called himself an "abolitionist," said these people were "the pitiful remnants of a decadent slave-owning aristocracy crushed by the brave Union armies seventeen years ago."

The first time I was taken to Priest Prairie I saw the pole with its cross-arm and fresh tracks beneath it where horses recently had run. The very spot seemed romantic to me. A fine-mannered old Negro said that a day or two before, the place had been used for a "gander pulling." A live goose had been suspended by its legs from the cross-arm. Its head and neck, from which the feathers had been removed, were greased with lard, and riders dashing by one at a time would seize the goose by the neck and endeavor to pull it from its support. The colored man told me that the gander pullers were not gentlemen, but were "pore cracker trash."

I came to know many of the "pore whites" and ate grits, corn-bread and white salt pork in their homes. Their language contained many quaint words. From them I heard much about hunting deer, bears and panthers in Gulf Hammock and the Suwanee River swamps. One night I went alligator-hunting with two of them. By means of a dark lantern strapped to his head one of the men would shine a reptile's eyes, fire a load of buckshot into its head, sever the spinal cord at its neck with a hatchet to keep its tail quiet, and haul the 'gator into the boat. Sometimes I helped both men get a large one out of the water. They were killed for their hides and teeth. It was one of these piney woods crackers, Pot-likker Johnson, who gave me my first lesson in playing checkers.

Another group of people at Archer was composed of families who were moving in from the Middle West, and were known as "Yankees." Then there were the Negroes, who out-numbered all the other classes three to one. They worked for the white people, cultivated small patches of land, and on Saturdays came to the cash and barter stores to trade cotton, eggs, sweet potatoes, and other produce for groceries, tobacco and cloth.

As money crops many people raised truck and shipped it to Northern cities. The vegetables grown for this purpose were mainly cucumbers, beans, and tomatoes. Sometimes the shipments paid well, but often the New York Commission merchants would report that the prices secured were only just enough to pay the express charges. News about all returns was quickly passed about the neighborhood. One evening when a neighbor dropped in to discuss the latest returns, he said that William Lipsey had just learned in Jacksonville that it was thought Northern people might develop an appetite for shaddocks. This was the first time I ever heard of people seriously eating grape-fruit.

There was a great deal of hunting. Nearly every man carried a gun when he came to town or traveled about the country. We would sometimes see six or more pale, lanky white men with wide-brimmed slouch hats riding together along the road, each with a gun across the front of his saddle. Often on Saturday nights there was much shooting, frequently mingled with the sound of running horses, hilarious hunting calls and rebel yells as some of the crackers made their way home after an evening in the saloons. Boys had guns before they were strong enough to hold them out and aim. People killed any wild bird or animal on which they were willing to waste a shot.

One of the first persons I heard speak against killing a bird was old Aunt Celie, whose cabin was in a cotton-field at Blue Pete. She said to me, "Honey, when you gits big enough to tote a gun don't never kill nary a mockin' bird. Every one of them little fowls takes kyer of some good man or woman what's daid, and when you hear one asingin' at night you knows dat some good soul done come back and is walkin' about. A sperit kaint never leave its grave lessen its mockin' bird hollers for it to come out."

I was twelve when Morgan Martin came to Florida. He had a .38 caliber Winchester rifle and nothing particular to occupy his time, so he often wandered about the country shooting at ducks, blue jays, bullfrogs, or any other wild creature he happened to find. He was seven years older than I, and I followed him around whenever he would let me. There was always the chance that one of his bullets might hit some creature which I could then examine at close quarters. In the yard he melted lead and poured it, a little at a time, into his bullet mold. It was wonderful to watch him reload his cartridge shells even though he would not let me help him.

One day when I was walking behind him across a recently plowed field, he stopped and pointed to what he said was a killdeer's egg lying in a little depression of the ground. He picked it up and carried it home. With a small steel drill he made a hole in one side and with a brass blow-pipe inserted in his mouth, blew out the contents. He told me he was going to make a collection of birds' eggs. The sight of that spotted egg fired my imagination. I, too, would collect eggs.

When Morge would allow me I accompanied him on his egg-hunts, and often I went alone, but without having the slightest idea of where any bird made its nest, or of what the names were of those I found. Morge knew very little of these subjects, but for every grain of information I gained from him, such as where to write for a blow-pipe and drill, the names of the few birds he knew, where a nest of a given species might be found, I paid him—paid him in eggs. Late in the month, he and Altie L. Quaintance planned to go to Horse Hammock, five miles away, to get eggs in a heron "rookery." I pleaded to be allowed to accompany them. Morge scornfully said that I could not keep up in the long walk, that the place was filled with snakes and alligators, and that anyway the morass was too deep for a boy of my

age. Earnestly I begged and contended that there might be
some nests in the shallow water near the shore which I
could reach, and if I found any I would give nearly all of
them to him. In the end he yielded.

Every incident of that day, April 27, 1886, is written in-
delibly upon my mind. The experiences were so wonderful
that I wanted to tell the world about them, and with the aid
of the druggist's wife I wrote the next year an account of
the trip, which, after a delay of some months, was published
in the *Oologist*, for January, 1888. The article contained such
significant sentences as these: "We prepared to wade, for we
had no boat—while the terrified herons quacked and flapped
over our heads," and again, "After gathering all the eggs we
could conveniently carry away we started for home." Among
the spoils of the day were eggs of the water turkey and five
species of herons and egrets. The article concluded: "That
night we slept peacefully to dream of herons, egrets, etc."

With the coming of summer Morgan Martin departed,
but left behind him two zealous bird-egg collectors.

One day early in 1887 my father permitted me to take
Snip and the buckboard and drive to Gainesville, fifteen
miles away, where I attended to a few errands for my mother.
At noon I went to the first public dining-room I had ever
entered. It bore the name, GOOD SAMARITAN RESTAURANT.
There was only one other diner. He sat across the table from
me. He was perhaps ten years my senior, was carefully attired, and had the confident bearing of an experienced man
of the world. I watched his nice way of eating and especially
observed that he took his soup from the side of his spoon.
I had not been much impressed with my teaching that this
was the proper way to use a soup spoon, but after observing
him for a time I became an ardent advocate of such a custom. It was usual in my neighborhood to speak to strangers
and try to make them feel at home in our country. So at
length I engaged him in conversation. He said very little

but smiled as I described birds and nests that I had found. He left the table without expressing any special interest in what I had said. This did not particularly disturb me as people seldom responded to my enthusiasm about birds.

I went to see Hovey Bell, a boy of my acquaintance. While talking with him, the man whom I had seen at the restaurant came in smoking a cigarette. After delivering some messages, he departed. I told Hovey that I had seen him in the restaurant and said I supposed he was a city man from somewhere. Hovey then told me that his name was Frank M. Chapman, that he was from New York and knew a great deal about birds.

I was amazed. I had never heard of Mr. Chapman, but the fact that he was a man who knew the names of birds greatly excited me, and I rushed out trying to find him. Disappointed in my quest I wrote him the next day hoping that I might get to see him again, but many years elapsed before I was to experience that pleasure.

Our common interest drew Altie and me together and when the next March, after Morge left Archer, we startled a ground-dove from her two eggs on a decaying pine stump, our fervor for collecting flamed anew. Chores about the house were shirked whenever possible and school duties became an abomination. We hunted eggs singly and we hunted them together. We exchanged eggs with each other and with collectors in other states, whose names we found in the *Oologist*. We talked of eggs and dreamed about them. We gathered eggs and blew them. We admired each other's eggs and quarreled about eggs. For months our lives were absorbed in the subject of eggs, while our fathers grumbled and our mothers prayed for us.

One day Father put me to work plowing near the house. The furrows were about one hundred yards long and ended at the rail fence. Over in the piney woods I heard a sparrow-hawk calling. Father was not in sight, so tying the horse to the fence with one of the rope lines, I went in search of the bird. It led me some distance to a deadening. Here many pine stubs contained old nesting-holes of the flicker. Sparrow-hawks laid their eggs in such cavities, so with a club I pounded on the base of the first one and then another of these dead trees hoping to frighten the hidden female from her nest. The search was unsuccessful, and after half an hour I returned to find Father guiding the plow which old Snip slowly pulled along. I hid in a pine sapling thicket and did not approach the house until darkness and hunger drove me in to face my father's displeasure.

For a long time neither Altie nor I had a bird-book, nor any money with which to buy one. I pored over the names of the birds in Lattin's catalogue of eggs, and merely by their names tried to identify the birds of the neighborhood. Altie had bought this catalogue from Morge for fifteen cents and, after finding he could get another free by writing for it, he traded it to me for eleven alligator eggs. Among the many birds which puzzled us was the kingfisher, which we in time decided was the "hoopoe" because of a picture we saw in a dictionary.

Our zeal was soon to lead us into trouble. One day at school I told Altie of a red-headed woodpecker's nest I had found the day before, and at the noon recess we went to examine it. In a slick, hard pine-stump ten or twelve feet from the ground I pointed out a newly made hole as evidence of the accuracy of my observation. I boosted him as high as I could and he climbed the rest of the way. To get the eggs it was necessary that the hole be enlarged so that a hand and wrist could enter. With the broken blade of a pocket-knife he cut and whittled away at the hard wood until the strain of holding on to the snag became too great and he slid to the ground. He boosted me up and I worked on the hole. Our labors resulted in finding one white egg.

As we neared the school-house in the edge of the piney

woods we saw no children playing in the yard and everything was still. This meant that school recess was over. With scratched wrists, flushed faces and moist, matted hair we took our seats. It was generally understood that we had probably been egg-hunting and our coming in late caused many eyes to shift expectantly from us to the teacher. Nor were their owners to remain long in suspense, nor be disappointed with what transpired. The teacher, a tall, raw-boned man at once announced he would make good his promise of two days before to punish the next boys who were "wilfully late." Before the entire school of perhaps thirty pupils he then and there proceeded to whip us soundly. I never did care for that teacher. One day, when as usual I had been unable to answer some simple question in grammar, he announced, "Gilbert is the most stupid boy I have ever seen. He doesn't know the difference between an adjective and a transitive verb." I did not question the truthfulness of the assertion, but very much resented the tone in which he made the announcement.

At three o'clock every day there was a fifteen-minute recess. With bruised backs and rebellious hearts Altie and I held a council of war and agreed we would go away and hunt eggs in peace. Our fathers were not at home and our mothers' wishes were disregarded. Securing such miscellaneous food as was available in the two kitchens, we fared forth. I also carried an old quilt at which Altie sneered and said that I must be a dude to want bedclothes when going on a camping-trip.

We kindled our fire that night in the woods by Levy Lake, eleven miles from home. Frogs by the thousands croaked in the darkness and barred owls came to the trees overhead and peered and hooted endlessly. Altie did not mind sharing my quilt with me I recall.

What a glorious experience it was to awaken in the forest the next morning! Redbirds began whistling with the first streaks of dawn and the morning chorus quickly swelled to a multitude of avian voices, virtually all of which were unknown to us.

We could hardly wait for the fire to heat the water for our tea, so impatient were we to be out watching the birds, hunting for nests and trying to name them from Lattin's catalogue. Skimming over the lake were numerous swallows. We found a water-logged boat which we bailed out and used in searching for their nests in the bushes along the shore. Altie was frankly skeptical about our chance of finding swallows' eggs in such a place, saying that he had heard some one say that up North the swallows build their nests in barns. I maintained that if there were no nests in the bushes we surely would find them along the tall reeds for I had seen the birds alighting there.

Returning from our unsuccessful quest on the lake we parted company for a time, Altie to hunt to the southward while I went northward through the hammock of magnolia, oak and palmetto.

Perhaps an hour after we separated I saw a turkey buzzard fly from the top of a large hollow oak stump about fourteen feet high. There might be eggs in there. I found a small fallen tree much decayed, but with a few fragments of limbs still attached. Hoisting this against the old stump I soon gained the top. Its shell was thin but very hard and was much like a gigantic cylinder set on end. Balancing on the jagged edge, I laboriously raised my improvised ladder and let it down inside. I had descended only a short distance when the support broke and with the upper end of the pole I was precipitated to the bottom of the cavity. The eggs were there—two beautifully spotted vulture eggs. I thrilled at their beauty and gloated over my find. But try as I might I could not get out of that hollow stump, and there I should probably have remained, as Allan Quatermain thought he should remain in the cave with King Solomon's jewels, if

Altie, after long searching, had not come within hearing of my tin whistle.

For three days we stayed away and then, starved-out, wended our way homeward one hot afternoon, exultant but not without apprehension of what might be awaiting our return. We had secured a few eggs, had learned a few more facts about the habits of birds, and I was suffering from a blinding headache.

I had saved my money as long as I could remember in order that some day I might buy a gun. My dream was realized when I was thirteen, and I promptly shot a grackle of which I was so proud that I took it with me when I went to bed. It proved to be covered with parasites which promptly swarmed over the bed, filling me with discomfort and my mother with dismay.

The next day the bird's body gave unmistakable indications that its removal from the house had become desirable. Reluctantly I buried it, but not until I had cut off the wings. These I tacked against the wall in my room where I could see them when I awoke in the morning. In a few days they disappeared. On the spot they had occupied nothing was left but holes where the tacks had been driven. Later I discovered them adorning one of my sister's hats.

I loaded my own shells and was saving with shot and powder. Now and then Mother gave me a few hen's eggs to trade at the store for ammunition, and sometimes I made a dime carrying notes for my sisters' beaux. Father for a time helped out by joining the neighborhood campaign against mockingbirds and woodpeckers, and gave me three cents apiece for all I killed. Woodpeckers destroyed corn when in the milk and mockingbirds pecked grapes. I was told that perhaps I could make more money at Arredonda or Kanapaha shooting robins in the strawberry fields, but these places were too far to reach on foot and the horse was always busy. The gun was my proudest possession. After the egg-laying season was over, I could, with its use, still give play to a pioneer boy's natural love for hunting and also satisfy my vaguely formed desires for intimate contact with birds.

I heard much talk of the "cash money" to be made by selling aigrettes. Hunting up Thomas Brown, I learned where the egret "flats" might be shipped and sold. Those of the large egret bearing from forty to fifty aigrette sprays were worth ninety cents. The scalps from the backs of the snowy egret would bring one dollar and twenty-five cents. I had never handled an egret and was not sure that I knew what an egret plume looked like. This is why, after a long bright day spent in Horse Prairie, during which a cold wind blew incessantly and my head ached bitterly, I came home with the skin from the back of a little blue heron in the white phase of plumage. It was only upon receiving an answer from a New York firm, to which I had mailed it, that I learned it bore no plumes and therefore was worthless to the feather trade.

It was one night some time after this when lying in the hammock on the veranda planning the future that a great idea took form in my mind. It came as an inspiration born of my experience and desires. The more I thought of it the more practical the plan seemed and my spirits began to soar. Dropping one foot to the floor to be able to push the hammock I was soon swaying to and fro with constantly increasing exhilaration.

"Stop making the hammock squeak," called my father, for I had broken one of the evening house rules when he was reading.

"Come in now and learn thy Sabbath-School lesson," added Mother a moment later.

As I entered the room Father laid down the *American Friend* he had been reading and handed Mother her Bible.

Both rocking-chairs were occupied, so with dangling feet I sat on a stool chair while Mother read about the Philistines overcoming the Hebrews in a battle, and how a man from the tribe of Benjamin ran to the city to tell Eli that his two sons, Hophni and Phinehas, had been killed. This finished, I had to repeat the golden text several times. Then Father read some commentaries from *Josephus*, "Profane History," he called it, looking over his glasses from time to time to assure himself that neither Mother nor I was missing any of the interesting points. Prayers followed as usual.

Through all this my mind was dancing with the scheme I was developing and as soon as escape was possible I hurried through the darkness over to the Quaintances and whistled Altie out of the house. I wanted his opinion and agreement. Swiftly I unfolded my plan. It was this: When we became men we would have a natural-history store in Gainesville, the county-seat, and sell birds' eggs. We must be partners so while one was out collecting, the other could attend to the trade over the counter. He thought the idea contained merit and said that we must also learn to mount birds and collect sea-shells for he thought that a brisk trade in these articles might be developed among the people of the town. We did not overlook the wealth to be acquired from buying egret plumes from the crackers and selling them at a handsome profit. As we talked our prospective business grew, and in our minds we had amassed a fortune, largely at the expense of birds yet unhatched, when his father called him in to bed and I went home.

As egg-collectors, Altie and I had started right, that is, all our eggs were in sets and with each a carefully filled-in "data blank" was always preserved. In our days afield we learned many things about birds. For example, we early discovered that when eggs are taken the bird soon produces another setting. I watched a sparrow-hawk's nest, from which the eggs had been removed, and found that another set was laid in nineteen days. I took these and in just nineteen days more a third clutch had been deposited. One spring I robbed a pair of red-headed woodpeckers four times, whereupon the birds built a fifth nest in a tree so high that I could not climb to it. In a few weeks a family of young woodpeckers with grayish-brown heads emerged from the cavity. A kind-hearted lady from the North once said to us: "Oh, you ought not to take all of the eggs you find in the nest. Let the poor bird keep some of them, so she can raise some young." She meant well, but, of course, she did not know that usually more harm is done by taking one or two eggs from a nest than by taking all of them.

The exchanging of eggs with other collectors required money with which to pay postage on the cigar-boxes in which we mailed them.

Although food was always abundant in our homes, and we were about as well off as most of the people we knew, there was little money in either household. To get funds for buying stamps I picked and sold wild blackberries at three cents a quart, when I could get a buyer for my product. At one time I arranged with Negro boys to trap quail and bring them to me for three cents apiece. I dressed and sold them about the neighborhood for five cents each. My profits were not large, for after selling about thirty of them the market became glutted. I tried working in a store for fifty cents a week and my dinners, but soon gave up the position. Then I hired to the blacksmith for three dollars a week. I liked this better, especially because the blacksmith promised to let me off two or three days a week when the season for egg-laying should begin.

The business section of Archer at this time consisted of four small general-merchandise stores, one drug-store, three saloons, a blacksmith shop, and on Saturdays a butcher shop. One cow a week, driven in off the range, supplied the neighborhood with fresh meat. My father bought beef every week, paying for it four and one-quarter cents a pound.

The first real bereavement of my life came when Altie went away to school and began laying the foundation for scholarship which was to make him one of America's most thorough and useful entomologists. The next spring I hunted eggs alone through the woods and fields about Archer.

I now suffered from the lack of companionship. There was now no one with whom I could talk about birds. I could not find anybody who knew, or even cared to know, how it was that young nighthawks, too small to fly or walk, might be found a hundred yards from the spot where they had lain a few hours before; why some coveys of quail, when startled by a hawk, broke into cries, but as a rule did not do this when frightened by a man or a dog; why two bald eagles dropping from a great height came within twenty feet of our barn and then arose without alighting; or the name of the bird that made deep croaks as it flew over the house on summer nights.

Not only was there no one interested in the subject that absorbed my life, but virtually everybody in the neighborhood pitied my parents for having a son who wasted his time and who was utterly worthless as a pupil or as a field-hand. I lived in a world to myself. Either I was unbalanced or everybody else was stupid.

The local educational facilities had greatly improved. We now used a large one-room school-house instead of Bauknight's buggy shed, and there was a bell on the roof. Sometimes, but not often, we had the same teacher throughout the whole term. Every year we started in with our studies about where we had begun the year before and went over the same subjects, using the same textbooks. One winter after the teacher was asked to leave because he could not manage the big boys, the county superintendent sent a man of a type I had not seen before. He was quiet and self-possessed in man-

ner and with grace and elegance that were most charming.
He was very kind to me and I read sympathy and understanding in his face. We were told that he was a graduate of
Purdue University. By the end of the first day I worshiped
him, and that evening at home I moved about and spoke
with a quietness that must have surprised my parents. I became desperately anxious to please him and for the first time
in my life I wanted to learn from books. I began to review
my grammar in a vain attempt to learn by self-teaching those
things which I should have known long before. After two
weeks he announced that he was going to leave, saying that
the school was a little different from what he had expected
to find and that he thought his duties lay elsewhere.

I was heart-broken at the thought that the very next morning there would go out of my life the most inspiring man I
had ever known. After supper I went to tell him and his
equally wonderful wife good-by. With me I took a ghastly
photograph of myself and six or eight complete clutches of
my choicest eggs and told him they were presents for him.
He must have been surprised and a little puzzled but tact-
fully he expressed his thanks, whereupon with swimming
eyes I made a hasty exit. Next morning I went to the station,
and keeping out of sight behind the corner of a box-car I
sadly watched my idols board the train and depart.

The spirits about the old hammock on the porch now sang
new songs to me in the moonlight. I must become an educated
man and learn to speak, walk, and act like that perfect gentleman. I spoke to my father about getting educated. He said
that the acquiring of an education was a splendid occupation
for any boy, and he reminded me that he had been trying to
impress me with that idea for some years.

"There is at least one thing thee can do," he added, "and
that is read good books."

My mind revolted at the suggestion. I thought of all the
books in the house, *Josephus, Talmadge's Sermons, The Siege*

of Jerusalem, Commentaries on the Scriptures, Gospel Hymns 1, 2, 3, and 4, and a dozen others of a similar nature. I did not want good books, my parents and neighbors read that kind of literature, and just look what it did for them. I wanted books that would make me like the wonderful teacher who had gone away, and I said so flatly.

The next day Father said, "Thee might read to advantage the lives of great men, such as Washington and Jefferson."

"But where can I get them?" I asked.

"I expect John T. Flemming has some books and may let thee borrow them," he mused.

Quickly I put the saddle on old Snip and galloped down to Flemming's store. Throwing the bridle rein over the hitching rack, I entered. Mr. Flemming, in seersucker coat, was standing outside the counter talking with three bearded men lounging on nail kegs. Waiting until there was a lull in the conversation, I said, with an assumed show of confidence, "Mr. Flemming, can you let me have the lives of Washington and Jefferson?"

For a moment he stared at me and then replied, "I'll give you the life of Span Wood, if you want it," at which his three visitors laughed loudly.

Span Wood was a worthless old Negro who loitered around the neighborhood. Snip carried me home empty handed.

I had heard that in life sometimes great fortune comes to one unexpectedly. It seemed that this had happened to me when one day out of the North there came a letter from a man who offered to buy all the birds' eggs I could collect the following spring, paying me one-third the price Lattin asked for eggs in his catalogue. In the hammock I read it over and over. This might mean college; at least it would mean culture-making books—many of them!

How I did hunt eggs that spring! Twenty-six sets of sparrow hawks' eggs I took and smaller numbers of shrikes, brown-headed nuthatches and screech owls. I raided another heron colony and collected three sets of turkey buzzards' eggs. One of the nests was in a hollow log, the other two were in small limestone caves. Every egg I could possily find I gathered and when the season was over found that I was to get about sixty-five dollars for my labors. Copying the man's address from the well-worn letter, I wrote him that I was ready to ship my specimens. In a few days his reply came, briefly stating that his plans had changed and he did not want the eggs.

The long hot summer with its gnats and mosquitoes, and rainy season followed, and in the autumn I went to the schoolhouse and again began the same lessons from the same old books. I was determined to get something useful from my eggs and wrote many letters with this in view. The Century Company did not have any second-hand books to exchange for birds' eggs, I learned, and a rich man, whose name I saw in a newspaper, did not reply. Perhaps he had no books to trade or maybe he had all the birds' eggs he needed.

In the end I made a very fortunate bargain. For all the eggs that were duplicates to my collection I received a copy of Coues', *Key to North American Birds*. This was my first bird-book. I have it now. On the fly-leaf is written the date of its arrival—January 16, 1891. It contained the first colored picture of a bird that I had ever seen. It was an illustration of a domestic pigeon, lying on its back with its stomach widely opened, like that of the unfortunate Zodiac man shown on the front page of the almanac hanging in Mother's kitchen.

That summer during Altie's vacation we bought for twenty-five cents a pamphlet on the *Art of Taxidermy* and learned after a fashion to mount birds. Soon I began writing to various schools and colleges offering my eggs and mounted birds for one term's schooling. I wanted especially to go to Earlham College, Indiana. My mother and brother both had been students there in the days when times were better. For a long time no encouraging replies came and then one evening a letter arrived from President Lyndon L. Hobbs, of Guilford College, North Carolina, stating that the College would accept my collection and give me in exchange my board and tuition for *two years,* if, as I had the time I also would collect and mount birds for the College Cabinet. That night the old hammock rocked and rocked but its squeaking brought no parental reproof.

CHAPTER II

AMABAT

IN THE YEAR 1891 the fall session of Guilford College opened on August 19th. A few days later I descended from the train at the Guilford Station carrying a telescope valise in one hand and a violin-case in the other. I had spent two days and nights in day coaches, lumbering along on accommodation trains and eating my meals, of fried chicken, pickles, bread, and jam, brought from home in a basket.

The college hack met the train, but there were not enough seats for all who had arrived, so two other boys and I set out to walk to the College. The road led straight away between fields and through second-growth woods. We passed a few small houses and in an opening in the trees I saw a log tobacco barn. Rain had been falling and the road was one continuous, sticky mass of the reddest mud that I had ever seen. Down the slopes rills of yellow water ran in the wheel-ruts, and on the sides of the road the ground was unbelievably slick. Having been accustomed to a sandy soil and a flat country I made progress with difficulty and three or four times my feet suddenly deserted me.

I was greatly interested in the numerous fragments of quartz and other rocks exposed on the banks of the roadside. I had never seen such rocks and thought that they must be very rare and valuable, so I filled my pockets with them. The letter from the President had said that I was to work to increase the "Cabinet," and I felt sure that these beautiful stones must have escaped the eyes of the less observant persons who hitherto had traversed this road. A mile from the railroad, we reached the College and I presented myself to Professor Perisho, Governor of the boys and Master of Archdale Hall. Very kindly, and quite seriously he acceded to my request that I be allowed to keep the rocks in my room for a time before placing them in the museum, and he suggested that I scrape the mud from my clothing, as it would not be long until dinner-time.

A little later the boys were lined up on the walk, and in double column we marched to the dining-room in Founder's Hall, a hundred yards away. The girls were already at their chairs when we entered. After a minute of silent grace we took our seats. A teacher at the head of each table filled and passed the plates. Then nine pairs of eager eyes watched her serve her own plate, and the moment she lifted her fork, nine other forks instantly went into action.

In the room were gathered about sixty young people, being something more than one-half of the total enrolment of the school. Many of them were from Quaker homes in North Carolina, two or three were from Virginia, and one callow youth was from far-off Florida. Nearly every boy had a girl as an "opposite." Such engagements were made for the school term. Some couples talked in an animated manner, others ate in silence. As I looked around the room I thought that I had never seen such a plain, uninteresting lot of people. The girls, especially, seemed to have an unfair share of homeliness. I mentioned this to one of the boys, who said, "Just wait until they get on their Sunday clothes." At First Day meeting I realized how much I had been in error.

It required two years of preparatory work and four years in college for a student to take all the studies that were offered at Guilford. After one of the teachers had examined my qualifications, I was assigned to the first-year preparatory class, which was the lowest in the institution. Second-hand books were secured and I began the training which I fondly thought would ere long make me like that wonderful teacher, who, for two short weeks, had taught our school at Archer.

One of the courses assigned to me was Latin Grammar. I hadn't the slightest conception of what the teacher and pupils were talking about, for I knew nothing of the meaning of such words as noun, verb, adjective, conjugation, and case. I would leave the class each day with my mind in a hopeless maze. The other students all seemed to possess much fundamental knowledge, of which I was totally ignorant. The class was taught by President Hobbs, a man of learning, tact, and forbearance. Sensing something of my bewilderment he did not call on me to recite for several days, but one morning, like a bolt out of the blue, he said:

"Gilbert, in the verb 'amo' what is the third person singular of the imperfect tense?" To which, at a venture, I replied, "amot."

"But, I asked for the imperfect case," he corrected.

"Oh," I apologized, "the imperfect; why that is 'amas.'"

Very quietly, he asked, "Gilbert, does thee play baseball?" That was something that I could answer with assurance, so I said "Yes."

He asked, "Is thee a good batter?" With becoming modesty, I admitted that I was not very good with the bat.

"Then," he said, slowly and impressively, "thee is an imperfect batter. 'Amabat' is the correct answer to my question. Does thee think thee can remember that?" I hastened to assure him that I thought I could—and I have.

However, President Hobbs evidently considered my case hopeless, for a few days later he told me to drop Latin and to begin English Grammar. This was crushing. I had thought that I left behind me in Florida that awful subject, and here at Guilford I must face it again. Before a class of pupils all younger than myself, there would be demonstrated my total ignorance of the subject as well as my hopeless inability to comprehend anything concerning it.

Various boys and girls had heard me declaim at length on the wonders of life in Florida, and had given me flattering attention while I told of encounters with water-moccasins and alligators, of camping in wild regions to collect eggs of birds, the names of which they had never heard, of climbing gigantic slash-pines to eagles' nests more than one hundred and thirty feet from the ground, of catching a ten-pound bass, and of a hair-raising but bloodless encounter with a Negro desperado. And now day after day before these same people I was certain to fail on recitation in the grammar class while young fellows from the farms, who had never taken a long railroad journey, who had never seen a palm tree, and who didn't even know the color of a nuthatch's egg, would glibly answer questions to the entire satisfaction of the teacher.

As I sat in my room and gloomily anticipated my first appearance in the grammar class next day my mind dwelt with bitterness on the fact that a girl who sat at our table in the dining-room would daily be a witness to my shame. She had manifested interest in my accounts of adventure and sympathy had shone in her eyes when I had exhibited the scar of a snake bite on my hand and the marks left on my wrist by an irate alligator. What would she think of me? Oh, Alas!

A week later, when we were leaving the class-room, she said to me, "Don't worry about that old grammar; you know a lot of other things that I don't know." And I remembered Whittier's little heroine who "spelled the word" one winter's day.

I had discovered, while in Florida, that with a little application I could memorize rules if they contained a slight suggestion of rhythm. I can still recite with ease some of the rules of syntax that I learned at Archer: "Verbs must agree with the subject in person and number." "Coördinate conjunctions join similar elements." "Subordinate conjunctions join dissimilar elements." But even yet, the meaning of these impressive declarations is obscure to me.

There were four red brick buildings at Guilford, also a few small cottages where some of the students lived and did their own cooking. There was a farm, the products of which came fresh to the table. The ample campus was shaded with magnificent oak, gum, tulip, and hickory trees. The College had an Endowment Fund of $40,000.

In Archdale Hall every room was furnished for two students. We cut the firewood for our stoves, also pumped and carried our own water. There was a bathroom in the building with a sizable tub, and the boys could build a fire and heat water whenever they wished.

In my room at night I found it very difficult to concentrate on the preparations of my lessons. My mind wandered constantly from the printed page. I would suddenly feel the need of a drink of water, or would leave my chair to close or raise a window. I would read again the last letter from my mother, or ask my room-mate which his parents owned, a buggy or a buckboard. I was interested in everything except study.

For weeks I was unutterably homesick and yearned for the sight of live-oaks and their long gray moss, for the magnolias and the palmettoes. I missed the rolling drum of the woodpecker on the shingles over my room at home. I longed for the odor of pitch pine smoke drifting from stick and clay chimneys across the cotton-fields when the sun was low. When I awoke in the night I never heard the riotious singing of mockingbirds, the soughing of great pines, or the measured hoots of a great horned owl. I chafed under the new order of things and paced my mental cage like an imprisoned panther from Gulf Hammock.

It was not until some weeks later, after the leaves had turned to red and gold, that I became aware of a charm in the country-side which I had not noticed. The rich brown of the broom sage in the abandoned fields with their boundary lines of gray rail fences and the blue haze that in autumn lingers along the horizon, I found were soothing to my spirits.

There came a day when I realized that I was becoming reconciled to life among the red hills of North Carolina.

A day student, Alden H. Hadley, and I developed a warm friendship. Our mutual interest in birds was the magnet that drew us together. I offered to show him how to skin birds if he would teach me to play a guitar. Any one who has seen his collection of birdskins at Earlham College and has heard my musical performances, will readily agree that I was the more successful instructor, or he the more apt pupil.

The museum, or "cabinet" as it was called in the college catalogue, was a room with shelves along two of its sides whereon was displayed a very neat collection of geological specimens placed there some years before by Professor Joseph Moore. The zoölogical exhibit consisted of an atrociously mounted gray fox and a splendid head of a buffalo, the latter being a gift from Joseph M. Dixon, a former student who had lately moved to Montana. In ethnology the one specimen was a large gray wool hat which had been worn by Nathan Hunt, an esteemed member of the Society of Friends, who many years before had passed to his reward.

The museum was to be the arena of my activities for the next two years. Here I unpacked and put on display my collection of birds' eggs comprising full clutches of more than two hundred species of North American birds. On Saturdays I roamed the surrounding country, gun in hand, seeking specimens of birds and animals to mount. I killed only a few, seldom wanting more than one pair of each kind. Gradually the collection grew. A crow, two blue jays, some woodpeckers, a muskrat and a pair of minks appeared on the shelves among various other specimens I had brought from Florida. These were exhibited and their habits and activities discoursed upon to students, visitors to the College, local farm-hands, in fact to any one whom I could entice to the museum, and who would have the patience to listen to me.

When talking about my specimens to a group of people, few of whom knew anything about the subject except what I told them, I was an entirely different individual from the boy who a few hours later in deep humility would be sitting in the grammar class directly across the hall. One of the teachers, a wise lady with a twinkle in her eye, after listening to one of my impromptu and perhaps pedantic talks, re-marked, "I think thee should remain in the grammar class for some time longer. Its influence is good for thee." I wondered what she meant by that statement.

The heroes at Guilford were the orators. A man's stand-ing among the students depended in large part upon his ability as a public speaker. Shortly after arriving I had seen an ascetic-looking man coming along the path.

"There's Joe Peele!" cried someone.

"Who's he?" I asked.

Quickly I was told that he was one of Guilford's greatest orators who had recently graduated. The year before he had been the winner in the State Inter-Collegiate Oratorical Con-test.

"His subject was 'Horace Greeley.' You should have heard him," my informant said radiantly. "I'll give you his opening sentence. 'The most memorable spot washed by the waters of the Hudson is Greenwood Cemetery, the necropolis of America's immortal dead.'"

The boys had two rival literary societies, the Websterian and the Henry Clay, and to one or the other every ambitious Guilford boy belonged.

On Friday nights the members met for speeches and de-bates. In their deliberations the most painstaking parliamen-tary procedures were practised. A copy of *Robert's Rules of Order* could be found in nearly every room. I was sure that I should have to learn to think and to speak before an audi-ence if I hoped ever to accomplish anything worth while in later years. I joined the Websterian Literary Society and found that I should be called on to take part in two debates each month. At an early meeting my name was announced as one of those who must shortly defend the negative side of the subject, "Resolved, that the South will eventually surpass the North in wealth and resources." Each speaker was to be allowed ten minutes. I went to work and for the next week thought of little except preparing for that speech. I searched through orations from Desmothenes to Henry W. Grady for thoughts, words, or ideas of any kind. I read *Wit and Humor of the Age,* and pored over the great speeches of Daniel Webster, and of Zebulon Baird Vance. I sought inspiration in the clouds, the trees, the sunsets, and the singing brooks. I wrote many pages, and read these aloud in a hidden retreat in a thicket of young pines.

The night came. The Society met. The President took the chair and appointed three boys as judges. The debate began and before long my name was called. I arose with calmness and with an assumed self-possession intended to be noticeable and confounding to the opposition. There were twenty-eight boys in that small room, but in a voice loud enough to be heard by an audience of five hundred I began:

"Mr. President and gentlemen of the jury. In these days of the telephone, steam engine, and rubber-tired buggies—comforts of which our forebears never dreamed—in these modern times it behooves us as citizens of a great Commonwealth to pause, to tear from before our eyes the curtain of the past and peer with earnestness down the long vistas of the future."

A loud guffaw broke the spell which I was so seriously trying to weave. It came from Ed Wilson, a senior, whom I held in great awe. He was not considered a particularly eloquent orator, but it was said that in debate his side usually won.

My speech was ruined. I stammered on for three minutes to keep from being fined and sat down amid scattering applause. My side lost the debate. I think that the last speaker for the affirmative stole away the hearts of the judges when he closed his impassioned appeal for the South with the words: "And gentlemen, we must never forget the imperishable glory that plays about the brow of the North Carolina soldier of the Civil War, for North Carolina troops were the first to fight at Bethel, charged farthest at Gettysburg, and were last to surrender at Appomattox." Thundering applause followed. I was obliged to speak every two weeks or be fined, but it was many months before I regained sufficient self-possession to make an extemporaneous speech of ten minutes' duration.

The first school term ended two days before Christmas and nearly all the students went home for the holidays. I remained at College and therefore was one of the first to receive a report card on the past term's work. I had made 30 on my English grammar examination. The grade necessary for passing was 70. This meant I must take the course all over again.

An entertainment was given every year by each of the boys' literary societies, as well as by the girls' society, the Philagorian. These were held in the collection-room in King Hall where the students sat and studied during the day when not on recitation. The money to erect King Hall had been provided by Francis T. King of Baltimore, a Quaker of the old type who felt that instrumental music was a little out of place in a Friends' School. In deference to his wishes no music had been produced in the building. I loved music, but my violin was the only musical instrument in the college and I possessed small skill in its use. Hence when the date for the Websterian entertainment approached and some bold spirits began to talk covertly about adding music to the program, I joined heartily in a plot to bring this about. We found a woman in the neighborhood who could play an organ and she agreed to be a partner in our villainy if we could get an organ somewhere. By the roadside, halfway to the railroad station, lived the widow Morris. Six of us went to persuade her to lend us her organ, and at length she consented. While every one was supposed to be at supper that evening we put the organ in a wagon and pulled it up to King Hall and placed the forbidden instrument on the platform. We were exuberant. We were going to show the old fogy teachers that the modern generation knew what it wanted and was going to have it. Like Hugh Wynn we had become free Quakers. Alas! our activities had not passed unnoticed. President Hobbs walked in upon us and said firmly: "Take that organ back to Sarah Morris." I still shudder when I think how nearly I came to being expelled for my part in the affair.

Shortly before Commencement the three literary societies treated the teachers, students, and general public to samples of their public speaking. These oratorical contests were the great events in the year. I had overcome my fear of Ed Wilson and no longer hesitated to face an audience. I developed a great longing to be one of those selected to deliver an oration for the Websterian Society, but I was only a first-year prep and such honors naturally were given to college students. How I worked on my bi-weekly speeches for the debates! If only I were good enough maybe I might be chosen.

The night came for the Society to select the representatives to compete for the annual prize, a Webster's International Dictionary with a metal stand. Six orators could be chosen, but no one was eligible who had previously won a contest prize. Various members were put in nomination but most of them declined to serve. When nearly every one in the room had been nominated and only four had been found brave enough to accept the responsibility, the President said that it would be a great reflection on the Websterian Society if it could produce only four orators this year. In the silence that followed a small boy who often had come to the museum to look at my birds and eggs, said, "I nominate Gil Pearson." It was a weak, squeaky voice that spoke, but that night I thought it the most musical one I had ever heard. Several voted for the motion and no one voted audibly against it.

A short time before this a teacher had given me two small circulars which she had received in the mail. They told of extensive killing of birds for the millinery trade. For several years not only egrets, but multitudes of little song birds had been killed in many parts of the country and their skins and feathers shipped to New York City and distributed to millinery stores everywhere. These tracts had been issued by an organization named the Audubon Society.

They gave me a theme for my oration. Combining what I learned from these circulars with what I had seen and heard of egret-killing in Florida, I produced in time a speech entitled, "The Destruction of American Birds." A teacher corrected it for me, "toned it down a little," she said, and I began to commit it to memory. Evening after evening the pine thicket, the oaks and hickories that surrounded it, as well as the blue sky above had that speech shouted at them over and over again until I was letter perfect, until every gesture, every movement of the body, every emphasis that I thought effective, was made almost mechanically. The last sentence I practised hundreds of times, not only in the woods, but in my room or wherever I was alone. Stepping forward with outstretched arms and with lifted eyes I cried, "O fashion, O women of America, how many crimes are committed in your name!" When after the contest that eventful night Ed Wilson said "Not so bad for a prep," my cup was full.

Commencement was fast approaching with examinations already casting their ominous shadows across the campus. The test I feared most, of course, was English grammar.

Beginning early in January the grammar class had met five days a week for the next five months, and I believe that I had not missed a single recitation. I had applied myself with the greatest diligence in order, if possible, to rid myself of that body of the death to which I was chained. Increased effort brought its reward. Among the records at Guilford College there is an entry showing that at the close of college in the spring of 1892 I was given in English grammar a grade of 58 —with only twelve more points I would have been through with grammar forever. Passing grades were recorded for me in penmanship, spelling, drawing, Bible study, arithmetic, and history.

As the students were leaving for their vacations the Treasurer of the College gave me a little money to go on a collecting trip I had outlined to him. I spent some days traversing the fastness of the Great Dismal Swamp and then went to Cobbs Island, Virginia. At the small hotel on the Island we were served daily with boiled eggs of laughing gulls, oyster-catchers, terns and clapper rails. Two dozen specimens of birds were secured and these, with a number of birds' eggs, were packed in my telescope valise. A lady whom I met loaned me ten dollars to go by boat to Washington. Here I took a room for one dollar, and living chiefly on bananas and crackers, spent nearly all the time for two days looking at the mounted birds in the Smithsonian Institution and reading their labels.

One of my chief objects in going to Washington was to meet and talk with that great ornithologist, Robert Ridgway. I found him at his desk in a balcony of the bird exhibition hall in the Smithsonian building and spent half an hour with him, during which I asked and received answers to many questions. In return he asked me if I had seen any ivory-billed woodpeckers. While we were talking a taxidermist brought for his inspection a magnificent male bird-of-paradise he had just mounted. I hoped also to see Major Charles E. Bendire, but was forced to content myself with enjoying a glimpse of his egg collection. Then after a night in a day coach I was back again on the campus at Guilford.

On November 10, 1892, Mrs. Lydia Blair, the principal of the preparatory department at Guilford, sent for me to come to her room.

"I suppose thee wonders why thee was not put in the grammar class again this fall," she said.

"Yes," I told her, "but I am very glad that thee has excused me from grammar."

"But thee has not been excused from grammar," she quickly advised me. "I believe this is thy birthday," she went on. "When was thee born?"

I told her in 1873. She looked at me for a few moments with kindly, musing eyes, then half to herself—"Nineteen years old and couldn't parse a sentence to save his life."

She extended her hand. "Thee may go now. Thee should pass grammar before graduating from the preparatory department next spring. Perhaps I can help thee. When I get a little more time I shall send for thee again"—but gratefully I record the fact that she never did.

All through that second school year a question troubled me, and as Commencement approached it loomed very large in my thoughts—what was I to do after the spring term closed? My credit for board and tuition, in exchange for my egg collection, would be exhausted. My cash income for the two years had amounted to just one hundred dollars, supplied by my father. I knew that it was now impossible for him to pay any part of my expenses in college, and for a long time I could think of no plan by which I would be privileged to stay at Guilford.

One day, when the spring was well advanced, Nerious English, one of the College Trustees, fell into my clutches and I took him to the museum. After showing him my collection and telling him of the hundreds of people who came to visit it, I enlarged on the value that it might become to the College if its growth continued and its interesting features were advertised to the public. I called his attention to the fact that not another college in the State had a museum of any kind. Then I explained the arrangement by which I had been going to school and my desire to enter the college department the next year. He told me to come to Founders Hall that afternoon and he would see that I had opportunity to present the matter to the Board of Trustees which would be in session.

No one ever put his heart into a speech any more than I did when standing before that group of serious men. How I blessed the Websterian Literary Society for the experience it had given me in thinking and speaking while on my feet. When I had concluded, Nerious English and some of the others made a few remarks, and a motion was passed authorizing the Treasurer of the College to allow me tuition, board, room and fifty dollars cash a year for my work in connection with the museum. I felt that my future was assured and told President Hobbs that I was going to prove to him that I was not an imperfect batter in everything.

James Peele Parker and I were chosen by the student-body to represent Guilford College at the Young Men's Christian Association's Conference to be held that summer at Northfield, Massachusetts.

First I went to Baltimore where I solicited and secured some money from Friends to enable me to extend my trip beyond that which had been provided for by the Guilford students. From here I went to New York City for two reasons: I wanted to meet Frank M. Chapman and to see the Brooklyn Bridge. I found Mr. Chapman in the museum building and had several minutes' conversation with him. As I was leaving he gave me some very sound advice. He told me that I had better get on a street-car rather than try to walk to the Brooklyn Bridge, for the distance was fully five miles.

Two delightful days I passed with Harvey C. Campbell of Lansingburg, New York. We had conducted some exchanges of birds' eggs a few years before and had much to talk about as we wandered over the hillsides that sloped to the waters of the upper Hudson. He showed me in an apple tree the first goldfinch nest I had seen.

At the Northfield Conference I attended Bible classes and the lecture courses given by Mr. Moody, Robert E. Speer, John R. Mott, and the distinguished Scottish educator and writer, Henry Drummond.

My journeys then led me to the World's Fair at Chicago. Here I saw and talked with Frank H. Lattin, editor of the *Oologist* and Carl Akeley, the African big-game collector. Returning by way of Richmond, Indiana, a day was spent in the museum of Earlham College where Professor Joseph Moore gave me, for the Guilford Museum, a fine mounted specimen of the passenger pigeon and a cast of an egg of that gigantic extinct bird, the *Æpyornis maximus*. And so with a mind filled with impressions of the great North I returned to Guilford College that autumn and entered the freshman class.

When Francis T. King passed away it became known that the ban regarding music had been lifted from King Hall. The Websterian Society took advantage of this at its next annual entertainment to present to the audience some gifted musicians. One whom I especially enjoyed was Miss Elsie Weatherly of Greensboro, a violinist. I was greatly impressed with her art, her grace, and her unusual beauty. No one had stimulated me so much since my idealized teacher in Archer six years before. That night I vowed that I would see her again soon if it were humanly possible.

From experience I learned that one may secure contributions for a worthy cause if one profoundly believes in its merits and if one looks a man directly in the eye and asks for his help. I discovered that I rather enjoyed collecting money for the Websterian Society. Also I found that I could raise money for the Guilford College Museum and make it possible for me to go on various collecting trips.

My second expedition to Florida for the museum was made in the summer of 1896. From friends of the College I had raised enough money to pay my railroad fare and also to buy alum, arsenic, and cotton for my bird-skins. From my home at Archer I made numerous trips, the longest of which was to the Gulf Coast. Here I hunted about old Tampa Bay, visiting some heron colonies, bald eagles' nests, and beaches where various shore-birds were found, but the only specimen I took was a gray kingbird. In Tampa I met a hunter named Highsmith, who lived in the palmetto prairie country of Manatee County and he invited me to visit him. By steamer I reached Palmetto on the Manatee River and for small cost a man drove me to a point several miles from town. Then by trail I reached Highsmith's small, one-room house. He was ill and unable to hunt with me, so I tramped alone and during the several days I was there secured three specimens, one a "scrub" jay that I shot, second, a Florida black duck given me by a wandering hunter, and third, a beautifully prepared skin of the swallow-tailed kite, which Highsmith had secured while hunting for deer and egret plumes in the Everglades not long before. Our food consisted almost entirely of corn-bread, jerked venison, dried grapes and boiled buds of the cabbage palmetto, all of which was most appetizing.

Mr. Highsmith told me of Captain Jim Bishop, head of a fishing crew, who lived near Terra Ceia Bay and said Captain Jim would take me without cost on a fishing cruise. Carrying my old telescope valise, containing my clothing, shot-gun shells and specimens, and with my double-barrel shot-gun on my shoulder, I made my way through the uninhabited wilderness to Terra Ceia Bay and arrived in the twilight just as the men were leaving for their fishing vessels. Captain Jim received me cordially and in his skiff we at once sailed away into the night. Some hours later we reached the schooner and a sloop on which the fishermen lived six days each week. I had not tasted food since morning and was thoroughly exhausted when near midnight I climbed supperless into a bunk.

In the morning I was awakened by shouts and the sound of running feet on the deck overhead. Coming out I found the men pulling off in small boats to surround a school of pompano that was breaking water near at hand. Time after time the net was run. About eleven o'clock boiled pompano and rice were served. I was so hungry and ate so rapidly that I soon doubled up with cramps and thought I was going to die.

During the week that followed the vessels were shifted to various parts of Tampa Bay. In a skiff I rowed to different uninhabited keys seeing what birds were to be found and occasionally taking a specimen. Captain Jim told me of Bird Key not far from the town of St. Petersburg and said many birds were breeding there. He was busy all day but one night he took me in his skiff and, after sailing many miles, the boat grounded on an oyster bar. The dark outline ahead, he told me, were the mangrove bushes of Bird Key.

I stepped overboard with my gun and slipped and stumbled among the oyster-covered mangrove roots until I reached the low trees. In the starlight I could see great nests above me and heavy birds began to flap away at my approach. Firing at a dark shadow that passed overhead, I secured a large male man-of-war bird with an expanse of wings of nearly eight feet. I also took a brown pelican and a clutch of pelican eggs. Suddenly the stars were blotted out and the sound of a conch shell reached my ears. It was the signal to return. It had become very dark, but the Captain's repeated blasts on the conch guided me to him. A storm was almost upon us. We pushed the boat into deeper water and set sail. In ten minutes the tempest broke with great fury.

Captan Jim unstepped the mast, covered himself with the mainsail and handed me the jib. I wrapped the man-of-war

bird in my coat and pushed it under the covering of the
prow. We were soon driven on a shoal. The rain fell in torrents for hours and the boat was nearly filled with water.
I held the dead pelican close to my body and bent forward
to shield it as best I could from the rain. By sunrise the sky
had cleared. Hundreds upon hundreds of man-of-war birds
rose from the island, wheeling in ever-increasing circles as
they attained altitude. The mass movement was like a great
rotating funnel. As the birds gained a height of perhaps one
thousand feet they left the formation and went sailing across
the islands toward the open sea. So far as I am aware, this was
the first time a bird student had visited the island that is
now known as Indian Key Bird Reservation.

Back in Terra Ceia Bay again on Friday afternoon my host
and his companions left me aboard the sloop. They were
Seventh Day Adventists and wanted to be at home from
sunset that evening until sunset on Saturday. I was to stay
on the sloop, cook my meals and await their return. Captain
Jim had pointed to a little house that was visible, probably
a mile and a half away, and said the owner kept a post-office.
After finishing my work of skinning a pair of roseate spoonbills I rowed ashore to mail a letter to my mother. A high
wind arose, forcing me to spend the night with the post-
master. The mail arrived that afternoon and he read to me
an account of the National Democratic Convention of 1896,
which had just been held. It told of a Nebraska orator who
had stampeded the convention and had been nominated for
President. The article stated that at the height of his oration
the audience went wild when he cried, "You must not press
down upon the brow of Labor the crown of thorns. You
shall not crucify mankind upon a cross of gold."

Two days later Captain Jim sailed me in his skiff out on
the tumbling waters of Tampa Bay and, waving an oar,
flagged down a little steamer bound from the Manatee River
to Tampa. From its deck I had my last view of him as, with

a smile, he waved his hand and headed for the sloop at anchor among the keys off Terra Ceia. With some knowledge of birds hitherto unknown to me, I returned in autumn to the class-rooms at Guilford as a member of the senior class.

The members of the Guilford faculty gave much attention to instruction in Bible study and in the cardinal virtues of correct living. Every student devoted an hour each week to recitation with the Bible as a textbook. We were required to go to Sunday School, First Day meeting, and Mid-week meeting. We attended the regular weekly gatherings of the Christian Endeavor and the Young Men's Christian Association. No card games were allowed, the use of tobacco was tabooed, drinking alcohol in any form was unthinkable, and, of course, there was never a dance. We did not look upon these duties and restraints as hardships; we accepted them rather as matters of course. Most of us had been surrounded with such influences from birth.

The daily assemblage of all students, which in many schools is called "chapel," was here known as "morning collection." In addition to prayer and a brief reading from the Scriptures, some member of the faculty or an occasional visitor would speak briefly or read a short article. I remember many of these morning talks. Particularly do I recall some of those given by President Hobbs.

Once in speaking of a highly esteemed man who had recently died, he said in substance: "If I were asked how a young man might in time attain to the very high moral and spiritual standard that guided the life of our departed friend, I should advise this course: Seek ever to dwell in the upper lighted chamber of your mind and studiously avoid descending, for even one hour, into the dark cellar of envy, intolerance and sensuality. When doubt arises as to which of two courses to pursue, always swerve to the path which, in your heart, you will recognize as the one leading to honesty of thought and purpose. Every temptation successfully overcome renders the outcome of the next encounter with the Adversary less in doubt. Such, I believe, was the philosophy that guided the life of this worthy man, whom we shall see no more."

Professor Perisho was very popular with the students and his talks to us were always received with eagerness. On one occasion I was so impressed with his talk about engaging in practices that would help develop the mind in self-control, that I bought some seckel pears, of which I was very fond, and, without any explanation to my room-mate, let them lie untouched on our study-table until they decayed. This was foolish, perhaps, but the act was quite in keeping with the spirit of the teaching at Guilford. I knew many boys and girls in those days who quietly engaged in some form of self-denial in their efforts to cultivate a sturdy self-restraint.

The six years I spent as a student at Guilford College were crowded with incidents that meant much to the boy from Florida's piney woods. I became an editor of the college magazine, president of my literary society, manager of the baseball team, and was captain of the football team that made the poorest showing of any team in the history of Guilford athletics. In my sophomore year I organized, and for three years financially managed, the Athletic Association, which I believe is still in operation.

One Saturday morning in the spring of my junior year I started for the woods with the object of collecting a pair of blue-gray gnatcatchers for the museum. A little later I heard one singing but for a time could not locate the performer. Then, all at once, I discovered him. He was sitting in his soft, lichen-covered nest saddled on the limb of a white-oak tree. With head thrown back he poured forth one burst of music after another. The little fellow undoubtedly was exquisitely happy. He seemed to love all the world and sang with a charming abandon as if he could not dream that any creature would want to harm him or his precious nest.

I could not raise my gun and as I walked home I reflected on the fact that never before had sentiment prevented me from killing a bird that I felt was needed for educational purposes.

I had various room-mates during those years at Guilford. There were Joseph Hare, tall, agreeable and bashful; Oscar P. Moffit, good student, self-possessed and always well groomed; Samuel H. Hodgin, homely, scholarly and fond of fun, food and folks; and Joseph E. Blair, ambitious, nervous, generous, the soul of honor, and a passionately loyal friend.

In my senior year I had another problem to worry about. What would I do after graduation? At Guilford I had received valuable collegiate training, but I wanted to attend some university where the general outlook was a little more worldly than that to be found in a denominational institution. I wrote to Harvard, Yale, Princeton and elsewhere, attempting to secure some position in connection with a museum where I could attend lectures at the same time, but there was no encouragement in any of the replies received.

One night at the College we had a lecture by Joseph Holmes, the State Geologist, who years later, while head of the United States Bureau of Mines, was to create the term "Safety First." It was the first address I had ever heard that was illustrated with stereopticon slides. His office was at Chapel Hill in connection with the State University. He was a man whose life was spent largely in the out-of-doors. I argued to myself that surely he would appreciate the yearnings of a student desiring to work in the field of natural history. I wrote asking if he could give me employment in his office so that I could attend the University. I built great expectations on making such a connection. He replied with a polite note expressing his regret that the State Geological Survey was unable to avail itself of my services.

After this disappointment I could see no hopeful future. I would have to return to my father's frozen-down orange-grove and little farm. I knew that Florida was a realm of moss-draped live-oaks and lily-covered lakes, but I also knew that it was a land of gnats, mosquitoes, rainy seasons and long cotton rows that shimmered in a blistering sunlight, wherein lurked headaches without number. The consciousness that I was not sufficiently resourceful to overcome the difficulties I now faced began to crush me. I became deeply depressed, and in my misery decided that after all President Hobbs had been right. I was indeed an imperfect batter.

CHAPTER III

PROBLEMS OF LIFE

THERE WAS a political upheaval in North Carolina in 1896. A reform group, known as the Populist Party, combined with the hitherto submerged Republican Party, had at the November election swept the Democrats from power. Consternation reigned. It was an unbelievable situation, and from all sides arose prophecies of dire evils to come upon the commonwealth. It was noticed that bluebirds had recently become scarce and some newspapers said that they had left the State rather than submit to Republican domination.

When the new Governor took office, the usual displacements began in favor of deserving Republicans and Populists. Southern Quakers were, almost without exception, Republicans, because from early times they had opposed slavery, and, in fact, had freed their slaves a hundred years before the Civil War.

One of those borne into office on that tidal wave was W. H. Worth, a trustee of Guilford College, who was elected the State Treasurer. I asked him if there would be a change in the Curatorship of the State Museum.

"Certainly," he replied. "The Governor is considering various men now to take Mr. Brimley's place. The selection may be made any day."

"If Brimley is to lose his position, why not give it to me?" I asked. "I'll graduate from Guilford soon." After a moment's consideration he answered, "I will speak to the Governor about thee to-morrow." A few days later Mr. Worth asked

46

me to come to Raleigh, and we went to see Governor Russell. He looked me over and asked if I would take charge of
the museum for less money than was being paid to Mr.
Brimley.

I said, "A Republican ought to be worth as much to the
State as a Democrat."

He smiled. "All right," he agreed, "you can have the job."

"Worth," he continued, "go to the Agricultural Board,
now in session, and tell the Chairman that I say elect young
Pearson Curator of the Museum. He can go to work now or
a little later, just as he pleases."

Mr. Worth left me in his office while he went to the State
Agricultural Building. The door opened suddenly and Professor Joseph Holmes came in asking for me. A clerk indicated where I sat.

"What do you have against Mr. Brimley? Isn't he a good
man? Why are you trying to take his position?" he demanded, all in one breath.

I explained the situation as I understood it.

"So, what you really want is to earn money to enable you
to come to the State University. Well, if you will withdraw
your application I think that I can induce the Governor to
keep Mr. Brimley, and I will give you work in my office.
Then you can take your college courses at the same time."
He spoke as if the idea was his own, not remembering,
perhaps, that I had written asking him to do this very thing.
Then he offered to pay me fifteen dollars a month for one
year.

"Make it twenty dollars a month for two years and I will
accept," I told him. That September I enrolled in the junior
class at the State University.

It developed that my duties in the office of the State
Geologist were not heavy, therefore I was often in the field
by daylight making a census of the birds found about Chapel
Hill as the seasons changed. On an area of wet meadowland

inside the east wall of the campus I one day flushed a woodcock, and at another time found some Wilson's snipe here.
Pileated woodpeckers at times appeared close to the college
buildings. Once I saw a wild turkey fly across the campus and
light just back of the Episcopal Church. Where the stadium
now stands I found the first specimen of the bay-breasted
warbler recorded for North Carolina. A few dozen birds
were collected and their skins preserved in the biological
laboratory.

I played a little football, was an editor of the college
magazine, spoke on programs of the Dialectic Literary Society, was elected an inter-society debater, and a junior class
orator. Biology and English were the studies that interested
me most.

In March I went with H. H. Brimley to the Newbern Fish
and Oyster Fair. Various dead birds were on display as examples of the game resources of the State. Here is the list
of what we found: brant and Canada geese, thirteen species
of ducks, Holboell's and pied-billed grebes, Virginia and
clapper rails, Wilson's snipe, woodcock, common and red-
throated loons, sanderlings, mourning doves, great blue
herons, flickers, pileated woodpeckers, herring gulls, and
royal terns.

About the first of April, Professor Holmes asked if I would
like to take a trip of ten days with him to Pamlico and
Albermarle sounds. I would have a chance to see various
water-birds and he wanted me to collect some specimens
for the State Museum and for the University. Eagerly I
seized the opportunity to extend my field experiences, for I
was already gathering data for a book on the birds of the State
that I wanted to publish some time.

With Professor Holmes went also two members of his staff,
Dr. Joseph Hyde Pratt, Mineralogist, and W. W. Ashe,
Forester. At Newbern we went aboard the little steamer
Lilly operated by the State Shell Fish Commission, and began

cruising through the sounds to the northward. We went ashore at Beaufort, Ocracoke, Wysocking Bay and other points where the members of the party found matters to study in their various fields.

After a busy day on the outer banks at Cape Hatteras we returned to the shore on the inner side of the island. From a little dock at the edge of the marsh we were to row to the *Lilly,* lying at anchor four miles off shore. A fresh wind was blowing from the south, and I pointed out to Professor Holmes that beyond a point of sheltering marsh a mile away the white caps were running. I suggested that we wait until morning. Our dingey was too small, I thought, to carry five men with safety in such a rough sea. He thought my fears were groundless, but I maintained my point so stubbornly that he finally said that I might stay ashore if I would arrange with a fisherman to sail me out to the boat at dawn. The other four men, whose experience with boats had been limited, rowed away in the twilight toward the lights of the *Lilly,* faintly showing in the distance. They could not reach the steamer, but after struggling all night in the seething waters of Pamlico Sound, were fortunately able to regain the shore, greatly exhausted and with the palms of their hands lacerated. Professor Holmes said that undoubtedly the weight of another man would have swamped the boat.

He had always been formal and a little distant with me, but after our Hatteras experience his attitude underwent a change, and when a few days later the trip came to an end at Elizabeth City, I felt bold enough to ask him to let me remain on the coast for a time, and to allow me thirty dollars a month for salary and expenses, until I returned. He acceded to my request without stipulating the length of time I could remain. It was five months before I returned to my studies at the University.

The experiences of that spring and summer left a thousand impressions imprinted on my mind. It was during this time that I found the first Louisiana herons recorded for North Carolina, and by much searching found four of their breeding-colonies. At Cape Hatteras I made the first stilt sandpiper record for the State, and at Great Lake, in the wilds of Craven County, discovered a colony of one hundred and fifty-one pairs of cormorants. It was, and still is, the only breeding assemblage of these birds that has been discovered by ornithologists along the Atlantic Coast between Florida and Maine. On North River I found three white ibises which had migrated from the South, and secured one of them for the State Museum. I know of no other record of this bird from the State. At Orton pond in Brunswick County I took a male water turkey with a nest and four eggs, which to-day may be seen mounted in a group in the State Museum in Raleigh. It was thirty-three years before another nest of the water turkey was found in North Carolina, although it is an abundant species farther south.

I waded swamps, labored through marshes, visited islands and traversed the long, hot beaches of the outer banks where I lived with fishermen and the crews of life-saving stations. Many times I lay down in the shade with wet cloths on my forehead to assuage the frightful headaches that unmercifully assailed me.

The three weeks spent in the unusually beautiful woods at Cape Hatteras yielded many items for my note-book. A nest of the bald eagle with its great clumsy young already on the ground beneath their nest; prairie warblers' nests made almost wholly of wool, gathered from twigs against which sheep had rubbed; wood ducks' nests, three in one day; and on the near-by grassy beaches shore-birds in swarms of untold thousands. Here and at Ocracoke, Morehead City and elsewhere, I talked with men who had long been engaged in shooting birds for the millinery trade. Terns had been shot by the tens of thousands, and their skins shipped to the millinery-dealers of New York. The young, of course, had been left to perish on the hot, sandy beaches where they had been hatched.

A fisherman showed me how to bring terns within gun-shot range. A number of them at the time were flying about searching for a school of minnows a hundred yards from our skiff. To a short stick he tied a white handkerchief, leaving two corners flowing, and threw it high in the air. As it fell a least tern darted forward and hovered over the floating object.

"See how easy it is to decoy the first one," he said. "Shoot that bird and another will come and you will soon have the whole flock here."

He told me that most of the killing had been done about shell lumps or sand spits where the birds collect to breed. "They don't like to leave their young," he explained. "At such places I have often shot strikers so fast that I had to put my gun overboard to cool the barrels."

During the conversation he made a statement which I had heard from many others along the coast. "There ain't one striker or gull in a hundred to what there used to be. We've got 'em about all cleaned out."

When I ventured to express disapproval of this wholesale killing of birds he was ready with his answer. "Pore folks have as good a right to live as city people. The good Lord put us here and the Good Book says, 'man shall have dominion over all creatures.' They're ourn to use." He voiced the sentiment of the great majority of the people he knew.

At Morehead City I met A. T. Piner, who had been a great plume-hunter. He told me of feather cruises during which he and his helpers had killed and skinned many thousands of terns and gulls, from Virginia to Florida. In relating his plume-hunting experiences, he talked with the same simple frankness that he used in telling about catching mackerel between Beaufort Inlet and Cape Lookout. In each case he was farming the sea for its products. To him and his neighbors the killing of birds and the catching of fish were both ordinary avocations of life. Joe Royal was another famous plume-hunter of Morehead City. He showed me entries in a record book to emphasize the great success which he had achieved on some of his trips. He also spoke of the growing scarcity of gulls and terns.

"It's got so it hardly pays a man to hunt them any more," he declared. "We ought to have a law to protect them until they can catch up their numbers again. If something like this ain't done the plume-bird business will sure come to an end."

There was a considerable demand for shore-birds. Those that brought the best prices were curlews, willets, plovers, yellow-legs and dowitchers, but turnstones, sanderlings, sandpipers and other species of the beaches were acceptable. They were shot wholesale, many hundreds often being taken by one gunner in a day during the spring and autumn migrations. There were shallow pools along the beaches where the birds gathered to feed. Some of the gunners would conceal themselves while others disturbed the flocks, which, in flying toward other feeding-grounds, would pass within range of the shooters. For hours they would be driven up and down the beach and the roar of guns was almost continuous. Several times I saw probably five thousand birds in the air at one time. Often they flew in such compact flocks that many could be killed at each shot. I counted more than forty that dropped at a single discharge of a gun. This shooting was done chiefly by poor people of the country, but the dead birds were eaten by gentlemen and ladies in Northern cities to which they had been shipped in barrels of ice.

Returning to Chapel Hill at the opening of the University in September, I found awaiting me not only the studies I must assume as a senior, but also the junior courses which I had dropped the first of April. Hence I faced a busy year.

When the Christmas holiday season arrived I remained at

the University. Railroad tickets were expensive. During my years at Guilford I had read one hundred and five books. In my note-book were the names of all of them together with the dates when I had read their last pages. I had not read them casually, but had perused them with great care, often reading a choice book several times. I was interested in the skill displayed by the author in building his story or developing his theme. I studied the structure of the sentences and committed to memory many passages which I can still recall with ease. I had not been able to learn grammar, but hoped by rule of thumb to acquire some small idea of how to write without too many grammatical errors. I had set myself the task of reading twenty additional books during the time spent at Chapel Hill, and I now occupied myself in this manner.

Nearly every day, however, short walks in the fields or woods were taken and notes made of the birds found. There were many on the campus during this Christmas period, and I have a record of twenty-one species on the college grounds at that time. There was a sapsucker, and numbers of chickadees and titmice. One day forty-two meadowlarks patroled the campus from gate to gate. The downy woodpecker, of course, was there as were also several flickers. Two of these I once discovered pounding around in an unoccupied room which they had entered through a broken window. Always there were bands of jays, and I saw one of them trying to catch a junco on the snow. A pair of sparrow hawks roosted under the eaves of the building where I roomed and the cries of killdeers could be heard day and night.

Several other boys spent their Christmas vacation at College. Some had shot-guns and did a good deal of shooting in the neighborhood. Birds were occasionally shot on the campus. One day I heard firing near the new East Building and looked out of my window just in time to see a flicker come to the earth with a broken wing. Several pigeons were shot and I saw one beating out its life as it lay on the wide stone step at the north entrance. These boys had been hunting in the fields earlier in the day and had killed some game. Now they were finishing their day's work with powder and shot among those birds of the campus which I had been observing with such pleasure.

The boys borrowed an iron pot from some one and that night on a box stove in a dormitory room prepared their feast. One of the participants gave me a list of the ingredients that were put into that pot and later were devoured by the hungry hunters. Here it is: 1 rabbit, 3 quail, 9 pigeons, 2 meadowlarks, 1 flicker, and 1 sapsucker—the very sapsucker which I had been watching for weeks as it fed on the cambium of its favorite tree. I myself had been wanting a sapsucker skin for the university collection, but I could not bring myself to shoot that bird even in the name of science, and I looked upon it as a pet. Now it had been killed by a boy who did not even know its name—and who never would have cared to know what its name might be. I brooded over the matter and wrote, for relief, a story of the hunt and the banquet which had followed. Under the title, "Life on the Holiday Campus," it appeared in the North Carolina University Magazine for February, 1899. So far as I observed, this literary effort made no appreciable change in the amount of shooting that went on in the neighborhood. No one reprimanded the boys. Shooting birds at pleasure was a common diversion practised at will. Why should this one incident cause any comment?

I collected a class of a dozen or more students and gave them talks on ornithology. We used the small study collection of bird-skins stored in the biological laboratory and also took various field-walks.

As the second spring of my residence at Chapel Hill approached I tried to induce Professor Holmes to keep me in his office for another year so I could get a Master's Degree and gather more data for the book on the birds of the State which I hoped he would agree to issue as a State Geological Survey publication. But he saw no particular need for such a book, and there was no important work to be done in his office for which I was especially qualified.

Then I wrote letters again to Northern universities, making various propositions which I hoped would enable me to attend one of them. All answers were of a negative character.

I was much interested in the Young Men's Christian Association and was President of this organization in the University. Quite unexpectedly I was offered the position of Assistant Bi-State Secretary for North and South Carolinas, and could assume the position at once upon graduation. The financial reward was alluring and my mother urged me to accept it, but after taking careful stock of my tastes, inclinations and faith, I realized that I should not enter this work as a profession.

Every Y.M.C.A. leader I knew and every minister whom I heard preach, believed in a literal interpretation of the Bible, or if he did not, he kept the fact well concealed. I had strayed from my early teachings. I held various beliefs that were not in accord with the teachings I would be expected to expound, and I wanted to engage in a work where I could be mentally free and honest in my declarations. Furthermore, I had determined I was going to devote thought and effort to arousing the people of North Carolina to the idea of protecting the birds that were being decimated on every hand, and I wanted to make my living in a field where I should constantly have opportunity for self-expression on the subject.

So I declined the offer that would take me into the field of religious effort and wrote to President Hobbs of Guilford College suggesting that he add me to his faculty and permit me to teach biology. To this he agreed, and it was planned that I should begin work the following September. To record my local ornithological observations I at this time prepared and published a *Preliminary Catalogue of the Birds of Chapel Hill,* but the printers did not give me a chance to correct the proof and I was not proud of the result.

On Commencement Day, 1899, a few of us seniors, selected by the faculty, delivered orations. Tam Boie's speech won the much-coveted Wiley P. Mangum medal for oratory, while R. D. W. Connor was a close second for the prize. The members of the graduation class received their diplomas from the hands of Dr. Nicholas Murray Butler, as President Edwin A. Alderman read our names. Then we doffed our caps and gowns and with high hopes started out to win our fortunes.

I went at once to Beaufort for Professor Holmes had arranged for me to do some work in the Marine Biological Laboratory, recently established there by the United States Bureau of Fisheries. My duties were most interesting and it was a great privilege to be associated with Dr. H. V. P. Wilson, as a member of his small staff.

One day I learned that Elsie Weatherly was spending some days at Morehead City just across the bay from Beaufort. She was the girl who so stirred me when she played on her violin at Guilford College and after that night I had seized every opportunity to see her. Instantly I lost interest in the laboratory with its mollusks, holothurians, echinoderms and other creatures which had been dredged from their muddy homes in the harbor. I took the first mail-boat for Morehead to contend with others for some share of her attention. Again I heard her play her violin, while I admired her black hair and her smiling blue eyes which always fascinated me.

The great verandas of the old Atlantic Hotel at Morehead were flooded on moonlit evenings with the songs of mockingbirds which surely have aided in the consummation of a thousand romances at this well-known summer resort. I lost all desire to go to Harvard or to any other university, in fact I decided that already I had spent too much time in school. I should have been out making money and getting in position to establish a home. I was afraid that some luckier man would get ahead of me. When not with her, miserably I paced my room, the dock, the veranda or the railroad track. Oh, if I only had money!

The last evening of her stay at Morehead, while tying my tie before dinner, I made a sudden desperate decision. I would tell her my story at once. She didn't say "yes" but she didn't say "no," and my spirits rose tremendously. The next day I whistled and sang and gave unusual attention to the comfort of the crustaceans and all the little finny creatures in the laboratory.

Late in the summer the North Carolina Yearly Meeting of Friends assembled at High Point according to annual custom, and the trustees of Guilford College met at the same time. On August 10th, in response to my request for an appropriation to equip a biological laboratory at Guilford, they voted me seventy-five dollars which they hoped I would make go as far as possible.

When College opened I faced the first biology class ever assembled in that institution since its founding sixty-three years before. Our only equipment was my collection of birds' eggs, about two hundred mounted birds, and one microscope for which I had spent thirty-seven dollars of my precious appropriation.

One evening a few days later I went to President Hobbs with another proposition. I asked that the College advance money for traveling expenses for me to go to Philadelphia where I would try to interest some members of the Society of Friends in contributing to our biological laboratory equipment. I reminded him that by writing letters in previous years I had secured help which had made possible various of my field-trips for the museum.

"They gave money for the museum, surely they will help equip a laboratory at Guilford," I argued.

But he thought the success of such a trip was doubtful, and said: "Thee might not raise enough money to pay thy expenses, then what would the trustees say?"

Whereupon I asked, "May I go if I advance my own money for expenses?"

"Does thee have any money?" he inquired.

"No," I told him, "but I will have some before long."

"Well, in that case I would not object, and thee may succeed. I hope thee does."

I had gone to Guilford with the agreement to teach a year for three hundred dollars, plus room and board. After a time I drew such portion of my salary as was due, and with a letter of introduction from President Hobbs, departed for Philadelphia. Upon arrival I went to see my fellow-Websterian, Edwin Wilson, now a Master at the Haverford School for Boys. He at once took me in charge.

When we started out the first thing he said was: "Don't forget you are up North now, always keep your overcoat buttoned, it looks better."

He introduced me to Dr. Isaac Sharpless, President of Haverford College, whose interest extended to •all Quaker institutions. He sent me with notes to people whom he thought might be helpful. Friendly Philadelphia! What delightful memories I have of kind-hearted people and brick houses with marble steps and mirrored busy-bodies on the sills of the second-story windows! I returned to Guilford with a substantial sum to start my laboratory, and with promises of more to follow.

Before the close of the school year a committee of three trustees visited the College to make arrangements about teachers for the coming term. I showed them around my laboratory, with its row of microscopes and other equipment. They sat down and I sensed that they had something on their minds. At length one of them spoke. There was an impression abroad that I did not entirely believe the Bible. Was this true? I told them that probably the rumor was correct, but that I should like to know of what particular heresy I was supposed to be guilty. Then one of them said that it was reported that I had flatly asserted that the sun did not stand still at the command of Joshua. I admitted that I regarded the story as only an interesting tradition, and I thought that no God, worthy of the love and respect of mankind, would stop the earth in its orderly turning through the heavens, to help the warriors of a barbarian chief slaughter the followers of another savage leader. No, frankly I did not believe that the sun stood still upon Gibeon, nor the moon in the valley of Ajalon. I added that I did not think much of the whale and Jonah story either.

"Thee need not be unduly disturbed by our question," one of them said. "Some very well-intended persons wanted us to ask thee about it."

Then they told me that they had decided to raise my salary 50 per cent for the coming year. I taught evolution as long as I remained at Guilford and never heard any further complaint about my unorthodox views. Quakers have always been broader minded than some uninformed people believe.

While at Chapel Hill I had to borrow some money, although I practised, as always, the most rigid economy, even to eating only two meals a day for a considerable period. Aunt Ann, the smiling, ample-proportioned colored cook at Guilford College had sent me money, a little at a time, until I owed her $160. By the close of my first year as a teacher at Guilford I had saved enough out of my salary of $300 to repay her in full, both principal and interest, and had sufficient change left over to jingle reassuringly in my pocket.

The next year I made another trip to Philadelphia, secured more funds and also gifts of equipment for the biological laboratory. While there I talked to various Friends about the great need for increasing the endowment for Guilford. I laid before them a plan for making an intensive campaign among the members of the Friends Church in North Carolina, with the view of inducing as many of them as possible to contribute to the endowment. The gifts might be very small, even twenty-five cents each from the members of large families. If anything like a considerable proportion of North Carolina Quakers would thus show their interest in the College, would Philadelphia Friends, I asked, be willing to supplement this with substantial gifts? They assured me that under such conditions their support would be generous.

Returning to Guilford, in great elation I presented the matter to President Hobbs, who was much interested and asked me to speak with some of the trustees. I joyously complied with his instructions and at once hurried over to Pomona to talk with one of them, J. Van Lindley, a prominent and well-to-do Quaker. He thought the plan a good one. The Chairman of the Board was Elihu E. Mendenhall. Borrowing a horse and buggy I drove to Deep River to confer with him. He said he would arrange for a meeting of the trustees as soon as practicable and that he wanted me to appear and present the matter. It was tentatively planned that I should stop teaching and undertake this financial campaign. The salary suggested was staggering. The sum was so large that within twelve months I would earn enough, I thought, to spend a year at Harvard—or to get married.

The trustees met at the College on January 9, 1901. Some hours later I saw them driving toward the station in the college hack. I hunted up President Hobbs.

"No one sent for me," I said.

He explained that the Board approved of my proposition, but thought I was too young and inexperienced to be entrusted with so much responsibility, and that one of the trustees, J. Elwood Cox, had offered to conduct the campaign I had outlined. So I went on teaching for thirty-seven dollars and fifty cents a month and Elwood Cox began the undertaking that was to increase materially Guilford's Endowment Fund.

In Greensboro at that time there lived a prominent educator, Philander P. Claxton. As editor of the North Carolina Journal of Education, he asked me to write some sketches about birds. After producing two or three of these he said that he could find a publisher if I would write enough of them to make a book. I talked it over with Elsie Weatherly, who encouraged me to do as he said, and volunteered to make many pen- and ink-drawings for illustrations. We both went to work at once—she with her drawing materials and I with a borrowed typewriter.

That spring I again took the Teachers' Employment Committee around the biological laboratory and exhibited our greatly increased equipment. My book would be out before long and would carry the name of the College on its title-page. No professor at Guilford had ever written a book, and I thought this ought to help me a little with the trustees. I told them of speaking in various towns and of working to get students to come to Guilford. I mentioned that more than twenty of my articles had been accepted by various periodicals, that there was some demand for more, and that it should not hurt the College to have a teacher whose name was appearing in magazines. I also pointed out that during the two years I had been teaching for them I had collected for the institution, in the way of money and equipment, much more than the College had paid me, and that the contacts I had made would enable the College to get additional financial support. All this was presented as argument why I hoped the committee would consider raising my salary.

The Chairman replied that they were looking to see where they could cut salaries. Then I told them I wished to get married and that in those times of high prices I did not feel that two people could live comfortably on less than $600 a year. They consulted, then offered to pay me $550, which I said I would accept if I could get nothing better. I loved Guilford and had many dreams of what I hoped I might be able to do to help in the building of its future usefulness. Still I had determined that if possible I was going to earn enough money to be in a position to establish a home. Therefore, I felt forced to seek a new arena of activities.

CHAPTER IV

PLANS CRYSTALLIZE

IN GREENSBORO, North Carolina, is situated a state institution for the education of women, known for many years as the State Normal and Industrial College. In the spring of 1901, I applied for a position there to fill a vacancy in the chair of Biology and Geology. The salary was to be $1000 a year. When the college year closed at Guilford, I went to Florida for a short visit with my parents, hoping every day to hear of my appointment to the new position I was seeking. At supper-time one evening there came a telegram from the blue-eyed girl in Greensboro, reading: CONGRATULATIONS, READ PSALMS 103-1. My mother at once quoted: "Bless the Lord O my soul and all that is within me bless His Holy Name." All the way back to North Carolina the wheels of the railway coach kept clicking on the rails, "I can marry her now, I can marry her now." However, when I met her, I was advised that this happy event would not take place for at least another year.

I found that among other courses I would be expected to teach botany. To review this subject I went to Harvard University that summer and took a botany course in what had once been Asa Gray's laboratory. Then going back to Guilford I put into my trunk my few household gods, including Darwin's *Descent of Man,* and sought lodgings in Greensboro.

One afternoon, a short time after the Normal College opened in September, while watching the young women of my biology class seated at many tables, peering into their microscopes, I began to wonder what practical use such microscopic work would be to them in after years. Often I had heard President Hobbs say: "Time is wasted which might be better spent." I spoke to the class and asked each member to look out of the window next to her and name for me the nearest tree. All complied but only one hand went up.

"What is it?" I asked.

"An oak tree," was the reply.

It was not an oak, but a maple—a beautiful silver maple. The weather was pleasant and the windows were wide open. I called attention to the notes of several birds that reached our ears. Not a girl in the class could give the name of a single one of them.

"You may return to your microscopes," I said.

That afternoon I called on Dr. Charles D. McIver, the President of the College, and asked how many of his graduates had taught school. He said that more than 60 per cent of them thus far had engaged in teaching.

"How many of my biology class will probably ever teach in a school where there is a microscope?" I asked. He replied that, of course, he could not say, but probably a good many of the thirty high schools in the State had a microscope of some kind.

Then I told him that I should like to make a radical change in the character of my biology work. In his hearty, friendly manner he asked what I had to suggest. I related my experience with the class that afternoon, and spoke of what had been running through my mind. Instead of having the students draw pictures of cross-sections of a fern's stem and the *Ligamentum nuchae* from a bull's neck, as revealed through a microscope, why not teach them about something they could see all their lives. Adjoining the College was a wonderful area of primitive forest, called "The College Park." It was not sodded, nor had it finished driveways or beautiful walks. There were great trees and thickets, logs and streams, and ferns. Here in spring bloomed violets, trilliums, anemones and blood roots. It was a wonderful bit of unspoiled wilderness.

"Let me have those woods for my laboratory for part of the time," I asked. "Permit me to teach these young women to know the red oak and white oak, the hickory, hornbeam, dogwood, and Jersey pine. Give them a chance to learn the names of the trees under which their pupils will play at recess. Let me teach this class to know the flicker, the great-crested flycatcher, the chickadee, and other birds that are needed to protect the crops of the parents who will send their children to school. These girls should learn to know the birds so they can tell their pupils about them—their correct names, where they migrate, and of what value they are on the farms and in the orchards. They should be given the opportunity to acquire that intelligent appreciation of nature that can come only from study of the outdoor life in the woods and fields."

This and much more I poured out to Dr. McIver during that interview. When my torrent of words had somewhat subsided he said he had asked me to come to the College in the belief that I could inspire the young women with a love for nature, and that he would leave to me the choice of methods I should employ.

Then he leaned forward in his chair saying: "I like to think of Agassiz as he

> wandered away and away
> With Nature, the dear old nurse
> Who sang to him night and day
> The rhymes of the universe."

I had a small collection of bird-skins for laboratory use and two field-glasses which I passed around among the students on our bird-walks. Lectures were given, notes taken, and examinations held. On the campus I pointed out birds and talked about them whenever I met a teacher or pupil who gave any intimation of interest. In a month my little book, *Stories of Bird Life,* appeared and most of my students, I believe, read it. It received some favorable reviews, which were the occasion for bringing me a letter which had much to do with my future work. It came from William Dutcher of New York City and was dated December 17, 1901. He spoke of having seen some mention of the book and asked where he might secure a copy. Then he told me that he had recently been chosen as Chairman of the Bird Protection Committee of the American Ornithologists' Union and that the Committee was anxious to have its "model law" to protect non-game birds adopted in all the states. He asked if I would not help to get it passed in North Carolina. He hoped that I would organize an Audubon Society to get behind such a bill.

The letter came at a most opportune time for instantly I saw the possibility of a friendly ally in my own ambition to secure laws to protect the birds of the State. However, I had never thought of working under the name "Audubon Society." In fact, I had a mild prejudice against the name, having seen a disparaging reference to it in some publication.

I replied to Mr. Dutcher, asking for further information. He sent me various useful leaflets. I also received others about this time, which impressed me very unfavorably, for their authors made claims that palpably were incorrect. The statements that birds designed for the millinery trade were skinned alive so their feathers would not fade, that the bird life of Connecticut had been reduced 75 per cent during the past fifteen years, and that all species of American birds soon would become exterminated, indicated the presence of extremists in the field of bird protection, whose writings could serve to mislead the uninformed, and would hurt our cause with thinking people.

After talking the matter over with J. Y. Joyner, the

WILLIAM DUTCHER

Founder and first President of the National Association of Audubon Societies, as he appeared in 1910.

State Superintendent of Public Instruction, President Hobbs, Dr. McIver, Miss Weatherly, and the members of the senior zoology class, I decided to act on Dutcher's suggestions. Thus, it transpired that on March 12, 1902, I faced an audience of some two hundred people in the college chapel to whom I spoke of the value of birds to the State: how they were being destroyed, and what, in my opinion, should be done toward rectifying the existing conditions. Before adjournment the Audubon Society of North Carolina was formed with 148 paying members enrolled.

The newspaper announcements of our action brought several letters of commendation. Within a few days I addressed two more audiences in Greensboro and soon accepted invitations to speak in Winston, Durham and Burlington. Articles and comments appearing in the daily and weekly press were generally encouraging, although one editor called my effort "Love's labor lost." "Bird Protection" was a new note in North Carolina, the idea was novel, and made good "copy" for the papers; also, the underlying idea appealed to many people.

Ten days after we started the Audubon Society I took part in the founding of another organization. This was the North Carolina Academy of Science, which was born in Raleigh on the afternoon and evening of March 22, 1902. I became one of its Fellows and was elected Vice-President, and later became President. Of course, I addressed this group of my scientific associates on the Audubon Society work and on the need for laws to protect our birds, and most naturally they gave hearty approval to both undertakings.

I continued to speak as often as I could get away from college duties and wrote articles for the newspapers, agricultural papers and school journals. I emphasized the economic and esthetic value of birds, the terrific slaughter of many species that was being carried on, and the desperate need of quick and effective legislation to protect them.

Dr. Philander P. Claxton had organized the Summer School of the South at the University of Tennessee, located in Knoxville. This was quickly to become the most largely patronized gathering for teachers in the South. He invited me to become a member of his faculty, teach ornithology, and give public illustrated lectures at night in the out-of-door auditorium.

When Elsie Weatherly was in college she had been a devoted pupil of Professor Claxton and I have always suspected that his seeming approval of me at this time influenced her in my behalf. We were married in her mother's home in Greensboro on June 17, 1902, and went at once to Knoxville where Dr. Charles Dabney, President of the University, charmingly introduced her at a reception as "the bride of the Summer School."

The weeks at Knoxville were very happy and very busy ones for me. My class in bird-study grew into several sections, each filling the class-room. People also came from town for the public lectures and the bird-walks. As time permitted I wrote articles for the newspapers, for Tennessee had no laws to protect its useful non-game birds.

Upon leaving Knoxville, Mrs. Pearson and I visited some friends whose attractive home was situated on the outskirts of Asheville. On the front lawn we discovered the nest of a pair of brow thrashers. It was about six feet from the ground and well hidden in a thorny bush. We became impressed with the frequency with which the parents brought food for their young, and decided to discover just how often they made such trips. A watch was kept by one or the other of us for many hours. Upon approaching the nest a parent bird would light on the ground, and after a glance around would hop along to the bush and ascend from limb to limb to the young. Each seemed to have its own stairway, one using one side of the bush, the other going up among the limbs on the opposite side. Through our field-glasses we could readily see the food which they carried in their bills. It seemed to be mostly the larvæ of insects, and often they appeared to bring two or more of them at a time. We found that one bird made such a journey on an average of every two and one-half minutes. The other worked more slowly, coming on an average of once every ten minutes. Perhaps it was the father bird.

One afternoon we heard a shot and hurried to the veranda just in time to see a boy aiming his small rifle at one of our thrashers. I shouted and ran out on the lawn. With him was his father, a well-dressed man carrying a cane.

"What do you mean by telling my boy not to shoot that bird?" he demanded with evident surprise and not without some heat.

In the ensuing conversation I pointed out the value of those birds to the gardens of the neighborhood and the pleasure the thrasher's song gave to the people of the household. I ended by urging him to talk to his friends about the need of a law in the State to protect such birds. He made no promises and the two went off down the road together, with the rifle still loaded.

It was the custom of the authorities of the Atlanta Public School System in those days to require all their teachers to attend an institute for two weeks just preceding the opening of the schools in September. The sessions were held in one of the large high school buildings. Dr. Charles D. McIver and I were engaged to take part in the institute that autumn. It was the custom every day that before the teachers scattered to different rooms for instruction they would meet in the assembly-hall. Here McIver would address them for three-quarters of an hour on educational problems and methods of instruction. Then I followed for a like period, speaking on mammals, snakes, and birds—mostly birds. I urged them to study birds, teach birds, and preach the need of bird-protective laws, for like North Carolina and Tennessee, Georgia did not protect its wild life.

The responsiveness of these teachers was so stimulating that I longed to devote my whole time to lecturing about birds and their protection. As we were always free in the afternoon it gave me opportunity to seek out and make the acquaintance of many prominent people on whose minds I tried to lay the burden of getting legislation enacted to create a state game-warden force. Upon the conclusion of this engagement Dr. McIver and I returned to Greensboro in time for the opening of College.

To the conscientious teacher there is a vast satisfaction in seeing the young mind develop and unfold before him. The spiritual and inspirational rewards to the teacher are profound. The students at the State Normal College came from all parts of the State. They were there from the peanut fields of Bertie and the watermelon country about Goldsboro. There were others who, of late summer evenings, had poured cobalt in the blossoms of the jimson-weed to kill the tobacco moths, and later had watched the glow of the fire from their fathers' tobacco barns of nights when the katydids were singing. From the far-away mountain coves of Watauga and the valleys of the Great Smokies others had been driven in carts to take the train to Greensboro. They had come from cotton factory towns and from homes with broad galleries and charming gardens.

Through the veins of virtually all there flowed the pure blood of the Anglo-Saxon. Their forebears had fought at Guilford Court House or Cowpens, or carried rifles up the steeps of Kings Mountain. Whatever they were they were the best that North Carolina could produce. They were destined to be the mothers of men who should fight the new and unknown battles of North Carolina's future. They had come to college to learn from books and from association with others, the inspiring things of life. And I, a member of the faculty, had the rare privilege of being one of their teachers. To me it was a glorious responsibility. I hailed with joy the approach of every day. I had found my place in life and here I would live and work and do my best to help raise the standard of literacy in North Carolina—the State of my adoption.

Eleven years before I had applied for Associate Membership in the American Ornithologists' Union, and in 1902 went to Washington, D. C., to attend one of its annual conventions, where I hoped to meet ornithologists with whose names I had been long familiar. During my absence Mrs. Pearson took care of my college classes. On the morning of November 18th, I went to the National Museum where the meetings of the Union were to be held.

An elderly gentleman preceded me through the door and I was just behind him when he reached the entrance of the assembly-hall. Here a young man handed him a slip of paper. He glanced at it and asked: "What is this?"

"It is notice of a meeting of the Audubon Societies, to be held to-morrow night."

"What are the Audubon Societies?"

"Societies to protect birds," said the other.

The older man returned the paper.

"I am not interested," he said. "I do not protect birds. I kill them."

I had not seen either one before, but I soon learned that the younger man was Harry C. Oberholser, and the other, Charles B. Cory, both prominent ornithologists.

Soon I met others, including Dr. C. Hart Merriam, John H. Sage, E. W. Nelson, Witmer Stone, Jonathan Dwight, Frederic A. Lucas, A. K. Fisher, William Dutcher, Thomas S. Roberts, Arthur C. Bent, William Brewster, Robert Ridgway, and Joel A. Allen—all names to conjure with in the ornithological world even at that day.

Three papers were presented that first forenoon, one of

these being my contribution on "Summer Bird Life of Eastern North Carolina." The sessions lasted three days. I heard all the papers and all of the discussions in reference to them and was especially glad to hear the report of Mr. Dutcher on the protection of North American birds; and the one which followed by Dr. Palmer on Federal game protection in 1902.

The Conference of the Audubon Societies was held on the evening of November 19th in Columbian University. Papers written by Olive Thorn Miller, Harriet E. Richard, Mabel Osgood Wright, Hilda Justice and O. B. Zimmerman were presented, and others spoke briefly. The program was short and was concluded before the evening was far advanced. The presiding officer asked if there were others who would speak. There were no volunteers, but Mr. Chapman stated that there was a young man present from North Carolina who had recently formed an Audubon Society and that perhaps he would have something to say. I was invited to the platform.

In my extemporaneous remarks I dwelt upon the great desirability of having laws to protect our birds, warden systems to enforce them, and a cultivated public sentiment to stimulate the activities of the wardens against market-shooters and plume-hunters. I urged that in all this work we avoid all semblance of hysteria; that we should present as evidence of our contentions only statements the truthfulness of which was beyond any question of doubt. I had been deeply disappointed to find that Audubon Societies of the rich and highly educated North were so small in numbers and so weak in finances, so I made bold to urge efforts for increasing membership everywhere and thus greatly augment the funds that might be made available for the payment of lecturers, traveling libraries and the distribution of literature.

What I said was well received and brought forth many expressions of friendly interest. I was at once asked to be a member of the National Committee of Audubon Societies, which had been organized the year before. Also, I was named as a member of the Bird Protection Committee of the Union, and in this latter organization was advanced from the status of associate member to a regular member. Many of the friendships I made on this visit to Washington were to last through life.

In Greensboro, Mrs. Pearson and I had rooms near the College. There was a lawn around the house with scattering trees, and there was a garden in the rear. It is amazing what interesting things one may observe about birds even in one's very dooryard, and I was ever on the lookout for material that could be used in that book on the birds of the State that must some day be written.

One afternoon from the window we watched a yellow-billed cuckoo raid a tent caterpillar web on a near-by tree. In five minutes it seized and swallowed nineteen of these hairy destroyers of the leaves of shade trees and of fruit trees. And yet, throughout the 48,580 square miles of North Carolina a man had just the same legal right to shoot a cuckoo that he had to kill a rat or a rattlesnake.

In the spring a pair of bluebirds appeared in the yard. I secured a box, cut a hole in one side, and nailed it to a tree. In this the bluebirds built their nest. We would stand on the top of the settee and peep into the box and count the blue eggs day by day until their numbers increased to five. Then one rainy night as the mother bird sat in the nest she must have heard the sound of claws on the bark outside. A moment later two yellow eyes blazed at the entrance, and a long arm reached downward. In the morning we found her chewed wing-tips under the tree and the blue and brown feathers were scattered about the lawn.

The male was disconsolate. All day he called anxiously, every now and then flying to the box and looking in the hole as if in the hope that his mate had returned when he was not watching. Early the next morning we again heard his notes, but now they were notably cheerful. Looking out we saw him on a limb, and a few feet away sat a female. About eleven o'clock she flew up to the box and looked inquiringly into the hole. We knew what this meant. Since she would have no use for the nest and eggs which it contained, we removed them. I wanted to make sure that the cat should not catch her, so with the aid of a wire I suspended the box about two feet below a limb. Another nest was made, four eggs were laid and once again the fur-covered agent of destruction climbed that tree. I have never seen a cat slide down a wire, but one morning the feathers of the female bluebird were blowing about the grounds.

Again the notes of the bereaved male sounded through the grove. Then he went away and we thought we should see him no more, but in just ten days he was back and with him was another lady bird! Something happened to the cat, and I buried it on a sunny slope at the back of the garden. Some weeks later four small bluebirds with ridiculously short tails were being fed on the limbs of the tree near our window. Three of them were raised but the fourth was killed with a sling-shot by a boy who violated no law in doing this.

It was about this time that the frightful headaches from which I had suffered from early boyhood took their departure. Mrs. Pearson had insisted that I consult an oculist and a pair of glasses was the result.

All that school year I continued to push the organization of the Audubon Society. Four circulars were printed and 75,000 copies were distributed. I delivered twenty-eight lectures and organized branches in several important towns. Many new members were enrolled. Gentlemen hunters and their families were my main supporters. They loved the out-of-doors and wanted market-shooting and plume-hunting brought to an end; while men who did not hunt seemed to take no interest in laws to protect wild life.

One problem that troubled me was this: Suppose we did get a law in the State to protect non-game birds, what reason could we have for thinking that more gunners would pay any attention to it? There had long been various local game-laws, but it was the business of no one to enforce them, except the general police officers. So far as I could learn, they rarely arrested any one for illegal hunting. If laws to protect quail, turkeys and deer were not enforced, could we hope for enforcement of a law to protect terns and gulls, as well as killdeers, woodpeckers, bluebirds and swallows? Would not cardinals and mockingbirds be caught and caged as of old? After all, what would be gained by passing another bird-law of any kind? It would take a lifetime, maybe several of them, to educate the population of the State to the point where no one would shoot birds whenever such an impulse came to him.

I had read that some of the Northern states had regular legal game departments that employed special officers known as game-wardens, whose sworn duty, and whose only business it was, to enforce the bird- and game-protective statutes. It was clear that there was no chance to induce our Legislature to appropriate any money to pay for game-wardens. The last Legislature had provided $100,000 for public education and educators were hailing with joy the fact that this increased appropriation would make it possible to have a four months' school term throughout the State. The people had begun to recover from the effects of the Civil War and the reign of the carpet-bag administrations that followed, but they still were very poor. No, North Carolina could provide no money for bird and game protection.

Gradually I worked out what I hoped would prove to be a feasible solution of this problem. I would ask the Legislature not only to pass a law to protect the non-game birds, but also to incorporate the Audubon Society of North Carolina with authority to appoint game-wardens who would work under the Society's jurisdiction. To get money to pay these men, I would ask that every non-resident who came to the State to hunt should be required to purchase a shooting license costing ten dollars; and that such fees should be given to the Audubon Society. One advantage of this arrangement would be that the protective work of the State would be entirely divorced from politics, which I learned was the bane of the game departments generally in the Northern states.

Upon consulting with some of the best lawyers I was told that my plan would never be acccepted by the Legislature. They pointed out that the idea of surrendering to a private society, prerogatives of State in this fashion, was unprecedented and unthinkable. They advised me to confine my efforts for bird protection to the class-room, the newspaper columns, and the lecture platform. But I found one brilliant attorney, Audrey L. Brooks of Greensboro, who agreed that the plan might be worth trying and consented to formulate my ideas into a bill suitable for presentation to the Legislature. When completed I sent it to Dr. T. S. Palmer in Washington, begging him for his criticisms, as I had been told that he knew more about the practical workings of game-laws than any man in America. Representative Westcott Roberson of Guilford County promised to introduce the bill in the General Assembly and father it on the floor of the House. Then I went to Raleigh and told my story to Governor Charles B. Aycock. He assured me heartily that I could rely on his active assistance.

The part of the State from which I most feared that opposition might come was the coastal counties of Currituck, Dare, Hyde and Carteret, where the annual killing of ducks, geese, and shore-birds was conducted on a large scale. This low country was also the haunt of the plume-hunters, who, aboard their sharpies or in shacks built on the beaches, for years had skinned and shipped to Northern markets the plumage of the fast-disappearing gulls and terns. In a last-moment effort to win support, and also to gather additional data for possible legislative debates, I left Greensboro on December 22nd. The journey necessitated my passing through Norfolk, Virginia, where between trains I visited the city markets. Here in barrels by the meat stalls, or hanging from nails by the vegetable bins, wild game was displayed for sale. There were ducks and geese and young swan. There were quail, killdeers, meadowlarks and little sandpipers. I saw several rails, also a large bittern, and hanging against one post I counted a string of forty-five cedar waxwings. Virginia, like so many other states, was making no effort to save its wild birds.

Starting at Mudon's Point, near the Virginia line, I worked southward through Currituck, Albemarle, and Pamlico Sounds to Cape Hatteras. I visited market-shooters and plume-hunters. I went to the duck clubs of wealthy Northern men. I examined the storage houses of local shippers where hung countless ducks, geese and occasionally swan, and saw dozens of barrels of these birds loaded on boats to be transferred to the railroad for shipment. I visited sheds where quantities of terns had been skinned for the feather trade. I saw men shooting wild-fowl from blinds and sink boxes, and at night watched the moving lights that gleamed from the prows of boats as hunters in the darkness silently rowed to the rafts of sleeping redheads and canvas-backs and fired broadsides into them at point-blank range. I traveled by sail-boats and horse carts, and afoot, and after covering two hundred miles in and out among the sounds, the marshes, and the islands, returned to Greensboro and girded for the legislative battle to come.

A few days later when the General Assembly of North Carolina met for its bi-annual session and the Governor's message was presented to the Senators and Assemblymen, it contained the following statement:

About a year ago there was formed, at Greensboro, the Audubon Society of North Carolina. The object of this society is to protect and preserve the game and non-game birds of the State. Already the Society contains a large membership of many of the best people in the State. We have heretofore paid little attention to the preservation of our birds, other than those which have been protected for the sake of game, but the birds other than game-birds are of great practical value to man. They render much service as destroyers of insects which are injurious to vegetation, as consumers of small rodents, as destroyers of large quantities of seeds of injurious plants, and as scavengers. Some of these birds consume more than their own weight of insects daily. In this way they are of great protection to our crops, and the little injury which they do to them is much more than counterbalanced by the service rendered.

There have been found in the State three hundred and twelve species of birds, but they become scarcer with each year. Many of them are almost entirely extinct. Our sea-birds have been almost exterminated for the plumes collected for the great millinery-houses. The Audubon Society will ask for the enactment of a law protecting all these birds. The Society will undertake the task of enforcing the law without expense to the State. I recommend a careful and favorable consideration of the plans which will be proposed by the Society.

With swelling heart I heard these words of the Governor and when soon afterward various members of the Legislature came to me, pledging their support and prophesying success, I believed that victory was at hand.

CHAPTER V

IMITATING SOLON

THE LEGISLATURE of North Carolina, which met early in January, 1903, for its bi-annual session of sixty days, was slow in getting to work. A United States Senator was to be elected and the Democrats went into caucus to determine whom they would nominate for this important position. A time-absorbing deadlock developed and I could not get Representative Westcott Roberson to introduce my bird-bill until the twenty-third of the month. It was referred to the Committee on Corporations which chanced to meet that very afternoon.

With two or three friends I spoke in its behalf, but we were given only a few minutes. Several of the Committee frankly showed their hostility, stating that the proposed measure was a long, involved, impractical one, and that to expect the Legislature to incorporate a private society with all the authority of a Department of State was a ridiculous idea. Upon motion it was referred to a sub-committee, and a newspaper reporter told me this was just a nice way of pigeon-holing the bill. He advised me to go back to my classes and forget about it.

Amazed, chagrined, and with difficulty realizing what had occurred, I went to my room in the Yarborough House to try to think. At dinner I saw one of the members of that sub-committee at a table with some friends. When he came out of the dining-room door I stopped him, and he agreed to talk with me for a few minutes in a corner of the lobby. After a little he consented to go to my room. Here our conference lasted for an hour or more, and he left with the promise that he would support the bill if his two colleagues would do likewise. Four days later I had the promise of their votes, also.

The next week the Committee on Corporations again convened, and, to the surprise of nearly every one present, the sub-committee reported that it favored the proposed law and urged that time be provided for me to explain in detail its provisions. For thirty minutes I spoke, restraining my speech as I always tried to do when I felt the invisible hand of Ed Wilson on my shoulder. The Committee was as responsive as I could possibly have wished and not only voted to report the bill favorably, but also decided to ask the Legislature to invite me to address the entire Assembly. Thus the first skirmish was won and my feeling of thankfulness was profound.

On February 11th, Roberson called up the Audubon Bill in the Legislature and moved that I be invited to address the Assembly before a vote was taken. Instantly a member sprang to his feet loudly voicing his objection to such an unheard-of procedure. I recall very distinctly his closing words: "Why, gentlemen, if we ask this Professor to address this body we will be setting a precedent for like requests from the friends of every other crank in the State who comes here with a freak bill."

His speech fired the Assembly and it seemed to me that every one in the Chamber at once took sides. Sometimes three or four were clamoring for recognition at once. A man whose daughter I had taught about birds warmly urged that the motion be adopted, and others followed his lead. One man shouted, "If we have nothing better to do than listen to a man talk about jaybirds and sparrows, we had better go home."

At length Speaker Gattis stilled the tumult with his gavel and said: "Gentlemen, the Chairman of the Committee on

Corporations moved that we invite Professor Pearson to address us for twenty minutes. We have already debated the matter for twenty-five minutes. I shall now put the motion to a vote." By a majority of two the Legislature voted to hear me speak and a Committee was appointed to escort me to the Speaker's desk. As I walked up the aisle I called mightily on the angel who guards over the Websterian orators of Guilford College and promised far-away Ed Wilson that I would be his worthy disciple. Perhaps a dozen of the Assemblymen left their seats and stood in the lobby near the door through which they could easily escape; others picked up newspapers or began to talk with their neighbors.

With every art practised by young Southern speakers of that day I poured out my story to them. I was in deadly earnest and perfectly at home on my feet for I knew my audience. They stopped talking, they laid down their newspapers. Those in the lobby drifted back to their seats. I told them of the robins and mockingbirds that sing in their yards, of the jays that even as I spoke were calling in the trees just outside the windows, and of the woodpeckers that had built their nest in the ball on the capitol dome above their heads. I talked of the great value of the birds to the State, and how they were being killed by an unthinking public, and that a Commonwealth which did not protect its birds gave hostages to Fortune. It was absolutely essential to hold the attention of those Assemblymen, and I sought earnestly to prevent them from anticipating the outcome of a single paragraph or even a sentence. I had been taught that a speaker must keep a bow-shot ahead of the thoughts of his listeners lest they weary, and he lose their attention.

I spoke with rapidity but with careful distinction, striving never to slur a word, never to repeat an idea, and never to allow my voice to fall at the end of a sentence. I knew positively that every man in that legislative hall heard distinctly, and clearly understood every word I uttered, and even before concluding I could tell by their faces that another battle had been won. When the vote was taken there was not a dissenting voice.

Shortly after my Raleigh speech, I received an invitation to address a joint session of the Tennessee Legislature "upon the subject of bird protection." It came as a formal resolution of the Senate and the House, and was endorsed by Governor James B. Frazier. Friends in Raleigh told me to accept, saying that they would see that nothing happened to the Audubon Bill in my absence.

Again I deserted my college classes and boarded a train for Tennessee. About midnight a pullman porter awoke me and said that A. B. Andrews, Vice-President of the Southern Railway, had sent him to tell me that we were blocked by a wreck, but that if I would join him in his private car, attached to the rear of the train, he would see that I reached Nashville in time for my engagement. An engine soon came up and pulling the car back along the track switched to another line, and brought us to Nashville next morning. I addressed the Legislature at eleven o'clock, spoke to the students of the Peabody Normal College in the afternoon, and hurried away on the return trip to Raleigh.

Something of the extent of the revolution which I was attempting in the matter of North Carolina game-laws can be shown in a few sentences. At this time it was legal to shoot deer, both male and female, throughout the entire year in twenty-three of its ninety-seven counties. In the other counties shooting was permitted for three months. Squirrels did not have the slightest legal protection in ninety-three counties of the State. One was not supposed to hunt opossum during one-half the year in fourteen counties, elsewhere these animals were not mentioned in the statutes. In eight counties, quail could be killed at any time, and there was no protection for wild turkeys in thirteen counties.

Rails, curlews, oyster-catchers, plovers, snipes, woodcocks, sandpipers and other shore-birds had no protection whatever except that there was a closed season of five months in New Hanover County. Ruffed grouse had short close seasons for shooting in four counties; and ducks, geese and swan in five counties. Elsewhere all these birds could be taken at any time of the year. Mourning doves could be shot or trapped at any time in eight counties. Robins, thrushes, meadow-larks, warblers, flickers, bobolinks, cardinals and other song birds might be shot, netted, or trapped by day or night at any time of the year. No one ever heard of a law to protect rabbits.

The shipping of game-birds to Northern markets was a common practice. No one thought of objecting to this any more than he would have opposed the shipping of potatoes, peaches, or cotton. Thousands of young mockingbirds were taken from their nests every year to be reared by hand. Those that survived could be seen everywhere. They were in cages hanging in the chinaberry trees at Negro cabins, on the porches of people living in towns, and on the galleries of planters. Many were sent to Northern cities, where they brought fair prices, as did the cardinals and nonpareils which also came from the South.

Game was common in the markets of the State. Grouse, wild turkeys and long strings of quail hung before grocery stores in the streets of such cities as Raleigh, Greensboro, Winston, and Charlotte. Quail, ducks, rails, snipes and robins could be bought almost anywhere in the eastern part of the State, and they cost but little. Country men and boys, both white and colored, shot and trapped game-birds every-where, and traded them at the "cash and barter" stores for food, ammunition, chewing tobacco, overalls or cloth for their women's dresses.

There were not, and never had been, any state officials known as "game-wardens." It was extremely rare that any one was prosecuted for infractions of the game-laws, although such violations were numerous. Once in a while some pot-hunter aroused the ire of a sportsman who would get a peace officer to arrest him for hunting out of season. Now and then a Negro would get into trouble. Gentlemen hunted game for their dining-tables and to give to friends, or if too busy or too inert, would hand a Negro some shells and promise him a dollar if he brought back a good bag.

There was considerable sentiment in the State for preserving the quail supply, this idea being fostered by sportsmen who did not want game to become scarce and by farmers who wanted to lease the shooting rights on their farms. However, birds were abundant and very good to eat; sheriffs were scarce, and, incidentally, enjoyed the flavor of game as much as any one.

It was to a Legislature composed of men who, like their fathers before them, had enjoyed wide liberties in hunting, that the Audubon Bill was brought. It contained a number of innovations, one of which was that its provisions should be applicable for the entire State. Furthermore, the exportation of most game, whether living or dead, was to be prohibited, except by permit under certain well defined conditions.

There was a section in the bill which gave the names of those species of birds to which no protection would be extended. I would gladly have reduced the length of this list, but public sentiment would not tolerate extending even a semblance of protection to English sparrows, crows, hawks, owls, blackbirds and ricebirds (bobolinks).

In another section there were listed the birds which should legally be considered game. It was the assumption that closed seasons had been, or would be, provided for them by county laws. In this category I had not included the "bullbat" or nighthawk, although it had always been shot as a game-bird. I knew I was taking a risk in trying to protect it, but when the bill was discussed in committee and on the floor of the

Legislature, it happened that no one mentioned it, and, of course, I did not do so.

When on February 12th the bill was being considered on its second reading, Assemblyman R. A. Doughton of Alleghany County, noticing me in the lobby of the House, left his seat long enough to ask me the correct name of the bird which in the mountains is called "joree." He at once returned to the floor and a few moments later arose and told the other Assemblymen that up in his country there was a bird named "chewink or towhee," which was very harmful to farmers because it pulled up and ate newly planted corn. This feathered despoiler of the fields, he said, should not have thrown around it the strong arm of legal protection.

Its name, he averred, should be added to the list of outlawed birds, and he offered an amendment intended to accomplish this end, but he worded it in such a manner that the bird's name was placed in the wrong paragraph. No member of the House noticed the mistake so the towhee became not an outlawed bird, but a legal game-bird and was so listed in the Statutes of North Carolina for the next twenty-five years.

With this addition the list of birds which the Legislature subsequently declared could legally be killed as game, read as follows: "Loons and grebes, swans, geese, brant, river-, fish- and sea-ducks, rails, coots, marsh-hens and gallinules, plovers, shore- and surf-birds, snipe, woodcock, sandpipers, yellow-legs, chewink or towhee, and curlews; and the wild turkey, grouse, partridge, pheasant, quail, dove, robin and meadowlark."

If the bill had been placed on its third reading immediately after its second reading, it would have passed without difficulty, but some one asked that it go over for a brief period so that he would have time to prepare a "beneficial" amendment, and the request was granted. Then trouble began.

Hotel men, guides, and boatmen who served visiting duck-hunters along the coast, sent petitions and delegates to the Legislature with claims that a ten-dollar non-resident license would hurt their business, as Northern duck-hunters would be kept from the State by such an outrageous tax. A man who for some years had employed several others to shoot terns and gulls for their skins and shore-birds for the markets, aroused the politicians of his county. Dr. Louis B. Bishop, a New England ornithologist who was a member of a North Carolina duck-hunting club, disapproved of the license feature and urged Dutcher to force me to drop this from the bill.

Roberson was slow in asking for a final vote in the House. A week went by. Two weeks passed. In less than ten days the Legislature would adjourn. Still Roberson did nothing. Finally, in reply to my proddings, he said he had decided that the bill was impracticable, for many farmers had written him that such a law would prevent them from leasing the shooting rights on their farms to Northern quail-hunters. Dutcher, discouraged, wired me from New York to strike out all sections of the bill except those designed to protect non-game birds. I declined to do this and sent hurried messages to sportsmen in Greensboro and elsewhere. They responded effectively and Roberson, concluding that after all his fears were unfounded, called up the bill and made a strong speech in its behalf. Various Assemblymen at once sent amendments to the Speaker's desk. The first one if adopted would completely destroy its efficiency, as Roberson vigorously pointed out. Another wanted it to go over until night to give him time to write an amendment. One man moved to table it. Several wanted their counties exempted.

Assemblyman Brittain arose and after a speech replete with scathing denunciations offered the following amendment: "Provided, that the senior member from Randolph [Mr. Brittain] may have one-half acre of cheap land, worth $1.00, set apart to him by the Audubon Society to be buried in and that same be exempt from the bird trust created by virtue of the provisions of the Audubon Bill, and that his widow and heirs at law be allowed to use the rabbit feet from said acre free from tax by virtue of any regulations of the Audubon Society, and that the game-wardens and all their understrappers take the necessary ghost notice when they enter said land."

After two hours' debate all amendments were voted down and the bill passed its third reading.

Three days later, which was March 6, 1903, the Senate gave its approval and the Audubon Bill at once became a law, for in North Carolina the Governor has no veto power. Thus was passed the first law ever enacted in any South Atlantic or Gulf state to provide for a state game-warden system. There were still seventeen states in the Union where no warden system had been put in operation, and in thirty-one states the law did not protect song and insectivorous birds.

Some of the Administration leaders sent for me and said that I must be careful about the type of men I appointed as wardens, for if these became obnoxious their activities would arouse the same resentment universally felt toward revenue officers. They also told me that they would watch our efforts for two years and if the plan did not work well they would take away our charter when the Legislature met again. I promised that we would do our best, and thanking the Governor, Roberson, and the leaders of the House and the Senate, took the train for Greensboro. At Durham I received a telegram of congratulations. It was from my senior zoölogy class, and read: WE JOIN THE BIRDS IN SINGING YOUR PRAISES. I still have that sheet of yellow paper.

One of these students was Virginia Brown, who after her graduation became my assistant in the College. She was unusually bright and her interest in zoölogy and botany was very real. Her love for these subjects was later to be reflected in the lives of her children. One of them, Robert Dick Douglas, Jr., in 1928 was one of the three boy scouts selected to accompany the Martin Johnsons on a wild-life expedition to lion-inhabited Africa.

A flood of applications for wardens' positions began to arrive. Most of the writers assumed that the positions would pay well. One offered to divide his salary, and reminded me that the more I paid him the more he could give me.

The next week the first annual meeting of the Audubon Society of North Carolina was held. Dr. Theodore S. Palmer came down from Washington to be our principal speaker. "Nothing succeeds like success," was the opening sentence of his address. Within twelve months from the date of its founding the Society had aroused a lively interest throughout the State in the subject of bird protection, and had been granted unheard-of legal powers. It had enrolled 917 members, had collected and expended $783.65, and had closed the year without a deficit. The world seemed very bright. We were going to save the wild birds of the State.

There was considerable publicity in the Southern newspapers at that time about our unique work in North Carolina, and various invitations reached me to speak before schools, colleges and civic organizations. Many people wanted to see and hear the young professor who was going about preaching a strange new doctrine. A flattering offer of a month's lecture work at the State Summer School of South Carolina arrived but the date conflicted with my engagement to return for six weeks to the University of Tennessee.

At Knoxville that summer I was appointed Chairman of the Committee on Program for the July 4th celebration held on the university campus. One incident of that day I remember with vivid clearness. After the parade had ended and all had gathered in the big assembly pavilion there were some

THEODORE S. PALMER

Eminent authority on wild-life legislation, for thirty-one years Vice-President and a director of the National Association of Audubon Societies. Photograph taken in the Roosevelt Bird Sanctuary, Oyster Bay, New York, in 1927.

demonstrations that had not been planned by the committee. The teachers from each state sat together. A spokesman for the Georgia group arose and said they were all proud that a certain professor from their state was on the faculty. Applause followed. There were two or three similar expressions from other states.

Then a North Carolina lady came forward directly toward me. She was smiling and in her hand was a large bouquet. She handed it to an usher on the platform where the hundred members of the faculty sat several rows deep. The usher turned to me. I arose, took the beautiful offering and bowed to the North Carolina delegation. At once the applause subsided appreciably, and an animated whispered conversation began. A horrifying thought assailed me, and turning I saw seated directly behind my chair one of North Carolina's most distinguished educators who had joined the faculty but three days before and of whose arrival I was not aware. He was a man of great prominence. His trail was big in the dust before I was born. I had taken the flowers that were intended for him!

When Mrs Pearson and I left Knoxville the last of July, men and boys in the evening were engaged in the popular summer sport of shooting swifts, martins, and especially nighthawks that were circling around over some of the vacant lots at the edge of the city.

We found the North Carolina mountains a cool retreat after the heat of Knoxville. The valleys and the slopes were vibrant with life. A snowbird was feeding its young within sixty feet of the hotel, the nest tucked in a hole in the bank near the walk. Scarlet tanagers were singing in the woods. A journey was made by trail up the side of Graybeard, and along the crest of Potato Top to the highest point of Mount Mitchel at 6,684 feet elevation. On the way we traversed forests of balsam, chestnut, and rhododendron, and rode through beds of ferns and acres of galax. We clambered

among masses of damp moss riotously covering rocks and
fallen logs, and passed through thick stunted growths where
the winter wrens were calling.

From the top of the great mountain whichever way we
turned our eyes rested upon a world of green hills. Below
white clouds filled the valleys. It was all strange, mysterious,
awesome, and wonderfully thrilling—this first trip of ours to
the high mountains.

Soon after the enactment of the Audubon Law the incor-
porators had met and elected officers and an executive committee. Dr. R. H. Lewis, a prominent physician in Raleigh,
was chosen President to succeed J. Y. Joyner, the State Superintendent of Public Instruction, who had been the Society's
first President. I was reëlected Secretary. Since the people of
the State had not been accustomed to paying much attention
to game-laws, we felt it our first duty to acquaint every one
with the nature of the existing statutes on this subject, also
with the further fact that machinery was now in motion to
prosecute people who violated them.

Warning notices, setting forth the nature of the laws, were
printed on sheets of linen and thousands were tacked up at
post-offices, court-houses, country stores, cross-roads and other
strategic points. Special leaflets on the value of birds were
printed and more than 125,000 were distributed. One thousand copies of the Audubon Law accompanied with letters
were mailed to the magistrates and judges of the State. Ten
readable books on birds and mammals were combined to
make up a library to be loaned to country school-teachers.
Fifty of these libraries were soon in use.

The shooting of nighthawks had long been a custom in
many parts of the State. Men would gather in open ground
near villages and shoot them from the air as they fluttered
about on summer evenings. Immense numbers were killed
every year, not only in North Carolina, but throughout the
Southern states generally. As a rule they were not eaten,

although sometimes Negro boys would run and retrieve them as they fell.

I have seen many groups of men engaged in nighthawk shooting when no one took the trouble to go about and pick up the dead and wounded birds. Why bother, at night the cats and hogs of the neighborhood would prowl over the shooting fields. One morning I saw a cat bring her kittens a live nighthawk with a broken wing. On occasions I observed ants eating at the wounds of disabled birds.

Now at least the law was on the side of the birds, and in attempting to handle this situation I wrote notices for the newspapers and went myself or sent men to many places to tell hunters that "bullbats" were now protected, because they were very valuable as destroyers of mosquitoes and other harmful insects. In most cases such shooting ceased after a warning had been given. Many of the hunters were young men of good families and not of the type who took pleasure in violating laws.

No money from the State would become available until the Northern hunters, some seven months later, should begin to arrive for the autumn quail- and duck-shooting. We had a little income from the fees of members whose numbers I was continually augmenting, and we set to work organizing our game-warden force. With great care men were selected here and there and the Governor, upon notification, would promptly send to each one a formal commission of authority. Mrs. Pearson wrote out the oaths which they were to take and in numerous other ways aided me in the work, for a large percentage of the daylight hours were necessarily devoted to my classes. With our small means we could not at first employ wardens on salary. Usually their pay was two dollars a day and expenses when on special duty. Later a few were engaged for fifty dollars a month and expenses.

Our first arrests were on September 9, 1903, when two young men near Greensboro, after being warned about shooting night-hawks, resumed their sport. A magistrate fined them one dollar for each of the four birds they had killed. The same day word came that a man near Charlotte, who had killed a wild turkey-hen out of season, was fined "one penny and costs."

The newspaper editors of the State, as well as various people who wrote letters for publication, continued their praise of the Audubon Society and its work. Early in September I spoke in Charlotte, Raleigh, and Washington, North Carolina, and in these towns organized branches of the Society. Every one seemed to be our friend, and it appeared that all good people were observing the bird laws and were frowning on any low fellow who did not do so.

But these expressions of good-will were not to continue without interruption. On September 22, 1903, the Raleigh *News and Observer,* under a nine-line caption, published a letter which in part ran as follows:

TO THE EDITOR:
Our community was very greatly shocked last week when it was learned that Mr. G. W. Anthony, one of the most wealthy and influential citizens of Burlington, had been arrested, charged with the killing of chimney-sweeps. On all sides are heard expressions of indignation.
For the past several months Mr. Anthony had been greatly annoyed by hundreds of chimney-sweeps infesting the chimneys. They congregated by hundreds, knocking down trash on his carpets and every morning his housekeeper had to clean up after the birds. One evening last week after the rain Mr. Anthony concluded to try to destroy them. He put a screen over the top of the chimney and [with straw] set the chimney on fire destroying several hundred. . . . The Honorable T. Gilbert Pearson, the chief manager and financier of the Audubon Society, read of the act and sent a man from Greensboro with instructions to one of the leading attorneys of this town to prosecute Mr. Anthony and he would see that he got well paid. Mr. Anthony was made to appear before a magistrate and was bound over to court to answer the charge of burning out his chimney-sweeps

that had been a continual menace and nuisance. Now, any one can see at a glance that the action was an injustice to Mr. Anthony....

If the Honorable T. Gilbert Pearson and his legion of women and children backers think that they can compel intelligent people to put up with a nuisance like this, he is mistaken. It may not be put in the paper, but so long as the abominable things worry the life out of housekeepers and endanger nice homes by carrying trash into the chimneys, to catch fire when it is dry, they are going to be killed, and they will not be electrocuted or given ether, but will go by the same old time-honored route, viz., burning out.

The truth of the whole business is that Mr. Pearson backed by the little children of the country, made the last legislature enact a very foolish law, under the pretext of protecting "song-birds," sea-gulls and others of the feathered tribe....

In his great zeal as the leader of this Audubon Society and in his efforts to protect the chinch-carrying sweeps, Mr. Pearson forgets that he is protecting them at the expense of good, well-meaning, honest people. The feelings of a man who is not conscious of having done wrong, in having to suffer disgrace by being arrested and brought before a magistrate, is nothing in Mr. Pearson's eyes, but when he hears the squeak of a sweeper his pulses thrill and he rings for an officer, and after seeing that there is enough funds left to pay his own forthcoming salary, he dispatches a message to spare no pains nor money in the prosecution—for the non-resident devil is footing the bill....

The magistrate before whom Mr. Anthony had been taken by the Audubon warden required him to give bond to appear and plead before the judge at the next term of the Alamance Superior Court. The *Burlington News* reported that Anthony said he was sorry that he had burned alive all those hundreds of birds, and the editor expressed a hope that the Audubon Society "will enter a plea of mercy in behalf of Mr. Anthony," and added: "At any rate the case has been the means of giving publicity to the laws along this line and will deter many from violating the same."

The Audubon Society entered no plea of mercy in behalf

of Mr. Anthony; in fact as it transpired he did not need help from any one as the trial judge before whom he pled guilty let him off without imposing a fine.

Thus, after being in operation seven months we had made four arrests for violations of the bird-protective laws, and had not lost one of our cases in the courts. The fines collected had totaled $4.01. Our efforts were succeeding.

CHAPTER VI

AT THE BOB-WHITES'S CALL

ONE MORNING when I was a small boy a bob-white dashed into the room where my mother sat knitting. A hawk came right in after it and in the confusion that followed she hit the hawk with a newspaper before it flew out of the door again. The bob-white crouched under a chair for a few minutes, then walked to the door, paused, ran across the veranda and flew down into the yard.

At Archer bob-whites at times fed in the backyard with the chickens. We knew them as "partridges." Often we would see or hear them within a few yards of the house. If they saw us they ran away or flew a short distance and stood hidden for a little while among the cow-peas. I caught two that went into our potato-house. Their scatter calls and conversational notes were heard about as often as were the voices of the mockingbirds, jays, and red-headed woodpeckers. In spring and summer the "bob-white" whistle was sounded continually.

As one sat calling on a rail of the scuppernong grape-arbor close to the house one day, I asked Uncle Pauldo why it gave the same notes so many times. The old Negro stopped hoeing the crab-grass among the young orange trees and made a great show of surprise at my ignorance.

"You don't even know about dat? Well, white chile, dat bird is a he one and when you hear him squawling dat-a-way hit mean he belongs to have a hen."

A little later in the pine woods I came upon a newly hatched family of them. The mother probably was brooding her young at the time for the first I was aware of their presence was the sudden desperate fluttering of the parent bird that sought to lead me away from the spot. Also, the ground was instantly alive with little yellowish brown bodies that ran cheeping in every direction and a moment later disappeared as if the earth had swallowed them. All my search resulted in the finding of just one infant partridge. As it crouched in my hand it seemed to be no heavier than a butterfly. Its tiny eyes were bright and the top of its beak still bore the little horn with which it had cut its way out of the egg-shell.

The life of the bob-white is filled with many alarms. All during the twenty-three days that the mother bird and her mate engage in incubation there is the ever-present possibility of disaster. Rats and hogs are fond of quail eggs and corn snakes, pine snakes, and black-snakes will clean out a nest if they find one. Cattle wandering about now and then step on nests. Self-hunting dogs and house cats will often catch brooding birds on their nests. Among the worst enemies are the red ants that enter eggs when they are pipped and eat the young alive before they can cut their way out of the shell. Always there are human enemies. One day a Negro showed me a nest containing twenty-two eggs which he then took away to boil for supper. He said he knew they were fresh because some were piled on others. "If they were addled they would all be in one layer," he explained.

When the young are hatched the responsibilities of parenthood are instantly increased. While sitting on the nest the scent from the bird is so slight that a dog passing within three feet in most cases would be unaware of its presence. But the young ones must be taken on little journeys in search of food, and the scent of the family in motion advertises its presence to every keen-nosed creature that comes along. So the mother bird with her young that I had stumbled upon in the pine sapling grove that day was filled with terror, and her cries were disturbing to hear. She would have little peace of mind until that brood was large enough to fly swiftly away when danger threatened.

She must ever be on guard. Coach whips were numerous and one of these long, slender, sharp-eyed snakes might find and easily swallow half of the family in a few minutes, or a butcher-bird might carry one away. Many dogs snap up little partridges for the pleasure it affords them. Heavy rains are to be dreaded. Some of the young may stray away and be lost. Others may get into wheel-ruts with the walls so high they can not climb out, and perhaps a wagon or ox-cart will come along. Sometimes a young one will fall into a deep hole where a forest fire has burned out an old fat-wood stump. In the autumn blue-darter hawks arrive from the North and spread terror and destruction through the fields and pine lands. Then the trapping and hunting season would begin. In the excitement of escaping enemies I have twice seen coveys dash against the side of a house painted white and some of the members in each case were stunned or killed. In short, so numerous were these birds' enemies in our community that each year about the same number of bob-whites inhabited the country-side. There is little wonder that through the centuries the bob-white was forced to develop the power of laying from twelve to twenty eggs in a nest.

Alex Darden showed me how to make a partridge-trap with sticks split from a yellow-pine fence rail. Four of these sticks were two and a half feet long and those of each succeeding set were two inches shorter. They were piled in such a way as to build a flat-topped pyramid about ten inches high. A piece of bark a foot wide served to close the final opening. Across this a green stick was laid and with a heavy cord wrapped about each end was securely tied to the bottom pair of sticks, thus holding the structure firmly together. A few minutes' work with a pocket-knife produced the three parts of a figure-four trigger. He raised one side of the trap, put the trigger in place and smiled, for his work was done.

Alex's face was yellowish-white like the sand of the "salamander" bed nearby. A wisp of bleached hair curled under each ear, his feet were bare. He was a Florida cracker.

Throughout the State and for a thousand miles to the north and to the west numerous other country boys, both white and colored, were making similar traps for it was autumn and coveys of partridges were numerous. Alex picked up the trap and I followed him through the recently burned piney woods. The stubble of the wire-grass clusters did not seem to hurt his feet, for they were hardened by long exposure. We climbed a rail fence and went along between rows of dead corn stalks where the beggar weeds grew thick. At the edge of a wild plum thicket he stopped and showed me a bare spot of ground on which I could see some scattered cow-peas and the tracks of birds. He had prepared and baited the place two days before. Here he set the trap and we went home.

The next day I went with Alex to the wild plum orchard. As we drew near we could see the trap was down, and could hear the thumps of the imprisoned birds as they struck against the slats trying to find a way through the cracks between them. Four partridges had been caught. He dug a hole under the edge of the trap, and thrusting in his hand and arm, brought them out one at a time and put them in an old corn sack. They were uninjured except that the feathers from the bill to the top of the head had been worn off as the birds tried to make their escape before we had arrived. He had two other traps, one of which had not been sprung, the other containing a mourning-dove. He pulled off the dove's head and thrust the body in his pocket—his mother would cook it for him. Alex sold his partridges to a man who kept a little store. He could get for them either four cents in trade for supplies, or he could have three cents "cash money" if he preferred.

That day I saw a crate of fifty partridges put into the open door of an express car when the accommodation train stopped at the Archer station. Near the door stood some barrels of iced fish from which water was spreading over the floor. There were also several sea-turtles lying on their backs with their front flippers sewn together. The fish and turtles had come from Cedar Keys. The expressman pulled the crate of birds well inside and waved his hand as the train moved away.

I was told that the partridges would bring ten cents apiece in Jacksonville. All over the southland that morning and every other morning for weeks to follow, live partridges would be put on trains for shipment to towns and cities where, quite as a matter of course, they would be sold for food as fish, beef, potatoes and cabbages were sold. Alex's uncle said that trapping birds was "nigger business," but he was a man who owned horses to ride when on rainy days he and his friends went out with their partridge-net. Sometimes they would catch three or four entire coveys in one afternoon.

Frequently I would range the fields with older boys who had guns. Now and then a meadowlark or flicker would be shot. Sometimes a mourning dove or two would be secured. Usually this was accomplished by creeping along the rail fence of a peanut field well rooted by the razorbacks which had been driven in from the woods to be fattened. Often doves were plentiful in such places and with gun pushed through a crack in the fence the hunter could now and then get two or three at a shot if he had patience to wait until several were close together. Not infrequently a hunter would come upon a covey of partridges running down a path or a cotton row and might get several when he fired. But when the boys went out for a serious partridge-hunt, a cur dog was taken along. At such time the trips were made along the borders of the open piney woods. When the birds were encountered the dog would race about barking and often some of the birds would fly up on the limbs of the trees. They sat very close and were hard to see, but when one was discovered it was easy to shoot. Alex made a famous shot one day of which the other boys talked for a long time. Late in the evening he saw a group of fifteen or more partridges going to roost. They squatted on the ground very close together and with heads pointed outward in all directions. He fired into the flock and killed eleven.

The Wood family at Archer had come from Boston. Mr. Wood was very fond of hunting partridges, or "quail" as he called them. When in the field he wore regular hunting clothes and took with him the first pointer dog that I had ever seen. Word soon spread about the neighborhood that he never shot a bird on the ground, nor in a tree. One of the bolder boys asked permission to go with him on one of his shooting-trips, but was refused. When I happened to see him crossing a field one day I hid in a fence corner and watched his movements. The dog ran here and there until presently it stopped with nose extended and tail pointed well out behind. When it took a step forward I heard his master say "Steady." The man walked cautiously forward until with an explosive roar the covey took wing. With incredible swiftness he raised his gun and fired, first straight ahead and then to the left. Two birds dropped and the dog ran out quickly and brought them to its master. Mr. Wood was known in the neighborhood as a sportsman, the name indicating a man who wore a hunting suit and who shot birds only when they were flying. All other shooters of the country were referred to simply as hunters, and virtually every healthy man or big boy who was not averse to tramping through briars or climbing rail fences, was a hunter at some time during the year.

It was a long time after watching that Boston sportsman through the cracks of a rail fence that I became responsible for enforcing the laws intended to protect quail in North Carolina. It was a well-known fact that for many years great numbers of them had been shipped to Northern markets, and when the shooting season opened in 1903 we expected that some people would attempt to continue the traffic, despite the fact that the Audubon Law now made this practice illegal.

One of our game-wardens in Greensboro was John Weatherly. He and I made frequent trips of inspection to the Southern Railway Station where the express from branch roads was unloaded for reshipment northward. We examined the labels of many packages, but discovered no quail. After some weeks of fruitless search, when I had just about decided that the quail-shippers had abandoned their business, I received an anonymous letter asking us to watch for a package which would be shipped from Silor City to Wallestine Brothers, Washington, D. C. A magistrate signed in blank several search warrants which we could fill in if we needed them. The first train from Chatham County contained a box addressed to Wallestine Brothers. It was a crate and we could see eggs through the slats. Nevertheless, we opened it and found that under a layer of eggs the receptacles were completely filled with the bodies of quail.

Two newspaper reporters came along just then and began a rapid-fire questioning. One of the things they wanted to know was how we happened to guess that the crate contained quail.

"There was no guess-work about it," Weatherly told them, "that dog of mine pointed the box for us." He patted the head of a little short-haired black dog that always accompanied him.

Within twenty-four hours the whole State had been advised that it was a perilous undertaking to try to smuggle quail through Greensboro, because a dog of unusual powers and sagacity was on constant watch. That fanciful yarn invented by Weatherly on the spur of the moment did more to check the illicit shipment of quail than all the subsequent prosecutions in the courts. The warden sold the captured birds at auction from the court-house steps and the proceeds, according to law, were forwarded to the State Treasurer.

While most of the shipments we seized were the result of information furnished in advance, now and then we made a discovery of our own. One evening I noticed a flat, square box of nice workmanship. Its weight aroused my curiosity. Upon removing the lid we found that it contained two dozen especially fine quail. They had been carefully cleaned and arranged in neat rows with their breasts upward in a nest of tissue-paper. The package was addressed to a lady in the fashionable residential section of Washington, D. C.

One day when a baggage-man was moving some trunks we noticed that one of the small ones seemed very heavy. When we stood it on end and shook it our suspicions were further aroused. It contained 334 quail. It was being transported as baggage and we were never able to locate the owner. One afternoon a telegram from Winston reached me saying, LOOK OUT FOR QUAIL IN EXPRESS CAR FROM HERE THIS EVENING. We were on hand when the train came in about dark, and were soon at work on the express packages, which were to be reshipped on the northbound train at midnight.

Weatherly began a systematic search while I sat on a crated carboy and watched his businesslike proceedings. I supposed the big jug under me contained moonshine, but I was not interested in illicit whiskey for our business dealt with birds, not liquor. The warden went through the express packages, consisting of a number of egg crates, butter firkins, and the like. There was a box of sweet potatoes, a half-barrel of apples, and even a cardboard carton which contained a dress suit. After this exhaustive search we left, grumbling about what a poor joke some one had played on us. The next morning I received a letter from Winston in which the writer said he hoped that we captured the quail about which he had wired me. He explained, "The quail were in a carboy, having been packed through a hole broken in the bottom."

A man in the outskirts of Greensboro kept a produce store, but seemed to do very little business. Like many other merchants, he bought quail which the farmers brought to town, but unlike the others he did not sell any. We tested this by twice sending a buyer to him shortly after we had seen quail delivered. From an upper window across the street in front of his door a watch was kept day and night for nearly a week. Now and then he shipped eggs and poultry to Raleigh, but never put any packages on the northbound trains.

One night we noticed that there were taken off the train from Raleigh two crates of eggs marked for transit to the North. They bore his label. Under a layer of eggs were many quail. At last we had caught him. It turned out that he had been sending his birds to Raleigh from which point they were shipped North over the Seaboard Railway. By some mistake these two crates had been reshipped to Greensboro, to be taken North by a Southern Railway train. It was three days before we could find that man to serve a warrant on him. Within an hour a prominent local politician hurried into my office and asked if I realized what I was doing in making that arrest. He told me that the merchant was the nephew of Judge So and So, who was a man of great influence and that I should at once withdraw the charge. This I declined to do and the case went to the Superior Court. The defendant's attorney belittled the seriousness of the offense and made the usual plea for mercy with the result that the man was let off with a very light fine.

One cold winter night, shortly before the train for Washington arrived, as Weatherly, another warden, and I were prowling around the depot, we paused by a truck loaded with mail-bags. Among them we noticed a burlap sack. Taking hold of it I could feel the bodies of quail concealed within. When the train stopped the three of us were between the track and the mail truck. A man suddenly approached on the opposite side of the track, snatched the sack of quail, and ran around back of the station, with us in hot pursuit. He doubled back through the waiting-room and out to the open door of the mail-car. Here a warden got hold of the sack, but it was jerked from his grasp and thrown into the car. Weatherly attempted to seize it but the mail clerk quickly dragged it beyond reach. The other warden jumped aboard the moving train and went into the mail-car. The clerk not only refused to deliver the birds, but stood over them and threatened the warden with arrest for assault on a United States mail employee if he so much as touched him. There was nothing for the warden to do but to get off at the next station and return.

I at once took the matter up with the Federal authorities in Washington and later was advised that the mail clerk lost his position for aiding and abetting violation of a state law. This case resulted in a government notice being sent to all railway mail clerks in the United States forbidding them to handle smuggled game.

Of course, we never found shipments of quail marked as such. Boxes of birds were always shipped under misleading labels, as for example: "Dressed poultry," "Walnut kernels," "Rabbits," "Medicine," and "Water ground meal." We found quail that had been inserted inside the bodies of dressed chicken, domestic geese and turkeys. Some of the birds that were seized showed evidences of having been shot, but as a rule they had been trapped. In hundreds of cases the feathers and often the skins were gone from the front and top of the head. I had only to remember those I had seen in Alex's trap twenty years before to understand how the injuries had been received.

During the five years ending in March, 1908, we made

sixty-three seizures of birds illegally shipped. These included 4 woodcock, 2 wild turkeys, 34 ruffed grouse, and 4,436 quail. At auction the confiscated quail averaged about ten cents each. We secured just ten convictions for all these violations. In about one-half of the cases the defendants were assessed small fines, others were given what the Court called "suspended sentences," which means they were not fined.

We had great difficulty in getting local officers to serve warrants for arrest of men who had been caught smuggling birds. Many people had begun to look upon the game-wardens with pronounced disfavor. The fact that we had sought the arrest of various prominent people who "had done nothing but ship a few partridges," did not enhance the popularity of the Audubon Society or its Secretary.

There were many quail preserves in North Carolina owned by wealthy Northern men, for the call of the bob-white makes a strong appeal to the man who enjoys sport in the open with dog and gun. At the time of which I write, near Greensboro there were a number of them. George J. Gould had a preserve of 10,000 acres; Clarence H. Mackay, one of 12,000 acres; and another controlled by W. Gould Brokaw covered 21,000 acres. In 1905, 153,000 acres of farm lands in Guilford County were under lease as quail preserves, for which the farmers received that year $7,500. In adjoining counties hunting leases were likewise extensive; in fact such holdings by Northern hunters were common in various sections of both North Carolina and South Carolina.

At that time it was customary for lessees to pay the taxes on farm lands and to receive in return the exclusive shooting privilege. In most cases farmers were furnished all the cow-peas they cared to plant to help increase the food supply for the birds. Much attention was paid also to the destruction of hawks, owls, crows and domestic cats, all of which were regarded as destructive to game-birds. Nailed on three sides of a building on the preserve of W. Gould Brokaw, south of High Point, I saw on Thanksgiving Day, 1906, 460 pairs of the feet of predacious birds and animals.

On the Mackay estate, near Jamestown, for thirty-five years steel traps have been used on poles to catch the hawks, owls and crows that alight on them. The superintendent told me that the traps were not operated in summer. While visiting with the President of the Thomasville Shooting Club, an attendant entered with a basket containing eighteen heads of hawks which had been brought in by farmers to claim the bounty of fifty cents each, offered by the Club. I took occasion to call attention to the identity of some of them and pointed out the very great economic value to the farm lands of such birds as the broad-winged, red-shouldered, and sparrow-hawks. After leaving I sent him literature on the value of useful hawks, and later he advised me that the Club had discontinued the payment of bounties.

It was a well-known fact that on the farms held under lease for shooting preserves quail were more plentiful than on the unleased neighboring farms. It was not an uncommon experience for a man with the use of dogs to find as many as twenty coveys of birds in one day, if he did not stop to hunt singles after they scattered. This was due to abundant food supply, protection against natural enemies and guarding against excessive shooting. The number of birds killed by the lease-holders was very limited compared with the abundant supply. It was a common saying among this class of men that it cost them ten dollars for every bird they killed.

On many of the preserves extensive kennels have long been maintained, and pointers and setters are trained and cared for in large numbers. The amount of money brought to North Carolina by quail-shooters has been very great. Many hundred, if not thousands, of guards, dog-trainers, stablemen, servants, and assistants were employed. Railroad fares, hotel bills, guns, ammunition, hunting equipment,

hunting licenses, payments for leases, and other expenses
ran into very large sums. Similar conditions obtained also
in sections of other Southern states where the quail naturally is abundant.

At one time a limited demand existed for live quail to
be liberated at various places in the State. The prices paid
for these ranged from three dollars to four dollars a dozen.
For dead birds farmers could get only from forty-eight cents
to seventy-two cents a dozen, according to local demands.

As the Executive Secretary of the Audubon Society, I had
the authority to grant permits to ship live birds to points
outside the State for breeding purposes. Similar authority
was exercised by State Game Officials in other states. From
1903 until the law of 1911 terminated the legal export of
live birds, I issued thirteen permits for total shipments of
639 birds. Not more than half this number actually were
shipped, however. The most of them went from one hunting preserve to another; and some were sent to the District
of Columbia to repopulate with quail the groves and fields
around Washington.

The State Game Commission of Pennsylvania desired to
purchase 10,000 quail to restock certain regions where the
birds had been decimated by over-shooting. Dr. Joseph
Kalbfus, Secretary of the Commission, came to Greensboro
and asked permission to have this number trapped and
shipped to his home State. I explained that the law did not
require the Audubon Society to issue shipping permits, it
simply granted us discretionary powers in such matters and
that I did not believe the Legislature ever contemplated our
permitting exportations of such magnitude. He departed
in a disgruntled mood and soon issued a statement to the
newspapers telling the world what he thought of the people
of North Carolina.

The Allentown, Pennsylvania, *Leader* of January 23, 1906,
published an article which said in part:

Dr. Kalbfus relates the appalling conditions that prevail in the Carolinas regarding the ruthless slaughter of game and other birds. Quail he found selling in the streets of Greensboro for twelve and one-half cents each, and large numbers are shipped to markets in Philadelphia, New York and Boston. Public opinion there does not favor protection of game-birds in any way, and the law is a dead letter. Protection is regarded as a "Yankee idea" to hamper and annoy people. Natives invade the groves at night where robins roost, and armed with torches, kill thousands of them. One Greensboro man who shipped thousands of quail out of the State was let off with a fifteen-dollar penalty. Migratory birds, game, insectivorous, and song, are cruelly and ruthlessly slaughtered with no fear of punishment by those who kill them.

On the North Carolina coast the wild water-fowl are killed without stint. Men from the North kill thousands of geese and ducks in and out of season and send them to the markets. Others follow the fowl in launches and kill simply for the love of killing. Pot-hunters abound on land and sea, and there are no protective laws for game that are regarded.

This and other quotations were reprinted in North Carolina papers, and I was not overly grieved that a visitor from a distance had driven home to the people of North Carolina some of the facts I had been seeking to impress upon the public mind.

The severity of the winters in the North has prevented quail from becoming so numerous as in more southerly regions where milder climate and abundant food supplies combine to make ideal environment for ground-feeding birds. When, therefore, the increasing destructiveness of hunters began to cause a decline in the numbers of quail, it was in the North that the failure of the supply was first apparent. Massachusetts sportsmen, loath to give up the sport of hunting these birds, began as early as 1850 to import live quail from the South.

Other states did likewise, and for more than eighty years the custom has continued, although many observers questioned the wisdom of such a course. Thus Dr. John C. Phillips believes that this Southern, less hardy stock inter-breeding with the Northern birds has produced a race less calculated to withstand successfully the rigors of a Northern winter. Quail shipments from the Southern states continued until sportsmen of the South, alarmed at the decrease of their game supply, appealed to the Legislatures and by 1912 had secured laws prohibiting further exportations.

Purchasers of live quail then turned to Mexico and from the states of Cohuila, Chihauhua, Nuevo Leon and Tamaulipas their wants have been supplied. For more than twenty years bob-whites have been coming across the border at Brownsville, Laredo, Eagle Pass, and elsewhere at an average annual rate of 34,600. For a time they could be bought for twenty-five cents each, but of late the price has risen to thirty-six dollars a dozen. They are the common Texas bob-white but are generally known as "Mexican" quail.

Alex Darden with his traps, and his uncle with his net, used to get thirty-six cents a dozen for the quail they took in the fields of Archer, but intelligent people in time put a stop to the practice that was hurrying the birds toward extirpation. Sometimes I wonder when our Latin-American neighbors will awaken to the threat which is hanging over the quail supply of their northeastern states. The surest way to send a wild bird to oblivion is to set a price on its head, and this is true equally of the quail that whistles among the pines by the Suwanee, and the one that calls from the chaparral of the Rio Grande.

In the United States the bob-white has passed the period in its history when, as a race, its existence seemed to be threatened. The days of the netter, the trapper, and the market-hunter are gone. The long hunting-seasons are at an end. Daily bag-limits have taken the place of the unlimited shooting privileges of former times. I have the photograph of

an Atlanta hunter with one hundred and sixty-five quail
hanging in strings from his shoulders. He had killed them on
a two days' hunt. The picture was made in 1913. To-day in
Georgia no one may take more than forty birds in a week.

In many states the Conservation Departments are engaged
in breeding quail, and thousands are being liberated annually. I have visited such breeding-farms in Massachusetts,
Maryland, North Carolina and elsewhere. The birds in pairs
are confined in small pens and the eggs are removed about
twice a week to be hatched in incubators or under bantams.
The quail does not care to begin to sit until she has available a double handful of eggs. As the bird in the pen is
not able to accumulate enough to arouse her incubating
instinct, she simply keeps on laying like any useful and con-
siderate domestic fowl. Fifty or more eggs are often produced
by one pair of bob-whites in a season. In 1932 a quail at
the Thomas Kinningham game farm in Georgia laid 171
eggs. Here and there private individuals are engaged in
raising these birds for the profit to be made by selling them
for breeding purposes.

The quail is a very useful inhabitant on farm lands by
virtue of the great numbers of insects and weed-seeds it con-
sumes. A planter once took me through his potato-field to
show me two coveys of quail that he said daily patroled the
rows. "They eat the potato-bugs and I have not had to buy
any paris green this season." He estimated that every quail
had saved him "one good hard silver dollar." There was
no occasion for surprise, therefore, when a little later he remarked that he allowed no hunting on his lands. In the
South the idea is abroad that quail eat the cotton boll-
weevil and the investigations of the United States Bureau of
Biological Survey have confirmed the truthfulness of this
impression.

In 1912 Ohio passed a law which prohibited the shooting
of quail for all time, and in 1913 the Michigan Legislature

provided for a closed season that still is in force. There is no land bird in the United States of greater fecundity than the bob-white, and with the leading sportsmen and the intelligent class of farmers both greatly interested in its welfare, its future in this country would seem to be abundantly assured.

Away back before the Pleistocene Age, the bob-white emerged and took its place among the birds that scratch and fly and call and give life to our continent. Where the first ones dwelt we shall never know, but their descendants spread until to-day their breeding range covers a wide area in the Western World. As through the years they gradually migrated into new areas, their size and plumage became modified to meet their various environments. There are those that developed black feathers, and reddish brown especially is a dominant color in some of the Southern forms. It is classified to-day into five species, each in turn being divided into various climatic varieties. But despite all the modifications that have been wrought in its appearance during the passage of time, there is one characteristic of the bird that has never wholly changed. The mating call of the bob-white that in spring rings across the wheat-fields of Virginia, is not far different from those that echo among the Maya ruins of Yucatan, or stir the sunlit savannas of far-off Venezuela.

CHAPTER VII

IN THE HAUNTS OF SONGLESS BIRDS

SOMETIMES I went to the Carolina Coast to visit the Audubon wardens and to see how the sea-bird colonies were prospering. One evening in 1907, when the waters of Pamlico Sound were rippling lazily in the push of an eastern breeze, Warden Jeannett pointed out Royal Shoal Island lying as a white streak against the northern horizon. Terns flew by, carrying minnows in their beaks, which meant that young were waiting to be fed on the land ahead. A little later a cloud of birds arose and by the time we dropped anchor in the cove thousands were on the wing filling the sea air with their shoutings.

Royal Shoal is a ridge of sand and bleached oyster shells, which year by year varies in size and contour according to the whims of the tides that sweep in from Ocracoke Inlet. Just now it was about eighty feet wide, perhaps five times as long, and was curved like a new moon. Its highest point was not three feet above the water. This lonely spot, eleven miles from the nearest land, was sought by nesting birds as it was ever free from marauding crows and snakes and furry raccoons.

From the deck we watched the terns settling down again to their nests. With breasts always toward the wind they dropped slowly to the sand in a great compact cluster, much as they had arisen when we first arrived.

A little later some left their nests again and shouted complainingly when Quidley, the engineer, went in the skiff to tong oysters for supper, but their cries did not continue long, for soon the darkness came. No sounds now reached our ears, except the lapping of waves against the launch and the occasional call of black skimmers whose deep, hoarse notes were reminiscent of the cries of hounds coming from a great distance through the starlit pine lands of Florida.

In the morning the birds awoke us and half an hour later we went ashore. The royal terns had laid their spotted eggs in little depressions which they had scratched out with their feet and shaped with their bodies. The nests were close together and when their owners were sitting it was difficult at a little distance to see the sand between them. I counted sixty-two nests in an area ten feet square, and estimated that there were at least 2,000 in the colony. Usually there was only one egg in a nest, but sometimes there were two.

Normally the little isle would have been teeming with young at this late day in June, but a storm-tide had swept most of the island and carried many eggs into the sea. Nearly a thousand had been left in a windrow at high-water mark. After this disturbance some of the colony had shifted to another part of the beach, which was occupied by skimmers. to these, however, the terns paid scant attention, merely scratching out their nests where they pleased, covering the skimmers' eggs with sand or kicking them aside.

Due to five years' protection, the birds had become unusually tame and one could photograph them within a distance of fifteen feet. It was a stirring sight, these thousands of white-feathered breasts and silvery-gray backs in mass formation on the beach or hovering in the air above. Everywhere were salmon-red beaks, white foreheads and long black crests framed against the gray-blue sea.

I noticed one tern, smaller than the others, with a black beak, the tip of which was yellow. Suddenly in amazement I realized that I was looking at a Cabot's tern. Its nest was close to the egg field and lying prone, I crept forward. When the bird flew I would work nearer and then lie still until it returned. Thus gradually I approached within seven feet of this wild creature that was so solicitous of her eggs. No less than twenty pairs of them had their nests on Royal Shoal. The discovery of this bird nesting so far north of its known breeding territory was a joy which can be appreciated by the field ornithologist, or by a diver who finds a pearl of great price.

When, back in 1903, we began protecting the breeding sea-birds in North Carolina, only five species were nesting on eight small islands. These were skimmers, and the Wilson's, least, royal and Forster's terns. The dainty least tern, formerly abundant, had become so reduced by plume-hunters that only six nests were found that season. Forster's terns were scarce, Wilson's were more common, and the big royal tern was the most numerous. In all about 1,700 sea-birds' eggs were laid on the North Carolina Coast during the first year of our guardianship. One hundred pairs of skimmers and Wilson's terns occupied Whalebone Beach in Carteret County, but a tidal wave engulfed all the eggs and the young. Laughing gulls had nearly disappeared and it was not until two years later that we found them breeding, eighteen young being raised in 1905.

All these coastwise species increased as the years went by, although natural agencies constantly took their toll. Thus, in 1908 all young laughing gulls, numbering about 160, were killed by a hail storm. In June of that year the tern colonies were washed by high waves. The birds nested again, but on July 28th a storm of great intensity broke upon the coast. It raged for five days and caused such high water in the sounds that our islands were swept bare of all life. Ten thousand eggs and nestlings were destroyed. The bodies of hundreds of young were washed ashore between Ocracoke and Hatteras. Warden Jeannett reported that the parents often alighted among them with food in their beaks.

Then a new threat developed. Men began to come from

the mainland and carry away boatloads of shells with which to lime their fields. To prevent the sea-birds' islands from being literally transported twenty miles to the mainland, I purchased for the Audubon Society both Royal Shoal and Legged lumps with the intention of holding them inviolate against such raiders.

Probably every wild bird has its natural enemies, and some creatures prey upon it or its eggs or young. In Southern tern colonies I have come upon crabs eating alive young terns struggling to come out of their egg-shells. Herring gulls along the Northern coast-line of eastern United States have driven the terns from many of their breeding islands, and the great black-backed gulls destroy the eggs and the young of the eiderducks. Some gulls live to a great age.

In May, 1889, a herring gull was shot and wounded in Bogue Sound, North Carolina, and Captain John L. Lewis of Morehead City placed it in his backyard and cared for it until its death on July 8, 1935. As the bird was in the white plumage when captured, it was then at least three years old; which means that this herring gull enjoyed a life span of not less than forty-nine years. This is the greatest age that has been recorded of these notably long-lived birds.

During his earlier years, "Kaiser" mated with another captive gull and young were raised. This, too, was unusual as we have no other knowledge of the species breeding south of New York State.

Crows are destroyers of wild ducks' eggs in the interior of North America. Fish crows, common along the coast, feed abundantly upon the eggs of terns, rails, herons and ibises. I have counted more than one hundred egg-shells beneath one pine tree where these crows were in the habit of perching. Depredations of natural enemies and losses by rain, snow, sleet, drought and storms serve to keep every species from increasing to a point where theoretically it would envelop the earth.

The shore-lines of the islands, outer beaches, and mainland of North Carolina when added together measure about two thousand miles. Some men whose work-boats sailed the adjacent waters claimed that since the terns ate fish they should be shot. Others have told me that "strikers" are useful in showing where to run nets with hope of success. When a flock is seen feeding, it indicated a place where schools of minnows had been driven to the surface by larger fish.

By 1905, feather-hunting, except for heron aigrettes, had been largely stopped, and sea-birds were showing a marked increase, prophetic of the day when, as a result of the Audubon Society movement, the coast-lines of the United States would again teem with these long-winged flyers of the sea. In North Carolina, the first Southern state to show an interest in protecting its water-birds, we were at that early date winning our fight against the destructiveness of man, but must ever remain powerless to contend with the actions of wind and tide. The losses of birds from natural agencies are many-fold greater than those wrought by man. When the two influences combine against any form of life, the future of that species is in grave danger.

Next to the bob-white, wild water-fowl long produced more revenue to the State of North Carolina than any other bird or group of birds. Early in autumn geese and wild ducks would begin to arrive from their breeding-grounds in the Far North. Black ducks came from eastern Canada and brant swarmed down the sea from the bleak, wind-swept headlands of Greenland. From the Dakotas and the great prairie provinces of Alberta, Saskatchewan, Manitoba, and beyond, the mallards, redheads, canvasbacks, pintails and scaups swept southeasterly across the United States to the coastal waters of the Atlantic and soon were teeming in the Carolina sounds. In Currituck, Albemarle, Pamlico and Core sounds, they gathered and fed in unnumbered legions.

Only the wood duck breeds commonly in Carolina, hiding

its eggs in the hollows of trees, sometimes at a distance of a mile or more from the water, to which the newly hatched young are probably carried by their mother. Now and then a black duck was reported to lay her eggs in the marshes of the State but I have never been able to prove this statement. Market-hunters for many years thrived in these waters. In Currituck County alone in the period from 1903 to 1909 local buyers paid not less than $100,000 annually to the 400 duck-hunters of that region, the fowl generally being shipped to Baltimore, Philadelphia and New York. Prices varied, but at times gunners received $1.60 a pair for redheads, and $2.75 a pair for canvas-backs. Canada geese were worth 40 to 50 cents each and ruddy ducks commanded 90 cents a pair. Often the daily bag of the market-hunter was a large one. I knew one gunner who took 100 ducks in one day. Exactly seventy-five of these were redheads and twenty-five were canvas-backs. I talked with two men who had come in from the sound with a few more than 200 redheads in their skiff. They received $140 for that day's work.

One of the Currituck Sound duck-hunters in those days was St. Clair Lewark. In the month of November, 1905, he, with three companions, received $1,700 for the 2,300 ruddy ducks that they shot and sold for shipment. The price for these birds had gone up recently. Only a few years previously they could have realized only eighty-five dollars for such a kill.

Two popular methods of shooting this species were at one time practised. One was to "sail up" the "boobies" as they lay in rafts on their feeding-grounds. Gunners in "batteries," which merely were floating coffins with canvas wings attached, were anchored about eighty yards apart on either side of a known flyway. Cruising sail-boats or launches would cause the birds to fly between the "batteries."

The other method was for a number of boats in semi-circular formation to approach a raft and gradually work it toward a marsh. Ruddy ducks do not like to fly over the land, so as the great flock gradually took wing every bird was forced to pass over or near some of the gunners. This practice was referred to as "ring shooting boobies." Later the practice was outlawed.

Mr. Lewark personally shot 282 ruddy ducks in one day, which was an unusually large bag. On another occasion he killed seventy-five canvas-backs, five swan, four Canada geese "and a few other ducks." His ammunition gave out and he stopped shooting before the day was over. He was firing from a blind on a point of marsh and his dog retrieved and brought to him the killed and wounded birds.

Just over the North Carolina line lies Virginia's famous Back Bay. It averages about four miles in width and fifteen miles in length. Its waters, which usually are fresh, grow large crops of wild celery which is dearly beloved by ducks.

G. W. Williams, a duck-buyer for R. L. Dyer of Norfolk, had a storage warehouse. Throughout the shooting season he would sail his boat to the different gunners who were operating in sink-boxes, batteries or blinds and buy their ducks. These he brought to Mill Landing, packed them in barrels with ice, and sent them to Norfolk by wagons, often as many as 1000 birds at a time. In the early years he paid 40 cents a pair for most species—four ruddy ducks were always counted as a pair. Redheads and canvas-backs brought from $1.00 to $1.50 a pair. Geese he bought for 50 cents apiece. He seemed to have had pretty much a monopoly on the duck-shipping business in Back Bay from 1888 until the sale of ducks was prohibited by Federal law, July 3, 1918. The harvest of dead ducks began for Williams early in October and continued for six months every season for thirty years.

At times, of course, the shooting was poor. Some days there was no wind and the ducks would fly but little, which meant that they would not come to the decoys. Cold, windy weather with a little rain or sleet is best for duck-hunting. "Weather

to kill canvas is weather to kill men" is an old proverb of the Hatteras banks. The life of the market-gunner was filled with uncertainties and discouragements just as is the life of the market fisherman.

There was so much firelighting of wild-fowl in Currituck County that the Audubon Society of North Carolina, in the winter of 1906-07, inaugurated an intense campaign to break up this illegal practice. Local men had proved to be largely worthless as game-wardens. Nobody wanted to arrest his neighbor.

M. W. Haynes of Tarboro, who was reputed to be a fearless man, was employed to take charge of the situation. He was supplied with five deputies and a stout gasoline-launch. Violations were numerous but it was difficult to secure prosecutions in the courts. Eight arrests were soon made for which the evidence was overwhelming, but seven of the offenders escaped without fines.

In Core Sound, Warden John Upchurch, with four deputies, worked during the greater part of January and February, 1907, and two arrests were made for shooting ducks by firelighting at night. The evidence produced was beyond question, but the Grand Jury found "Not a true bill."

The next winter Haynes prosecuted thirty-four men in Currituck, twelve of whom pled guilty and were let off with nominal fines; the others were acquitted. During the hunting season of 1908-9, he and his deputies secured the most convincing evidence against thirteen men. Ten of these were dismissed by the Court without even a reprimand. In January, 1908, Game Warden James H. Evans operating in Currituck County was fired on by a man illegally hunting ducks at night. Shot struck him in the face, hands and body. He was able to keep after the offender until he recognized him. No conviction resulted.

It was all very disheartening, but I whistled to keep up my courage and kept making speeches and writing newspaper

articles telling the people of the State about our valuable wild life and insisting that we must preserve it.

To acquaint myself as thoroughly as possible with the entire wild-fowl hunting situation, I took many trips to the sounds of the Carolinas during these years, and while I shot but little, I sought to acquire personal experience in the use of all the devices employed by man to circumvent the wild-fowl. With the best of guides I engaged in point shooting, sink-box shooting and battery shooting; also I accompanied gunners who went "dusking" for black ducks in the woods on the Hatteras banks.

Daylight duck- and goose-hunting was carried on by use of decoys. A "stool" usually consisted of a few live geese, more rarely a few live ducks, and generally from a hundred to two hundred wooden decoys, or "idols," as some Carolina hunters called them. From association with the local guides I acquired much of the lore of the professional duck-hunters. I became familiar with the best way to place decoys; how to rise in the battery to shoot brant; but never to show a head or arm when flock-shooting teal. I learned something of the hunting to be expected during days of different weather conditions; how to get the geese decoys to call; and how far to lead with a shot at a flying duck. I learned to speak the language of the market-hunter. I met his family and ate and slept in his home. I listened to his sorrows and to his hopes. I became familiar with his point of view on life.

As laborers hoeing their sweet potato ridges in the fields beyond the coastal swamps; or like men sitting in their offices in far-away cities, the market-hunter, too, had hopes and joys and sorrows, and the ever-present problem of making a living for himself and family. Reared under a similar environment, the man in the sweet potato field and the worker in the office might easily have been market-hunters, so much do the accidents of birth and the influences in youth shape our lives. For a million years, the forebears of the man to-day

DUCK TRAP BAITED WITH CORN

One of thirteen visited by the author in a Virginia marsh in one day in the autumn of 1935. The use of such traps has long been illegal.

PUNT GUNS

Long employed by market hunters for shooting wild ducks along the coast from Maryland to North Carolina. Their use is now illegal.

who never shoots, were hunters of birds and other animals for food.

While greatly disliking the occupation of the market-hunter, and although busily engaged in trying to devise means of destroying his busines, I found it impossible to despise him, if in his heart dwelt honesty and friendliness and his eyes reflected a love of clean mirth. It was the system which encouraged the over-killing of the bird supply that must be changed.

It was interesting to watch the bald eagles that in winter and spring came to pick up crippled ducks. I have seen one of these great birds keep an injured coot diving until it was so exhausted that it could no longer stay beneath the surface. Then the yellow claws of "Cloud Wings" closed upon it and the end came quickly. Sometimes royal contests took place in the air as one eagle sought to rob another of his booty. The market-hunters seldom disturbed the eagles, but guides and sportsmen from the mainland usually shot at every one that came within range. Their great nests, several feet in thickness, often have a weight of more than half a ton, and I have seen many of these aeries in gigantic trees along the coast and about fresh-water lakes from the Adirondacks to South Florida and westward to the Continental Divide in Wyoming and all along the coast to southern Alaska. In autumn eagles in the northern part of their range drift southward and many appear in the sounds of the Carolinas.

Three varieties of geese and about twenty-five species of ducks came regularly to the waters along our Atlantic Coast. A few other ducks and five additional geese made their appearance at rare intervals. Whistling swans are common along the coasts of Maryland, Virginia, and in the North Carolina sounds of Currituck and Albemarle. Also they may be seen in Mattamuskeet Lake, in Lake Erie and elsewhere. They have not been shot extensively since the feather trade has stopped, their flesh being too tough for most epicures.

A well-cooked cygnet makes a fairly acceptable dish, I have often been told.

The legal open season for shooting wild-fowl in Currituck during the beginning of this century began November 10th and extended until April 1st the following spring. Thus the period for hunting was four months and twenty days. However, the closed season applied only to shooting over decoys—without decoys one legally could kill ducks at any time. This famous duck-hunting county did not permit shooting on Saturdays, Sundays or Wednesdays. The reason for the existence of these rest days, or "lay days," puzzled me for a time. As one of the chief industries of the county was killing ducks and geese for market, and as it was to the interest of the gunners to get all they could, why had these very hunters caused to be enacted a law supposed to prevent them from hunting three days every week? The first Currituck man I questioned readily gave me the answer, which I found quickly leaped to the lips of every man of whom I made a similar inquiry. He said: "We have lay days because they help us to kill more fowl."

Then he explained that when the ducks were shot too continuously they leave the eel grass and celery-beds of the sound and go up to Back Bay or down into Albemarle Sound, or across the outer sand banks and rest on the ocean all day, returning only at night to feed. Therefore rest days did not exist for the protection of the ducks, but to keep them from leaving and thus redound to the benefit of the shooters.

The market-hunters of the North Carolina coast were never enthusiastic about the Audubon Law. In the beginning we had the support of many of the best people in that section, and in Currituck County a branch of the Audubon Society was formed. S. M. Beasley, representing the county for a time in the Legislature, supported the work with all his strength. The rank and file of the gunners, however, resented "outside interference," and felt that the people of the county should be left to do as they wished with "their" game and fish. They became much opposed to the Society when its wardens began to arrest them for infractions of the game-laws. In time this led to a situation which was described in the Wilmington *Star* (N. C.) for August 4, 1906:

The Audubon Society has become a factor of the politics of Currituck County. A Gunner's and Fisherman's League has been organized in opposition to the Society. In the primaries held there they virtually carried everything their own way. Their candidate for the Legislature, Pierce Hampto, was nominated by the largest vote ever polled there. Currituck is a good fishing and hunting county and the members of the League are violently opposed to the Audubon Society.

There was another class of men on the Carolina coast who had great interest in wild-fowl. This was composed of Northern sportsmen who owned shooting-club properties and who came South on one or more occasions during the winter to enjoy an outing and the abundant wild life of the marshes and sounds. They shot moderately and as a class scrupulously observed such game-laws as then existed. Their presence meant much financially to the State. They had large investments in club-houses, shooting marshes, boats and other equipment, and the salaries they paid to local men to serve as boatmen and marsh guards ran into large figures. These sportsmen were a considerable source of income to the farmers of the near-by counties for they bought quantities of grain to feed the ducks to keep them on their preserves. Visiting these clubs on various occasions, I always found that their chief problem was how to deal with pot-hunters who poached on the ponds on their marshlands.

Among the more famous of these clubs were the "Pea Islands," "Currituck," "Currituck Sound," "Narrow Island," "Monkey Island," "Lighthouse," "Deal Island" and "Grassy Point." Sometimes I heard club members discuss the possibilities of getting laws to stop the sale of wild-fowl in the

United States, and expressions were common that legal action of this character might in time become necessary. Ducks and geese were abundant but the opinion prevailed among these men that the killing was excessive and that the time might come when we should see a pronounced diminution in their numbers. Impressed by this thought, I began, on December 21, 1906, a newspaper campaign warning the people of North Carolina that in time the market-hunter would destroy our wild-fowl supply.

It was the custom at these clubs to register a list of the game taken by the members. I made notes from one of the record-books which revealed that during the preceding shooting season the twenty-one members of the Club had secured about 4,000 ducks and geese, and I was advised that the expenses of the Club were such that it cost the members about twelve dollars for each bird taken. At some other clubs the cost per bird was rated at from four to five times this amount.

Of extreme interest to me were the Canada geese decoys that lived in great numbers along the coast. One saw them in many places. They wandered about the yards of the club-houses, and honked from goose-pens of the market-hunters and from the fields of others who never shot. Long ago the early settlers had begun raising geese from wing-tipped birds taken during the winter shooting. Now they were plentiful. They did not mate very readily, and a man who had twenty-five or thirty might feel himself fortunate if a dozen of them were paired. Some never mated, but if once a gander selected his goose and she accepted him, they were usually seen together both winter and summer. When the female is brooding, her mate is very solicitous, and with beak and wings will readily attack the man who approaches her.

At Poplar Branch men showed me a gander which local history claimed had fallen wounded from a flock sixty-one years before. Unassailed by Cupid he had associated with the other geese in the yard for thirty years and then one spring gave the key to his heart to a comely young goose, and since that time he had never strayed from her side. One man pointed out a goose which he said had been courted by various ganders, but never would mate with any of them.

"She has been pretty much of a flirt, I guess, and the ganders finally got tired," he sighed. Then added, "the last three or four years none of them ain't paid no attention to her. She has been put on the shelf."

Occasionally a goose that had long been associated with others of the home flock without exhibiting the slightest mating instinct, would suddenly become interested in a bird on a neighboring farm. It might be that the two were totally unacquainted, but one would be attracted by the honk of another and they would call back and forth for days. If not shut up they might start across the country through marsh, field and briar thicket in their attempts to meet. Sometimes a man would put all his unmated geese in slatted goose-coops, load these in his cart and drive to another farm some miles away where they would be liberated with others. Two or more matings might be the result.

Some years ago an unmated wild goose was worth about a dollar but a pair of mated birds would bring five dollars. Their attachment for each other is very pronounced and gunners often take advantage of this fact when using them for decoy purposes. In staking or anchoring them out in V-shaped formation a gander would be placed at one end of the line and his mate at the other. Their mild alarm at thus being separated a few rods would cause them to call repeatedly, and their honkings would stimulate the other decoys to do likewise, thus producing a loud clamor likely to attract the attention of the wild geese moving at a distance.

The instinct to migrate is very strong in these great feathered breasts and although such a bird is raised in captivity it may join the wild geese and never return. To prevent losses the tip of the goslings' wings are clipped, which renders flight impossible for all time. In March, when migrating geese are passing overhead, I have seen decoys look upward and honk and flap their wings as though they heard the call of the North, and longed to join the wild ones in their flight toward the frozen pole.

The waters of our South Atlantic seaboard are abundantly supplied with forms of vegetable and animal life that serve as food for water-birds of many kinds. Hence, loons and grebes abound here in their season, and on nearly every Southern buoy and channel-stake, a tall, black cormorant sits. Herring gulls from the New England Coast and beyond, come in winter and eat stranded fish on the mud flats or tower aloft to drop clams to break them on the hard-packed beach. Wilson's plovers make their nests on the dry sand and chase each other in mimic combat about the shores. Clouds of shore-birds swirl over the islands like leaves in a gale and in quiet lagoons the herons feed. Clapper rails chatter ceaselessly in the salty marshes, and flocks of geese go clanging by in endless procession. Beyond the ocean surf there are petrels and jaegers, and sometimes great white gannets come to sail and wheel and plunge where the bluefish run. But from them all, never a song is heard.

There are calls and whistles and quacks, there are grunts and honks and harsh cries in great variety, but the typical birds of the open sounds and the sea and the wet beaches do not sing. After all, a lilting strain would seem out of place if rendered to the accompaniment of a pounding surf or the tolling of a bell-buoy tossed in a hurrying tide.

CHAPTER VIII

FROM A REFORMER'S DIARY

THIS CHAPTER deals chiefly with the movements of a pioneer crusader on various fronts during the years 1904-1906, which are typical of the way his time was employed for nearly a decade.

The term "Audubon Society" had been coined in 1886 by Dr. George Bird Grinnell, who, in the February issue of his magazine *Forest and Stream*, gave this name to a society started "for the protection of American birds not used for food." As a boy Dr. Grinnell had been a pupil of Mrs. John James Audubon, living in the home of her younger son, Victor Gifford Audubon, in "Minnie's Land," near what is now 158th Street and Riverside Drive, New York City. Her husband, then deceased, had written and published the monumental work, *The Birds of America*. Its text and its illustrations of birds from drawings by the author, inspired young Grinnell to become a bird student, and later a bird-protectionist.

In Grinnell's first announcement, he advertised that men or boys might become members of the new society by signing a pledge either to "refrain from killing, wounding, or capturing any wild bird not used for food," or "not to rob, destroy, or injure the nest or eggs of any wild bird." Women and girls could join by agreeing "not to make use of the feathers of any wild bird, as ornaments of dress or household furniture." No membership fees were required; therefore, after securing about fifty thousand signatures, chiefly those of school-children, it became necessary to abandon the enterprise in January, 1889.

127

Seven years later, William Brewster, a member of the Board of Directors of the Massachusetts Fish and Game Protective Association, revived the name by organizing "The Massachusetts Audubon Society for the Protection of Birds." Inspired by this new movement, several other state and local Audubon societies soon came into existence.

In the autumn of 1901, it was decided to form a National Committee composed of representatives of these State Audubon Societies. This was formally organized the following April, and at the next meeting which was held in Washington in November of that year, I became an active member of the group.

Early in 1904 I had occasion to go North, and sailing from Norfolk reached New York the afternoon of February 10th. I had advised William Dutcher, Chairman of this National Committee, of my coming, and to my surprise and great delight he met me at the dock. Tall, handsome, with neatly trimmed beard, and friendly eyes shining through rimless spectacles, the sight of him was indeed warming to the heart of a stranger arriving in the great city. He took me to his home at 525 Manhattan Avenue, where I met Mrs. Dutcher and their daughter Mary. It was to me an evening of great delight. I remember particularly his account of helping in the campaign of the Humane Societies to stop the shooting of domestic pigeons at traps.

He entertained me with a player organ, putting in one paper music roll after another. With great animation and with evident relish he worked the pedals vigorously and manipulated the various stops with quick and confident movements, as he rendered "The Blue Danube," and some of his favorite hymns.

Another man in New York whom I wanted to meet was William T. Hornaday. As a boy I had been thrilled while reading his book *Two Years in the Jungle*, which told of killing elephants, orang-utans, and other animals for a taxidermist's establishment, and his account of the money he made in this way aroused my youthful cupidity.

I found him at the Bronx Zoological Park. Seldom had I met any one who was so responsive and friendly. His manner completely captivated me. His careful attention to all my remarks was most flattering. Later, when some one asked me about my visit to Hornaday, I replied with all sincerity that I came away feeling that he was about the biggest man I had ever met.

I called on Colonel G. O. Shields in the office of *Recreation*, at 23 West 24th Street. There were many book-cases and on the walls were hung drawings of birds and game mammals. On the floor were spread some large, heavy-haired black and white pelts, and Mr. Shields told me they were skins of the cattalo, which had come from the ranch of Buffalo Jones. A cattalo, he explained, was a cross between a cow and a buffalo.

During that summer I again gave a lecture course at the University of Tennessee, and in August went to Tallulah Falls, Georgia, to address the Convention of the State Horticultural Society on the importance of enacting laws to protect the birds of the State, and the need of forming a State Audubon Society. It was here that I had my first experience with the mistakes of a stenographic reporter. Later I read that I was supposed to have said, "Song birds scratch away the snow so that they can get worms from the dead leaves beneath."

Autumn came, and on the hustings hundreds of orators were explaining to the voters of North Carolina the virtues of various candidates for office. It was the bi-annual period when many promises are made that beneficial laws will be enacted at the coming session of the Legislature. Some of this talk concerned our Audubon work and I heard of at least a dozen proposed changes in the bird-protective statutes. A man, formerly a member of the Society's Executive Committee, began proclaiming that the Audubon Law must be amended so that a non-resident shooter could take out of the State more than the fifty dead quail which were allowed. Robert Glenn, Governor-elect, declared loudly and at great length that the non-resident hunting-license law should be repealed, contending: "It is a shame that an invited guest, who comes to this State to hunt, should be required to provide himself with a license." Like many others, he believed this law a violation of the social amenities demanded by Southern hospitality. I was kept busy running about over the State trying to check various insidious rebellions against our state-wide game-law.

In the midst of this disquieting and trying period, William Dutcher called me to New York to discuss a matter of much importance. I arrived on the morning of November 25, 1904. He explained that a wealthy man, Albert Wilcox, had become interested in our National Committee of Audubon Societies and was willing to help us in a substantial way if we would take certain steps which he recommended. I was to have luncheon with Mr. Wilcox that day so that he could look me over and talk about his plans.

I met him in his office on Nassau Street. He said that he was deeply concerned about two great evils which existed in our country: one, the terrible destruction of birds and game animals; the other, the abuses being heaped upon the Negroes of the Southern states. I did not talk much about the second point, but had something to say about bird and game protection. After luncheon he said, "Now, we will go and see Mr. Dutcher."

At Dutcher's office on the tenth floor of 141 Broadway, he made a brief and businesslike statement that if we incorporated the Audubon Committee as a National Association, not merely for the protection of birds but also for the benefit of useful mammals, and if I would devote approximately one-half of my time to the Association, he would contribute $3,000 a year for at least two years and would provide in his

Thayer but my best was not good enough. All I could get him to agree to was to be a lay member of the Finance Committee and to make a subscription of $500.

In Cambridge I called on William Brewster and asked him for $100 for the Endowment Fund. He gave me his check and was thus enrolled as the first life member of the Audubon Association.

Two ladies on whom I called agreed to become life members. One of them, Miss H. E. Freeman, asked me to dine with her, after which she took me to the Boston Society of Natural History to attend a lecture. This was January 18, 1905. The speaker was E. H. Baynes and his subject "The American Buffalo, a Plea for its Preservation." He was not particularly effective, because he was nervous and his slides were not very good, but he was very much in earnest. After his address he attempted to form a society for the protection of the bison, but was prevented from doing so by the outspoken opposition of various members of the Natural History Society. Before leaving I told him that if he came to New York he would find support for his undertaking. Doubtless he received the same advice from others and on December 8, 1905, the American Bison Society was organized in New York City. Baynes soon became an able and entertaining speaker, and his lectures were responsible for the organization of many bird-clubs through the country before his premature death on January 21, 1925.

On January 30, 1905, the first meeting of the Board of Directors of the Audubon Association was held, and the following officers were elected: William Dutcher, President; John E. Thayer, 1st Vice-President; Theodore S. Palmer, 2nd Vice-President; T. Gilbert Pearson, Secretary; and Frank M. Chapman, Treasurer.

A few weeks later, in Raleigh, I met an Asheville man who said that western North Carolina was up in arms against me, that I was charged with dealing dishonestly with the local

Audubon Society, and that there would be a meeting in Asheville that next night to agree on a legislative bill for incorporating an independent Audubon Society for western North Carolina which would take over the hunting-license money now being collected by the State Society in that region. Stopping in Greensboro only long enough to see the State Audubon Treasurer, I went to Asheville.

The meeting was held in the home of an officer of the Asheville Audubon Society, who had started the trouble. Perhaps twenty business and professional men were present. He was asked to state his charges against me, which he did, although laboring under evident embarrassment. He said that he had sent to our Treasurer the monthly contributions of the Asheville Audubon Society which I had agreed to duplicate and use the combined sum in employing a local game-warden, but that for some months I had not paid any money to the warden who, therefore, had not been serving the community.

I read a sworn statement from the Treasurer, saying that for some months past no money had been received from the Asheville branch. I then called upon the Asheville game-warden, who stated that despite the fact that the Asheville contributions had been withheld I had paid his full salary regularly and that he had been on active duty constantly. It was a tense moment when that group of men realized how they had been misled by one of their number. Sheet-lightning played along the heights. A check for the back payments due from the Asheville branch was demanded by one of its members, and was produced, and the plan to present a bill to the Legislature was dropped.

It was said that great injury had been perpetrated on the Audubon Society of North Carolina and a rank injustice had been done to me. A strong endorsement of the State Audubon Society and a fulsome vote of confidence in its Secretary were at once adopted. A Committee was quickly named to prepare notices for publication in the papers next morning, advising the public that the Asheville group was squarely behind the State Society and its Secretary, and that a mass meeting had been called at which I would address the people of the city. The Committee did its work thoroughly and the next day I spoke at length to one of the largest and most friendly audiences I ever faced in North Carolina.

After shaking hands with dozens of people and looking into scores of smiling faces, I took the night train for Greensboro where I found a message that required me to hurry away to clear up some Audubon Society troubles in Richmond, Virginia. Life indeed had become very full of duties and responsibilities.

The Third Annual Meeting of the North Carolina Audubon Society was held on March 17th. Our Legislature had just adjourned and in my report I was able to list the passage of several new game-laws which we had advocated. Among these was one prohibiting the shipment of shore-birds to markets outside the State, one for the further protection of quail and wild turkeys, and still another to prohibit the killing of deer when they are swimming. The Society that year had distributed more than two million printed pages of game-laws and pamphlets telling of the usefulness of birds, had secured convictions for violations of the game-laws in sixty-six cases, had fed the hungry birds during the great snow-storm, had confiscated eighteen illegal shipments of game, and had continued constantly the work of newspaper publicity. I also reported that the recently enacted New York law prohibiting the sale of ducks had caused a drop in prices of wild-fowl in Currituck County of 30 per cent.

Then after a trip to Currituck and Washington, D. C., I reached New York March 30th. Here several days were spent calling at business offices trying to get men to become members of the Association or to make donations to its work. These efforts were amazingly barren of results. I then proceeded to Boston. On April 8th I addressed a large audience in Huntington Hall on "The Mission of the Audubon Society." On April 19th I wrote William Dutcher: "Have to-day completed the round of the six names of men given me by John E. Thayer. I visited their offices and, in all cases where they lived in Boston, their residences also. With one exception they were all away." I got no money. On April 20th I wrote: "I enclose one application card and five dollars. Several men whom I attempted to see were away, and one turned me down in a very rude manner."

I made two friends in Boston who were most helpful. Charles W. Dimock was a member of the Massachusetts Fish and Game Protective Association. He extended to me the use of a desk in his office. He and Augustus Hemenway helped prepare a circular of appeal which we mailed to 6,000 people. The enrolment of a hundred sustaining members and five life members resulted, making just $1,000 in return from this circular. I also talked with a woman who agreed to mention the Association in her will.

All the following summer I worked in the two Carolinas, visiting bird colonies, having conferences with our wardens, lecturing, enrolling Audubon members, and sending out many thousands of circulars, and scores of news-letters for the press.

The Audubon Society in North Carolina was making such progress as a non-political state game-protective department that both Dutcher and I were anxious to put the same plan in operation in other Southern states. At this time there was no state game-warden system in any state south of the Ohio or Potomac rivers except in North Carolina. Therefore, in 1905, to arouse further support of our bill pending in the South Carolina Legislature, I accepted an invitation from the State Summer School at Clemson College to conduct classes in bird-study and give public lectures. I also lectured at various other points in the State.

That summer we organized the Audubon Society of South Carolina in the office of O. B. Martin, State Superintendent of Public Instruction, on July 10, 1905. United States Senator Benjamin R. Tillman was elected President; Dr. H. N. Snyder, President of Wofford College, Vice-President; O. B. Martin, Secretary; and Governor D. C. Hayward, Chairman of the Board of Directors.

I then visited different towns and enrolled more than forty sustaining members and collected their first annual fees of five dollars each. Also, I organized an Educational Department of the State Society and collected a fee of twenty-five cents each from 225 school-teachers.

Early in August one of those wholesale, useless slaughters of birds which always make my blood boil took place in eastern North Carolina. Purple martins to the number of 100,000 or more established one of their amazing late-summer roosts in a grove surrounding a resort at Wrightsville Sound. They created inconvenience and annoyance to the people of the immediate neighborhood and the proprietor of the hotel determined to get rid of them. A company of men assembled late one evening and all began firing into the thickly massed birds. The hunt was quite satisfactory, or the slaughter was frightful, just as one may look at the subject. Estimates of various observers, based on partial counts, indicated that 10,000 or 12,000 were killed. In addition, immense numbers were wounded and many fluttered about the fields and road-sides for some days.

With lance at rest I went for these men. Martins had been protected by the Audubon Law for more than two years. Some of the shooters claimed that they did not know that they were violating any law, and probably this was the case. We secured the names of twelve who had wielded shot-guns that night and convicted them without difficulty, although the fines imposed were nominal. We drove the offending martins from the neighborhood with burning tar barrels, placed in such a position that the dense smoke drifted through the trees the birds were occupying.

With the newspapers and sportsmen behind our efforts in South Carolina, the prospects of securing our Audubon Law continually grew brighter, and when the Legislature convened in 1906, I was invited to address that body in the capitol building on January 17th. My work in Columbia continued until I was called away by Dutcher to attend the convention of the National Association of Game and Fish Wardens and Commissioners held in St. Paul on January 25th to 27th.

After this Minnesota meeting Dr. Palmer and I went through the game markets of Milwaukee and Chicago and had conferences with the game-wardens at these places. In Chicago I recall being impressed with the immense quantities of wild ducks displayed along South Water Street. Then, after conferring with our Audubon workers and game officials in Indianapolis, I started for South Carolina, but was caught by a telegram and deflected to Richmond in the interests of a pending bird-protective bill.

In the South Carolina Legislature there was a deadlock over a bill affecting the State's experiment in handling the retail sale of liquor. All bills, therefore, were being held up. I worked like a beaver, in Columbia, exhausting every device I could think of to get our Audubon bill considered, but the Legislature adjourned without its having been brought to a vote.

While there I occupied my spare time in getting letters sent to United States Congressmen urging their support of the Babcock Bill designed to protect all birds and other wild animals in the District of Columbia.

A little later I was in Pinehurst, where Leonard Tufts, proprietor of the Carolina Hotel, introduced to me some of his friends who seemed much interested in learning of our work, but before I left, my entertainment cost them $300 in membership fees.

Personal campaigning for membership was then conducted in Philadelphia, after which I worked in Georgia, speaking, among other places, in the Lawton Memorial Hall at Savannah, where Mrs. H. B. Skeele had arranged for me to give a lecture.

Not long after this I again found myself in Florida, this time to make a search for bird colonies along the lower Gulf Coast, a region little known to ornithologists. It was the hope that if some were found on government-owned islands we might be able to have them declared Federal bird reservations.

One night on the Manatee River, in trying to jump from a launch to the dock, I slipped and fell into the water. After being pulled out the Captain of the boat said very seriously, "I feared that you would get into trouble. Don't you know that in shallow-water cruising it is bad luck to wear a white cap?"

I had not heard of this before. Disregarding the warning, I was wearing my cap again, one evening when I went aboard a small schooner leaving Marco for Key West. We had sailed only a mile or two when the boat ran upon a submerged bar from which it was floated only after much labor.

About midnight a storm struck with great force. The sheets running to the end of the main boom were torn from their deck fastenings and the mainsail put on a performance which must have aroused the envy of all the witches riding the wet sea-lanes that awful night. Then the rudder jammed and for hours we were driven shoreward toward Cape Romano. During one of his more quiet moments the Captain shouted through the wind: "Why in h—— did you bring that d——d white cap aboard this boat?"

Two days later in attempting to tie up at the dock at Key West, I did the amateurish trick of stepping into the bight of a hawser and was jerked overboard after first coming into violent contact with the shrouds. When the doctor from the marine hospital had patched me up and the effects of his chloroform had somewhat subsided, I revived sufficiently to ask about my cap.

"Your Captain said to tell you that he did not salvage it," the doctor smiled.

On July 8, 1905, Guy Bradley had been shot by plume-hunters while serving the Audubon Society as a guard to the Lake Cuthbert rookery in south Florida. He was buried in a lonely cocoanut-grove at Cape Sable and the Florida Audubon Society erected an appropriate monument over his grave. William Dutcher raised, by subscriptions, a sum of more than $1,500 to purchase a house for Mrs. Bradley and her children. I saw her in Key West, and together we picked out a house which she said that she wanted.

In a few days I was back in Greensboro, nursing a dislocated shoulder and two broken ribs. My discomfort was not rendered any easier by a case of the whooping cough that just at this time took possession of me.

Propped in a chair at home, with one arm bound to my side and with adhesive tape over my broken ribs, I coughed out a report for my secretary to send to Dutcher. While in Florida I had found several colonies of herons, ibises, cormorants and brown pelicans nesting on government-owned islands along the stretch of the Gulf Coast I had traversed. Three of those which I had discovered ornithologically were soon made Federal bird reservations.

Georgia was another state that Dutcher and I had decided ought to have an Audubon Society, which should be incorporated by the Legislature as a state game commission, and already I had done some preliminary campaigning on the subject. As soon as I was able to travel I went to Georgia to resume the enrolling of Audubon memberships, and to make plans for the introducing of our bill in the Legislature. Soon

I was sending checks to New York in envelopes bearing the stamp of various Georgia post-offices.

But Dutcher did not leave me long among the red hills of Georgia. He wrote that it was very important for me to attend the eighth annual meeting of the League of American Sportsmen to be held in Buffalo.

These meetings usually had attracted many wardens and commissioners. Speaking to such audiences gave me opportunities to urge game officials to enforce the laws for the protection of non-game birds, a duty which in many states was not being taken very seriously.

The gathering in Buffalo was disappointing. The fact was, the League already was showing signs of disintegration. On June 10, 1906, I wrote to Dutcher: "The League meeting was not very well attended. Not more than sixteen men were in the room at one time. Only one Buffalo man came to any of the sessions."

Long ago I had formed the habit of soliciting memberships for the Audubon Association on all opportune occasions, and I fear on many occasions that were not particularly opportune. One of the new members I secured on that trip was George Eastman, who gave me a check for life membership when I called at his office in Rochester.

I now returned to Georgia and resumed the work of enrolling members. Many new contacts were made, and in Macon we organized the Georgia State Audubon Society on June 30, 1906. P. J. Berckmans, a prominent horticulturist in the State, was elected President, and Martin Calvin, Secretary.

Dr. Palmer and Mr. Dutcher both having approved the Audubon bill I had drawn for Georgia, I induced Senator Alsobrook to introduce it and in about a week it came up for a Senate Committee hearing. There was some opposition, but this was overcome and the Committee gave the bill a favorable report.

But we were to fail in the end. A substitute bill was presented which would place in the School Fund the money to be derived from the non-resident hunting-licenses we had proposed. If the Audubon bill should be passed without the revenue-producing feature, it would be worthless. This rival bill brought on a fight that split the Legislature and a Kilkenny cat episode ensued. We killed the bill of our opponents but did not have enough support left to pass our own bill, and the Georgia Legislature adjourned with nothing gained for bird protection.

One day in August when a special train on which William Jennings Bryan was traveling, drew into the station at Greensboro, we learned that death had just claimed Dr. Charles D. McIver. He had been accompanying Bryan and the end came suddenly while he was conversing with friends. The loss of this widely known Southern educator was a shock throughout the South Atlantic States. To me it was a keen personal loss. He had long been my friend and we had often spoken from the same platform. At this very time we had an engagement to go together to Ohio where we were to make addresses before a convention of high school principals. His life's work had terminated at the age of forty-six.

Dr. McIver was a man of irrepressible good humor and he was very fond of stories, which he told with unusual effectiveness. At his funeral at the cemetery in Greensboro I saw a little group of intimate friends, Walter Hines Page, Dr. Edwin A. Alderman, and others, standing apart from the crowd. They were retelling some of his stories.

That autumn I lectured in various states, and I recall in particular the occasion at Asbury Park when I addressed a convention of the Federation of Women's Clubs of New Jersey. I named many of the feathers I could see on the hats in the room, and described methods employed in securing them. I concluded by offering a resolution condemning the wearing of aigrettes, and it was adopted.

One day in New York Albert Wilcox sent for me and said that he was much pleased with my work and had decided to leave to the Association more than the $100,000 he promised, to insure my future work. That he carried out his intention was revealed after his sudden death on August 13, 1906. From his estate the Association received $320,000.

W. Gould Brokaw had a 21,000-acre shooting preserve in the center of the finest quail territory in North Carolina. His Scottish gamekeepers annually raised also several thousand pheasants for shooting purposes. I was one of Brokaw's guests at a shoot held on Thanksgiving Day, 1906. Gunners were stationed in a field a few hundred feet apart. A line of beaters came through the woods rattling bushes and striking trees with their sticks. The pheasants ran before them until coming to the edge of the woods they encountered a low net hundreds of feet in length.

We could see the birds running back and forth, looking for an opening through which they might creep, until, upon the near approach of the beaters they took wing, a few at a time, flying over the net and coming directly toward the gunners. As they swiftly passed over the shooting-stands they presented marks which tested the skill of the hunters. After luncheon the sport was continued until evening when some of the guests departed, each with two or more braces of birds. My education regarding hunting-practices was progressing. I had witnessed a typical example of battue shooting as practised on some estates in Europe.

Chapter IX

ON THE FIRING-LINE

THE YEAR 1907 was an anxious period for the small scattered groups of people in this country who were actively engaged in trying to stem the tide of wildlife destruction. The legislatures of more than forty states held sessions and into their hoppers were poured many bills having for their purpose the liberalizing of the modest restrictive laws on hunting then existing. The only membership organization trying to work on anything like a national scope was the Audubon Association, and our funds for maintenance and for campaignings, even with the income from the Wilcox legacy, totaled only $17,978 for the year. Much of our legislative effort at this time, as well as for many years to come, was necessarily defensive in nature, but whenever possible, aggressive programs were attempted.

In Texas a state game-warden system to be supported by money derived from hunting-licenses was established this year. We expended $1,582 on this campaign.

With literature, news-releases and correspondence, we aided John H. Wallace, a former member of the Alabama Legislature, in his successful efforts to create the office of State Game Warden, and to provide for a system of deputy game-wardens. Our Vice-President, Dr. Palmer, went to Montgomery and explained the necessity of such legislation to many of the Senators and Assemblymen. This law was enacted February 19, 1907, and by October, Mr. Wallace, who was appointed State Game Warden, had secured convictions for violations in eleven of the sixty-six counties then in the State.

Financial aid was extended to the Michigan Audubon Society, which, under the leadership of its Secretary, Jefferson Butler, killed a bill to legalize the shooting of meadowlarks. A bill to provide bounties on kingfishers, great blue herons and English sparrows was opposed, and in the end the bounty was made to apply only to English sparrows. A bill to give a bounty on "chicken hawks" was urged by farmers, but the Audubon Society was able to bring about its defeat.

In Maine an attempt to take protection from gulls because of their destructiveness to drying fish and to fish scrap scattered on farms as fertilizer, was overcome.

The Audubon Association unsuccessfully supported a proposed measure in New Jersey to stop the spring shooting of wild-fowl and shore-birds; however, we were influential in preventing the passage of a measure designed to add doves and flickers to the list of game-birds.

Dutcher repeatedly visited the Legislature of New York State in the interest of bills which we hoped would prevent the sale of wild-fowl in close season, and which also would abolish the cold storage of game. However, it was found impossible to get such bills even brought to a vote.

Oklahoma took a forward step, through the initiative of the Farmers' Union, by stopping the trapping of quail, mourning doves and meadowlarks.

About this time West Virginia adopted the Model Law to protect non-game birds, and California established its hunting-license system, reduced the daily bag-limit on ducks from fifty to thirty-five, and took protection off all fish-eating birds, except "gulls and blue and white cranes."

Two field-agents were employed by the Association at the beginning of the calendar year of 1907, and the weight of their energy and skill was at once noticeable. One of these was William L. Finley, of Portland, Oregon, already a notable photographer of wild life, and a man who had been helping the Association's work from time to time. Complaints had become numerous that the varied thrush, Lewis's woodpecker and certain other birds were doing great damage to the fruit-growers of Oregon; and in spite of Mr. Finley's most heroic efforts to head off a bill which would permit farmers, orchardists and gardeners to kill any bird they considered harmful, it passed both houses of the Legislature. In the end Finley induced the Governor to veto the measure.

Edward Howe Forbush was the other agent the Wilcox money made possible for the Board of Directors to employ. In January his legislative work began with the introduction of two bills into the Massachusetts Legislature—one to protect the larger gulls, the other to stop spring shooting of wild ducks. The gull bill alone was passed. He helped to secure a measure, introduced by the Fall River Natural History Society, to protect loons, eagles, and useful hawks and owls. He aided Dr. George W. Field in getting a law to establish a reservation for the fast-disappearing heath hen on the island of Martha's Vineyard, and the Association appropriated money to aid in its development. The Legislature also authorized the expenditure of funds for republishing *Useful Birds and Their Protection,* by Forbush.

In Connecticut Forbush aided in getting laws to stop spring shooting of shore-birds, and to prohibit the sale of upland game-birds; and in New Hampshire assisted the State Audubon Society in getting legal protection extended at all times to the wood duck, upland plover and killdeer.

The most pronounced legislative reverse in 1907 took place in Missouri. This state had long been a paradise for market-hunters and game-dealers. Back in 1889, sportsmen's groups led a fight to put a curb upon the traffic in game but those who profited by killing and selling game-birds and game mammals were too strong to be overcome. In 1901 an Audubon Society was organized in Missouri, and its officers and members joined with the sportsmen in renewed efforts to stop the terrific slaughter of wild life that was going on ceaselessly. However, the game-dealers were able to retain their attorneys in seats in the Legislature and nothing was gained that year. Similarly, and for the same reason, virtually all game legislative protective efforts failed in 1902. But public interest had become awakened, and in 1905, under the leadership of Harry R. Walmsley, of Kansas City, there was passed an almost ideal game-law which extended protection to non-game birds, provided more restrictions on the killing of game, and set up a state game-warden system to enforce these laws.

After receiving this set-back, the market-hunters and game-dealers organized "The Missouri Country Produce Dealers Association," and soon their paid agents were campaigning in every part of the State to create sentiment for the repeal of the Walmsley Law. Large sums were expended in printing and postage. This work was so effective that various candidates for the Legislature, known to be in sympathy with the existing game-law, were defeated at the polls.

The Legislature in 1907, therefore, was controlled by the game-dealers. Even the Governor was with them, and when their repeal law was passed he promptly gave it his approval. By this measure the entire game-warden force of the State was abolished. Does and fawns were allowed to be killed either by day or by night. Streams could be seined and game fish sold in market. Quail, ruffed grouse, woodcock and prairie chickens could be bought in the markets, or from men hawking them on the streets. The commercial interests had regained their "rights" to exploit to the last fin, fur and feather of wild-life resources of the State.

In North Carolina, within ten days after the General Assembly met in January, a flood of local game-bills had been introduced. Collecting these typewritten documents from the Chairman of the Game Law Committee in each house, I examined them with care, and found several that were very harmful. For example, there was one to permit the shipment to market of woodcock from Dare County; another making it lawful to kill "yellow hammers" and "jay birds" in Chatham County; and another to repeal all provisions of the Audubon Law in Granville County. These and other proposed measures of like nature were killed in one of several ways. First, I would go to the member who had introduced a bill of this kind, and point out to him the objectionable features. If he persisted in pushing his measure, I would get from him the names of his constituents wanting this law, go to his county, and try to induce them to drop the matter. Sometimes when there was much local sentiment to be overcome, I would call a public meeting in the court-house or a church, or a school building, give a talk on bird protection, and explain why the Audubon Society was trying to preserve the birds. Usually this settled the matter. When a bill could not be handled in this manner, I would ask the Game Committee of the House or of the Senate to wield the big stick.

In February, while I was busy in Virginia, a company of duck-hunters and game-dealers from Currituck, who controlled the politics of that county, appeared without warning in Raleigh, and demanded an immediate joint-hearing by the Committees on Game Laws. They wanted to repeal the provisions of the Audubon Law that had laid restrictions on their shooting. The committees listened to them but declined to take action until they had heard what I had to say. In the end, the Currituck proposition was rejected.

Although local county game-laws were the bane of our state-wide efforts, there seemed to be little logical reason for opposing those which were intended to put further restrictions on excessive shooting. I advised with many of the representatives and often drew such bills at their request. This year in a number of counties the shooting season was reduced by two weeks, and a state-wide law, which I advocated, to prohibit the killing of woodcock during their nesting season, was enacted. Another act made it illegal to sell game-birds during those months when it was unlawful to kill them.

Victory came in South Carolina, February 18, 1907, with the passage of our bill to incorporate the Audubon Society of that state with all the powers of a state game department, this measure being almost identical with the North Carolina Audubon Law. After a conference with B. F. Taylor, of Columbia, President of this new society, it was decided to secure the services of James Henry Rice as Executive Secretary, and we authorized him to select, appoint and direct the work of deputy game-wardens.

It was during the hectic days of January, 1907, that I responded to a hurry call from Washington, D. C. The House Committee on Agriculture had struck from the Agricultural Appropriations Bill all provision for maintaining the Bureau of Biological Survey, and friends of bird protection stood aghast. If this committee's action should be approved there would come to an end all governmental effort for educating public sentiment to a better appreciation of wild birds; no further scientific investigation of the food habits of birds and mammals would be carried on and no more effort would be made to enforce the Lacey Act for governmental coöperation in enforcing certain state game-laws.

It was reported to be the declared purpose of Congress to transfer to the Smithsonian Institution all the Survey's work, "which in its judgment has no bearing on agriculture" and "so far as the enforcement of the game-shipping laws was concerned this work might be transferred to some bureau connected with the pure food law." Congressman J. W. Wadsworth announced that after the fullest investigation it had been decided to abolish the Biological Survey. It was currently supposed that this movement emanated from powerful cold-storage interests as the Survey's influence was being felt in the efforts being made to break up the extensive business of keeping game in cold storage throughout the year.

The Biological Survey of the Department of Agriculture had come into existence on July 1, 1886, as a modest "Division of Ornithology and Mammalogy" at the behest of the American Ornithologists' Union. In 1905 its name had been changed to Bureau of Biological Survey. It was regarded by ornithologists as their particular agency in the government organization.

When, therefore, this attempt was made to destroy it, William Dutcher was one of the first to sound an alarm and call for the filing of protests with Congressmen, urging that the usual appropriation of $52,000 should be continued. I at once went to Richmond, since some of the Virginia delegation in Congress held positions of great influence in Washington. In fact, Lamb of Richmond was the ranking Democrat member on the House Committee on Agriculture. On January 28th I had interviews with the Governor, the Commissioner of Agriculture and other politicians. They signed telegrams which I took to the telegraph office and sent to all of the ten Congressmen and the two Senators from the State. Newspaper men were interviewed, and messages were sent to many prominent Virginians requesting them to communicate with their representatives in Washington and ask that they stand by the Biological Survey.

Going then to Norfolk, I dispatched messages, signed by many influential men of that city, to each of the Virginia Senators and to all Virginia Congressmen. The next day I was in Greensboro keeping the wires humming with telegrams from North and South Carolina politicians to the Washington delegations from those states. Among other personal messages was one to "Pitchfork" Ben Tillman, whom I knew very well.

Mr. Dutcher in New York, and Forbush in Boston, were engaged in similar work.

It was not long until a wire reached me from Congressman E. Y. Webb: WE HAVE JUST RESTORED BUREAU OF BIOLOGICAL

SURVEY AND PLACED IT IN AGRICULTURAL BILL; and I sent on the good news to Dutcher.

But the end was not yet, as it was found that the appropriation for the salary of the Chief of the Survey had been omitted.

When the bill reached the Senate the appropriation for the Chief was included. Having thus been modified since leaving the House, it necessarily was referred to a Conference Committee of the two houses.

I rushed to Washington and buttonholed every member of that Conference Committee, and had interviews with many of their closest friends. Letters inspired by Dutcher were pouring into Congress by every mail. One afternoon, about three o'clock, while I was waiting near the closed door of the conference-room, Senator Simmons came out and told me the Conference had agreed that the Chief should continue to have his salary.

So the Biological Survey was not destroyed, nor was its appropriation reduced. However, a great threat was left hanging over it, as the appropriation bill approved March 4, 1907, contained the following paragraph:

And the Secretary of Agriculture is hereby directed to investigate and report to the next session of Congress to what extent, if any, the work now being done by the Bureau of Biological Survey is duplicated by any other Department of the Government, and to what extent the work of this Bureau is of practical value to the agricultural interests of the country.

The Audubon Association was almost wholly dependent on the field-studies and publications of the Survey for information as to the economic value of birds which was so essential in our educational and legislative campaigns. For this and many other reasons it became our plain duty to get letters and resolutions of approval of the Survey's work into the hands of the Secretary of Agriculture. For several months we kept accumulating such testimony, some of which required much time and effort.

The International Conference of Cotton Growers and Cotton Spinners had a convention in this country that autumn. It was the most influential body of agriculturists that would meet during the year. After assembling in Washington, the delegates went to Georgia for two days' deliberations. Reaching Atlanta about the time their special train arrived I found that five hundred cotton men had assembled. I at once hunted out Harvey Jordan, President of the Southern Cotton Growers' Association. He had taken the lead in getting the Audubon Law to protect non-game birds adopted in Georgia four years before, and I thought he would be just the one to get a resolution approving the Survey's work. He flatly refused my request, saying that it had been decided before leaving Washington that no subjects whatever, other than those already agreed upon for discussion, would be considered at the Southern sessions.

"I was very active in insisting that such a plan should be adopted," he said, "so you see I am not in position to do anything for you, and I see no way whereby your resolution can be considered."

After some delay I secured an introduction to James MacColl, of Rhode Island, who was President of the Congress. He told me the same story and said that he could do nothing for me. As he turned away he remarked: "Of course, if some delegate should spring a resolution from the floor he might possibly get consideration, despite our clear understanding that no new topic shall be given a hearing."

Some delegates from North Carolina came along, and I recognized two men with whom I had been a comrade-at-arms in a hard-fought political convention. I asked one of them if he would introduce the resolution. He answered that he had never even heard of the Biological Survey about which I was so excited.

"I wouldn't know what to say if some one asked me a question. No, sir, I'm not the man you are looking for, not by a long shot."

"Introduce it yourself," said another. "We'll back you in the convention for anything you want. I have the power to appoint delegates to represent my North Carolina organization. Here, get in line."

We were near the table where delegates were registering. Soon I had a badge, an invitation to a reception to be given by Governor Hoke Smith, and other documents.

The next morning the Congress convened in the State Capitol. Mayor Joyner of Atlanta welcomed the delegates to "the Gate City of the South," and presented to the President a fourteen-inch "Key to the City."

When the meeting was open for business I was the first man on his feet. I read my resolution of endorsement of the Biological Survey and moved its adoption. "Second the motion," said a North Carolinian. "The gentlemen are out of order," declared the President. "The resolution is hereby referred to the Committee on 'Growing and Handling Cotton,' it cannot be voted on here unless it has first been considered and approved by that committee."

I then learned that there were three committees of the Congress, all to have meetings that afternoon at two o'clock. At twenty minutes before two I was at a door on which was tacked the notice: COMMITTEE ON GROWING AND HANDLING, and there I stayed until a Capitol employee came and unlocked it.

At the end of the room facing the hall was a small table with two chairs. I took a seat in one of these and spread out some papers before me. While the room was filling a gentleman whom I suspected was the Chairman approached. I gave him my name and said that I supposed he needed a secretary and that I was willing to serve if he so desired. He replied briskly that the Committee itself would select a secretary.

Some one spoke to him just then, and I went down the aisle and said a few potent words to one of the North Carolina delegates. As I walked toward the front, the Chairman called the Committee to order and asked for nominations for a secretary. A voice answered, "I nominate Gilbert Pearson of North Carolina." There being no other candidate the vote was unanimous, and the Chairman handed me a sheaf of resolutions which had been introduced during the morning session.

That afternoon was a busy time for me, taking down minutes and trying to interpret the unfamiliar speech of Egyptians, Englishmen, Austrians, and other foreigners. There was a tremendous amount of talking and of offering motions of various kinds, and the meeting wore on until the Chairman said that the time had come to adjourn, and that no other resolutions could now be considered that day. I arose and said that I held one in my hand which I felt sure the leaders of the Congress would expect us to consider and report in the morning, and that it would cause no debate. Quickly I read it.

"I move its adoption," said a North Carolinian. "Second the motion," called another.

The next morning at the main convention, the report of the Committee on Growing and Handling Cotton was called for at once. The first of its resolutions caused a commotion and much opposition. After lengthy debate, it was re-referred for further study. The second and third resolutions suffered similar fates. A delegate, securing recognition, complained that the entire forenoon was being consumed with the business of this one committee.

"I move that the entire report be returned to it for further study," he cried.

"Second the motion," yelled a dozen voices.

By that time I was on the platform, and before the Chairman could put the motion, I shouted, "Mr. Chairman, I am secretary of that Committee and I have here one resolution of the greatest importance that we are anxious to have passed. It will cause no discussion."

Without waiting for recognition by the President, I read it and despite the calls for various men seeking to interrupt me, I followed with a three minutes' speech on the vast importance of memorializing Congress to preserve the Bureau of Biological Survey so that it could continue its work of discovering what birds eat the boll-weevil and other insects that were destroying the Southern cotton crop. To drown the clamor of those who were contending that I was out of order, I spoke so loudly that the sound of my voice must have swept down Capitol Hill and crashed along the façades of Whitehall Street.

A vigorous "Second the motion," came from a voice with a strong Tar Heel accent, and the Chairman, ignoring the unparliamentary proceeding of considering a new motion while a motion for adjournment is pending, put the question to vote. Down on the convention floor one minute later I reached under a seat for my derby hat, and leaving the room, wired Dutcher that the resolution he wanted had been adopted at twelve o'clock M. on October 8, 1907.

In January, 1908, I decided to pay a visit to South Carolina, and help in any way I could with getting the State Audubon Society work more rapidly under way. This society had been responsible for enforcing the state game-laws for nearly ten months, but up to the present time had secured only eleven convictions, and rumors of many law-violations were reaching me.

In Columbia I worked with State Senator Christenson on the drafting of a bill for some further restrictions in the game-laws, and introduced Miss Mary T. Moore, our new Audubon Association school-lecturer to Mr. Martin, State Superintendent of Schools. Together we made plans for her to begin at once lecturing on birds and bird protection before teachers' groups and in the schools of the State.

In Aiken at that time there was a large hotel, the Park-in-the-Pines, patronized in winter by wealthy Northerners. Here I met John R. Bradley, who entertained me in his room most of the afternoon with stirring accounts of his hunting expeditions. He told of crossing Africa and of the methods he employed to safeguard his men against crocodiles when fording streams, and of how fires were kept burning around their camps at night to prevent raids of lions or leopards. He said he was proud of the fact that of his safari of one hundred and thirty men, he did not lose one during this jungle trip of eleven months.

Not long before we met he had returned from a trip to the Arctic. Purchasing a substantial Gloucester schooner he had expended $10,000 in reinforcing its sides and prow with steel and had sailed north to the realm of the walrus and the polar bear. He said that he had left one of the party at Etaw to pass the winter with the Greenland Esquimaux.

"He has food and other supplies for a stay of two or three years," he added. "He is Dr. Frederick A. Cook, a member of the Explorers' Club of New York."

"Will Dr. Cook make a dash for the North Pole?" I asked.

"We are saying nothing about that," was his brief reply, and began to talk of other matters. The next year the world was electrified by the news that Dr. Cook claimed he had reached the North Pole.

Mr. Bradley invited me to come to see him the next time I was in Florida. In Palm Beach sometime later I found that he was the proprietor of the Casino, which could be reached in a few minutes' walk by following a palm-bordered path leading from the Royal Ponciana Hotel. His place of entertainment, I was told, was an unusually successful business venture, being, in fact, the Monte Carlo of America.

From Aiken, I went to North Augusta and spent part of

the day at another winter hotel patronized by Northern people. This was called "Hampton Terrace." On the bill-of-fare I saw "quail," and the clerk at the desk told me they had 3,000 of these birds in cold storage. From others I learned that the managers of the hotel employed men on salary to hunt quail, and that they had almost wiped out these birds in the surrounding country over a radius of fifteen miles. As the sale of the quail was a violation under the State Audubon Law, I, of course, reported the case for prosecution. Later I was told that the proprietor claimed it was unethical of me to report him to the game-warden after I had been his guest, but he overlooked mentioning the fact that I had been a paying guest.

The next day, in Kershaw, I found quail for sale. When I reached Charleston, a fruit- and bird-dealer in King Street tried to sell me robins for the table. He had many of them in cages which was quite legal at that time. Quail and mourning doves were on the printed menus of the two largest hotels, and, in fact, the non-sale-of-game law was being openly violated throughout the city.

One day I crossed the Savannah River to Augusta, Georgia, and visited a local egg-collector, Dr. M. T. Cleckley, and found that he was buying and selling birds' eggs. He gave me the names of two men whom he was paying to collect for him, one of them being a well-known ornithologist, who soon afterward felt that he had just cause for becoming one of my critics.

At Georgetown non-resident hunters were shooting without the required hunting-license, and two of them told me they had no intention of buying a license since "no one pays any attention to game-laws in this country."

Such were the conditions in South Carolina in 1908. But soon things began to improve, for Mr. Rice was very zealous, although his means were limited and public disregard of game-laws for a time was very general.

We had been seeking to get a game-warden system established in Florida, but without avail. The bills were always killed by the House Committee on Game Laws, the Chairman of which we had recently learned was an attorney for the East Coast Railroad Company. This railroad did a good business in carrying shipments of food-fish and, therefore, was supposed not to look with favor upon laws for restricting the commercialization of game-fish and incidentally game-birds. Mr. Henry M. Flagler was the head of this organization, as well as of an extensive hotel system along the east coast of Florida. Early in March, having occasion to go to that state, I secured an appointment with him at Palm Beach, and sought to convince him that if fish and game were properly preserved it would be a continuing means of bringing more tourists to spend money at his hotels and on his railroad. In the end he said that although he had "no influence at the State Legislature," he would be glad to examine any bill I might prepare, covering the subject we were discussing. I did not take long to get copy for a state game commission bill into his hands. When the State Legislature met again, the attorneys for the East Coast Railway, who had blocked our previous legislative efforts in Tallahassee, introduced a bill similar to the one I had prepared for Flagler. Whether the gentleman gave the measure his heartfelt support I cannot say; but I do know that it was not until five years later that a game department was created. I was in Tallahassee at the time this occurred, and urged the Governor to appoint as state game-warden some man of experience and real interest in the subject. However, he appointed a young man, E. Z. Jones, who was earnest but knew virtually nothing of natural history, and events subsequently showed that he was not particularly skilled in the game of politics as then played in Florida.

For Jones's second annual report published in 1915, I prepared an article on "Florida Bird Life" and also a list of the 350 birds for which I could find records for the State. It encouraged us very much to find that he was willing to publish such articles for there was little in them about game-birds. He did not last long in office for, after two years' service, the Legislature abolished his department.

In 1917 I again appeared before committees of the Florida Legislature, this time being accompanied by Dr. W. F. Blackman, President of the Florida Audubon Society. We remained in Tallahassee until the Legislature enacted our bill to recreate a state warden system, but Governor S. J. Catts refused to sign it despite our pleadings. Not until 1925 was a state game commission law passed—it still remains on the statute books.

But to return to 1908. I had so much confidence in the plan of having State Audubon Societies serve as department of state for handling wild-life protection matters, and thus keeping warden appointments out of politics, that I was extremely anxious that Georgia should adopt the Audubon Game Commission Law as had North and South Carolina. My bill to bring this about did not come to a vote in the legislative session of 1906, but when that body convened on June 24, 1908, I was again in Atlanta ready for battle. Within six days the bill had passed its second reading in the House without one dissenting vote, and soon it was on its way to the Senate, where I was told it could not at once be considered.

I, therefore, left Georgia to fill various lecture engagements, stopping in Greensboro to dictate a hundred or more letters. Then I returned to Atlanta and found that strong opposition to our bill had developed. After days and nights of effort, during which I had very little outside assistance for there were no sportsmen's game-protective associations in the State and our newly formed Audubon Society was very small, I saw it defeated by a margin of four votes on August 7th. Again we had lost.

One night that year, while lecturing before a large audience attending the annual meeting of the Indiana Audubon Society, the stereopticon from which my pictures of birds were being thrown on the screen gave some trouble. Usually when a speaker experiences a difficulty beyond his control the sympathy of the audience is very much with him. Sometimes I have thought that there are those in the hall who feel more concern than does the lecturer. If he is an experienced speaker he usually has no difficulty in saying something to fill in the interim. On this occasion, when for a short time no picture was being projected, the bright light reflected from the screen revealed to me a lady in the front whose face exhibited marked emotions of sympathy. "There," I thought, "is a woman very sensitive to the suffering of a speaker." After the lecture she spoke to me. It was Gene Stratton Porter. She invited me to spend the rest of the evening with her and some friends.

The next morning I boarded a train with her and her daughter, and for some days was a guest in her attractive log house, "Limberlost Cabin," at Geneva, Indiana. We had pleasant times talking of birds and flowers and books, and calling on her friends. One day while driving out in the country she pointed to a field where she said she had been told there was once a swamp called the limberlost. At this time I read her book *Freckles,* five million copies of which have since been sold. The dummy of a book she was preparing on *Birds of the Bible* had just been assembled, and she graciously asked me to examine it and give her my opinion on the undertaking. I found she was using the pictures of some American birds to illustrate the Asiatic species mentioned in the Bible. In my library there is published copy of *Birds of the Bible* with a very friendly letter that begins: "You gave me small encouragement about writing this book; but I am sending you a copy just the same. I have put in three years on the text and five on the illustrations, and then you see by text, I did not contract to go closer than a member of the family of each species."

In some of the South Atlantic States there have long been fox-hunting clubs. It is the custom of Southern gentlemen to chase wild foxes which are jumped by the dogs in the woods. If one is captured uninjured its life usually is spared. Once, however, about this time I rode to hounds where unusual standards existed. Dashing across fields and over fences and ditches with other riders was very exhilarating; and frankly I state that I have always been stirred by the voices of running hounds. But a poignant memory of that day is of discovering upon our return that we had been chasing a captive fox that had been liberated just before the chase began. In a pen I saw two others whose feet had been injured by the steel traps which some place out in the forest had deprived them of their liberty. They, too, would be chased by dogs, maybe the next day—or perhaps the next.

CHAPTER X

NIL DESPERANDUM

WHEN THE Legislature of North Carolina met in January, 1909, I journeyed to Raleigh for a conference with the President of the Senate and the Speaker of the House. At their request, I suggested the names of those to be appointed as members of the Legislature's Committees on Game Laws.

A little later I was in Richmond, Virginia, where I addressed six hundred adults in the Jefferson Hotel and spoke three times in the City Schools. Then in Raleigh I appeared before a joint session of the legislative committees on game-laws and secured favorable reports for my bill to stop the sale of quail.

Just after this it became necessary to marshall our forces to prevent the state non-resident hunting-license being modified in such a way that it could easily be evaded. On February 5th our bill prohibiting the marketing of quail passed the Senate after a stormy debate of an hour and a half.

An invitation had come to address a joint session of the two Houses of the Arkansas Legislature in behalf of a bill to establish a game-law system in that state. The leaders of the Administration in Raleigh told me that the enemies of the Audubon Society were well in hand, that the quail bill would surely be passed by the House and that I ought to accept the invitation. Therefore, I went to Little Rock and spoke to the Arkansas law-makers in the old Capitol building which was soon to give place to the present modern structure. From here I went to Austin, Texas, and lectured to the students of the State University. One evening was spent with Captain M. B. Davis, who for a modest remuneration was serving as our Audubon Association's agent for Texas. He was a picturesque old man with long flowing locks and was a most engaging raconteur—relating his experiences with General Lee's Army, and later as a Texas ranger, fighting Indians and bad men along the border.

In Austin and San Antonio I met several people who gave me vivid accounts of the extensive killing of birds and game mammals going on in Mexico. Men from the States were invading Mexico and slaughtering wild life at a frightful rate. Some of them lived in freight-cars shunted on railway sidings. They themselves hunted, and they employed natives to kill for them. Deer, ducks and wild turkeys were piled in the freight-cars and brought across the border where they were sold at a good profit.

The Mexican armada method of shooting ducks was described to me by men who had witnessed the scenes of which they told. Many guns, sometimes a hundred, would be arranged on a platform in such a manner that half of them could be fired at a time. The armada was built on the shore of a shallow lake frequented by wild ducks, which in autumn had flown there from the far Northwest in their search for food and safety. Men, wading beside the horses they led, would gradually work the swimming ducks to a point directly in front of the guns and within shooting range. Then a battery of fifty guns would hurl 13,650 leaden missiles of death into the thickly clustered water-fowl. As the startled survivors roared upward the second battery of fifty guns discharged its smothering broadside.

These and other accounts of the slaughter of bird life were given to me by Texans and by Mexican government officials. They advised me that there was not a game-law in Mexico, except in one or two states where there existed certain restrictions on the hunting of wild sheep. These gentlemen expressed the hope that I would go to Mexico and talk the matter over with the President—Don Porfirio Diaz—whose power was sufficient to bring about any reform in which he became interested, and whose name for thirty years had caused evil-doers to tremble.

Following their suggestion, I started with letters of introduction southward over the great cactus plateau of Mexico. My train left the United States at Laredo, passed onward through Monterey, San Luis Potosi, and Queretaro, whence after climbing to an altitude of more than ten thousand feet, it dropped down to the Valley of Mexico. The first night in the capital city I was installed in the quaint old Jardin Hotel. I was given an enormous room, ceiled with paper-covered cloth, sagging in the center, as if fastened only along the walls. Rats used this for a race-course and a fighting field all through the night and until dawn peeped in through the dingy windows.

The first letters I delivered were to Colonel Porfirio Diaz, son of the President. This courteous and gracious gentlemen spoke English fluently and I soon learned that he was interested in agricultural chemistry, architecture, polo and big-game hunting. He was busy directing the erection of public buildings to cost three million pesos. He had won these government contracts he told me by competitive bidding. In his automobile, driven by himself, he took me about the city. Once he halted to examine a workman whose eyes were so inflamed that he could not see to walk. A passer-by was called and a doctor summoned. Again he stopped his car suddenly and springing out accosted a policeman who was beating a boy. The lad it seemed had just stolen a banana from a fruit-stall. I do not know what was said, but the beating stopped and the policeman walked away in one direction and the boy ran off in another.

In his home, surrounded by a high iron fence and protected by guards, he showed me mounted heads of mountain-

sheep, deer and other trophies of the chase. He handed me
a Mannlicker-Schoenaure rifle that had been especially built
and presented to him by the manufacturers. It was beautifully engraved and when I threw it to my shoulder I found
that it fitted me exactly. Of course I expressed my admiration
for such a beautiful gun.

He smiled happily, "You like it? Ah, it is yours."

I gasped, but fortunately collected my wits enough to remember that when a Mexican says "It is yours," he does not
mean that he is giving it to you.

Two days later in the great bull ring I saw dozens of
people throw their canes, parasols and costly hats at the feet
of a popular matador, majestically circling the arena. He
had just neatly dispatched a charging bull with one thrust
of his sword and was receiving the tumultuous applause of
the multitude. Although he continually bowed his appreciation for the gifts showered upon him, he did not pick up
any of them. Two *banderilleros* who followed promptly restored the objects to their owners, as was customary and
proper.

Colonel Diaz seemed to think well of my proposals for
preserving wild life and arranged an interview for me with
his father. President Diaz received us in a great room in the
Castle of Chapultepec, perched on its rocky hill at the end
of the Paseo de la Reforma. Its furniture had been installed
by the unfortunate Emperor Maximilian during those hectic
days in the 1860's when he was maintained on the throne of
Mexico by the soldiers of France.

My plans for beginning bird and game protection in
Mexico were confined to these few fundamentals: provide
a close season on hunting during the spring and summer
months; stop the killing of egrets for the millinery trade;
prohibit the export of game; charge a non-resident hunting-
license of twenty-five pesos; and make the rurales a national
game-warden force. The President asked many questions as

to how the plan worked in other countries. The interview lasted for half an hour, and at its conclusion he said, "I think that the wild birds and mammals should be preserved," then turning to his son, asked, "Would you be willing to organize a society advocating needed measures of this nature?" When the Colonel replied that he would gladly do so, the President said: "When you have done this I shall present the subject to the Senate."

We walked out on the upper terrace of the Castle and lifted our eyes to the great volcanoes, Popocatepetl and Iztaccihuatl, the tops of which towered more than two miles above us. I tried very hard to pronounce those names with young Porfirio, at first seriously, and then with some amusement, repeating the words over and over again. I decided that people with small linguistic accomplishments had much better use the English equivalents, "The Giant" and "The Sleeping Lady."

Colonel Diaz seemed much pleased with his father's reception of the plans suggested, and asked me to furnish him with copies of bird- and game-laws in force in the United States, and to provide him with literature on the value of birds. We returned to the center of the city, and leaving my host I went to the city market where I discovered the bodies of great numbers of ducks selling for a sum equivalent to five cents each in United States money.

In the central plaza by the Executive Palace I paused to listen to the band, whose beautiful music filled the plaza and the surrounding streets and flowed into the homes of the people. There was much passing to and fro. Some listeners leaned against the walls of the buildings and others sat at ease on their serapes. Suddenly I noticed a woman lying on the ground near the cathedral door. Her body was shaking as if convulsed by sobs. Turning to a young Mexican attorney, with whom I had exchanged a few remarks, I indicated the prostrate figure and asked him what he supposed was the matter. He glanced at her, then with slight shrug said "peon," and turned his attention again to the music.

With some earnestness I asked him to speak to her and learn if she had been injured. With evident reluctance he walked over and touched her lightly with his foot. She lifted a tear-drenched face and I saw that she was perhaps eighteen years of age. After talking with her a minute or two he told me that she had arrived that afternoon with an old peon and some burros loaded with her mother's orange crop. It had taken two days to reach the city. She had planned to get some cotton cloth so that her mother could make her a new dress, but her father was in purgatory and as it had been so long since she had been to the cathedral to have prayers said for him she was told that it was necessary for her to leave all her oranges there. She felt very unhappy because she could not have a new dress to wear at the fiesta to be held in her village before long.

As I sat there and reflected on the suffering that innocent people have often endured through religious institutions, I recalled that the great Cathedral of Mexico City, with its chapels adorned with priceless objects of gold, occupies the spot where a teocalli of the Aztecs once stood. There, in 1520, when the city was known as Tenochtitlan, Cortez had help-lessly looked on while Indians sacrificed to their gods some of his soldiers they had captured. On top of the teocalli the Aztec priests cut the hearts from their living victims, while all about them the air pulsated with the throbbing music of war-drums made of serpent skins.

I turned homeward toward the Rio Grande, nearly a thousand miles to the northward, bearing with me a photograph of my new co-worker, and a book which he had translated into Spanish. Both presents bore the inscription of the giver, *Porfirio Diaz, Hijo*. The title of the book is *El A. B. C. del Cultivo del Maiz*. As yet I am unable to read the book but I understand that it deals with the growing of corn.

As the trail bore me across the cactus plains and through maguey plantations, where peons in sombreros make and consume that atrocious drink they call "pulqué," I had the feeling that my trip south of the border might be productive of worth-while results in the protection of wild life. But I had not yet comprehended the full significance of the word *mañana,* nor did I anticipate that two years later President Diaz and his engaging son would become political refugees from the land of their birth and labors—nor had I any inkling of the trouble awaiting me in North Carolina.

Arriving in Raleigh after an absence of three weeks I met at the entrance to the Capitol a newspaper friend who told me that my bill to stop the sale of quail had been killed in the House of Representatives. The quail merchants of the State had secured the coöperation of the shippers of ducks and geese from the coast counties and had been able to prevent its passage. This, indeed, was a blow. For six years no game-bill in Raleigh which I favored had been defeated, nor had one become a law over my opposition. The situation was getting serious. The killers of birds were becoming too well organized.

A little later I met a Senator who told me that some of his colleagues had worked a trick and slipped through the Senate a bill most harmful to the policy of state-wide administration of the game-laws. Senator Fred P. Latham, representing Beaufort, Martin and Washington counties, had introduced as S. B. 1234 "A Bill for the Better Enforcement of the Game Laws of Bertie and Currituck Counties," and asked that it be placed on the Calendar. Without any discussion, this was done. Such a request was not uncommon when a legislative session was nearing its end. By this means the bill was kept from going to the Committee on Game Laws.

That same evening its proponents called up the bill, had it read by title only, and it passed its second and third readings. It had not been printed, in fact few bills ever were

printed, the State usually not going to this expense. So
Latham's bill, I understood, passed the Senate with less than
a dozen knowing what it contained. When it reached the
House it had been referred to the Committee on Game Laws
where it was resting when I arrived. The Chairman of this
committee had advised my senatorial friend of its character
and he in turn told me.

It was thought that the best course was for the Senate to
recall the bill, to expose its contents and to kill it. We re-
paired to the Senate where in a few minutes the necessary
action to recall the bill was taken. Then I went across to
the House to wait until the demand should be presented and
the bill ordered to be returned. As I entered the Chamber
I heard a fiery speech in progress, my name being mentioned.
What I heard in substance was at follows:

This man has accumulated great wealth at the expense of the
tax-payers of North Carolina, and we gather from the daily press
that he and his family are even now wintering in Mexico [the
orator shouted]. He is a Czar to whom the State has surrendered
all its authorities over the birds and mammals which roam
your farm and mine. He even induced this Legislature to establish committees on game-laws to handle game-bills instead
of referring them, as heretofore, to their proper committees—
the Committees on Propositions and Grievances. You know and
I know that we cannot pass a game-law affecting our counties
except with his sanction. It will soon be so that if you want to
kill a woodpecker on your own land you must first ask him.

What had happened was that I had been seen to enter
the Capitol and my enemies in the House had demanded
that the House stop its consideration of the general school
bill, the special order for that morning, take S. B. 1234 out
of the hands of the House Committee on Game Laws and
give it immediate consideration. Without understanding the
reasons for such a sudden change of action, but impressed
with the vigor of the proponents of the motion, the Assembly

voted to discontinue the debate on the school bill and take
up Senator Latham's local county game measure. This bill
provided that the Audubon Society should no longer have
jurisdiction in the counties of Bertie and Currituck, and that
the money collected from non-resident hunting-licenses in
those counties should be kept by them instead of being sent
to the State Treasury where it became subject to the checks
and vouchers of the Audubon Society. The counties would
use half of the money for the School Fund and the remainder
to hire county game-wardens.

Twice in my life I had seen groups of men bent on lynch-
ing some unfortunate Negro, and now I was to see something
akin to mob-spirit in action in a legislative hall. Excitement
ran high as men told of the large sums of money which they
claimed the Audubon Society received from the non-resident
hunting tax and of the great benefits to be derived if half
of these funds could be used for the education of the poor
barefooted farm-boy. Dozens of men, fired with local patri-
otism, sprang to their feet and sent up amendments to include
their counties with Bertie and Currituck. They wanted to
share in the wealth which they imagined the Audubon Society
was enjoying. I heard men tell how we were getting thousands of dollars from license fees in their counties each year,
when I knew that these counties had never yielded a dollar
to the game-fund. Others spoke glowingly of the splendid
game-law enforcement which they would have in their counties if they could only be free from the Audubon Society,
while I knew that if the Audubon wardens were withdrawn
those counties would have no game-law enforcement at all,
for they would have no license money to use. I knew that the
illegal shipping of quail and the shooting of game out of
season would again become rampant in various regions where
we had been able to check it.

In listening to some of these speeches an outsider might
readily believe they were discussing funds that ran into

millions of dollars. The published report of the Treasurer showed that during the preceding fiscal year the total receipts from the sale of hunting-licenses and confiscated game in the entire State of North Carolina amounted to only $8,776, or an average of $89.55 for each county, and this had been the year of our largest revenue.

I knew many of the men who spoke against our work that day. Some were sincere, but were misled and were speaking without understanding. There were others whose friends the Audubon wardens had prosecuted, and there were also the representatives of the market-hunters and the shippers of game who had smarted under our administration. One of those who voted against us had warned me six weeks before that he could no longer support the Audubon Society unless I would allow him to amend the Audubon Law so that he could ship woodcock to Northern markets. Governor William Kitchen, to whom I appealed, said that his law partner, Mr. Travis, was working with me. That was true, but the Governor's brother Paul, also in the Legislature, was one of our outspoken opponents.

There were many men who fought valiantly to maintain the state-wide game-law in defense of the Audubon Society. One called attention to the fact that the Society had never cost a tax-payer of the State anything unless he had been caught violating a game-law. Mr. Graham, the Speaker, declared among other things: "Until the Society was organized there never was an efficient game-law in North Carolina." Another stated: "If this opposition bill is passed game protection will be set back ten years."

In North Carolina at that time there was no organization actively interested in wild-life protection, except the Audubon Society. We did not have game-protective associations upon whom we could call for help in the struggle. The Women's Clubs had not developed an interest in birds to a point where they would think of taking part in legislative activities. Only a few people here and there had a special interest in such matters, and these were scattered throughout the State and were without lobbying experience. Dr. R. H. Lewis, a prominent and beloved physician in Raleigh, was the President of the Audubon Society. He did what he could by coming to the Capital. So did Colonel Fred Oldes, the historian, and a few other loyal friends, but mostly it was a lone battle that I had to wage.

So thoroughly had our enemies done their work of misleading uninformed members of the Legislature into believing that here was a good chance to get large sums of money for their counties, that there was no stopping the Latham Bill. It was passed after it had been amended by adding the names of many other counties which wanted to run their own game-law affairs and have more money, so they thought, for educational purposes.

In the Senate there was another long fight, which consumed much of the law-makers' time for two days and a night. The Raleigh *News and Observer* of March 6th stated: "For stubbornness of contest, resourceful resistance on the one hand and determined aggressiveness on the other, no fight during the present session of the Legislature is comparable to that which has waged fiercely about the bill designated as the anti-Audubon Bill."

At length the Senate restored to the Audubon Society thirteen of the counties that had been removed from its jurisdiction by the House, and the bill was carried by a margin of four votes. It provided that on May 1st the new law would become operative in fifty-two counties, forty-six being left under the authority of the Audubon Society.

When a man has given for years the best within him to a cause in the righteousness of which he has implicit faith and has seen that cause grow and bear abundant fruit, he feels that it must necessarily continue to stand. He feels that its worthiness is so unmistakably apparent to all intelligent people that they will never permit its usefulness to become impaired. He may persuade himself that no one could possibly oppose his creed or differ from him in his faith, unless that person were inspired by malice, jealousy or intolerance. My plan from the beginning had always been to keep game-law enforcement out of politics and I fondly thought I had set up such a machine. But experience had shown that wherever money is involved there are always people ready to resort to political practices to get control of it.

Disappointment and chagrin were my companions as I sat in the railway car returning to Greensboro on May 7, 1909, after the most bitter legislative defeat which I had thus far suffered.

Dutcher, always sympathetic, wrote me, "what was done was a positive loss to the State and was instigated by pure self-ishness. Unfortunately, there are a great many people in this world who care little except for themselves, and provided they get what they want, they give little thought for what is best for the rest of the people."

Among other disquieting thoughts was the fear that this action by the Legislature of my own State would work adversely against the Audubon bills which I had drawn for immediate passage in Arkansas, Florida and Georgia.

However, all was not lost. In the comments of the papers of the State I do not recall seeing a single editorial that spoke unkindly of me or of the Audubon Society. Many letters came with assurances that the "rebel counties" would return to the fold at the next Legislature. But I knew that at least some of them never would. No one could expect Currituck County willingly to consent to be ruled by state game-laws as long as ducks and geese came to its waters and the market for their bodies continued.

In our Audubon counties during the year that followed we successfully conducted one hundred and thirty-three prosecutions for violations in the bird- and game-laws. It was a sad experience to be unable to respond to numerous urgent calls to prosecute violators of the bird-laws in those counties which had withdrawn from our jurisdiction and were without game-wardens to protect their wild life.

As I look back upon those years I realize how woefully inadequate were the funds at our disposal for carrying on what was supposed to be a state-wide undertaking. We received no state appropriation and our entire income came from the $9.50 received as our share from each non-resident hunting-license, a few small sums from the sale of confiscated game, and the fees and contributions of our members and friends.

The entire income of the Audubon Society of North Carolina for the eight years, during which I was the executive officer, amounted to $71,316.21, of which sum $16,592.20 was received from membership fees and gifts secured by my personal solicitation. My total remuneration for the eight years of service was $9,875.

When our Society was incorporated in 1903, we had engaged twenty-nine wardens and this number gradually was increased to 100 in the year 1910. We expended for this service $35,995.29 and successfully conducted 855 prosecutions. These dealt in part with the killing in close season of deer, opossum, ducks, quail, turkeys, meadow-larks, robins and other legalized game-birds and mammals. There were many others for killing cardinals, nighthawks, martins, flickers, bluebirds, gulls, herons, and other non-game birds. Still other convictions were for hunting on lands without the owners' permission and for non-residents shooting without hunting-licenses. All money collected from fines as provided by law was paid into the State School Fund.

Through the Audubon Society, North Carolina had been the first Southern state to provide for a game-warden system and the most of the work which we had conducted had been new to the people of that section of our nation. In efforts

for wild-life preservation North Carolina had been the
pioneer state in all the vast region lying south of the Ohio
and Potomac rivers.

When in January, 1911, the Legislature again assembled,
the Audubon Society distributed a pamphlet: "To the Governor and Members of the General Assembly of North Carolina," in which we stated that more than half of the counties
which had withdrawn from the operations of the Audubon
Society had no game-wardens, and no hunting-license money
with which to pay for such officers, and that the killing of
game in those regions, therefore, was going on unchecked.
We recommended that the Legislature cancel the Society's
charter and establish a Game Commission with state-wide
authority. We also urged that all local game-laws be abolished
and that hereafter only those state-wide in their application
be enacted. Illustrating the extent to which county game-laws
had grown, the report stated:

In 1909, legislative sessions were held in five of the Canadian
Provinces and in all of the states of the Union but five. The
total number of game-laws enacted was 220. Of these North
Carolina alone enacted 69, all but one being local county measures. As a result [of this tendency] our game-laws have become
very complicated, and to-day constitute a tangled mass which
no man can understand. The United States Government, which
every year publishes a sheet showing the open seasons for hunting in the various States of the Union, and the Provinces of
Canada, is now forced to publish two of equal size, the second
one containing only the game-laws of North Carolina.

Many of the counties did not wish to give up the game-
protective work which they were receiving from the Audubon
Society, and felt that this would be the case if a politically
appointed game-warden system were established. Other counties wanted to be "free" whether or not their game was protected, and still others took no special interest in the matter
one way or the other. Therefore, no action on the measure

we had proposed was taken by the Legislature and still more county game-laws were enacted. From that time on every two years the Audubon Society of North Carolina came forward with a bill to establish a State Game Department, and just as regularly it was defeated and more local laws came into being. All this time the bird and game statutes were being violated throughout the State, and the law-violators had little to fear for there were few game-wardens "to molest or make afraid."

The Raleigh *Times* for February 25, 1919, speaking of our bill for that year stated:

Opposition to the state-wide game-law, and the appointment of a game commission developed from two sources and the bill was laid on the table on motion of Senator Tracy. In the first place, the Audubon Society bill abolished all local game-laws. . . . In the second place, the bill would take out of the county treasury and put into state depository, the money collected under the game-laws.

Attached to this clipping in my records is a note penned by that sane naturalist and staunch wild-life protector, H. H. Brimley of Raleigh, who had sympathized with every move to establish state-wide control of game-law enforcement. It reads: "*Sic transit gloria mundi! Nil desperandum!* Bee Gum Branch stands like the Pyramids against the State abolishing the ten dollars it hopes to receive the year after next from the sale of a non-resident hunting-license!"

So it came about that it took the Audubon Society sixteen years to induce the General Assembly of North Carolina to abolish the Audubon charter which back in 1903 it had granted after a campaign of half that many weeks.

A State Game Commission was not created until 1927, but Currituck, Hyde and Dare counties, with their duck-hunters, succeeded in remaining independent in wild water-fowl matters until 1935, when public sentiment finally overcame their resistance and the most famous wild-fowl hunting region in eastern United States came under the yoke of state control.

Although the North Carolina Audubon Law had been mutilated by legislative action early in 1909, I still had plenty of work to do. Writing letters and articles on bird protection, holding conferences, and lecturing kept me busy. I spoke at Hampton Institute, at the Virginia State Educational Conference, and before the Indiana Nature Study Society. I gave my presidential address before the Eighth Annual Convention of the North Carolina Academy of Science, delivered a series of lectures at the University of Tennessee, and prepared the Audubon Association's "Report on Bird and Game Protection in America" for the National Conservation Congress.

Much work was required at the Georgia Legislature, where a most vigorous but unsuccessful attempt was made to get legislation to support a game-warden system by income derived from proposed resident and non-resident hunting-licenses.

Nonpareils were flooding the markets of Philadelphia, and playing the rôle of an amateur detective I uncovered a number of bird-trappers in the Savannah region. In the end we stopped this traffic through some of the transportation lines, especially the Merchants' and Miners' Steamship Company.

Money was desperately needed for the National Association, and the Board of Directors planned that William Dutcher should give special attention to soliciting memberships in New York and Pennsylvania; Mr. Forbush was to do the same in New England, and I was asked to do similar work throughout the West. Dutcher was beginning to feel the strain of his many years' work, and often said he was neglecting his insurance business on which he depended for a livelihood. In May, 1909, he wrote me: "As far as I am able to do so, I am shifting responsibility, because the day will soon come when it will be shifted whether I want to have it so or not; and, therefore, I want you to work this proposition out yourself, as you will have to do on all occasions not very far in the future."

So I went ahead and planned work in Milwaukee, Chicago, Madison, Indianapolis and elsewhere. It was during this trip that I saw the only passenger pigeons I was ever to behold. There were two of them, and they were in a cage in the Cincinnati Zoological Garden. This was in the year 1909. On September 1, 1914, the last one of these died, and the race became extinct.

About this time I gave illustrated addresses to large audiences in North Carolina, at Winston-Salem, at the State University in Chapel Hill, and before the National Farmers' Congress in Raleigh, where, quite naturally, I spoke on "The Value of Birds to the Farm."

Also, I completed my bulletin on birds and their value for the North Carolina State Department of Agriculture, 50,000 copies of which were at once published and distributed.

Later in the year, Dutcher wrote that he wanted me to join him in New York and go to Syracuse to attend the annual convention of the New York Forest, Fish and Game League, where he had made an engagement for me to speak. The League was an influential body and its recommendations regarding game-laws had much weight with the State Legislature. Our "Model Law" to protect birds was now in force in most of the states, but it did not distinctly prohibit the sale of the feathers of any bird unless it could be shown that these came from some individual bird that had been illegally killed within that state. In 1907, and again in 1908, Dutcher had tried in vain to get a law in New York State to stop the sale of the feathers of all native protected birds. He now planned that I should try my hand at accomplishing this end. Perhaps the State League of Sportsmen could be induced to help us if, in my talk, I was able to secure their interest and good-will.

I spoke for at least half an hour, urging the need of removing game protection from the realm of politics, and thereby uplifting the general standard of the warden forces. Particularly, I emphasized the desirability of requiring all applicants for appointment as game-wardens to stand a civil service examination. Also, that after a warden has once qualified and is doing good work, he should not be removed for political reasons. I urged that wardens should study to learn the names and appearances of the various birds and animals they are to protect and, as opportunity arose, be in position to speak to granges, schools and other gatherings on the beauty of wild life and the importance of preserving it.

My Syracuse speech was so well received that Dutcher arose and said he would send me to speak to any sportsmen's club that might desire to have me visit their community. The program of the day stopped while at least twenty men came forward giving him their names and addresses and asking that I plan to address their clubs.

There was a formidable hurdle to be cleared, however, if the plumage bill was to succeed at the next Legislature. The support of James S. Whipple, State Game Commissioner, must be secured. His influence was so potent that in 1908 he had prevented the Audubon Feather Bill, introduced by Assemblyman Francis, from even being reported out by a legislative committee. Dutcher said that he had criticized Commissioner Whipple for his lack of interest in the matter, and that he felt sure that now he never would be able to induce the Commissioner to support an Audubon Society bill. He had heard that Whipple thought well of me after our lecture trip together in northern New York the year before, and he wanted to see if I could possibly secure his support to our measure. We went to Albany, and while Dutcher remained at the Kenmore Hotel, I went up to the Capitol. Whipple demurred for a time, but finally said he would do what he could to help me get the bill passed if I would promise to keep Dutcher away from Albany. Dutcher smiled broadly when I returned and made my report. "The condition he imposes is very easy to comply with," he said.

All the way back to New York we discussed plans for the battle with the feather milliners, which would begin when the State Legislature should convene in January.

Chapter XI

THE FEATHER FIGHT AT ALBANY

F OR A LONG time New York City had been the headquarters for the North American millinery trade in the feathers of wild birds. Plumage of slaughtered birds came to this city from all over the United States and from the tropical countries of the world. Here they were trimmed, dyed and arranged into a thousand different creations for hat decorations. Distributing agents shipped the products of the manufacturers to local milliners in every state in the Union. In time, laws, public sentiment and a changing mode reduced the extent of the craze for the feathers of small birds. However, a great business in aigrettes and certain other plumage continued to flourish.

In 1910 I was called upon to take part in securing legislation to bring about the destruction of this industry which employed thousands of people and involved investments of millions of dollars. I went to Albany early in January as legislative agent for the Audubon Association to try to secure a law making it illegal to sell aigrettes and the plumage of other native birds. My experience in securing legislation had been confined to Capitals in the Southern states, where I felt at home and knew the types of men I should meet, but in the New York Legislature I had not a single acquaintance, and I had the idea that I would find these Northern men to be shrewd, resourceful and particularly formidable.

There was something terrifying about the situation in which I found myself, but I mustered up courage and began to make the acquaintance of Senators and Assemblymen. At first I did not say anything to them about the bill to be introduced but merely tried to establish friendly relations. In the evenings I joined groups of them in the Kenmore and the Ten Eyck hotels, where often we exchanged stories. My specialty was anecdotes and tales of the South, told in the dialect of the Negro plantation-hands. Soon I knew many of the younger men; but to become really "one of the boys" I made a desperate effort to cultivate a taste for beer. They never suspected how I suffered in those deliberate but futile efforts to take a drink. Beer, to me, was, and is to this day, an abomination—too strongly reminiscent is it of the bitter waters which, as a boy, on many a Summer's day, I was forced to drink from a quassia cup to ward off attacks of ague and break-bone fever.

It had been planned that Assemblyman James Shea of Essex County should introduce our plumage bill as soon as the Legislature convened. At the Stuyvesant Hotel I tried to see him on the morning of the sixth, and found him just entering a cab with his wife and baby, hurrying to catch a train.

"They didn't give me a chance to introduce the bill yesterday," he called out to me as he drove away.

In the office of the Secretary of State I filled my application as a lobbyist—I had never done that before. Down South they always seemed glad to have a stranger come around, if he had a good story or two to tell and a couple of extra cigars in his vest pocket. At this office I learned that all the members of the Senate and the Assembly were going home for a few days. I asked why they wanted a vacation so soon when they hadn't done any work, but the clerk didn't trouble to answer.

That night I mailed Dutcher a new membership fee secured from George F. Seward, whom I had met on a train; and the next morning I left to fill a speaking engagement at Ticonderoga.

It developed that the Legislature met only four days each

week so there were not many of its members in Albany to interview on Fridays, Saturdays and Sundays.

Large audiences assembled by sportsmen's organizations and grangers greeted me the next few weeks in Watertown, Henderson, Syracuse, Newark and ten other New York towns. The men whom I had met at Syracuse in December certainly had been effective as advance advertising agents. In all these places I told of our proposed plumage law and, without exception, secured hearty resolutions of its approval. One day I spoke at the annual gathering of state game-protectors in Albany, following Dr. Palmer who had come from Washington for this meeting.

State Game Commissioner James S. Whipple, with whom I had established very friendly relations, took me as his guest to Canton, where he spoke on forest preservation, and I urged protection of birds. Our reception by the large audience was little short of an ovation. Mr. Whipple was feeling particularly good when we were returning to Albany, so I took the opportunity to suggest that he become a member of the Audubon Association, and he at once agreed.

I visited various people to get their support, among them Bishop Potter of Albany, officers of the sportsmen's club of Troy, Mr. Godfrey, President of the State Grange, and Mrs. Elmer Blair, President of the New York State Federation of Women's Clubs. Dutcher was sending thousands of letters throughout the State asking people to write their legislative representative to vote for saving the birds. The replies he received from Senators and Assemblymen were sent to me and helped me to determine just how to approach each one of the writers.

The form of our bill to stop the sale of the plumage of wild birds proved to be unsatisfactory to some and had to be redrawn. It was referred to Dutcher and to the Association's attorney, Samuel T. Carter, Jr. Dr. Palmer was consulted, telegrams exchanged, various Senators and Assemblymen gave advice, and the wording was worked over and over. Mr. Whipple and the counsel of his Commission, John K. Ward, of course, were among the first to be seen and their opinions sought. Whipple's influence was paramount. It was so great that Senator James White said he would decline to introduce the bill unless Whipple would support it; and Assemblyman Shea declared that, while he did not mind fighting Whipple, he knew that Whipple could beat him on any game bill. At length everything seemed to be pretty well ironed out, and on January 24th Senator White introduced our bill, and two days later Mr. Shea placed the measure before the Assembly.

I was told that the bill must rest for a time, that if we pressed either of the game committees for a quick consideration it would be to our disadvantage. So I accepted a call by telegraph to meet with the game committees of the Virginia Legislature in Richmond on January 31st. Two days later, with Mrs. Pearson I boarded a train at Greensboro and, in company with Dr. Palmer and Mr. Carleton, State Game Commissioner of Maine, started for New Orleans where I was to preside at the sessions of the Fifth Convention of the National Association of State Game and Fish Wardens and Commissioners, which were to begin February 5th. Representatives from the game departments of twenty states attended this meeting. The hospitable New Orleans people showered entertainments upon us, and the occasion was enlivened by the street parades and general gaiety incident to the Mardi Gras.

In our talks Dr. Palmer and I took every opportunity to impress the delegates with the need of strengthening the game-laws in their states, and especially emphasized the importance of enforcing the statutes which extended protection to non-game birds. Although I was already engaged in about all the work that one man should undertake, I accepted the election as President for the Game Commissioners' Association for a term of two years.

The day after the Convention closed, Dr. Palmer, Dr. George W. Field of Boston, and I decided to go to Buras, near the mouth of the Mississippi River. The train ambled reluctantly along through the fields and scattered orange-groves of the Delta. When near the levee we could see that the surface of the river was considerably above the railway tracks. A strong, gusty wind blew the rain against the car windows, and it was cold. At length we agreed that we could do nothing on the lower river if we ever succeeded in reaching Buras, so since it was nearly noon we decided to leave the train, secure some food, and return to New Orleans that evening. We got out on the platform of an isolated store, the back part of which was used as a residence. Tall pilings lifted the structure above the marsh.

My companions were not enthusiastic about the prospects of a dinner of cheese and crackers. With the consent of the store-keeper I invaded the rear part of the building, found his wife, and asked her about cooking us a dinner. She yielded only after I promised to help. While Palmer and Field with growing appetites sat by a stove in the parlor and listened to the rain outside, I supplied stove-wood, peeled potatoes, and prepared for the oven two mallard ducks I found hanging on the back porch—"French ducks" our hostess called them. These, with hot biscuits and preserves, combined to make a meal of which my companions still speak at times with enthusiasm.

A bill to establish a State Game Commission was pending in the Mississippi Legislature, and I was asked by its sponsors to go to the Capital and advise with them regarding its provisions. The bill covered sixteen pages of legal-cap paper and was a most formidable-looking document. The changes I suggested, including the insertion of an anti-plumage clause, were accepted, and the Governor told me he would urge its adoption in that form.

The North Carolina Audubon Society work of late had been carried on largely by correspondence, with the help of an able secretary in the Greensboro office; but now it became necessary to spend a week in the State before returning to Albany. In the meantime, I tried to arrange by telegraph for committee hearings on our New York plumage bill, but upon reaching Albany found that the milliners had thus far been able to defeat any plan being made for a hearing and another waiting period became necessary.

I renewed the work of getting votes pledged for our bill and devoted many active hours to combating Assembly Bill No. 765, intended to permit sale of foreign game-birds during the close season for hunting in New York; and to denouncing Assembly Bill No. 359, to extend the duck-hunting season to February 1st. At this time I recorded among our supporters the name of James W. Wadsworth, Jr., Speaker of the Assembly, and Franklin D. Roosevelt, a member of the Senate. The former afterward served one term in the United States Senate and later became a member of Congress; the latter served as Assistant Secretary of the Navy during the World War, and in 1932 and again in 1936 was elected the President of the United States.

One night while in New York City, I went with Samuel T. Carter, Jr., to the Hotel Astor where a dinner was to be given in honor of Commander Robert E. Peary by "The Canadian Camp and seventy-five other sportsmen's organizations of this country and Canada." Shortly after the dinner began, a gentleman approached and said that the Rev. Dr. Edward Judson, Master of Ceremonies, had asked that I come to the speaker's table.

Commander Peary gave an account of his recent discovery of the North Pole, and was presented with a bronze wreath. Dr. G. Lenox Curtis, President of the Canadian Camp, proposed toasts to the President of the United States, the King of England, and Mrs. Peary. Captain Jack Crawford, the "poet scout," read some of his poems, and others made short speeches. Then, with not more than two minutes' warning, I was introduced to the audience. Seldom have I been more surprised than I was with what occurred three minutes after I had arisen. It was thus described in the New York *Times* the next morning, March 16, 1910:

A little thing called out a Roosevelt demonstration. An incidental remark about the ex-President electrified the three hundred present, so they broke into wild applause, sprang to their feet and waved their napkins. It was T. Gilbert Pearson who made the remark that fired the enthusiasm about Col. Roosevelt, in telling the story of how President Roosevelt had set aside a small island as a breeding-place for birds.—[There had been neither law nor precedent for this action, but he had realized the need for it and had done it.]

"He's the man who always does things when they are to be done," he went on; "Oh, he's a great and many-sided man," and the audience turned itself loose.

The next morning two representatives of a New York City newspaper called to see me, one a photographer and the other a lady who asked me to tell her about the Audubon Society, while she made notes of what was said. I did not catch her name, and when her account of the interview was published I was surprised to find that my engaging visitor had been Mrs. Howard Chandler Christy.

Despite all our efforts, time dragged on at Albany without any date being set for a hearing on the Audubon Plumage Bill. However, personal work among the members of the Legislature, and especially the letters from constituents coming to them in ever-increasing volume, were having their effect. Day by day, I was correcting the lists in my note-book. Names that had been in the column "opposed" or "doubtful" were being transferred to the "favorable" group. Every day our prospects looked brighter. If those unseen forces that control the destiny of legislation would only permit our bills to come out of the committees so that our friends in the two Houses could register their votes!

We could learn nothing of the attitude of the Governor since he declined to deviate from his policy of not indicating his opinion regarding pending legislation. Dutcher issued more mimeographed letters and the office force sent them to Audubon Society members, sportsmen, grangers, members of women's clubs and, in fact, to almost any list of New York State people that could be procured. Twice I sent letters to all the members of both Houses, and on March 2nd and 3rd placed in the Capitol post-office for each of them a newly bound set of our forty-one "Educational Leaflets" and our twenty-one "Special Leaflets." These contained twenty-seven full-page pictures of birds reproduced in colors. This was a popular move. In fact, it proved to be almost too popular for our pocket-book, as many Senators and Assemblymen wrote asking for additional copies for their friends. Some wanted ten, others twenty-five or even a hundred.

Finally, on March 9th, more than two months after the Legislature had convened, the Assembly Committee on Forest, Fish and Game gave a hearing at which the Audubon Bill was discussed. A goodly company of witnesses and spectators was present. In the room many mounted birds, bird-skins and samples of hat plumage were on exhibit, which caused one newspaper writer to report: "the place looked like a taxidermist's shop."

Our bill provided that Section 98 of the Conservation Laws should be amended to read: "No part of the plumage, skin, or body of any bird protected in this section, or of any birds coming from without the State, whether belonging to the same or different species from that native to the State of New York, provided that such birds belong to the *same family* as those protected by this chapter, shall be sold or had in possession for sale."

Our main object was to stop the sale of aigrettes, the plumes growing on the backs of the snowy egret and American egret during the spring and early summer. These birds at that time were rarely seen in New York State, hence the words "same family," were employed to insure their protection by giving them the same legal status as other members of the heron family commonly found in the State and already protected by law. As worded, the bill also prevented the sale of the feathers of virtually all the species of North American song-birds should the fashion for such millinery trimmings again return, nor would it be necessary to prove that they had come from birds killed in New York State.

Mr. Dutcher, S. T. Carter, Augustus S. Houghton of the Camp Fire Club of America, Mr. Cook, attorney for two interested ladies, and I testified in behalf of the bill. Judge Julius Meyer, representing the Eastern Millinery Association; Benjamin Feiner, attorney for the Feather Importers' Association of New York, and several of the milliners in person, defended the rights of the feather dealers. Mr. Feiner read an article recently published in the *Outlook* magazine, in which it was claimed that egrets and other herons that we desired to protect were injurious birds and should not be conserved.

Mr. Feiner contended that egrets were not killed to get the feathers, but that their plumes used in the feather trade were shed feathers picked up from the ground. We maintained that the egrets were killed for their plumage in the breeding season, which necessarily caused the young to die of starvation. Feiner said the man for whom our Society was named did not think egrets were so important and he was supposed to be a great ornithologist. He said that Audubon did not object to his friend, Dr. Bachman, killing egrets, and read Audubon's account of one of Bachman's shooting expeditions to a colony of breeding herons.

Finally, Allison Brothers, milliners, announced that they sold $200,000 worth of egret plumes a year.

The hearing lasted about three hours, and as Dutcher wrote next day to a friend, "part of the time the temperature was very hot."

We had done our best to impress the Committee with our side of the question, but another fortnight was to elapse before its report was given. In the meantime, we were encouraged by an action of the Legislative Committee of the Republican League of Clubs of New York State, which on March 15th asked all Republicans in the Legislature to support our bill.

On March 23rd the Forest, Fish and Game Committee reported our bill favorably to the Assembly. Three days later, March 26th, the New York *Times* published an editorial, thirteen inches long, under the title: "Piffling Legislation." It dealt with the Audubon Plumage Bill pending in Albany and a similar one that Dutcher had caused to be introduced in the New Jersey Legislature. In part, it ran:

Sentiment and sentimentality are generally strong not only in Albany, but in most other state capitals. If common sense and good judgment were as plentiful we should have fewer absurd and undesirable laws.

There are already laws in force to prevent slaughtering song-birds. It is not proposed to stop the killing of wild game-birds for the markets. But the feathers of those birds must not be sold. The proposed law prohibits the sale, but neglects to indicate any other way to dispose of the feathers. They must not be used to stuff beds or cushions unless they can be obtained for that purpose without a commercial transaction. The feathers may be given away and accepted as gifts. In other words, women may continue to wear feathers if they can get them....

What sane argument and good example cannot do to arouse women to a sense of the bad taste and cruelty of wearing feathers and stuffed birds, the law cannot be expected to accomplish. Such laws are made to be broken with impunity and the presence of a multitude of such laws in the statute books helps to create a general contempt for the law.

[Further it stated:] Birds-of-paradise and ostriches are not protected in New Jersey, a fact which will cause consternation among the native ostriches and birds-of-paradise.

It was now the milliners' turn to be happy. They hailed this editorial from a great New York City daily with delight, and in order that no New York Assemblyman should miss seeing it, a marked copy of the editorial page containing this article was sent to all of them. The covering letter, dated April 4, 1910, was signed by that able attorney, Benjamin F. Feiner. Even now, as I read his communication, I feel that if I were not better informed on the subject than was the average Assemblyman at that time, I should be deeply impressed with the logic of its conclusions.

At this time there was a good deal of talk about money being liberated in the Legislature to help defeat our bill. Mr. Shea and some others believed that this was true. Some rather unpleasant things had occurred in the Legislature the previous year or two and I took it the present talk was merely a surmise based on what had taken place in the past. We, therefore, were somewhat surprised when, on April 9, 1910, an article on the subject boldly appeared in the New York *Mail*. It had been written by the staff correspondent of that paper then working in Albany.

The caption read, BLACK HORSE IN RAID ON BIRD BILL— $12,000 FUND FOR CAVALRYMEN TO BRING DEATH TO PLUMAGE MEASURE.

The article began:

Although consensus of cynical comment pictures the black horse cavalrymen as so disorganized and routed by recent exposures that they would not even accept a spotted orange by way of forage, there outcrop now and then whispers of secret raids by small groups of the sable rangers.

The millinery and feather dealers of New York City are said to be the victims of a hold-up, either accomplished or planned. . . .

The bill was up for its third reading this week, but went over until Tuesday. "I shall fight to pass that bill as I have fought for no other bill I ever introduced," said Assemblyman Shea.

The corridor rumor tells of a fund of $12,000 partially subscribed. It is said that this week-end, the last before the bill comes up for final vote, a tremendous effort will be made by the lobbyists to raise more money in New York to defeat the bill. Whether this money will ever get to the Legislature only the go-between will ever know.

I was asked whether the Audubon Society was responsible for this newspaper story, it being intimated that it might have been a move on our part to intimidate some honest objections to our bill. I said we had nothing to do with it and wired Dutcher suggesting that the telegraph to Senator White that he did not inspire the black horse cavalry story, nor did he approve of it. He did so and he made his statement strong.

When the plumage bill came up for final vote in the Assembly, the fight for the milliners was led by Alfred E. Smith of New York City, who contended that the passage of the bill would destroy a great industry. He was very strong in his opposition and made good on the statement which had been attributed to him, that he "would fight against this bill to the last ditch." In later years Mr. Smith's interest in the conservation of wild life underwent a marked change for, in 1928, when he was a candidate for the Presidency of the United States, and I asked him whether, in the event of his election, he would support Federal legislation to protect migratory birds, he wired: MY WELL KNOWN RECORD ON CONSERVATION IS YOUR GUARANTEE OF SYMPATHY WITH THE MOVEMENT YOU SO ABLY REPRESENT. In his opposition to the passage of the Audubon Feather Bill he was joined by others, among them Mr. Glore of Brooklyn, who said the bill was a "crime" and that "no man should vote for it."

Contending for its passage were Messrs. Shea, Dana and others. One telling point that Feiner had made against us at the committee hearing was that not a single species of New

York song-bird was being used in the feather trade, and that we were trying to get the Legislature of New York to protect birds of other countries that did not want them protected. This time we had the answer to this charge and it was in Mr. Shea's possession. By the merest chance we had learned that department stores were selling bows of ribbon, each with a bird's head sewed on it. In Albany I purchased some of them. They were called "Chanticleer Bows." The heads they bore were those of the skylark.

Skylarks had been introduced from Europe and liberated on Long Island, and some of them had been known to breed.

When one of the opposition had concluded the talk in which he laid much stress on what he regarded as our weak point, Mr. Shea arose and said that he held in his hand several heads of a species of song-bird that lived and sang in New York State, "and here is the receipt of a bill of sale showing that they were purchased only yesterday in a store on Pearl Street, here in Albany, almost within the shadow of the building in which we sit." He called on the Assemblymen to vote for his bill which would save from slaughter one of our most charming song-birds—the world-famous skylark.

After the debate had gone on for an hour, Mr. Merritt, the majority leader, took the floor, urged the passage of the bill and moved the "previous question." I could hardly believe my ears when the result was announced, the victory was so sweeping. On April 12, 1910, we had won in the Assembly by a vote of 108 to 15. That evening was one of rejoicing by some of us in Albany.

Dutcher was relentless in making speaking engagements for me. Three nights after the Assembly vote I lectured in Connecticut, took a train at four o'clock next morning for Washington City and in the afternoon addressed a convention of the Daughters of the American Revolution in Continental Hall.

In the Washington audience, I discovered sitting in the

back row Dr. Palmer and another good friend of the Association, Frank Bond. When the meeting concluded, rain was falling in torrents. The committee in charge of affairs had ordered a taxi-cab to be waiting for me, and when I emerged, husky policemen were busy keeping women from taking possession of it. Other uniformed minions of the law made a lane through the crowd for Palmer, Bond and me and without ceremony we hustled into the car. As we drove away, Palmer spoke about the ladies left standing in the rain, and asked, "What has become of that Southern chivalry of yours?"

The press of the country was ringing with the struggle at Albany. Friends of the birds were having many things to say in support of our work.

Some of their statements were extremely inaccurate—such as describing birds being skinned alive for the feather-trade; or the "heads pulled from living songsters to satisfy a foolish fashion." The cartoonists were busy. One showed "Chanticleer Hats Now Under Investigation." One was a picture of a woman's hat on which birds had built a nest and were feeding their young. Another hat was adorned with twigs on which birds were feeding. One cartoon depicted a silk-hatted milliner with manacled wrists coming from his store with a detective's hand on his shoulder. Columns were printed giving the opinions of people who operated millinery stores. Women milliners were quoted as saying:

"I know why they're springing that bird bill; the men are just receiving our bills for Easter hats."

"I protest against any man's dictating in any way what any woman shall wear."

"I suggest that every man who votes for such a bill be promptly boycotted by every woman of his acquaintance."

One said: "Women will now buy their feathers in other states. It simply will result in the discouragement of home industries."

THE CHANTICLEER BOW

Its sudden appearance in women's-wear stores in 1910 was effective in securing the passage of the New York law that stopped the sale of feathers.

SMUGGLED BIRD PLUMAGE

Feathers of the goura pigeon and birds of paradise seized by the customs authorities at New York. This one shipment was valued at $73,500.

Under the caption, "The Feather Fight at Albany," one irate woman denounced it as "The silliest, most wicked, and most nonsensical bill I ever heard of."

Several days later the Senate Committee on Forest, Fish and Game Laws gave its hearing on the plumage bill. The milliners were there in greater force than ever, and the large room in which the hearing was held was filled. Judge Meyer and Mr. Feiner, of course, were present, and again told the story for which their clients contended, that egrets were not killed to get the aigrettes used by the trade, but that the plumes were feathers that had been shed.

In rebuttal I exhibited scalps of egrets bearing the skin from the backs of the birds with the plumes still attached, and explained that these were samples of goods constantly being received in New York from Florida and South Carolina plume-hunters.

The Committee reported our bill favorably and after another wait of fifteen days, on April 21st it came up for consideration in the Senate.

One of our opponents, Mr. Frawley, maintained that its passage would throw out of employment an army of 20,000 people and confiscate business interests to the sum of $17,000,000. But the tide now was running strongly in our favor and after the bill was amended to allow milliners until July 1, 1911, to dispose of some of their feather stock, the bill was passed with only three dissenting votes.

The machinery we had set in motion to bring pressure to bear on the Legislature, now was turned on to Governor Charles Evans Hughes. Dutcher felt confident that he would approve of the Audubon Bill, and said to me, "The fight is finished, you had better go away from New York and get a little rest."

I returned to North Carolina and H. H. Brimley and I were on the point of leaving for some shore-bird investigations on the coast of that State, when a telegram came from

Dutcher, recalling me to Albany. Governor Hughes had granted the milliners a hearing on the plumage bill.

The company that gathered before him on May 3rd was a large one. We had more witnesses for our side than we could possibly use. Among them were some who had shown no special desire to help us during the heat of the battle while the contending lines were swaying first one way and then the other, but who now volunteered their services and were eager to make speeches.

In vain I searched the face of Governor Hughes that day to ascertain, if possible, what effect the arguments of either side were having upon him. He neither smiled nor frowned, nor did he show that he was pleased or displeased at anything that was said. Only once, as I recall, did he speak. He asked Palmer for the citation of a recent decision of the Supreme Court of Louisiana, upholding a somewhat similar law in that state. At the conclusion he announced that he would take the matter under consideration.

We parted that day for a time with Judge Meyer and Mr. Feiner. They had made a good fight, developing to the limit every point that could be turned to account for their side. They had shown much resourcefulness, but had always been square. They were foemen worthy of any man's steel.

On May 7, 1910, Governor Hughes affixed his name to the Audubon Plumage Bill, and it became a law. Congratulations poured into the office from all over the country. "The most important law ever enacted for bird protection," was the expression most often heard, for it was generally believed that in stopping the wholesale feather trade in New York there had been sounded the death-knell of the wild-bird feather business throughout the civilized world.

It was William Dutcher who planned and executed the feather fight in Albany. He was responsible for all that took place in winning the struggle, and his was the ever-present worry about the money to finance the campaign. I always have been grateful to him for allowing me the privilege of serving as his field marshal, and I cherish in my memory certain generous words which in the moment of triumph he said to me when our opponents had been driven from the field.

CHAPTER XII

PITCHING A TENT IN GOTHAM

WHEN THE feather campaign at Albany had been concluded, H. H. Brimley and I carried out our plan for a little rest in the open. On an almost uninhabited peninsula, the northern tip of which forms the right bank of the inlet at the mouth of Cape Fear River, North Carolina, we went into camp and for several wonderful days saw no human being except our Negro waiting-boy.

There were two or three old fields, but a forest covered most of the country. There were stunted oaks of weird and fantastic shapes, and back of them grew towering pine trees. Toward the sea the woods terminated along the crest of a line of ancient dunes, from which one looked down on a sandy plain extending half a mile to the ocean. Between the sand hills and the beach were long shallow ponds thronged with yellow-legs, plovers and various sandpipers. Egrets and other herons stalked in the shallows. Alligators were in sight at all hours of the day, the tops of their flat heads and occasionally their backs being visible. In the early morning their deep bellows roared over the flats and reverberated among the dunes.

In the woods numerous signs of deer and wild turkeys were in evidence, and at night the shouts of chuck-will's-widows were heard from every side. Here I found my first nonpareil's nest, and made other notes for use in the *Birds of North Carolina,* to be published later. In the salt marshes clapper rails now and then broke into discordant cries as they called to each other along the slick, muddy banks of Dutchman's Creek.

What peace and contentment of mind we found sitting on the dunes in the evening, looking at the sea birds, and watching the breakers throw up their white hands as they struck the hard-packed beach!

Then would come the curlews, rank on rank, sweeping by from regions somewhere to the southward. We spoke but little at such times. Human speech seemed a sort of desecration in these surroundings. Fervently, we promised each other, and every evening renewed our vow, that never, never, would we leave this place to return to that world hideous with honking automobile horns and the endless clanging of street-car gongs.

Never have I known a man who enjoyed hunting and camping more than Herbert Brimley, and seldom have I known a hunter who killed less game despite his unusual opportunities. Any one knowing him even slightly can sense the deep love of the open which pervades his mind.

One evening during this camping-trip we were moving along the beach, he being about two hundred yards ahead of me. Away up by the inlet was a small fort. Suddenly Brimley stopped as a flock of curlews came in from the sea. He made no attempt to shoot, but grounded his gun and watched the birds as long as they were in sight.

I attempted to interpret the feeling that motivated his actions by a few simple lines which I called

THE EVENING FLIGHT

The shadows are long on the beaches,
  A stillness creeps over the lea,
And far on the dark, heaving sky-line
  The sun is awash in the sea.

Low down o'er the slow-rocking waters,
  Where the shark and the bluefish hide,
The swaying ranks of the curlews
  Sweep in with the rising tide.

Whence have they come in the offing?
   From what realms of the outer waste?
What means their plaintive calling,
   And why do they know such haste?

What is it that beckons them onward,
   As the beams of the setting sun
Gleam red on their burnished pinions,
   Like the flash of yon evening gun?

They rise and clear the headlands,
   Then sink toward the sandy plain,
They sweep along o'er the marshes,
   Then out to the sea again.

Lo, far away in the distance
   In the hush of the fading day,
Where the sky and the ocean mingle
   The curlews have passed away.

And I stand bereft on the island
   In the hush of the fading light,
For my heart has gone with the curlews
   As they passed in their evening flight.

Mr. Dutcher had planned a trip to Europe to attend an Ornithological Congress in Germany, and to look after some personal matters in Switzerland. Therefore, shortly after my trip with Brimley in May, 1910, I returned to New York and was soon left in charge of the Audubon Society office with its staff of four clerks. There was much correspondence and there were many legislative bills to oppose. As examples, there was a bill in Louisiana to remove protection from gulls and terns because they were supposed to be destructive to the shrimp industry; and another one to repeal the law protecting robins, because some people preferred to have the robins they ate killed legally. There was even one to abolish the State Game Commission, the campaign for the establish-

ment of which we had financed, and the local work for which
had been led by our agent, Frank N. Miller.

We joined in a fight at Albany against a bill which would
permit the sale of wild ducks until March 1st, and supported Whipple's measure to enlarge the state game-warden
force. Forbush was to study the feeding habits of the starling
in New Jersey and Pennsylvania, and scientific collecting
permits were to be secured. In fact, there were a hundred
matters to attend to, including the ever-urgent necessity of
raising money to meet the Association's expenses.

I corresponded for some time with Mrs. Russell Sage about
the killing of robins then carried on legally in all of the
Southern states except Louisiana; and one day in May she
yielded to my pleadings and sent her check for $500 to use
in starting a special campaign for these birds in their winter
home. Not only were robins shot by day, but of nights tens
of thousands were killed with sticks and brush as men, carrying lights, attacked them in their vast roosts in titi thickets
and cedar swamps where they collected as the sun went down.

At once I engaged E. J. Sawyer to prepare a colored drawing of a robin singing among the apple blossoms. Reproductions of this picture, accompanied with a leaflet, were in
time distributed to the extent of more than 5,000,000 copies.

Just here I digress long enough to say that our first legis-
lative victory for the robin came on March 1, 1912, when
Virginia passed our bill for its protection. Mrs. Katherine H.
Stuart, our field-agent for that state, and Mrs. E. H. Harris,
President of the Virginia Audubon Society, led this fight.

When the bill came up for consideration in the Senate, a
battalion of school-children appeared and their leaders were
permitted to march up the aisle to the presiding officer and
present a petition bearing 10,000 names, asking that man's
friend, the harbinger of spring, should be accorded the protection it deserved. The plea was greeted with applause and
the bill passed by a large majority.

Governor William Hodges Man sent me the pen used in signing the bill. Mr. Rex Brasher was employed to paint a picture of a robin singing in a blossoming dogwood bough. To this the pen was attached with an appropriate legend, and then the framed picture was presented to Mrs. Russell Sage.

In 1913 North Carolina adopted our robin bill for eleven counties, but the representatives of nearly ninety counties refused to give up their legal right to enjoy that Southern delicacy known as "robin-pie."

In Florida Mrs. Katherine Tippetts, President of the St. Petersburg Audubon Society, was the skilled strategist who led to success the attack against the time-honored custom of killing robins. One of the guns she fired was a mammoth petition presented to the legislature. It was so large that so far as I was able to learn no one had the courage to count the names. The signatures were written in double column on sheets of paper which, when fastened together, made a document seventy feet in length. The Florida robin bill became a law on May 20, 1913.

What may be considered a robin political casualty occurred in North Carolina early in 1912. One day when Mayor Bennet Nooe of Pittsboro was out of town, the aldermen suspended the ordinance against shooting inside the incorporate limits, and getting their shot-guns all five of them led the bird-hungry citizens on a robin-hunt. There was snow on the ground and the robins had come into town in great numbers to feed on cedar-berries.

When the Mayor, upon returning, learned what was taking place, his wrath was kindled. He said no one had any right to fire off guns in the town and he held the aldermen to be especially culpable. He tried to have all the gunners fined, but failed. The aldermen in great glee then proceeded to amend the ordinance they had flouted by providing that it was all right to shoot robins in town until March 1st. Mayor

Nooe then resigned. In a letter to me he wrote: "It is estimated that about four thousand robins were killed during
the few days the birds were here. This, of course, does not
include the country, but just in and around the town."

In most of the Southern states we failed utterly to secure
state legislation to protect the robin. Our financial resources
were small and we had to rely largely upon local volunteer-
workers, and these were few and, as a rule, not overly effective. Influential people generally seemed to take no
particular interest in the subject. Not until 1913, when the
Federal Migratory Bird Law was enacted, were all the gaps
filled up, and it became illegal to shoot robins anywhere in
the United States.

Mrs. Russell Sage was known to be wealthy and very kind-
hearted, and after she had helped us to start a campaign to
protect robins I sought her financial aid for a wider field of
work in the southern states. This resulted a little later in a
talk with her attorney, Robert W. de Forest, who asked me
to tell him about the Audubon Association's accomplishments, and how we handled our money. When my explana-
tions were finished, he asked me what we would do with
$5,000 if such an amount should be given to us. I at once
told him that we would use it for educational work in the
Southern states, especially in the schools. His next statement
pleased me greatly, and I made a record of his words upon
returning to the office. He said, "You have made the impression on me that I hoped you would and I am authorized by
Mrs. Russell Sage to say that she will give to the Audubon
Association $5,000 a year for three years to be used for your
educational work in the South."

This momentous event took place on the morning of June
11, 1910. I say "momentous" advisedly, for it was the beginning of a phase of the Association's work which in time was
to enrich the thoughts of many millions of children through-

out the United States and Canada, and greatly hasten the development of the public mind in favor of wild-life preservation.

One morning in 1910, while the negotiations with Mrs. Sage were progressing, a gentleman called at the office and introduced himself as "Mr. W. W. Grant." He said that the friends of William Dutcher ought to send him a couple of hundred dollars to use for entertainment while in Europe, but that Clinton Abbott had suggested he talk with me before attempting to raise the money. I felt sure that many of Dutcher's friends would gladly contribute for almost any purpose which they thought would be pleasing to him; but knowing Dutcher as I did I replied that I believed that he would be much more pleased to have money subscribed to the cause of bird protection.

After a few days several of us met at a luncheon and decided to raise a fund for the Association as a memorial to Mr. Dutcher's recently deceased daughter, Mary, to whom he had been deeply attached. I agreed to help prepare and mail out the appeal letters from our office over Mr. Grant's name as Chairman of a special committee, but preferred that as an officer of the Association my name should not be used as one of the group soliciting the money. Mr. Grant suggested that I also sign his name in writing acknowledgments of gifts and answering any inquiries that might arise. The response to our circular appeal and to Mr. Grant's personal efforts among his friends was most gratifying.

In the latter part of June I left the office correspondence in the hands of Mr. Bowdish, and soon was again with my classes in the summer school at the University of Tennessee. My mind was filled with joy and thanksgiving. The great aid extended by Mrs. Sage and the Mary Dutcher Memorial Fund! What a report I would have to make to Dutcher upon his return!

One day I received a card from him mailed in Germany,

telling me that I must study the German language because I would find this of the utmost importance when I began working abroad. There was a man in the University teaching German grammar. I had never even learned English grammar! Still I could speak English after a fashion. Maybe I could learn to speak some German. I employed the German professor to be with me at such times as we were both free. It was a struggle. In time I was able to say, *Das ist ein Fenster, Das ist mein Hund,* and a few other equally startling declarations; but soon determined that I should learn sentences more in keeping with my tastes and interests, for example—*Ein Bier? Danke nein!* and *Ich rauche meine Pfeife gern.*

But as soon as the summer school had ended, it became necessary to give up this fascinating subject and go to Atlanta. The milliners of the State had joined with the market-hunters, and it was feared that they would kill our bill for a non-political game commission, which they eventually succeeded in doing, just as other milliners shortly before this had scuttled our New Jersey plumage bill.

Soon after Dutcher returned to New York in July, a luncheon was arranged by a number of his friends, and he was asked to tell about his trip to Europe. He had attended the Fifth International Ornithological Congress held in Berlin, May 30 to June 4, 1910, and had read a paper on "Some Reasons Why International Bird Protection is Necessary." He had spoken of the world-wide traffic in the feathers of birds used in the millinery trade, of the shipment of European song-birds to America as cage birds, and of the trade that was carried on in lapwings, quail and gray partridges shipped to America for food. He had suggested that the Ornithological Congress urge the forty-three countries which had participated in the Second International Peace Conference to enter into an agreement that they would all prohibit the importation and the exportation of birds or their feathers of any species. He took a keen pleasure in announcing that the Congress had appointed a committee to communicate with the officers of the Peace Conference at the Hague on the subject.

The surprise for Mr. Dutcher was then announced and a check for $6,550, the recently collected "Mary Dutcher Memorial Fund," was handed to him as a special endowment for the Association. For those who knew Dutcher, it is not difficult to imagine how deeply touched he was by this gift to the Audubon Association made in the name of his dear departed daughter.

On October 16, 1910, Dutcher wrote me a beautiful letter upon learning that Mrs. Pearson and I had named for him our second son, born two days before. I was never to hear directly from him again. He had not been well since his return from Europe and was greatly troubled by the loss of a sister and by complications that consequently arose. Also unmistakable evidence exists that at this time he felt much hurt by criticisms of his management of the Audubon Association. He had devoted many years to its work without rewards of any kind. He had received no salary and neither medals nor printed eulogies had been bestowed upon him. He did not desire these things, but he did yearn for the goodwill and the coöperation of all those with whom he labored.

Arriving in New York on October 20, 1910, I learned that the previous morning he had been stricken with paralysis, a condition that deprived him of the power of speech or of the ability to express his desires even with the use of a pen. For nearly ten years he was to continue in this most unfortunate and helpless condition. Thus ended the work of one who deeply loved his fellow-men as well as the birds; whose smile came from a heart overflowing with kindness and whose honesty of purpose, tolerance and unselfishness made of his life at once an inspiration and a benediction.

Suddenly losing the leadership, the inspiration and constant counsel of Mr. Dutcher was a heavy blow, but the work of wild-life protection must be carried on; and I had long known that he wished me to be his successor. This meant that I would have to give up my State Audubon Society work in North Carolina and come to the North to live.

My associates on the Board of Directors said to me in substance: "Handling the Association the coming year is your job. Defend the wild-life of the country as best you may. Raise what money you can and spend it along the general lines of the budget we have handed you. Save a thousand dollars, if possible, and pay on our indebtedness. If we can do this regularly for eight years our deficit will no longer exist. We will have frequent meetings to discuss the Association's problems. Come to us when we can give advice or be of help in any way. Count upon us for all reasonable backing." At least that is the way I interpreted their action and that was the way it worked out.

It was felt by the Board that Dutcher, even in his unfortunate paralytic condition, should be reëlected President of the Association as long as he should live, therefore the by-laws were amended to clothe the Secretary with virtually all the authority of an active President.

When under the new by-law I was reëlected Secretary on January 4, 1911, I already had nine years' constant experience with Audubon Society organization work, for nineteen years had been writing and speaking on bird protection, and for twenty-four years had been a student of field ornithology. For nearly a quarter of a century I had been in turn an egg-collector, a bird-collector, a college professor of biology, a summer-school teacher of bird-study, an amateur nature photographer and a student of hunting methods in many fields. For seven years I had been the head of a state game-warden force, a lobbyist at State Legislatures and at Congress, and I enjoyed a wide acquaintance with Audubon Society workers as well as with state and Federal game-protective officials and had intimate knowledge of many of their problems. I, therefore, was not a novice in the duties I was assuming.

For an office we occupied one room on the thirteenth floor of a building at 141 Broadway. Our office staff consisted of Beecher S. Bowdish, as Chief Clerk; a bookkeeper, two stenographers and an office-boy whom we referred to as "junior clerk." The combined salaries of these five employees had cost $3,271.15 for the year 1910.

We had three part-time field-agents: Edward Howe Forbush in New England, William L. Finley in Oregon and Captain M. B. Davis in Texas. Miss Katherine Stuart, working under the Sage Fund, had recently been engaged for her full time in Virginia.

Our income for current expenses during that year had been $31,340, which included gifts of $7,000 from Mrs. Sage, and $16,327 interest accruing from our endowment invested in bonds and mortgages. The remainder was from membership fees, gifts, and sale of leaflets, books and slides.

A map published at this time shows that there were thirty-nine State Audubon Societies. They were all separate organizations, each determining its own policies. Only four of these held membership in the National Association. Seven local societies also were affiliated to the extent that they paid one membership fee, the same as any individual.

It will be seen, therefore, that the Audubon Societies over the country contributed but lightly to the expenses of the national work. They all had their own obligations to meet and their income was not great. Besides the Societies in North and South Carolina, only the fourteen-year-old Massachusetts Audubon Society had the year before enjoyed an income exceeding one thousand dollars, and the others had received only very small sums. Several of them for years had been rendering good service, and were virtually the only groups actively working in their states to cultivate an interest in the study and protection of non-game birds. Many, however, were

"State" societies in name only and most people did not even know of their existence. I recall that from one Commonwealth I received letters from two groups of people, both calling themselves the State Audubon Society. Inquiry revealed that neither group had heard of the other, although one had enjoyed a paper existence for several years.

The membership of our Association at the beginning of 1911 consisted of 110 life members who had paid one fee of $100 each; and 1,140 sustaining members who were each paying $5.00 annually. At the annual meeting of the members, always held the last Tuesday in October, the directors were elected. These were eleven in number and served for five years each, the terms of some of them expiring each year. The Board at this time was composed as follows: Dr. J. A. Allen (2nd Vice-President), Frank M. Chapman, Dr. Jonathan Dwight, Jr. (Treasurer), and Dr. Herman C. Bumpus, all of whom were members of the Scientific Staff of the American Museum of Natural History. Also, there were Dr. Frederic A. Lucas of Brooklyn, Dr. George Bird Grinnell, W. W. Grant, and the writer (Secretary) of New York City; William Dutcher (President) whose residence was in New Jersey; Dr. Theodore S. Palmer (1st Vice-President) of Washington, D. C., and William Brewster of Cambridge, Massachusetts.

All but W. W. Grant were active in the American Ornithologists' Union; eight were Fellows, one a member and one an associate member of that body. Most of them had long been leaders in the Audubon movement. I have already mentioned the part that some of them had taken in this work. Dr. Allen and Frank Chapman had been prominently associated with every movement for bird protection in the New York City region since 1886, including that of the New York State Audubon Society, which had been very active since its founding in 1897. All the directors were greatly interested in the success of the National Association, but in examining the records for the year that had just closed I found that five of the eleven had not paid membership fees. I doubt if any of them had been asked to pay a fee, so glad were Dutcher and I that they were willing to take time to attend an occasional Board meeting, and to give advice from time to time. Heretofore, meetings of the Board of Directors had averaged two a year, but it was thought that in future these should be held more frequently. A small Advisory Committee was appointed. To suit the convenience of some of the Board members, the meetings were held in the American Museum of Natural History. In fact, during the first nineteen years of the Association's history the directors met only once in the Association's office. During this period few of them ever called to see how we were getting along, and I used to yearn for the more frequent sight of some of these older men. However, the most of them had their own special fields of primary interest, so logically I could not expect them to devote a very great amount of time to the consideration of problems for the solution of which I was being paid a salary. I had long been fighting my battles pretty much alone anyway.

From my early years I had looked with awe upon the names of Brewster, Chapman, Dwight, Dutcher, Grinnell, Lucas and Palmer, who were among the most prominent of American ornithologists. It was true that I was older now, but so were they. My reaction when meeting them now was somewhat like that of a man returning to his alma mater and finding on the campus a group who had been seniors when he was an insignificant freshman. With Dutcher and Palmer I was always much at ease; they, too, were devoting their lives to wild-life preservation and came constantly into contact with its complicated problems, and hence were understandingly interested in all the details of my work.

I was fully aware of the task that lay ahead of me, to try to build up and keep going a large organization in the field of wild-life preservation, a field in which others had attempted similar tasks and failed. But with a certain confidence born of many years of experience in the various lines in which I should have to work, I had undertaken the task with deep interest and with no special apprehension as to the outcome.

How lonely a stranger can be in a great city, I was to learn in full measure. With the beginning of Dutcher's illness, I lived alone in New York City for fourteen months. My modest salary made this course necessary. Mrs. Pearson and our three children were in North Carolina where at intervals I visited them. My few acquaintances were widely scattered, and I can recall only two New York homes into which I entered during that period. One of these was that of Rex Brasher, then a struggling young bird artist who was living with his brother and a niece in very modest surroundings in Brooklyn.

Most of the people I met entertained on a scale that I could not afford to repay in kind, so I sought to avoid rather than to welcome their hospitality, and buried myself in work. I went to the office early, and returned late in the day to the Endicott Hotel, at Columbus Avenue and West 81st Street.

In my room I read reports on wild-life protection subjects, composed newspaper articles on the Association's work, and wrote out letters to be typed next day. When my brain grew overly weary, I walked the streets for exercise, sometimes wandering down Broadway to 42nd Street or on to 33rd.

The thousands of people I saw were all strangers to me. Generally they seemed to be on pleasure bent. The expensive cafés and cabarets were thronged, and men and women poured in and out of theaters. Only on rare occasions did I enter one of these places of amusement. The feeling of depression and loneliness that seized upon me on these excursions to the "Tenderloin," or to the "Rialto" etched itself deeply upon my mind. To this day I never find myself alone at night in that part of New York without the return of vivid and harassing memories. The old feeling of poverty and loneliness lays hold upon me. I flee from The Great White Way and hurry home.

Sometimes visitors from the South or the West say to me, "How grand it must be to live in this great city!"

"Yes," I sometimes say, "it is wonderful, if you have friends and a little money to spend."

To my mind the great opportunities for service which the National Association had before it at the beginning of the year 1911 were:

First, secure laws to protect the non-game birds in those states that as yet had not made such provision.

Second, continue the fight to make illegal the traffic in feathers of wild birds used in the millinery trade.

These were distinctly Audubon Society undertakings, and no other societies had shown any special activities in these fields.

Third, coöperate with sportsmen conservation organizations in their long-continued efforts to preserve an adequate game supply by means of increasing the legal restrictions on hunting, where needed, and lend our aid for the establishment of state warden forces where these did not now exist.

Fourth, to create numerous reservations for wild birds and useful mammals and provide special agents to guard them.

As a large part of our work, we should increase our educational campaigns, by means of the press, lectures, and literature.

We must always be prepared to meet, so far as possible, the attacks made on our wild-life protective laws; and by keeping informed on the problems in our field throughout the country, be in position to discriminate between vital and relatively unimportant subjects on which to expend our limited time and means.

And finally, build strongly the financial structure of the Audubon Association, without which all our work would ere long elapse into hollow declarations and weak ineffectiveness. In these policies I believe that all the directors and 95 per cent of our members heartily concurred.

The growth of the Association had been modest but steady since the beginning, and, of course, I was extremely anxious that it should continue to expand. The first year of my executive stewardship I was so fortunate as to have for current expenses $36,599, which not only carried the work on a scale fully equal to that employed the year before, but also enabled us to pay off our entire indebtedness of $7,780.55. Well remembering the unhappiness caused by debts in former years, I had every intention of living within our means. It, therefore, became my set policy never to assume an obligation or recommend to the Board a new commitment without knowing where the money was to come from to meet the additional expense, and through all the years of my administration there was never a departure from this principle.

There were those who sought to impress me with the idea that it was better to run into debt: "Then you can call on your members to make up the deficit," they argued. "In this way you can do more work and can show a greater total income at the close of the year." But I had enough to think about without worrying over debts, and felt that careful business men would approve of a "pay-as-you-go" policy, and that many would be inclined to give, or to bequeath money, to an organization operated on what seemed to me to be a sane and conservative financial basis.

By the year 1911, the country was rapidly becoming aroused to the subject of wild-life preservation, and numerous game- and bird-protective laws were in operation in every state. Records compiled by Dr. T. S. Palmer showed that during the previous ten years, 1,324 game-laws had been enacted. Of these 316, or 25 per cent, came into existence in that local game-law championship state—North Carolina.

Going back farther into history, we find that the first colony to adopt a game-law was Connecticut, in 1677. The last state to adopt its first game-law was Oklahoma, in 1890. The Massachusetts Bay Colony, in 1694, was first to give protection to any kind of game in summer, by rendering it illegal to kill deer between January 1st and July 1st. New York followed in 1705 with a closed season on deer from January 1st to August 1st. Three years later it went further and was the first state to stop the killing of grouse, heath hens, wild turkeys, woodcock and quail during the breeding season. The first bag-limit law in the United States was adopted by Iowa in 1878. This applied only to prairie chickens and grouse. One could continue to kill as many other birds and mammals as he chose. In 1883 Maine put a bag limit on moose and deer, and the same year Wisconsin adopted a bag limit to help protect its rabbits.

By 1911 the principle of having special officers to enforce game laws was operating in forty-one states, and hunting-licenses were required in thirty-three states. The custom of using for game protection the revenue derived from the sale of hunting-licenses was becoming well established. Hunters thus were paying the bills for prosecuting game-law violators; and in return were supposed to have a better chance to secure some game when they went a-hunting.

Long strides had been made in behalf of the sorely persecuted gulls, terns and song-birds of the country. The Model Law to protect non-game species, prepared by the Bird Protection Committee of the American Ornithologists' Union in 1886, was at once accepted by the New York Legislature. Few other states received it kindly until 1901.

In 1902 the National Committee of Audubon Societies was formed, and soon took over and greatly enlarged the legislative efforts which had been inaugurated by the Union. In January, 1905, this Committee became incorporated as the National Association of Audubon Societies.

By January, 1911, the Model Law, now generally known

as the Audubon Law, had been adopted in all the states and territories except ten. Those still neglecting to extend protection to their non-game birds were: Idaho, Kansas, Montana, Nebraska, Nevada, North Dakota, Oklahoma and Utah, and the territories of Arizona and New Mexico.

As it was the Audubon Societies that for years had been actively contending for non-game bird protection, it was very natural for the general public to look upon it as a song-bird society which also had a strong interest in gulls and egrets. It was a fact, however, that the National Association of Audubon Societies had been responsible for establishing the state game-warden forces of Louisiana, Oregon, and North and South Carolina, and had busied itself with many other game-protection matters.

Some well-meaning people, fond of referring to themselves in a rather exclusive way as "bird lovers," cried out against all "sportsmen." They seemed unaware of the fact that in the ranks of the hunters there were those numerous strong, influential men who, by hard work in legislative lobbies, had secured nine-tenths of all the existing laws for wild-life preservation. One might go further and say that virtually ten-tenths of the wild-life legislative protective work had been done by those who were killers of game-birds or game-mammals; or else had been so at one time. Dr. George Bird Grinnell of New York City, founder of the first Audubon Society, was an active sportsman, as was William Brewster who in Massachusetts organized the first permanent State Audubon Society. This was true also of William Dutcher, G. O. Shields, William T. Hornaday, Theodore Roosevelt, E. W. Nelson, E. H. Forbush, Frank M. Chapman and Thomas S. Roberts, as well as almost any other outstanding wild-life preserver one may choose to name.

In a word, the fight to preserve the wild life of America had been waged in large part by a class of those men who had tramped the forests and fields and marshes, gun or fishing-rod

in hand. They had long enjoyed intimate contact with the
wilderness, and had fallen under the spell of the secrets it
had revealed. To them the rustling of fallen leaves, the
tapping of a woodpecker on a dead limb, the whisperings of
wind-blown branches and the echoes from lonely glens were
inspirations. Many of those who sensed these values felt a
responsibility for helping to save some of the wild environment for the uses of posterity. Many others who did not
engage in field sports with rod and gun undoubtedly saw and
felt these things, but there is little record of their accomplishing any practical reforms for the saving of wild life.
It is to hunters of the type I have mentioned that we must pay
our homage for leading all of the effective movements that
brought about legal measures for the relief of our hard-
pressed wild birds and mammals, and which, in many cases,
have saved species from extirpation over large regions.

For three hundred years white men in North America
destroyed wild life almost at will, and the majority of those
who hunt to-day would be exterminators were it not for the
legal restraints brought about chiefly by a comparatively
small but broad-minded minority of their fellow-hunters.

Upon taking over the duties that Mr. Dutcher had been
so successfully performing, I not only experienced the exhil-
eration that comes to one whose position has been advanced,
but I had to bear the brunt of the opposition of certain
forces that had added much to his problems.

There had existed for some time a suspicion on the part
of a considerable number of ornithologists that the Audubon
Association was working to prohibit all scientific collecting
of birds. Five years before this date Dutcher, I and some
others had been dropped from the membership of the Bird
Protection Committee of the American Ornithologists'
Union. The explanation given at the time was that the newly
formed Audubon Association alone was sufficient to look
out for bird protection, but many of us believed that this was

not the real motive for the action. Dr. A. K. Fisher was appointed to succeed Dutcher as Chairman of the Union's Bird Protection Committee and retained this position for eighteen years. During this period the Committee seldom functioned, very rarely even making any report to the Union.

Nearly every active ornithologist at that time was engaged in collecting birds, and the use of the opera-glass in making identifications was in little vogue. Most "sight records" were looked upon as questionable evidence.

Some of the strongest dislike of the Association which I inherited centered in Washington. I went to see Dr. E. W. Nelson of the Biological Survey, to have a frank discussion about the matter, but he refused to talk with me. He said it would be a waste of time to enter into the matter. I tried to talk to a brilliant young naturalist named Alexander Wetmore. He knew who I was, but when I spoke to him he replied that he believed he had not met me, and turned abruptly away. Dr. A. K. Fisher frankly was hostile and said that if the Association did not actually advocate the stopping of scientific collecting it at least was to blame for what was taking place, because it was arousing interest over the country in birds which reacted against collectors.

A much larger group of men that had little good to say of us was the rank and file of sportsmen who, judging by the pronouncements of officers of some of the state and local Audubon Societies, felt that the National Association at heart wanted to stop all hunting. Therefore, we were rated in their minds as theoretical, impractical bird-idolaters. It was not entirely illogical for them to feel this way, for some writers and public speakers connected with Audubon Societies constantly were holding "sportsmen" responsible for all the crimes committed by pot-hunters, market-hunters and general game-law violators. Such would-be reformers, whose experiences were so limited that they could not differentiate between the various classes of men who use the gun, conveniently grouped all hunters under the name "sportsmen" and pointed to them as "game exterminators."

To try to win the confidence of suspicious ornithologists and the good-will of the best class of sportsmen without whose coöperation we could not hope for success in legislative reforms were two of the tasks with which I was faced. How far I succeeded in these undertakings is not for me to say, but through all the years of my work I have sought as best I could to expound the doctrine of tolerance and moderation in dealing with controversial problems, for, after all, few people are as bad, as insincere, or as foolish as their opponents often would have us believe.

CHAPTER XIII

SOME EVENTS OF 1911

IN 1911 THE National Audubon Association was the one sizable organization devoting its entire energies to the field of wild-life preservation. Letters or circulars on the subject appeared now and then from the pens of individuals, and the bulletins of the Biological Survey and of some state departments were of great value, as was also the educational effect of the increasing law-enforcement work by state game administrations.

The Association was fully conscious of its obligations to do everything in its power to resist the all but overwhelming forces that were commercializing the wild life of the country. The game-dealers were still rampant and the feather milliners of New York remained a serious threat, for we knew they had no intention of allowing the anti-plumage law in New York State to go into effect on July 1st without an effort to accomplish its repeal. There had been another state election; the Republican Administration had been overthrown and the Democrats were to apply the new broom and sweep up all "blundering and unwise legislation" that had been enacted by the Republicans. Mr. Alfred E. Smith, who in the Assembly the year before had headed the unsuccessful fight to prevent the passage of the Audubon plumage-law, was now the Assembly leader.

Assemblyman A. J. Levy, from New York City, introduced the bill that was intended to repeal our state feather law. A copy of it reached our office on February 8th. At once I wrote Mr. Gurrett, Chairman of the Assembly Committee on

Forest, Fish and Game Laws, asking that the friends of the birds be granted a hearing before his Committee. No reply was received. I wrote again. Still no answer. I wired him on March 11th, 20th, and 21st, vainly trying to get his promise that we could meet with this Committee.

The newspaper publicity of the milliners, meanwhile, was wide-spread and formidable. We engaged in similar propaganda, and also mailed thousands of letters and circulars in opposition to the Levy Bill. Dr. Henry Fairfield Osborn joined in the campaign, as did Madison Grant, A. S. Houghton of the Camp Fire Club, Dr. W. O. Stillman of the Humane Societies, Dr. W. T. Hornaday of the Bronx Zoological Park, Mrs. Emmons Crocker of the State Federation of Women's Clubs, and others. There were many others who bore arms with us in that somewhat bitter legislative contest in 1911.

On April 18th we were cheered with the news that Governor Woodrow Wilson had signed our plumage bill which had passed the New Jersey Legislature a few days before.

Finally, on April 26th, a hearing was granted and several of us journeyed to Albany and presented arguments in favor of retaining the plumage law.

A number of feather-dealers were in attendance. They produced two dozen good-looking young women whom they thoughtfully seated facing the members of the Forest, Fish and Game Committee. These constituted Exhibit A for the milliners, who explained that they were representative of several thousands of girls engaged in the millinery trade who would lose their only means of earning a living if the Audubon feather law were not abolished.

The lawyers for the milliners contended that no cruelty was practised in procuring the aigrettes used in their trade, and as authority for the statement laid much stress on an article published in the New York *Times* about ten days before. From this I quote:

M. Mageul Grisol of the Museum of National History in Paris, has written a letter on the white heron harvest of Venezuela to J. E. Grillet, President of the Syndicate Chamber of Manufacturers of Feathers for Ornament. As ammunition to repel the attacks of the Audubon Societies this letter is being widely circularized among the milliners and feather-dealers, much distressed at the realization, growing daily more acute, that after July 1st, aigrettes and many other feathers can not be sold legally in the State.

In part, Mr. Grisol says:

"The white heron and other wading birds follow the natural law, which every year at a fixed period compels them to moult —that is, these birds, aiding themselves with their beaks, scatter hither and thither the magnificent feathers which are their ornament and which are bound to grow still more beautiful. Everywhere on the ground, as well as on the tree branches and on the bushes and thickets, they leave their feathers which at that moment must form the happiness of the natives and of the workmen busy with the harvest thereof. There are some *Garzeros* where daily from three to four kilos of these magnificent feathers may be gathered.

"I had with me six men for the gathering of the feathers and the daily result was from about 600 to 700 grams per man at the time of the highest moult. As a total I may calculate that as an average of three months I obtained from 450 to 600 grams a man per day. I knew another *Garzero* in the City of Guerico, called Chauguangal, which gives yearly 125 to 130 pounds of feathers gathered or picked up as I said above.

"I could cite more than fifteen *Garzeros* in which one proceeds always in the same way, and which render yearly at the moulting period a total of about 1,200 pounds of feathers.

"It is very rare for the natives to kill the herons. It would be only in the case of necessity for their sustenance. The birds furnish, through their feathers, one of the most appreciable revenues of these rich countries."

When this testimony had been presented, I brought in a man to testify in rebuttal. It was plain to see that the appearance of this surprise witness was disconcerting to some of the opposition. The man was A. H. Meyer. A digest of his testimony, to which he made oath, is as follows:

I wish to state that I have personally engaged in the work of collecting the plumes of these birds in Venezuela. This was my business for the years 1896 to 1905, inclusive. I am thoroughly conversant with the methods employed in gathering egret and snowy heron plumes in Venezuela and I wish to give the following statement regarding the practices employed in procuring these feathers.

The birds gather in large colonies to rear their young. They have the plumes only during the mating and nesting season. It is the custom in Venezuela to shoot the birds while the young are in the nests. A few feathers of the large white egret (*garza blanca*) can be picked up of a morning about their breeding-places, but these are of small value and are known as "dead feathers." They are worth locally not over $3.00 an ounce, while the feathers taken from the birds, known as "live feathers," are worth $15.00 an ounce.

My work led me to every part of Venezuela and Colombia where these birds are to be found and I have never yet found or heard tell of any *garzeros* that were guarded for the purpose of simply gathering the feathers from the ground. No such a condition exists in Venezuela. That story has been put forward for commercial purposes. The natives of the country, who do virtually all of the hunting, are not provident in their nature and their practices are of a most cruel and brutal nature.

I have seen them frequently pull the plumes from wounded birds, leaving the crippled birds to die of starvation, unable to respond to the hungry cries of their young in the nests above. I have known these people to tie and prop up wounded egrets on the marsh where they would attract the attention of other birds flying by. These decoys they leave in this position until they die of their wounds or from the attacks of insects. I have seen the terrible red ants of that country actually eating out the eyes of these wounded, helpless birds that were tied up by the plume-hunters.

To illustrate the comparatively small number of dead feathers which are collected, I will mention that in one year, I and my associates shipped to New York eighty pounds of the plumes of the large heron and twelve pounds of the little recurved plumes of the snowy heron. In this whole lot there were not over five pounds of plumes that had been gathered from the ground. The plume birds have been nearly exterminated in the United

States and Mexico, and soon they will no longer exist in tropical America.

The subject of repealing the Audubon feather law had worked around to an argument on whether or not egrets were killed for their plumage. The milliners had contended that the aigrettes of commerce were simply cast-off feathers, while we claimed that they came from birds that were shot in the nesting season. To which of the two testimonies would the Committee give credence, and would its belief in the truthfulness of the matter have anything to do with the way it would vote? From the faces of the members I felt confident that it would obey its political leaders and decide against us— and this is exactly what it did; its report favored the passage of Levy's repeal bill.

I never have understood the strategy of our opponents in delaying action by the Assembly, for our strength now was growing daily. May passed and June was waning before we learned that a test vote was about to be taken. The Chairman of the Senate Committee on Forest, Fish and Game was Franklin D. Roosevelt. On June 20th he wrote: "The Levy Plumage Bill comes up in the Assembly sometime this week, and I sincerely hope that I will be able to prevent its passage."

At this critical time I was forced to go South. We had expected that by this time the plumage bill would be out of the way and arrangements had been made for the Ninth Annual Meeting of the Audubon Society of North Carolina to be held on June 22nd. At this meeting, in Greensboro, I formally turned over the duties of Secretary of the State Audubon Society to P. D. Gold, Jr., and returned to New York.

The Levy Repeal Bill came to a vote just before midnight on June 29th. A majority of the entire membership of the Assembly must vote in favor of a measure if it is to pass, and seventy-six is a majority. At the roll-call only sixty-six of those present answered "aye," and we had won. Twenty-four hours later, July 1, 1911, the Audubon Plumage Law of New York State therefore became effective, and millions of dollars' worth of millinery goods went into the discard.

But the New York feather-men still had plenty of fight in them. The next morning after the death of the Levy Bill, a millinery firm, Sciama & Company, filed a petition in the United States Court of the Southern District of New York, asking that an injunction be granted restraining the state officials from enforcing the plumage law. Mr. Thomas Carmody, Attorney-General for the State, asked the Audubon Association for assistance in opposing the granting of this injunction, which, of course, we furnished. On October 13th, Judge Ward refused to grant the injunction and thus another battle was won for the birds.

In the meantime, New York milliners had sent to the State Game Commission a great quantity of feathers accumulated from the four corners of the world, and asked the very natural question which of these could be used and which could not legally be handled under the law that prohibited the sale of any bird belonging to the same family of any native bird protected in New York State. The authorities asked my help, so taking Waldron DeWitt Miller with me as a feather expert, I went to Albany. Mr. Miller readily gave the information desired. Sixty-eight lots, many of which represented numerous species, he declared could legally be sold; and the species included in the fifty-eight other lots were declared prohibited.

The first case for violation of the New York Audubon Anti-Plumage Law resulted from the following advertisement which appeared in the New York *Evening Telegram*, for September 5, 1911:

"Elegant fur rug cheap; aigrettes, and other things. Phone 2568 W. Morningside, 430 West 119th."

This was read by Joseph V. Sauter, Chief of Division,

Forest, Fish and Game Commission of New York State. At the address given he found Mrs. H. B. McCulloch, who offered to sell him four bunches of aigrettes. It was a small case, but it was a violation, so she was arrested and brought for trial on September 6th, in the Harlem Police Court. The trial was postponed to September 7th, when the case was again postponed to September 21st. The lawyers asked for further postponement, to await the result of the injunction proceedings instituted by Sciama & Company in the Federal Court of the Southern District of New York: so the case was called for October 5th. It was then postponed to October 19th, and from then until October 23rd. Then it was referred to another court and, having many things to do, I lost track of subsequent procedures.

Another measure attracting much attention in the New York Legislature this year was the Bayne Bill to prohibit the sale of all game birds belonging to the same family as protected species found in the States, regardless of whether they had been killed in this country or abroad.

Dr. George Bird Grinnell, editor of *Forest and Stream,* had sounded the call for stopping the three-hundred-year-old American custom of selling game, in an editorial published February 3, 1894. For a time he received little support, but in 1897, Montana, New Mexico and Texas translated his teaching into legal statutes. By 1911, nineteen states, whose combined areas exceeded one-half of the area of our whole country, had enacted non-sale-of-game laws. New York State at this time forbade the sale of grouse, quail and woodcock, if killed within the state.

In 1909, at the convention of the New York State Forest, Fish and Game League, held in Syracuse, William Dutcher had pointed out that New York was a fence for the sale of game shipped from other parts of the country and demanded that this should be stopped. As an example of the extent of this traffic, it may be mentioned that some time before this a game-law official had seized 50,000 game- and song-birds that were being held illegally in one New York City cold-storage warehouse.

Dr. William T. Hornaday was largely responsible for the introduction of the Bayne Bill in 1911. Despite all the support given it by the New York Zoological Society, the Audubon Association, the sportsmen's groups and many individuals, it made slow headway, until the Hotel Men's Association of New York had it amended to permit the sale of European grouse, blackcock, plover, partridge, quail, and various forms of deer imported from abroad. There was also tacked to it a rider providing that pheasants, mallards and black ducks raised on game farms could be sold. This was a portion of Dwight W. Huntington's game breeders' bill, which now for the second time was pending in the Legislature. With the support of the game-dealers' lobby, the bill now made rapid progress. The measure passed both houses with scarcely a dissenting vote, and on June 26, 1911, became a law.

Thus was cut off America's greatest market for the ducks and quail of the Atlantic Coast States, and for grouse and prairie chickens from the West. Furthermore, the Bayne Law proved to be a very important step in encouraging the breeding of game on game farms. However, no records seem to be available as to the numbers of such birds marketed the next few years but we do know that during the two years following the passage of the Bayne Law 492,400 dead game-birds from foreign countries were brought into the Port of New York.

The Audubon Association was active this year in legislation in various states besides New York:

In New England our agent, E. H. Forbush, was busily engaged with legislature efforts. Dozens of bills affecting wild life were under consideration. Here, as well as in New York State, commercial gunners were seeking to repeal the laws which forbade the taking of wild-fowl after January 1st. They wanted the privilege of killing ducks and geese until these left on their spring migration.

In the Rhode Island Legislature, friends of the birds vainly tried to get a law to eliminate stray dogs and cats; and we sought to make provision for the appointment of a state ornithologist.

We had given up our long fight to get the Audubon Society of Georgia incorporated with the legal standing of a State Game Department, and this year supported, until it was enacted, a bill to establish a politically controlled State Game Department.

But all our work was not in legislative halls, and many kinds of duties arose which claimed our attention. There was a letter from August Belmont, who thought it was unjust that he, who had financial interests in a shooting-club in South Carolina, should be required to pay ten dollars for a non-resident hunting-license when he went to that state to enjoy himself in the field with dog and gun. To convince him that such a law was needful and desirable, and then to induce him to pay $100 for a life membership in the Audubon Association, were tasks in which I was fortunate enough to succeed.

One man protested because *Bird-Lore* carried an advertisement of a magazine known to encourage traffic in birds' eggs. He declared: "It is like a church paper which advertises cheap whiskey at cut rates."

There were complaints of the killing of song-birds by Italian laborers in New Jersey. An agent from our office searched out the offenders and secured the necessary evidence to convict these hunters.

A correspondent reported that members of a club raised mallard ducks, baited them through a wire runway for half a mile, then threw them into the air where they were shot as they flew back to their pond. In the game-laws there was no provision that covered such a case so we turned the matter over to a humane society that was actively enforcing the law against shooting live pigeons from traps.

In August, 1911, many thousands of birds selected for their nightly roost a group of shade trees in Montclair, New Jersey. Their presence was very distasteful to people living in the immediate region, and one of the householders employed a colored man to shoot into the trees at night. An account of this occurrence ran through the press of the country. The statement was made that "great numbers of robins, grackles and other useful birds were being destroyed." "Unnecessary Slaughter," "Butchery," and "The Barbarians of Montclair," were some of the newspaper head-lines that were used. We received a flood of protesting letters. From the tone that ran through some of them, it seemed that the writers felt that the Audubon Association was in some way responsible for the whole business. One frankly stated that the Audubon officers were not alive to their duties, for if we had any real interest in bird protection we would never have permitted such a scandalous occurrence.

I sent a representative to Montclair to investigate the matter. When the man who had wielded the gun was hailed into court, it was revealed that he had shot on only two evenings and that the total slaughter had amounted to five starlings and twenty-three English sparrows. English sparrows were not protected by law, and seven years later New Jersey transferred the starling to the list of birds that any one may kill if he so desires.

Interest in the subject of attracting birds about the home was developing rapidly under the continuous campaign of the Audubon Society, and about this time Ernest Harold Baynes imported from Germany a mechanical device for making the Von Berlepsch type of bird nesting-box. He thus became one of the first to engage in the commercial manufacture of bird-attracting apparatus.

Among our other duties during the spring months had been that of finding a new location for our office, where we could have more space and where rents were not so high. I hunted up Broadway from Liberty Street to 72nd Street for a location to meet our needs, and on April 15th we moved into two rooms at 1974 Broadway, on the corner of 67th Street.

Our attempts at guarding a few egret colonies had met with such poor success that of recent years the Association had made small efforts in this direction. Frequently we received reports that men were killing egrets in Florida and selling their plumes to tourists or shipping them to the North. There was little that we could do about the matter, for the few county wardens in the State did not interest themselves in such matters, the Federal Government could provide no guards, and our financial position was not strong.

The number of white egrets in the United States at that time was at the lowest point in history. Gulls and terns were showing a marked increase under our guardianship, but many feared that in the South Atlantic States egrets would become extirpated. Their plumes were now selling in London for eight pounds sterling per ounce, or for more than twice their weight in gold.

I determined that a very serious effort to protect these birds should be made. The other members of the Board approved of the idea if I could raise the money to carry out such a program. Field investigations were instituted, ten small breeding groups were found, and men were employed to guard them. Seven of these heronries were in South Carolina, and there was one each in Florida, Georgia and North Carolina. There was also a prosperous colony of snowy egrets on the property of E. A. McIlhenny, in Louisiana. At a cost of $250, accruing from the Mary Dutcher Memorial Fund, we bought Bird Island, a thirty-five-acre area in Orange Lake,

Alachua County, Florida and O. E. Baynard, who arranged for its purchase, served as our guard for the season.

We felt sure that there were other rookeries of egrets, especially in Florida, but were without the means of financing the necessary field explorations to find them, or to protect the birds if any were found. In our colonies that summer, the egret population numbered about 1,650 birds, of which 250 were the small snowy egret.

This year marked the beginning of the Audubon Association's renewed efforts to guard the egrets, herons, ibises, spoonbills and water-turkeys of the Southern swamps; efforts which, despite numerous set-backs, were to grow in extent and effectiveness until our country was again to be enriched by the presence of many hundreds of thousands of these exquisitely beautiful creatures.

Eleven years had elapsed since Dutcher had made his survey of the Maine coast and had reported twelve colonies of herring gulls. I determined to go to Maine and learn what had been happening in the meantime as a result of our warden service.

Early in July, 1911, I joined Arthur H. Norton of Portland, who knew more about the wild life of the Maine coast than any other man, and our journey promptly was begun. The herring gulls had greatly increased. On the island of No-Man's-Land we estimated that no less than 20,000 were nesting. It is believed that for about a hundred years this had been the most southern point along the Atlantic Coast where this species had regularly bred. When, therefore, we landed at Metinic Green Island, off the lower part of Penobscot Bay and I came upon a herring gull's nest with eggs, Norton's joy was delightful to witness. We were then about twelve miles south and west of No-Man's-Land. The nest had been built, perhaps, by the first pair of herring gulls that in recent times had pioneered south of No-Man's-Land. The next year some bred on Martha's Vineyard,

Massachusetts, and twenty years later they had colonized in Connecticut and New York.

Numerous additional islands came into use by these birds until, when Robert Allen and Arthur Norton cruised the Maine coast in 1931, they found seventy-seven islands occupied by breeding gulls.

Norton and I worked our way farther up the coast till we came to the mouth of the Bay of Fundy, where lies a Canadian possession known as Machias Seal Island. Here, the lightkeeper's dog was amusing himself by digging Leach's petrels out of their burrows. One hundred and forty-seven of their bodies lay in an area of less than one acre. I spoke to the lighthouse-keeper about the law protecting them. He said that he doubted if the laws of New Brunswick covered such birds.

I went to Fredericton and, after considerable search, found a copy of the New Brunswick Game Act. This provided that, with the exception of blackbirds, crows and English sparrows, "Any gull, pheasant or any small birds which frequent the fields and woods" were protected. Clearly, the laws of the province did not extend to the little petrel of the stormy sea, so I gave the lighthouse-keeper twenty-five dollars to send his dog to the mainland for the rest of the summer and made plans to take further action.

Soon I made a formal request of the Department of Marine and Fisheries of Canada, which caused a communication to be sent to all lighthouse-keepers in the Dominion, dated from Ottawa July 29, 1911, directing them to afford protection to all wild birds nesting in the neighborhood of their lighthouses.

An event occurred this year that gave the Audubon Association more publicity than had any other subject up to that time. It came about in this way. One day I received a telephone call from a lawyer saying that he had some clients who wanted to start an organization to protect game-birds and game-animals, and that he had been asked to learn if I would care to talk with them on the subject. Of course, I answered "Yes."

At his office I met H. S. Leonard and another man whose name I do not recall. They represented the Winchester Repeating Arms Company, which, they said, was going to start an organization to preserve game-birds and mammals from undue killing, for "as the game decreases our business grows less." Mr. Leonard asked if I would accept the job of running such an association. He then said his company would provide $5,000 or $10,000 as a fund to start the work and that their sales-agents would enroll members whose fees would help keep the organization going.

I thought his plan contained much merit and said so, but pointed out that to build and operate a national organization much more money would be needed. Also, I said that if it was to the interest of the Winchester Company to protect game, such protection likewise should help to preserve the business of other gun and ammunition companies. I gave it as my opinion that they should be able to pledge a sum of not less than $25,000 a year for five years, if they expected to build a going organization of a national scope. A little later Mr. Leonard returned to New York and handed me a list of pledges that had been made by various companies which, in the aggregate, amounted to the sum I had mentioned, and again asked if I would accept the proposition he had made.

In the meantime, I had given the matter some thought, and I asked, "Why not give the money to the Audubon Association to finance a game protective department of its work?" He went away and soon sent me a letter formally inviting me to become President of an American Game Protective Association, which would at once be incorporated; or, if I preferred, the money would be given to the Audubon Association, provided it would be used for game protection and that I should be the one to direct the work. The letter stated that if the money went to the Association the donors would ask for no representation on its Board of Directors; nor would they seek in any way to control or to influence its policies. As such a gift would about double the Association's income they said it would be agreeable with them if half my salary should come from this fund, and they thought the salary should be raised from $3,000 to $6,000 a year.

The matter was reported to the other members of the Board and a meeting called. The fact that these companies had raised a considerable sum of money for game protection leaked out, and we learned of one or more men who tried to get control of its expenditures.

Our Board was divided on the subject of accepting the proffered gift, but the majority voted to take it. Instantly there was a cry that the Audubon Association had sold out to the gun people who wanted to kill all the birds of the country. This came chiefly from men who had no connection with our organization. Some of it was from a man who, we had reason to believe, was chagrined because the money had not been given to him to spend. I decided to wait a little while and see how the public reacted to the matter, before advising Mr. Leonard of the action of the Board. Within a week or two it became apparent that to accept a large sum from this source would continually make us vulnerable to the attacks of some of our enemies who would neglect no opportunity to misrepresent the motive for our action. Therefore, the Board rescinded its former action. We thanked the companies for their offer but advised that they form a separate organization.

A representative of one of the affiliated commercial groups then asked me if I would not consider accepting their first offer. I appreciated their implied confidence in my ability to build up a large game-protective society but told him my interest was in all forms of wild life, especially all kinds of birds, and that I preferred to stay with the Audubon Society where for so many years I had been working.

The gun and ammunition companies incorporated the American Game Protective and Propagation Association on September 25, 1911, and engaged John B. Burnham, then in charge of the game-warden force of New York State, to become its President and general executive. Mr. Burnham was well equipped for this position. He had hunted in many parts of the country, had a broad knowledge of existing game conditions and enjoyed a wide acquaintance with game-protective officials.

The idea that any board of directors should fail to accept a gift of $125,000 was such an unusual news-item that the story of our declining this offer must have been printed in virtually every paper in the United States and Canada, and the commendations we received were numerous.

In our educational work that year many lectures were given, news-letters were sent monthly to the press of the country, and 406,000 copies of our Educational Leaflets and 370,000 colored pictures of birds were issued.

Necessarily much attention had to be given to the raising of money for the Association. Circulars and personal letters were employed, and I asked help from nearly every person with whom I became acquainted, if that person impressed me as an encouraging prospect. When, in October, the Treasurer's report for the year was presented, it showed that the Association had received an income of $44,600, an increase of $6,000 over the previous year. We had employed four clerks in the office, four agents in the field, thirty-nine part-time wardens to guard water-bird colonies, and had sent *Bird-Lore* free to our members and junior leaders. These things had all cost money and the Board was pleased to find that there was a comfortable cash balance remaining in the treasury after all bills for the year had been paid.

Some people were kind enough to say that we had accomplished much for the cause we represented. However, not every one thought this way. Mr. John Lindley, a New York attorney, and a former member of the Association, in declining to make a contribution wrote: "My reason for not contributing is that it seems to me that there is relatively nothing done in the way of practical bird protection by any of the so-called Audubon Societies."

On November 3, 1911, when the American Ornithologists' Union convened in Philadelphia, Mrs. Pearson joined me there, and in a few days we came to New York City to look for a place to live, as we were now planning to move here the following January. Mr. and Mrs. William Beebe graciously insisted that we should locate near them at University Heights. They took us to see a house in Loring Place, which seemed to meet our needs, and there we have ever since resided.

CHAPTER XIV

BIRD RESERVATIONS BY ORDER OF THE PRESIDENT

THE FIRST United States Government bird reservation created by executive order was Pelican Island in Indian River, three miles south of Sebastian, Florida. Its establishment, destined to be of much historic interest in the realm of bird preservation, took place on March 14, 1903, as the logical result of three happenings and the courage of President Theodore Roosevelt.

The first of this trio of events was a visit by William Dutcher and Dr. T. S. Palmer to the Florida Legislature, resulting on May 29, 1901, in the passage of a law to protect the non-game birds of that state. The second was Frank M. Chapman's insistence that a guard be placed over the bird colony on Pelican Island, which he had visited in 1898 and again in 1900. The third was the efforts of Dutcher, Palmer and Frank Bond to find a way to protect these birds.

One of Mr. Bond's associates in the General Land Office was C. L. DuBois. It was he who suggested that Pelican Island might be declared a Federal bird reservation, as the land belonged to the Federal Government. The plan was approved by the Secretary of Interior, an order was prepared, and the President signed it promptly. It set forth that the island "Is hereby reserved and set apart for the use of the Department of Agriculture as a preserve and breeding-grounds for native birds."

The Secretary of Agriculture could do nothing in the way of employing a guard for the island, as he had no appropriation from which money could be allocated for such a purpose. However, Dutcher agreed that the Committee on Bird Protection of the American Ornithologists' Union would provide the warden service. The year before it had employed Paul Kroegl, living on the mainland two miles away, to serve as guard; and on April 4, 1903, the Secretary of Agriculture appointed him warden of Pelican Island. It is interesting to note that he seems to have been the second Federal game-warden ever appointed in any capacity, the first one probably being Buffalo Jones, game-warden of Yellowstone Park. A month after Kroegl's appointment, the Florida Audubon Society furnished him with a naphtha launch to use in going to the island.

When, back in 1855, Dr. Henry Bryant landed on Pelican Island, he found it inhabited not only by pelicans but by thousands of egrets and a small number of great blue herons and roseate spoonbills. Now, however, no nesting birds were left except pelicans, whose number, according to Mr. Chapman's estimate, was nearly 3,000. Formerly the birds had built their nests on the low-growing mangroves that crowded the four acres of the island. Cold weather in the 'Nineties killed these trees and by 1903 only a few of the trunks and large limbs remained; necessarily, therefore, most of the birds now built their nests on the ground.

The unusual period of the year when this colony engaged mainly in domestic duties was most surprising. Warden Kroegl annually made careful note of the time when the birds began to build their nests, and found that during fourteen of the seventeen years of his stewardship the first eggs of the main laying period were deposited on the following dates:

December 1, 1903	October 27, 1907
November 18, 1904	October 25, 1908
November 18, 1905	October 20, 1911
November 1, 1906	September 30, 1912

October 3, 1913   September 14, 1916
September 18, 1914   August 29, 1917
September 8, 1915   August 23, 1918

The unusual activities of this pelican community were various in their nature. The marked tendency to commence egg-laying each year at an earlier date than the year before, resulted during the passage of sixteen years in a total gain of sixty-nine days. And why did their chief breeding period begin in the autumn?

One hundred miles to the westward, the pelicans on the Gulf Coast regularly began laying their eggs in April. Furthermore, the breeding periods of these curious birds at Pelican Island are not fully indicated by the foregoing list of nesting dates.

Colonies of water-birds rarely nest a second time in the same year, unless during the early part of the breeding period the eggs or young have met with disaster; and even then this does not always occur. But this colony seemed not to have been governed by the accepted rules of conduct usually obtaining in such assemblages of birds. Here is a somewhat typical, chronological account of happenings on Pelican Island during a period of three years:

1906.—*February 15*—Young pelicans began to die, evidently from exposure; and in a few days seven hundred had perished. Only one hundred and fifty young survived.
April 15—Old birds begin to nest again, and four hundred young were raised.
November 1—Still another egg-laying period began.

1907.—*March*—Young able to shift for themselves and a second nesting now took place.
April 2-4—Island flooded by storm tide which drowned all of this second brood and killed many adults.
June 1—On this date there were one hundred new nests with eggs and young
June 15—All old birds left the island, and the abandoned young perished.

October 7—Birds arrived and began to nest. Egg-laying began 20 days later.

1908.—Cold weather early in the year killed five hundred young. The colony was the largest in all its known history—eight thousand adults using the island according to the warden's report. Many were not breeding birds.

April—Early this month the birds began to lay and six hundred young were raised.

October 25—General egg-laying again began.

The story of the weird actions and calamitous happenings of this haphazard colony runs on and on. Sometimes the birds nested once and sometimes twice a year. In 1907 there were three distinct egg-laying periods. Storm tides or freezing blasts from the North took their toll every two or three years.

In 1914, following a most propitious start the previous October, the old birds deserted their offspring before they could care for themselves. Every young pelican died and the old birds, as if tired of so much domestic labor and responsibility, took a rest and no new nesting activities were begun until the autumn. I have sometimes wondered whether two or more distinct groups of pelicans did not use this island, each with a separate breeding period.

The National Association of Audubon Societies in 1905 took over the cost of maintaining the warden on Pelican Island. We built, and for many years operated, the patrol boat *Audubon*, but leased this at nominal cost to the Biological Survey in 1919.

For nearly twenty years Pelican Island suffered only occasionally from human molestation. The largest known killing by man was in 1918 when unknown parties one night clubbed to death 400 immature birds. In 1922 houses began to appear nearby; and by 1924, nearly all of the birds, alarmed by these human encroachments, had departed and established themselves on an island in Mosquito Lagoon. Many fishermen do not like pelicans because of an exaggerated idea of the amount of valuable fish they consume. On March 15,

1924, I visited this new nesting-place of the Indian River pelicans and counted more than 1,200 young birds that had been killed during a raid by fishermen. Not more than 20 per cent of the young escaped destruction.

In October, 1925, the island was set apart as the "Brevard Bird Reservation." Government funds were scarce, and the Florida Audubon Society, with some aid from the National Association, has sought to provide necessary warden service.

Mr. Frank M. Miller of New Orleans organized the Louisiana Audubon Society in 1902. The next summer he visited some of the uninhabited islands off the coast of his state where sea-birds breed and learned they had been extensively shot for their feathers, and that their eggs were taken for food or for shipment to St. Louis "to be used in the making of the delicate films on photograph plates."

He had read about the Pelican Island Reservation and concluded that a reservation for sea-birds should be established in Louisiana. He went to New York and laid the proposition before William Dutcher. In Washington, Frank Bond's examination of records in the General Land Office proved that some of the bird islands Mr. Miller was talking about were government property, so President Roosevelt again was appealed to and on October 4, 1904, the Breton Island Bird Reservation was created by decree. This included Breton Island, which was six miles in length, also Old Harbor, Freemason, and other small islands and sand-bars.

The islands contained little vegetation except rank beach grass and a few bushes. They were popular breeding-places for laughing gulls, skimmers and five species of terns. In winter many ducks flocked to the lagoons of Breton Island, and numbers of golden plovers were reported to arrive here every year about April 28th, after their long spring flight across the Gulf of Mexico.

To the westward of the reservation lay the marshy mainland of Louisiana, bordered by numerous low, grass-covered islands. The control of seventeen of these was secured by Mr. Miller for the Louisiana Audubon Society on a lease granted December 31, 1905, by the Lake Borgne Levee Board. The rent to be paid was forty-five dollars a year for the 3,000 acres involved. Laughing gulls and three species of herons nested here.

The neighboring Battledoor Island and its keys aggregating another 1,000 acres, were bought from the State for twenty-five cents an acre. Here was the abode of many gulls, skimmers and terns.

For the islands Mr. Miller had bought and leased, he arranged with trappers to clear out the raccoons, prophesying that 5,000 would be taken and then the birds would be safe from natural enemies.

The guardianship of this vast domain of seven hundred square miles devolved upon the newly incorporated National Association of Audubon Societies, for there were no state game-wardens to enforce the provisions of the Audubon Law adopted that year by the State Legislature, and the Biological Survey had no money it could use to guard the birds of Breton Island. A boat was purchased and two men were employed to maintain a patrol among all those barren islands that dot the sea between the Chandeleur's and the Louisiana mainland.

The first careful summary of breeding water-birds of the region was made by a special agent of the Association, H. H. Kopman, in July, 1908. His estimates of the ten species of water-birds nesting on twenty-nine islands were: snowy egret, 40; black-crowned night heron, 220; Louisiana heron, 8,900; least tern, 50; Caspian tern, 45; Forster's tern, 625; Cabot's tern, 3,000; royal tern, 4,500; black skimmer, 2,525; and laughing gull, 46,000—total, 65,905. This indicated a fair breeding stock for most of the species.

Mr. A. C. Bent, cruising with Captain Sprinkle and his assistant on the Audubon patrol boat *Royal Tern,* in June,

1910, estimated that at Grand Cochere Island alone there were 3,500 occupied nests on June 8th.

Mr. Herbert K. Job, who was in these waters with President Roosevelt in 1915, spoke of the amazing numbers of birds they encountered.

During my own visits of inspection in 1916, and again in 1918, I made no attempt to arrive at estimates, but was convinced that royal and Cabot's terns were more abundant than had been estimated by Kopman in 1908. Nearly every year there were heavy losses of eggs and young by storm tides, but because of our warden service human molestation on any extended scale had ceased.

The Audubon Association continued its wardenship of these islands for fourteen years, or until 1919, when the Government Biological Survey assumed control, and at a nominal fee we leased to it our large gasoline-driven boat. A few years later the Survey relinquished its patrol work in this region, turning over these efforts to the Louisiana State Game Commission.

William Dutcher and Frank Bond kept up their search for other bird colonies on government territory. Within four years after Breton Island had been set aside for the birds, fifteen other areas likewise were so established by Executive Order. One of these was Stump Lake, North Dakota. The others were small islands off the coasts of Florida, Louisiana, Washington and Oregon; and two were in Michigan. One created on October 10, 1905, was Indian Key not far from St. Petersburg, Florida, where one wild summer night back in 1896 I had waded ashore and secured a pelican and a man-of-war bird before Captain Jim Bishop blew his conch to warn me of the coming storm.

Naturally, the friends of the birds had been advertising the fact that our country had a President who was dedicating islands and lakes to the birds by simply signing his name to papers. Around Congress there was some talk that the chief executive had no legal right to do such things. "On what meat doth this our Cæsar feed?" they began to ask.

To take care of the matter, a bill was introduced in Congress providing that it should be unlawful to disturb birds on any United States lands which had been set apart as breeding-grounds for birds by law, proclamation, or *executive order*, except under regulation by the Secretary of Agriculture. In this inferential way the President would be granted authority to issue executive orders creating bird sanctuaries on public lands. The bill attracted no special attention and was not opposed. It passed both houses and, by receiving the signature of President Roosevelt, became a law June 28, 1906.

All national bird reservations established by executive order until 1908 were for non-edible water-birds, but now the claims of the wild ducks and geese were brought to the front by the creation of two water-fowl refuges of great importance. One was Lower Klamath Lake in southern Oregon and northern California, which was dedicated to the birds August 8, 1908. It was fifteen miles in length and nearly half as broad. On all sides it was surrounded by a belt of tule marsh, miles in width, and floating islands of tule dotted its surface. In addition to having colonies of white pelicans, Farallon cormorants, Caspian and Forster's terns, grebes, and blue herons, it was a famous breeding- and resting-place for Canada geese and many kinds of ducks. Here market-hunters thrived. One hundred and twenty tons of wild-fowl had been shipped from this region in one year. In January, 1908, Dutcher wrote William L. Finley of Portland, Oregon, and asked him for a report on Klamath. Finley had furnished information that made it possible to bring protection to the great Three Arch Rocks bird assemblages in October, 1907, and he knew more about bird colonies in Oregon than any one else. He had visited Klamath in 1905, and the report he now filed in response to Dutcher's letter was the means of

Lower Klamath being declared a bird reservation seven months later.

The Audubon Association at once undertook to guard the lake, supplying a man and a boat for this purpose. Duck-hunters and other disturbers were held in check and the birds flourished. I found hosts of them late in May, 1915, when with Finley and Bruce Horsfall, I went over the region. There were many distinct breeding colonies of water-birds. To me the most striking assemblage was on a floating island where great blue herons were nesting. I have seen the nests of these birds in many situations: in sycamores in Indiana, in an oak-grove on a hill in Nova Scotia, in tall pines and cypresses many places in the Southern states and on the bare ground along the Texas coast, but here at Lower Klamath a unique condition existed. At least seventy nests were built on piles of tules which the birds had built to a height of from two and one-half to three feet. Over some acres the rushes were mashed flat and the nests stood up like altars erected to some god of the marshlands.

The Association's old patrol boat wore out, so in the summer of 1917 we built a new one, the *Grebe II,* but it was not destined to continue long in service.

Lower Klamath received its water from a run that came in from the Klamath River. The run contained a water-gate, and on October 12, 1917, this was closed, for there were those with influence at Washington who wanted the lake to dry up so they could sell its black alkali bottom to misguided "home-seekers" from Iowa or Nebraska or from wherever such people come. At first the stoppage of the water seemed to have no great effect on the lake, and for a time we constantly expected the flow to be renewed.

The story of the fight to save this reservation is a long and painful one. It involved the appointment of government and California State commissions to study the subject, and the pulling of many wires by friends and foes alike. At length

I was told by Mr. Mede, Assistant Secretary in the Interior Department, that on the very next Monday the water-gate would be opened and the lake would be saved. But an unfortunate news release given out by the Agricultural Department awoke the water-power interests on the Klamath River and the gate was not opened.

In 1919 Mr. Finley wrote me that most of the water in Lower Klamath had evaporated and the marshes were parched. "To complete the destruction," he said, "fires were started months ago in the vast tule marsh. Not only the surface but below the surface into the tule roots and the peat, the fires are burning continually."

Later I received a letter from the Reclamation Service, which said that if the Audubon Association or some other group or individual would pay for having a dyke built to protect the ranches already established, it was thought the rest of the lake could be allowed to refill. The cost was estimated at $150,000, but where could we find such a sum?

One hot day in 1927, I drove over much of what had been Lower Klamath Lake. I did not see a ranch, although I was told that there were a few somewhere. I saw only weeds— miles and miles of thickly growing weeds—and the only living creature we found was a scrawny, venomous snake that crossed the road and paused by the wheel track to shake his rattles at the two perspiring men in the car. Farther on we came to open flats over which whirlwinds chased each other like ghosts of the wild life that had departed. In despair, almost in bitterness, I fled. It all seemed so useless to spend one's life trying to aid in saving some of America's beauty spots and the wild creatures that inhabit them. Why worry because one's dreams as a bird-protector come to naught? How many people really care whether pelicans or herons or ducks live on? After all, why bother about such things? Speeding over miles of paved highways and drinking beer under shady arbors is so much more important anyway.

About one hundred and seventy miles northeast of Klamath Lake was another large body of water. The two were similar in appearance and their fates have paralleled each other strangely. Appropriately, even prophetically, some one had named this lake Malheur. It lies in the arid sage bush country of Harney County, Oregon. Ornithologically it was discovered by Captain Charles E. Bendire, in the early 'Seventies, but its wonders were brought to public attention by William L. Finley who, with Herman T. Bohlman, in the year 1908 spent five weeks photographing in its marshy vastness. Finley's report to the Audubon Association was the means of its being declared a Federal bird reservation on August 18th of that year.

One day in 1916, with the game-warden, Triska, I witnessed its amazing spectacles of bird life. Among the feathered hosts were avocets, grebes, killdeers, phalaropes, stilts and willets. There were three kinds of terns, also redheads, ruddys, cinnamon teal and other ducks. As our little boat proceeded, white pelicans, glossy ibises, cormorants, gulls and great blue herons came into view. There were thousands of Canada geese. Wings were everywhere in the tules, on the shores, among the interminable jumble of islands, on the water and in the sky. It would have been an easy matter to shoot a boat-load of birds. But such things were not being done here although before Finley's trip the egrets had been cleared out by plume-hunters. Now it was a vast bird nursery, more than one hundred and forty square miles in extent and no one with a gun was permitted to enter its precincts. In efforts to control natural enemies of the birds, more than 4,600 muskrats and many mink had been trapped the previous winter.

A disquieting story reached me. The Governor of Oregon and members of the State Land Board had left the region just before my arrival. It was said they claimed that the land belonged to the State and steps were to be taken to clear up this title and drain the lake for farm lands. A railroad was being pushed into this region and the lake bottom, when once the water had been removed, would make a magnificent farming community.

I rushed to rail-head and sped to Washington to tell the story to Frank Bond, our staunch friend in the General Land Office.

This was the beginning of a fight for the possession of Malheur Lake, which was to continue for nineteen years before a settlement could be reached. On one side were the Biological Survey, the Oregon Audubon Society and the National Association of Audubon Societies, trying to save the lake for the birds; the opposition came from the State of Oregon through its engineering department, abetted at every turn by commercially minded persons who wanted the region drained for farm lands. Finley, for many years President of the Oregon Audubon Society and the Western field agent for the National Audubon Association, was the active director in many of the hard-fought battles that ensued.

He led an effort in the State Legislature to pass a bill to cede to the United States Government any rights that Oregon might have in the lake. The bill was defeated. He was the moving spirit in an Initiative to declare Malheur Lake the "Roosevelt Bird Refuge." Money was necessary for the campaign, so I solicited funds and sent our Oregon friends more than $2,000.

The contest that followed was a bitter one. The issue at stake on November 2, 1920, was that if the people of the State voted our way the birds could keep their old home; but if we lost the election, the lake was to be destroyed and its dried bed sold for the benefit of the State School Fund.

Just before election, the would-be land developers widely distributed a card showing a picture of a little girl and a white pelican, which bore the legend, VOTE FOR THE BABY. From all the feathered inhabitants of Malheur, our opponents cleverly chose the pelican on account of the popular prejudice against it as a fish-eating bird. An avalanche of adverse ballots lost us the Initiative election.

The Soliciter of the Department of Agriculture decided that the Government had some rights to the water of the Silvius and Blitzen rivers, without which the lake would soon evaporate. By 1921, therefore, plans were completed for filing an injunction restraining the State from making too free use of the water.

But the injunction was never filed. Just at the most effective moment an Oregon Congressman descended on the Biological Survey for a parley. This resulted in calling a conference at Salem, Oregon, where the matter might be discussed under Western skies. Here a representative of the Survey, like Solomon of old, proposed to divide the disputed property, except that in this case a dyke instead of a sword was to be used. But Oregon would not agree to partition the lake into two parts by a dyke; what it wanted was all the water for its citizens. So the matter dragged on.

The Eastern Oregon Live Stock Company secured large holdings south of Malheur, and in time diverted the waters of the Blitzen on to the desert to make hay lands for stock. Ranchers to the north of the lake likewise used the flow of the Silvius and before many years Malheur Lake became a barren waste. No wild life was left. The earth was baked and cracked and burnt; and in the alkali dust curled the whitened forms of fish, and the horns and heads of long-dead bison came to view. Malheur, the Wonderful, had become Gehenna, the Place of Death.

Years went by, during which a few ranchers grazed cattle or raised meager crops on the edge of what formerly was the lake-bed. Every spring and autumn ducks and geese came over, circled about for a time and, finding no place to alight, continued on over the uplands of gray and purple sage. Now and then a wandering gull flew by with a discordant cry. The

Which is Best for Oregon, this BABY or this BIRD?

THE MALHEUR BIRD RESERVE

Would take from Oregon 47,000 acres of its most valuable school lands.

Would prevent irrigation and reclamation of a fertile and productive country.

Would continue a shallow mosquito breeding swamp which harbors mainly worthless inedible birds such as this.

The people of HARNEY COUNTY ask Portland for fair play.

VOTE 317 X NO

VOTE FOR THE BABY! 317 X NO

Schwab Printing Co., Portland, Oregon   Published by JAMES DONEGAN, Burns, Oregon

A DEADLY CAMPAIGN DOCUMENT

Its wide distribution just before the Oregon election in 1920 destroyed the chance to save Malheur Lake, our most important reservation for water-fowl.

MALHEUR LAKE REDEEMED

As the lake bottom began to fill in 1935, after the site had been completely dry for many years.

greatest area for water-birds in all óur vast Western country was no more. The friends of the birds were too few and their arms were too weak to withstand the combined attacks of politics and commercialism.

Thus time passed, until 1934, when unbelievably good fortune befell. Mr. Jay N. Darling, the new Chief of the Bureau of Biological Survey, secured funds from the Public Works Administration and for $675,000 bought the Live Stock Company's holdings, of 64,717 acres which lay athwart the Blitzen, cut the dam, and waters again began flowing into the parched basin of Malheur. That fall, in migration time, the 4,000 acres of water that already had accumulated were covered with happy ducks, and the settlers were rapidly departing.

Right on top of this came another great stroke of fortune. Under laws passed in 1917, and in subsequent years, the State of Oregon had asserted title to beds of navigable lakes and declared that all meandered lakes were navigable. This included Malheur. The Government brought suit and on April 15, 1935, the Supreme Court decided that Malheur Lake belonged to the United States Government.

Six other bird reservations were created in 1908 along with Klamath and Malheur. Of these most interesting was Chase Lake, North Dakota. Eight years later I was to have the pleasure of photographing white pelicans in this, the most eastern known breeding-colony of these great birds.

But a new reservation, the largest ever established, was soon to claim the attention of bird-protectionists.

One day back in December, 1903, the schooner *Yeiju Maru* dropped with the tide down Yokohama Bay, and with her crew of eighty-seven Orientals and with ample supplies for killing and skinning birds, sailed eastward into the Pacific. She reached the uninhabited island of Lisiansky in mid-ocean near Midway Island on January 8th, and the slaughter of nesting sea-birds began. Ten days later a fierce gale destroyed the *Yeiju Maru* and ten of her men who happened to be aboard at the time. The steamer *Iroquois,* chancing to pass that way, brought to Honolulu news of the presence of the Japanese poachers, and the United States Revenue Cutter *Thetis* went out to investigate. It returned in June with seventy-seven disconsolate Japanese hunters and taxidermists, but left on the island 335 large packing-cases estimated to contain plumage of 300,000 sea-birds, which had been intended for the European millinery market.

A few weeks later Professor W. B. Bryan of the Bishop Museum in Honolulu came to New York City and called to see William Dutcher, who unsuccessfully sought to arrange with President Roosevelt an interview in order that Professor Bryan might acquaint him with the colossal killing of sea-birds that was going on in our Pacific Islands. Returning disappointed to Honolulu, Professor Bryan wrote to the President on October 13, 1904, and related some of his observations regarding the work of the Japanese feather-hunters over wide ranges of the Pacific Ocean of recent years. He spoke of finding 40,000 tern-skins ready to ship from the Island of Marcus after one schooner-load had already sailed. He stated also that during the past six years one of the largest of all Albatross colonies had been wiped out of existence. He urged that United States Government vessels visit our outlying islands at least twice a year for the purpose of putting to an end the commercialization of the oceanic bird life.

Less than a month after this letter was written, John Hay, Secretary of State, instructed our Ambassador in Tokio to discuss this matter with Japanese authorities. Soon the Minister of Home Affairs in Japan issued instructions to stop, if possible, such feather cruises.

The next month, on December 17, 1904, a certain Max Schlemmer, former manager of the Pacific Guano and Fertilizer Company of Honolulu, applied to the Governor of Hawaii for a ninety-nine-year lease on Lisiansky, Laysan and French Frigate Shoals Islands. One of Schlemmer's proposals was, "I will agree to protect the birds; but ask for the privilege of killing annually the number stated in my previous letter; the skins of the birds to be turned over to the Territorial Government for sale, and a royalty of 10 per cent of the net realizations from the sale of the skins to be retained by the Territory, the balance to be paid to me."

From Laysan Island alone he stipulated that he should have the right to take annually 21,800 birds of fifteen species, and in addition, "all there could be killed of frigate birds."

Dutcher learned of what was in the wind, and his letter of February 20, 1905, to the Secretary of the Interior, boomed like a giant fog-horn across the waters of the Pacific. Soon it was announced that Max Schlemmer's proposal had been declined.

Much might be told of what took place in those islands during the next five years, but here I will remark only that on February 3, 1909, President Roosevelt signed an order creating the Hawaiian Islands Bird Reservation. It ran through five degrees of latitude and twenty degrees of longitude, and included all the important bird islands of the Western Hawaiian group.

The most extensive bird colony in all this vast area was situated on Laysan Island. So numerous were the birds that resorted here to breed, which in a large measure were Laysan and black-footed albatrosses, the guano which accumulated was considerable. The collection of this guano, together with the eggs of the birds, had been an industry in which men frequently had engaged for a number of years.

Max Schlemmer could not abandon his hope for making money by the killing of birds for their feathers. Some months after the islands were created a bird reservation, news reached the ears of Professor Bryan that another raid by Japanese poachers was in progress. He at once communicated with Washington, and Dr. Palmer, representing the Biological Survey, promptly took the matter up with the Revenue

Cutter Service. The *Thetis*, then lying at Honolulu, was dispatched to Laysan on January 11, 1910.

Arriving there, it was found that the feather-pirates had already wiped out half of the bird population and twenty-three Japanese bird-killers were brought back to Honolulu, together with 259,000 pairs of wings and much other plumage. The feathers of at least 40,000 additional birds all ready for shipment to the millinery markets of Europe were destroyed before the *Thetis* sailed for home. In due time the poachers were deported to Japan and action taken against Max Schlemmer under the immigration laws for his part in the enterprise. He was charged with importing alien laborers, but nothing came of the case.

Some one suggested that reservoirs on Western reclamation projects should be made sacred to water-birds, and so, on February 25, 1909, the President issued executive order to this effect for seventeen artificial lakes situated in Arizona, California, Idaho, Montana, New Mexico, Oregon, South Dakota, Utah, Washington and Wyoming. As yet the Biological Survey had no one in charge of bird reservations, whose business it was to inspect them. In the summer of 1916, it was arranged that I should go and see what some of these new reservations looked like. Several were visited and I unhesitatingly advised the Survey to abandon some of them. A body of water lying between steep mountains and with an annual rise and fall of at least twenty feet, is not a good place to grow duck food.

One day after a long hard trip to Kachess, Clealum and Bumping Lake in the heart of the Cascade Mountains, I arrived at a small railroad town. On the side of a two-storied frame building was a sign, none too skilfully painted, but yet distinctly legible, HOTEL—MEALS 25 CENTS AND UP. Hopefully, I entered a door around which the most flies were buzzing. There was a short counter and two tables. A young woman was in charge.

"I have just read your sign; what does 'and up' mean?" I ventured to ask.

Promptly, with an accent that must have been acquired somewhere on the Wabash, she answered:

"Thirty-five cents, with napkin and brown gravy."

My guide and I were among the best paying guests she had that day.

Mr. Darwin, the State Game Warden of Washington, kindly put at my disposal a small steamer and I went up Puget Sound to see three other government bird reservations of which little was known. Ediz Hook and Dungeness Spit I found to be attenuated sand spits extending into the Straits of Juan de Fuca from the northern side of the Olympic Peninsula. They were covered almost from end to end with drift logs, in places piled four or five deep. Over much of their area no bird could have reached the ground unless it was an unusually gifted and persistent woodpecker with a strange fascination for saw logs.

Across rough water to the northward lay Smith Island Refuge. It contained a few flat acres and was adorned with a lighthouse. At low tide a narrow ridge of rocks was exposed, where during the cold months black brant sometimes to the number of a hundred would climb out to sun themselves for a time.

However, Ediz Hook, Dungeness Spit and Smith Island are not typical of the Federal bird reservations scattered along the coast of our Western States, five of which are of very great importance to sea-fowl. They were ceded to the birds by President Theodore Roosevelt in 1907 and in 1909. It takes but a sentence to name them: Flattery Rocks, Quillayute Needles, and Copalis Rock, Washington; Three Arch Rocks, Oregon; and Farallon Islands, California. The Farallons are quite the best known. From ornithological literature there may be assembled a lengthy list of scientific observers who have written of the birds that frequent these islands that were discovered by Ferelo in 1543 and described by Sir Francis Drake in 1579.

They have long been popular with eggers, and being situated only about thirty miles from San Francisco, a ready market for this product was close at hand. We learn that in 1850 the Farallon Egg Company was organized to collect and transport to the near-by city the eggs of sea-birds—especially murres. During the next five years this company is believed to have sold in the neighborhood of four million eggs, and as late as 1873, 500,000 eggs were handled in a season. Mr. Leverett M. Loomis wrote that in 1896 the annual harvest had dwindled to 7,645 dozen, or something more than 91,000 eggs. He said that the price of the eggs from the Farallons had dropped to twelve and one-half cents a dozen.

Mr. Loomis gave these and other facts to William Dutcher and urged him to request the United States Lighthouse Board to stop this egg-collecting business. Dutcher did this on October 3, 1896, with the result that on December 10th the following order was issued by George F. F. Wilde, Commander, United States Navy, Naval Secretary: "The Board desires that the lighthouse-keepers shall be prohibited from engaging in the business of collecting or selling wild birds' eggs on these islands in any form."

When in the rush to get as many executive orders for bird reservations as possible signed by President Theodore Roosevelt just before he went out of office, it was but natural that Dutcher and Bond should think of the Farallon Islands, and they were included among the twenty-five executive orders handed to the President at this time. The order creating the Farallon Bird Reservation received his signature on February 27, 1909.

The sea-birds that breed here in great numbers are the tufted puffin, Cassin's auklet, pigeon guillemot, California murre, western gull, two species of petrels and three kinds of cormorants. Here, as elsewhere, gulls perform their work of eating the eggs of their bird neighbors. William Leon Dawson wrote in 1911:

Our presence was hailed with glad acclaim by the gulls, who, though somewhat fearful for their own treasures, are always eager for an excuse to plunder "the ledges." In fact, the Larine outcry always seemed to be nine-tenths make-believe, being intended to alarm the galleries instead of voicing a personal anxiety. Obedient to the tradition, the murres begin to shift and edge away when the gulls assured them that yonder object picking its way carefully over the rocks is dangerous. It looks harmless, but who knows? A gull swoops near to the ledge and shrieks, "Fly for your lives, you fools!" The timorous obey promptly; the rest crowd to the edges. Fear becomes panic, and panic rout; while the gulls swarm down to feast on the abandoned eggs.

Big Lake in eastern Arkansas was a famous shooting-place for wild-fowl market-hunters, and for several years a legal battle was waged between them and the members of the Big Lake Club, whose house stood on a knoll at the end of the lake. The Club sought to prevent any one but its members and their friends from shooting the ducks, so purchased a strip of land all around the lake and employed guards to keep off trespassers. But this did not stop the market-shooters, so the Club secured court injunctions against a number of them. The marketmen retaliated; at least they were supposed to be responsible for various shots fired at the club manager, who on one occasion was wounded.

One night there was a fire of mysterious origin and by morning nothing was left of the fine club building but smoldering embers and a great brick chimney. No prosecution followed, for one cannot be convicted of arson without good evidence.

In the midst of all this agitation, it was discovered that the original survey of the land about the lake had been fraudulent, and the hearts of the market-hunters were made glad.

Then, certain friends of the birds in Washington, finding that Big Lake and its immediate environs was still government property, saw a chance to dispose of both the club men and the market-hunters. They prepared an Executive Order for making Big Lake a bird reservation, and this was signed by President Woodrow Wilson, August 2, 1915.

As usual, it was placed under the care of the Biological Survey but also, as usual, no money was available for guards. In the report of the Chief of the Survey, four years later, he stated that of the sixty-eight bird reservations under his care, he was able to employ only eighteen wardens and eight of these were in service for part time only.

Some months after the proclamation, I visited Big Lake in company with Mr. Visart, a Federal warden employed to enforce the Weeks-McLean Migratory Bird Law. When the boat that took us over the lake left its muddy landing, it also contained four other men, with their guns and decoys. These were deposited in two shooting blinds. Before long, we came upon three other blinds, each containing its quota of two hunters with wooden decoys bobbing about with their heads ever pointing into the wind.

"Who cares anything about the Government's orders to keep out?" one of the shooters asked me.

The next year the Survey managed to transfer a guard for temporary service at Big Lake, who, with the aid of the Arkansas State Game Commission, did good work in stopping some raids of the numerous poachers. It took a good deal of effort the next few years for the Survey, with little money and with hostile local sentiment, to prevent the killing of ducks on Big Lake. Many men of the region had shot here most of their lives, and they continued to kill ducks, and by means of motor-boats and automobiles ran them across the Missouri boundary where they could be shipped to the markets of the Middle West.

Gradually, however, the Survey got control of the situation, and a fearless Federal judge of the district greatly aided matters in 1921 by fining a poacher $500, and by sending his associate to jail for six months after relieving him of fifty dollars, which seems to have been all the money he could raise.

The reservation is about five by nine miles in extent and covers 8,937 acres.

Malheur, Klamath and Big Lake for a time were the most important government bird reservations for ducks and geese in the United States, but there was to come a day when of the three, Big Lake alone would offer refuge for these strong-winged flyers of the sky.

President Theodore Roosevelt issued fifty-one executive orders to create bird reservations. President Taft established ten during his stay in the White House, and eleven more were called into existence by President Wilson. Later Presidents have added to the list. These vary greatly in size and in usefulness to birds. Some are mangrove keys, perhaps thirty feet wide and a hundred feet long; while others, as I have shown, are large and extremely important refuges for wild life. Ninety-seven such refuges were created between March, 1903, and May, 1935. Of these, eleven were later abandoned and two were transferred to other departments of government. We now have many additional government refuges of great value to bird life, but most of these came into existence through other means than by order of the President.

Chapter XV

SCHEDULE "N" AND WHAT FOLLOWED

THE FEATHERS of birds probably have served as human decorations ever since man developed sufficient pride to adorn his person. However, it was not until modern civilization developed a rage for their use in decorating women's hats that birds of bright plumage began to suffer greatly from the human race and an immense trade in their feathers was started.

The campaign against this deplorable industry in America began when William Brewster, speaking at a meeting of the American Ornithologists' Union in New York City on October 1, 1884, so stirred his hearers that a committee was appointed to work for bird protection. Dr. George Bird Grinnell followed with the formation of the first Audubon Society in April, 1886.

Articles on the destruction of birds written by J. A. Allen, William Dutcher, Frank M. Chapman and George B. Sennett, of the Union's bird-protection committee, were published as a separate supplement in *Science* for February 26, 1886, and served for many years as the basis of the educational work carried on by the defenders of bird life.

How extremely difficult it was to make progress in this field of reform was illustrated by an article in a New York City paper, printed thirteen years after the supplement in *Science* had been issued. It was a report of the proceedings of a meeting of the New York State Audubon Society held in the American Museum of Natural History, in 1899. It stated: "About 150 persons were present, most of them women, and fully three-fourths of the women wore birds, or parts of birds, in their hats, a practice on which the Society frowns."

Agitation, however, continued, and before long the Millinery Merchants' Protective Association of New York proposed to make a treaty with their adversaries. There was a sharp division of opinion as to whether such an offer should be accepted. Negotiations were opened, however, and on April 21, 1900, a three years' contract was entered into by the milliners and the organizations that were opposing their feather trade. This stipulated that the members of the Millinery Merchants' Protective Association pledged themselves to stop dealing in the feathers of "gulls, terns, grebes, humming-birds and song-birds," and to discontinue their trade in heron aigrettes and American pelicans after January 1, 1904. .The bird-protectionists agreed "to endeavor to prevent all illegal interference on the part of game-wardens with the millinery trade" and to refrain from aiding in the passage of laws that would interfere with trade in the feathers of domestic fowls or of foreign birds other than those mentioned. It was signed by George Legg and Charles W. Farmer for the milliners, and by Frank M. Chapman for the New York Audubon Society and by William Dutcher for the American Ornithologists' Union.

This, as well as a somewhat similar agreement with Baltimore milliners about the same time, and another with the Western Millinery Association in 1904, soon lapsed but some of the dealers continued to observe their promises.

In the meantime, back in 1897 another force had entered the field of bird protection in the person of George F. Hoar. He printed a petition bearing the names of many birds, which it was alleged had signed it, asking that their lives be spared. This gained wide distribution. Then through friends in the Massachusetts Legislature, he secured the passage of a law which rendered it illegal to have in possession the feathers of protected birds. The statute was very explicit as to just what was meant. It provided a fine of ten dollars for any one who "wears such feathers for the purpose of dress or ornament." The law was so drastic that a woman chancing to cross the State with a feather on her hat could be arrested and fined. The courts promptly declared it to be unconstitutional.

The next year Mr. Hoar, as a member of the United States Senate, introduced on March 14, 1898, a bill intended to prohibit the importation, sale or shipment of feathers for millinery adornment in the United States. At a meeting of the American Ornithologists' Union, held in Washington that autumn, Witmer Stone, then Chairman of the Union's Committee on Bird Protection, told of what Senator Hoar was trying to do, but it was the consensus of those present that the bill should not be supported. It was feared that if the importation of foreign plumage were stopped, the killing of our American birds would greatly increase, as few laws existed for their protection. With the powerful milliners actively fighting the Hoar Bill, and the friends of the birds afraid to interfere in its behalf, the Senator's second attempt to suppress the feather trade came to naught, as did also his third undertaking launched the next year.

Fourteen years went by during which the Audubon Society and allied interest had secured bird-protective laws in most of the states, but no one had again attempted to prohibit the importation of foreign plumage.

In the mail one morning in December, 1912, I received a letter from Dr. Henry Oldys of Silver Springs, Maryland, in which he recalled the vain efforts of Senator Hoar in 1898. "Now, however, conditions are different," he wrote. He went on to suggest that it was the job of the Audubon Association to stop the importation of birds' plumage by means of a provision inserted in the new Tariff Act then being drawn. Soon afterward, while in Washington I had a talk with R. A.

Doughton, a North Carolina Congressman of my acquaint-ance.

He told me that I should communicate with Oscar W. Underwood, Chairman of the Ways and Means Committee, if I hoped to have a voice in shaping the Tariff Bill; and that I must ask for permission to speak when the Committee con-sidered Schedule "N." "Write that down," he advised. "Re-member it is Schedule "N.""

I wrote to Mr. Underwood but was told that all the time available for considering this schedule had been assigned to others. At once I sent a letter to more than one thousand Audubon Society members urging that they write to Mr. Underwood and ask him to invite me to appear before his Committee and present some facts on the feather trade. Also, I again made a formal request for an appointment in the name of five institutions and associations.

He replied by wire: ALL ALLOTTED TIME TAKEN BUT WILL ARRANGE TO HAVE YOU HEARD UNDER SCHEDULE.

Hearings on the schedule dealing with feathers were to begin on January 29th. I had accepted an invitation for that night to address the Women's Auxiliary of the New York Zoological Society at the Colony Club of New York City, but William Beebe agreed to take my place. In Washington I was joined by Dr. William T. Hornaday, to whom I had com-municated my plans.

On the appointed morning I appeared in the committee-room armed with documents and samples of millinery plum-age then in general use. The printed program for the day showed that several importers of feathers were to speak before I did. These men took so much time that the Committee adjourned for the day just as my name was reached. Dr. Hornaday then asked to have his name included among the speakers for the next day, and this was granted.

We talked over our strategy, and it was decided that he would ask to have the importation of all millinery plumage prohibited, and that I should present a proposition based on the law adopted by New York State, viz.: prohibit the importation of all birds belonging to the same families as those protected in the United States. If the Congressmen took the position of some state legislators, that they could not be expected to pass a law to protect the birds of other countries, they would have the alternate proposition before them for consideration. This was the plan we followed the next day; I taking occasion to state that if we could not have the whole loaf we wanted a half loaf.

When after the hearing we took our hats and departed, we felt pretty sure that our proposition would have favorable consideration.

We were soon asked to provide the exact wording of the two plans we had presented for consideration, and this we did promptly.

In the end the Committee agreed to ask that the importation of the plumage of all wild birds should be prohibited. This proviso of the Tariff Bill in due time passed the House, but when it reached the Senate trouble began.

I will here reproduce my editorial on this subject as published in *Bird-Lore* for July-August, 1913:

The paragraph in Schedule "N" of the Tariff Bill which plans to prohibit the importation of the feathers of birds, except those of the ostrich and domestic fowls, did not fare well at the hands of the Finance Committee of the Senate to which it was referred after having successfully passed the House of Representatives. The Chairman of this Committee distributed the different schedules among various sub-committees for detailed consideration. Thus Schedule "N" fell into the hands of Senators Charles F. Johnson, of Maine; Hoke Smith, of Georgia; and William Hughes, of New Jersey. The millinery interests worked energetically and desperately on these three law-makers, and eventually induced them to adopt a provision which, if it finally becomes a law, will in a large measure nullify the effect of the anti-importation proviso.

The Sub-Committee, after having evidently reached a conclusion on the matter, reluctantly granted the friends of the birds a hearing. This was done suddenly and without sufficient warning to admit of the presence of some who, had they known in advance, would have gladly availed themselves of the opportunity to be there. There were present, however, Dr. W. T. Hornaday, of the New York Zoological Society, Mr. E. H. Forbush, of Boston, representing the National Association of Audubon Societies, and Dr. Henry Oldys, of the District of Columbia Audubon Society. The scant impression which the array of unanswerable facts presented by these gentlemen seemed to make on the Sub-Committee was a subject which occasioned comment.

So the Sub-Committee made its report to the Finance Committee, and the Finance Committee, adopting its suggestion, recommended to the Democratic caucus of the Senate that the feather paragraph be amended so feathers or plumes of birds commonly recognized as edible or pestiferous can be imported.

Think of it! The feathers of any bird which any one eats at any place on this green earth, or any bird which any interested person may be pleased to catalogue as a pest, may be imported under this provision! Mr. L. S. Crandall, of the New York Zoological Park, has compiled for Dr. Hornaday a list of 1,622 birds which he considers game-birds. But remember, the Senators have not said "game-birds," but went much farther and said "birds commonly recognized as edible." Few of us would think of calling robins, nighthawks, bobolinks, flickers, white ibis and night herons "game-birds," and yet in a number of our Southern states these, and also several other species, are "commonly recognized as edible," so their feathers may be imported. In Italy there is hardly a bird that flies, walks or swims but what is "commonly recognized as edible," which would mean that the feathers of European song-birds could be imported with impunity. Where is the thing to end, and who is the official who will dare to say that any feathers whatever shall be debarred from importation?

Then, too, pestiferous birds are placed on the unprotected list; but no authority is given for determining just what birds are pests. The city dweller says the English sparrow is a pest, the suburban gardener declares the starling is a pest, the rice-planters say bobolinks and blackbirds are pests, the corn-grower declares the lark and dove to be pests, the chicken-raiser votes that hawks are pests, the propagator of fish says herons and kingfishers are pests, sailors vow petrels that warn them of coming storms are pests, the man with a chimney says the swift is a pest, the Southern grape-grower swears the mocking-bird is a pest, and, under the proposed law, whosoever will, may call any bird in the world a pest, and ship its feathers to this country to enrich the pockets of the selfish, greedy traffickers in the plumage torn from the bodies of slaughtered mother birds.

United States Senators will soon be elected by a direct vote of the people, and they will listen right now to what their constituents have to say on important public issues, if the constituents will only speak freely and insist on being heard.

Just before going to press, word was received to the effect that the Senate Finance Committee has decided to strike out the entire feather proviso except the clause which prohibits the importation of heron "aigrettes"!

During the campaign we engaged in many efforts to influence Congress in behalf of the measure. One undertaking was a motion-picture exhibit.

Mr. E. A. McIlhenny of Louisiana, had caused a film to be made revealing with pitiless accuracy the method of securing aigrettes. Into a large colony of snowy egrets which he has long nurtured near his home on Avery Island, "plume-hunters" entered and from a boat shot egrets about their nests. The film faithfully showed the hunters pushing through the bushes in their quest, showed the birds falling dead or wounded before the gun-fire, and revealed the helpless young left in the nests. Then there was the camp scene on shore, where the backs of dead birds were skinned for their feathers and soon a line of drying scalps were waving gently in the breeze.

Mr. McIlhenny lent us this film. We engaged a hall near the Capitol and invited the members of Congress to come and bring their wives and friends. At four o'clock on the appointed day, Dr. Hornaday explained our feather proviso and introduced me. I made a short talk and commented on the film as it unrolled. Before I had finished more people arrived. Dr. Hornaday again spoke and I followed with my remarks, and our operator started the film going. These performances were continued with new audiences until about ten o'clock that night, when people stopped coming and we went out for refreshments. We were fighting the most important battle that has ever been waged for the suppression of the feather traffic of the world and its results were destined to be profound and far-reaching. And now, once more, I shall revert to *Bird-Lore* and quote from one of my editorials in the September-October, 1913, issue, written when these matters were fresh and vivid in my mind:

It will be recalled that the Democratic majority refused to accept the House provision on this point, and, after first mutilating the feather proviso almost beyond recognition, finally eliminated the entire clause with the exception of heron "aigrettes." Thus the matter stood until August 16, when Senator George P. McLean of Connecticut made a most forceful and exhaustive speech in support of his amendment to restore the House feather proviso in the Tariff Bill. His address brought forth many favorable comments from Senators and some adverse remarks as well.

One of those who took issue with Senator McLean was the Hon. James A. Reed, Senator from Missouri, who, in speaking of the killing of egrets, unburdened himself as follows:

"I really honestly want to know why there should be any sympathy or sentiment about a long-legged, long-beaked, long-necked bird that lives in swamps, and eats tadpoles and fish and crawfish and things of that kind; why we should worry ourselves into a frenzy because some lady adorns her hat with one of its feathers, which appears to be the only use it has?"

And again:

"If the young are then left to starve, it would seem to me the proper idea would be to establish a foundling asylum for the young, but still let humanity utilize this bird for the only purpose that evidently the Lord made it for, namely, so that we could get aigrettes for bonnets of our beautiful ladies." ,

Think what a distorted mind and heart this poor man, James

A. Reed, must have inhabiting the body which has been granted the breath of life for a time by the same God who created the egrets, and who doubtless gives as much heed to cries of the dying young birds as He does to the heartless utterances of the ignorant Senator.

Senator McLean and others interested in the bird-protective measure had little to fear from a man of the caliber of Reed. Our greatest opponent has been Senator Hoke Smith of Georgia, who has fought the feather proviso with all his might ever since the Tariff Bill came over from the House; also he has not been at all modest in claiming great credit for the passage of the State Game Laws of Georgia, which he declared shows that he is a true believer in bird protection.

This same Georgia law contains a clause expressly permitting the importation of birds' feathers into Georgia for millinery purposes.

Never before, of recent years at least, has the United States Senate been deluged with such a flood of letters and telegrams from indignant constituents on any subject as that which poured into Washington this summer demanding favorable consideration of the anti-feather importation proviso in the Senate.

The result was that Senator Simmons of North Carolina, Chairman of the Finance Committee, recalled from the Senate the feather section "for further consideration." He again referred it to his Sub-Committee which had previously undone the House proviso. This Committee met on Sunday, August 31, and voted to stand by their former decision to allow the milliners to continue in their nefarious work of importing birds' feathers. The Finance Committee so reported to the Democratic Caucus, which met on the night of September 2. The next morning the Washington *Post* reported:

"For five hours last night Democratic Senators fought out the question of whether or not the plumage of wild birds should be permitted to be imported into the United States. The Senate Committee had first agreed to a modification of the drastic prohibition of the House. This modification was denounced by the Audubon Society and other lovers of birds, anxious to stop their slaughter, as tending to make the House provision absolutely ineffective.

"The fight for the House provisions was led by Senators Lane and Chamberlain of Oregon. The caucus at first decided to stand by the Committee. The two Oregon Senators bolted, and others supported them. Party managers then found the spirit of insurgency too strong, and the House paragraph was adopted. This absolutely prohibits the importation of the plumage of wild birds except for scientific and educational purposes."

The next day, September 3, 1913, the Senate passed the proviso without opposition, and on October 3rd the new tariff bill received the President's signature.

Thus ended the campaign which we fondly thought would put a stop to the feather traffic and thus bring to a happy conclusion the movement started by the American Ornithologists' Union thirty-eight years before.

Not long after this law was enacted by the United States Congress, a similar one was passed by the Canadian Parliament largely through the efforts of Dr. C. Gordon Hewitt, Dominion Entomologist and Consulting Zoölogist. This went into effect January 31, 1915. It was not quite so drastic as the United States law, in that it did not prohibit the importation of "the plumage of wild birds ordinarily used as articles of diet." However, it was sufficient to be a great help in sounding the death-knell of the millinery trade in the country of our neighbors in the North.

There were stirring times about the steamship piers of New York City in the autumn of 1913. Women returning from European ports could not leave the wharf until they surrendered the bird feathers adorning their hats. Many such passengers were arriving by every ship. They continued to come. Hundreds and even thousands of travelers were relieved of their decorations so proudly borne aloft as evidence of recent visits to London or Paris millinery-houses.

The great bulk of the feathers were "aigrettes" purchased in European shops where the latest style of hat trimmings were always available in exchange for American dollars. In the seizure-room of the Customs Department I saw three great chests that were filled with these contraband goods.

Women also lost their feathers at Pacific Coast ports, and at the borders where trains crossed from Mexico or from Canada. The United States Customs officials were actively enforcing the new law prohibiting the importation of the feathers of wild birds. Many of us took a certain grim satisfaction in what was happening, and stories of the clipping of feathers from women's hats made good copy for the newspaper writers.

Women were willing to pay such high prices for feathers that a brisk business in the smuggling of plumage soon developed, for there was no law against the sale or the wearing of such adornments once they were in this country. In the open markets were displayed the head-crests of the goura pigeon, the down of the marabou stork, and the wonderful decorations of birds-of-paradise. Paradise plumes especially were desired, and many subterfuges were employed to get them into the country.

On the night of January 29, 1916, government Federal agents caught two men in Texas as they waded across the Rio Grande River near Laredo. They were carrying a trunk which, when opened, was found to contain the skins of 527 male birds-of-paradise in magnificent plumage.

Another seizure of contraband plumage in New York this same year brought on some prosecutions in which we had a small part.

The Steamship *Kroonland* docked at Pier 59 North River at 2 P.M., November 26, 1916. Angelo Tartaglino, Chief Steward of the ship, came to the gate where J. C. Rothschild, Customs Roundsman, asked him if he had any contraband. Tartaglino answered "No." However, Rothschild was suspicious, and taking him aside discovered a wide cloth belt, which Tartaglino said he was wearing because he was sick. The sack circled his body and two extensions from it reached to his knees. The "life-belt" contained 150 bird-of-paradise plumes, and the man soon confessed that he had seven more belts aboard ship. He further explained that he had been approached by a man in London to bring these packages over and deliver them on the dock to a tall stranger with drooping mustaches whom he would find awaiting.

The seven belts were found to contain 950 paradise plumes and 849 crests of the goura pigeon. On December 15th Tartaglino was sentenced to Trenton prison for eleven months and fifteen days, and paid a fine of $500. While in jail it was discovered that the chef at Shanley's Café was sending him checks monthly. The two men were brought before the Grand Jury where in time the whole story came out.

Tartaglino confessed that he was an agent for Arthur Arbib of the New York Fashion Feather Company, and that this was his second trip. He stated that another Italian named Felice Strado had been a smuggler for Arbib for some time and that he had bought Strado's business for $200. He was to receive $300 for each consignment he brought to New York.

Arbib then came forward and confessed. His store was raided and paradise and goura feathers in great quantities were seized on the theory that they were the feathers which had been brought on Tartaglino's first trip. Tartaglino, however, advised that on his first trip he had examined the contents of only one of his life-belts, and that it contained only paradise plumes. He was unable to swear whether he had brought any goura. The Court, therefore, ordered the Customs authorities to return to Arbib the goura crests. There was such a great quantity of these that it required seventeen cartons, three feet square and four feet long, to contain them. They were worth $100,000 or more when seized. Arbib was fined $4,500 for conspiracy and $500 for smuggling, but, on account of poor health, escaped a prison sentence. Investigation proved that the goura and paradise which many of the large department and women's furnishing stores in New York City were selling, had been purchased from Arbib.

It could not be established that these had been smuggled, and the courts ruled that they could not be confiscated. On July 16, 1919, by order of the Assistant Secretary of the Treasury, 150 goura plumes valued at $8.00 each, and 150 paradise plumes valued at $35 each, were presented to the Audubon Association for educational purposes. When I went to the seizure-room to receive these, I learned that the assistant United States Treasurer had authorized the sale at public auction of all the remaining confiscated stock, which was estimated would bring the Government $150,000.

I communicated with the Biological Survey and the National Museum, and both institutions applied to the Treasury Department for the confiscated goods to be used for educational and exhibition purposes. Their request was granted, and thus the feathers were kept from the market.

There were various other incidents connected with this case. For example, the smuggler for Arbib delivered the plumage to the home of a man in New York to which Arbib would go and get them. This householder never came to trial for when arrest was imminent he committed suicide. A lawyer who was supposed to be the brains of the conspiracy was saved from arrest by the timely arrival of instructions from high political sources in Washington, D. C., that he should not be prosecuted.

The Audubon Association secured from the Customs officials and from Game Commissioners a considerable variety of plumage that had been seized in their law-enforcement activities. Thinking it would be of interest to many people to see an exhibition of the different feathers still popular with millinery connoisseurs, a series of exhibits were arranged, each specimen accompanied with a label showing the name of the bird and the value of the decoration as appraised by a jobber in the feather trade.

These collections were presented to forty-five museums in twenty-seven states. These exhibits were valued at more than

$20,000. Other samples were sealed in boxes and placed in our storage-room.

Then, one day, I spread newspapers on the floor of my office and called in three clerks. Two young women with scissors cut up a large pile of the finest feathers of goura, marabou and birds-of-paradise. The other clerk and I signed affidavits as to the number thus destroyed. These affidavits, with a sworn statement regarding the few feathers kept in our possession, and the receipts from the museums through the country, were filed with the Government.

With the election of a Republican President in the year 1920, it became apparent that a new Tariff Act would be drawn. Here, then, was our chance, and we took full advantage of it. Over strong opposition of the millinery forces, the Ways and Means Committee was induced to amend Schedule "N" in such a way that if any one offered the plumage of wild birds for sale they must produce proof satisfactory to the Customs officials that these were imported legally before October 3, 1913. When announcement was made in the press that this change was pending in the New Tariff Bill, there was much excitement in the millinery emporiums. Advertisements appeared offering paradise plumes for $65 that the week before were bringing $125. By the middle of September the price sagged to $29.50, and the day before the Tariff Bill became a law they were bringing only $15.

The feathers we see in the New York millinery trade to-day mostly are the dyed plumage of chickens and domestic ducks. Occasionally some one violates the feather law in the hope of making easy money, just as others steal automobiles, rob banks or smuggle coolies.

The world traffic in feather millinery reached its height in the period between 1870 and 1908, and the quantities of plumage used during these years was beyond calculation. The dried skins of tanagers, kingfishers, parrots, humming-birds, terns and hundreds of other species came to the millinery markets in millions from virtually all the countries of the world. As a single example, in an auction-room in London, where great sales took place monthly, there was displayed in June, 1900, in one lot, white egret plumes that had cost the lives of more than 24,000 birds. In Paris I examined the records of the Customs Department of the French Government and found that between 1890 and 1929 bird plumage had been imported to the extent of 45,797,583 kilos, or something more than 50,327 tons!

The three great centers of the feather trade of the Western World were New York, Paris and London. I have spoken of how North America dealt with the problem. There is little to say about restrictions having been adopted in France.

In England the earliest effective opposition to all this holocaust of slaughter was voiced by Professor Alfred Newton, of Magdalene College, in an address at Norwich, England, in 1868. The campaign emanating from him and his associates caused Parliament, in 1869, to prohibit the killing of seabirds along the shores of the British Isles. The Royal Society for the Protection of Birds, from the day of its foundation in 1889, actively advocated the suppression of the feather traffic. At a conference early in the year 1908, attended by representatives of that Society, the British Museum, the Linnæan Society, the Zoological Society and the Selborne Society, a bill to stop the importation of feathers for millinery purposes was proposed by James Buckland. After some modifications had been agreed to, it was redrawn by Montague Sharpe, Chairman of the Society for the Protection of Birds. It was introduced in the House of Lords by Lord Avebury on May 5, 1908, and passed July 21st, but was not adopted by the House of Commons. Agitation continued without abatement and the campaign led by the Royal Society for the Protection of Birds never ceased and its bills regularly appeared in the British Parliament. In 1920 a few interested people under the leadership of S. Massingham, and ably supported by Mrs.

Reginald McKenna, organized as The Plumage Act Group, and were especially active in supporting "The Importation of Plumage (Prohibition) Act" which was introduced in Parliament by W. Trevelyan Thomson. It passed Parliament and received the Royal Assent July 1, 1921. It went into force April 1, 1922. It was not so all-inclusive as the United States law but had a tremendous effect in saving wild bird life. When it became a law fifty-four years had passed since Alfred Newton launched his first attack on the feather traffic before the British Society in Norwich in 1868.

Feathers are still used in the millinery business in various parts of the world but we see little of it in America, although visitors to Paris find evidences that the French milliners every few years attempt to revive the demand for such articles of adornment.

CHAPTER XVI

THE BIRD TREATY WITH CANADA

I T WAS not until about the beginning of the present century that the United States Congress exhibited any special interest in the welfare of wild birds. To be sure, birds' eggs had been mentioned in the Tariff Act of 1894, but only to the extent of prohibiting the importation of those not used for food, unless they were intended for scientific purposes.

Shortly before Senator Hoar's fruitless attempt to prohibit the importation of feathers for millinery use in 1898, Assemblyman John F. Lacey of Iowa introduced a bill on July 1, 1897, to encourage the introduction and propagation of useful birds. It failed of passage. At the next session he presented another which provided for stopping the inter-state shipping of game killed in violation of state laws, and for authorizing the Secretary of Agriculture to regulate the importation of foreign birds and other wild animals. It made illegal the importation of the mongoose, "flying fox," English sparrow, starling or other injurious species. This bill became a law May 25, 1900. In later years it was amended to include some additional measures.

The Lacey Law was the first bird-protective statute the United States Biological Survey was authorized to enforce. At this time, also, there were a few Federal statutes for protecting game in Alaska, Indian Territory, the District of Columbia, and on certain other government properties, including the twelve National Parks that then existed. These laws, important though they were, never attracted the public attention as did a series of efforts to secure government control of migratory game-birds which soon were to begin their troublesome course through Congress.

Merely as an accommodation to his political party, George Shiras, III, the naturalist, entered Congress as Representative from Pennsylvania in 1903, with the avowed intention of serving only one term. While working on the subject of government control of pollution which spread disease from one state to another, it occurred to him that if the Federal Government assumed the obligation of destroying harmful migratory germs, it could with equal consistency use its police powers to protect useful migratory game-birds. This line of reasoning led him to introduce into Congress, on December 5, 1904, "A Bill to Protect the Migratory Game Birds of the United States."

From long experience in various hunting-fields, he knew that this class of birds was inadequately protected under state management; in fact, in a number of states no game-warden system at that time existed. He did not ask for a committee hearing on his bill, but stated that for the present he merely desired to have it printed and circulated for the purpose of arousing discussion among game commissioners, naturalists, the five million sportsmen of the country, and others.

Upon his retirement from Congress, Representative Weeks and Senator McLean undertook the task of enacting his plan into a law. Their measure became known as the Migratory Game Bill. It had many admirers and a few friends; but people were busy with other matters, and although the Audubon Association and some individuals now and then spoke a few kind words in its behalf, no one on the outside of Congress made any effective effort to have put into statutory form the theory which Shiras had advanced.

Several years passed and then the newly organized American Game Protective and Propagation Association came upon the scene. Its officers decided that the slumbering Weeks-

McLean Bill should at once have their attention, and on March 6, 1912, engineered a hearing in Washington before the House Committee on Agriculture and the Senate Committee on Forest Reservations and the Propagation of Game. Federal and state game-protective officials, as well as representatives of twenty-three associations, and societies, presented their comments to the committeemen. This was the first large gathering of people ever assembled in the halls of Congress to work for the passage of a bird-protective bill.

I was the only speaker that day who did not urge the enactment of this bill just as it stood. My contention was that it should be amended to include protection for migratory insect-eating birds as well as migratory game-birds. In a short time it was amended in this manner. The change brought to the measure many recruits, who cared little for preserving game-birds to shoot, but who were interested in saving song and insectivorous birds.

There followed an extensive campaign under the leadership of John B. Burnham, President of the American Game Protective Association. There was constant fighting, both in Congress and out of it, on the all-absorbing subject of the Government's assuming an authority over the fortunes of migratory birds heretofore exercised wholly by the states. A great deal was said and written about the unconstitutionality of such a law. Senator Elihu Root held that if the principle involved was embodied in a treaty, it would then not be subject to scrutiny by the courts; consequently, on January 14, 1913, about six weeks before the Migratory Game Bill became a law, he introduced a resolution in the Senate looking to the possibility of securing a treaty for bird protection between Canada, the United States, and countries to the South. It was not acted upon.

One of the opponents of the Weeks-McLean Bill was Frank W. Mondell of Wyoming. In a speech delivered in the House, February 23, 1913, he declared:

This is, in my opinion, the most revolutionary, the most far-reaching legislation, in its possible and probable effect on our system of Government, that has been presented to Congress in the sixteen years during which I have been a member of this body. If this bill should become a law no man who voted for it would ever be justified in raising his voice, against any extension, no matter how extreme, of the police authority and control of the Federal Government.

It takes from the States control over everything that flies, save some birds of the grouse family, bats, and butterflies, and it authorizes a clerk in a bureau of the Agricultural Department to designate as crimes, punishable by imprisonment in Federal penitentiaries, the slightest infraction of the prohibitions contained in the bill against the capturing, the killing, or taking of any bird that flies anywhere in the Union save those few which never migrate.

Under this legislation a bureau of the Agricultural Department could promulgate a regulation having the force of law under which a farmer shooting a crow in his corn-field could be hailed before a Federal grand jury, indicted, fined and imprisoned—fined not exceeding $100 and imprisoned not to exceed six months. Regulations could be promulgated under which a barefooted boy in any state of the Union, snaring a lark or reed-bird, taking a shot with his air-gun at the smallest and most insignificant of the feathered tribe, could be indicted, tried, condemned, and immured in a Federal penitentiary....

Pass this bill and every barrier standing against the assertion of Federal police control in every line and with regard to every act and activity of the American people is broken down, and we no longer have a Government of self-governing States but are well on the way to an empire governed from this Capital.

These remarks were delivered with great vehemence.

However, in about ten days after this speech, viz., on March 4, 1913, the Weeks-McLean Migratory Bird Bill, having passed Congress, received the signature of President Taft and became a law. Money for its enforcement was necessary and $50,000 was placed in the hands of the Secretary of Agriculture for this purpose. One of his first duties, however, was to make and to promulgate regulations listing the migratory birds that could be killed, and stating when and how they might be taken.

The tentative regulations, prepared in the Biological Survey by Dr. T. S. Palmer, Dr. A. K. Fisher, and Wells W. Cook, were ready for distribution on June 23, 1913. Before becoming effective, they were advertised for three months to give the public time to study them and to register its opinion.

The Audubon Association was much pleased with the regulations, which extended protection to useful non-game birds in those states that had not as yet adopted the model Audubon Law. Robins were to be protected everywhere, thus finishing one of our special campaigns; and ducks could be killed for only three and one-half months each year. Furthermore, sixty-two species of water-birds, which had been heavily shot, were not to be taken for the next five years.

During the three months following the publication of the proposed regulations, public hearings were held by government officials in Omaha, Boston, New Orleans, Wilmington, and in Washington, D. C.

Strong objections were voiced in many places. What had the Government to do with birds when the laws of every state declared that they belonged to the people of the state in which they were found, and the courts had repeatedly upheld such statutes? In fact, some group was against every hunting restriction proposed. How were these malcontents to be satisfied? Secretary Houston needed advisers throughout the country to help him solve his bird-regulation problems both now and in the future. Who was to hold the bridge with him?

The answer was given in an Associated Press dispatch, issued from Washington, D. C., July 21, 1913:

The Department of Agriculture announces the selection of fifteen men prominent in the protection of game and other birds in various sections of the country to advise Secretary Houston in framing regulations to make the new Federal protection of migratory birds effective. To these men, who will serve without remuneration, will be referred certain questions arising in connection with the tentative regulations recently published by the Department in connection with the Act of March 4, which gives the Federal Government jurisdiction over the migratory birds of the United States.

The names of the fifteen appointees were as follows: John B. Burnham, New York, Chairman; F. W. Chambers, Utah; Prof. L. L. Dyche, Kansas; W. L. Finley, Oregon; E. H. Forbush, Massachusetts; Dr. George Bird Grinnell, New York; Dr. William T. Hornaday, New York; John F. Lacey, Iowa; Marshall McLean, New York; T. Gilbert Pearson, New York; George Shiras, III, Pennsylvania; George John C. Speaks, Ohio; W. P. Taylor, California; John H. Wallace, Alabama; and Major Bluford Willson, Illinois.

By Presidential proclamation the final draft of the regulations under the Weeks-McLean Law went into effect October 1, 1913, and with its meager appropriation the Biological Survey set out to see that they were observed.

The number of wardens which the Survey could employ to enforce the provisions of this law was extremely small, and naturally there were comparatively few arrests. Such cases as were made were turned over to the Department of Justice for prosecution.

The constitutionality of the Weeks-McLean Bill had been discussed for several years, and many briefs and opinions were published. The most formidable was by George Shiras, III. It was printed in *Forest and Stream* for November 24, 1906, and occupied thirty columns and contained more than 20,600 words.

Shortly after the regulations went into effect in 1913, Colonel Joseph H. Acklen of Nashville, Tennessee, received an appointment, without pay, as Chief Federal Game Warden. He was a lawyer and was one of those active friends of the new law who felt that a test case should be carried to the Supreme Court of the United States to determine its constitutionality. An opportunity soon came.

In Jonesport, Arkansas, there lived at this time a young man, Harvey C. Schauver, who occasionally indulged in the recreation of hunting. One winter's day he went gunning on Big Lake, but finding no ducks contented himself with shooting a couple of coots. He had shot coots in the past whenever he felt so inclined, just as did any other person in the region. Colonel Acklen learned of this act and calling on the young hunter advised him that he had broken the Federal law, as coots could not be shot as late as January 13th. Mr. Schauver was much surprised and at once said that he would go before the nearest Federal judge and plead guilty. This did not suit Colonel Acklen's plans, and he insisted that Schauver must plead not guilty, in order that whichever side won, the case might be carried to the Supreme Court. Reluctantly, Schauver agreed to this as a patriotic duty. Colonel Acklen, as the United States Game Warden, was to see that he was prosecuted and, at the same time, as President of a certain duck club, he was to provide the necessary funds for Mr. Schauver's defense. Everybody interested understood just why Colonel Acklen was proceeding in this manner. On May 27, 1914, the trial took place before Judge Jacob Trieber, presiding in the United States District Court at Jonesboro, Arkansas. The judge promptly declared the Migratory Game Law to be unconstitutional and dismissed the defendant. The case was appealed by the Government and in time reached the attention of the Supreme Court.

Mr. William S. Haskell, attorney for the American Game Protective Association, filed a brief for upholding the law. It was signed by thirty-eight conservation organizations. The Department of Justice assigned one of its staff, E. Marvin Underwood, to represent the Government before the Supreme Court.

At Mr. Underwood's request I aided him with data on various points, and on October 12, 1915, one year and nine months after Harvey Schauver shot those coots, his case came before the Supreme Court. I was with Mr. Underwood that day and heard him give his argument. That evening in his home, while we sat at dinner discussing the happenings of the day, he said that some of the Supreme Court Justices undoubtedly were hostile to the law. The questions they had asked, and the tone in which they spoke, convinced him that they were decidedly unfriendly.

Five months of suspense passed by, for the Supreme Court did not report on the Arkansas case until March 13, 1916, and even then it did not settle the question for which we so long had waited for an answer. The Court simply referred the case back to the Department of Justice, with an order that it be argued again.

The friends of the statute were not anxious for a rehearing of the Arkansas case and let the Department of Justice become aware of this fact. We knew that an adverse decision would destroy any hope of concluding a treaty approving the principle of government control of migratory birds.

Back in February, 1913, one month before the Migratory Game Law was enacted, Senator McLean of Connecticut had re-presented Senator Root's resolution calling for a treaty to protect migratory birds. It had been adopted, the President had taken action, Great Britain had indicated its willingness for a conference, and a treaty between these two countries had been drafted to protect birds migrating between Canada and the United States. Therefore, throughout the most of 1913, all of 1914 and 1915, and until late in 1916, the friends of wild birds were on the anxious bench. On the one hand, they were backing the Biological Survey in its efforts to organize bird-protective work under the Migratory Bird Law and contending in the courts to establish its constitutionality; while on the other hand the struggle went on to get the bird treaty adopted which would end all constitutional questions involving the Government's right to assume the guardianship of migratory birds.

The work of preparing the treaty had devolved upon the Biological Survey of the United States Government and the Commission of Conservation of the Canadian Government. Of course, these officials consulted with other people, and differences of opinion arose. One of these I shall mention. It seemed extremely important at the time but developments have shown that after all it did not matter very much one way or the other.

In discussing the time of year to be named during which ducks, geese and swans could be taken, I said to Dr. E. W. Nelson, Chief of the Biological Survey, and to Dr. C. Gordon Hewitt of the Canadian Commission of Conservation, that here was a golden opportunity to abolish all spring shooting of wild-fowl. They both heartily agreed and stated that this certainly was one of the important treaty provisions they had in mind. For several years this subject had been a perennial source of bitter contention in the State Legislatures of the land. Ducks were known to mate while on their winter feeding-grounds in the South, hence if they were shot during their spring migration many pairs would be broken and less young would be raised that summer. Game-conservationists, therefore, had become strong advocates of prohibiting the shooting of water-fowl after the 1st of February. Opposed to this view were numerous gunners who wanted to shoot ducks in spring as long as any could be found, and they had the active support of cold-storage operators and hotel men, who in those days constituted a formidable opposition, and often defeated conservation measures.

The actual wording of the treaty was to be prepared by the Biological Survey and sent to Canada, where Dr. Hewitt was expected to be the leading spirit in getting the Provinces lined up to support it. Everything proceeded as planned and, on June 23, 1915, the treaty was returned from Canada to Sir Cecil Spring-Rice, British Ambassador in Washington. The Arkansas case to test the constitutionality of the Migratory Game Law would have to be argued soon. Already more than a year had elapsed since the appeal was taken. If the case was heard and should be lost before the treaty was ratified, we probably never could get Congress to agree to such a treaty. The situation, therefore, was critical; but Sir Cecil was overwhelmed with matters connected with the World War, and forgot all about the treaty until the next spring when Dr. Hewitt got someone to jog his memory. Senator McLean, meantime, was eagerly waiting its arrival at the State Department so that he might bring it up in the Senate for adoption.

On March 8th Dr. Nelson wrote asking me to come to Washington at once. He had secured the treaty from Sir Cecil and it was now in his possession. Political pressure was demanding that it be amended so that either country could permit spring shooting of ducks and geese. I found him deeply troubled. He spoke of the urgency of getting Congress to approve of the treaty at once as any day the Supreme Court's decision might be announced and prevent its adoption; and yet he thought that if the treaty were not delayed long enough to prepare for the concession, the Middle West had sufficient influence to kill the treaty when it came up in the Senate. He said that John Burnham and various others agreed with him that as a war measure, it should be amended so that wild-fowl hunting would be possible until March 10th. He wanted me to use all possible influence to get other people to agree to his plan, and he wished me to urge Dr. Hewitt to have the Canadians accept such a change. To this I could not consent. It would keep open the whole spring-shooting question in the duck-shooting states and would mean no end of trouble. If we did not yield to this pressure, we could now stop spring shooting for all time in both countries.

A few days later Senator McLean, who was the leading spirit in bird protection in Congress, wrote me, "If it is a case of treaty this session, or an agreement to let the treaty conform to what the Secretary of Agriculture is bound to grant anyway, it may be wise to concede." Other co-workers expressed the same sentiment.

Much of the demand for a spring-shooting clause was coming from Illinois and Missouri, but other Western states, also, were shouting for the same change. I received on March 26th a telegram from the Des Moines County [Iowa] Game Protective Association, consisting of "sixteen hundred hunters of southern Iowa," which said: WE STAND PAT FOR A MIDDLE ZONE TO INCLUDE IOWA OPEN SEASON ON DUCKS, GEESE, AND SO FORTH, OCTOBER 1 TO MARCH 31, AND OPEN SEASON TO APRIL 15 ON SNIPE.

On April 21st State Conservation Commissioner Shireman of Indiana advertised in the Indianapolis *News* that he would receive petitions from sportsmen asking for spring shooting and would forward these to Washington.

The Middle West continued its bombardment. Congressmen and Senators were constantly calling on Mr. Houston, Secretary of Agriculture, and demanding that he should assure their constituents that they could have their wishes in this matter.

Finally, the Secretary told Dr. Nelson very plainly that the people of the dissatisfied Western region must be placated. Dr. Nelson, splendid man that he was, was in a frightful dilemma. He had long been opposed to the shooting of game birds during the mating season, and to be forced to yield on this point was wormwood to his soul. On the other hand, he was fully conscious that the fifty-two Congressmen who had requested him to provide for spring shooting probably could cause the elimination of all appropriation for the Biological Survey. I contended that he had overestimated the strength of the Congressmen who had talked to him and to Secretary

Houston, and at length said that, while the Audubon Association had never publicly attacked the Survey, I was determined to recommend that we do so on this point unless within two days he should assure me that the date February 1st would be retained in the treaty. He replied on April 3, 1916, that he was coming to New York at once and asked if I would not call a meeting of the Executive Committee of the Audubon Association.

Six of the directors, gathered informally in the American Museum of Natural History, heard his story. Frankly he told us he was faced with the question of giving these mid-western Congressmen what they wanted or of running the very great risk of having the Biological Survey abolished. He reminded those present that two attempts to eliminate the Biological Survey by cutting off appropriations had failed only by narrow margins. He gave us a long list of people whom he said had agreed not to fight him in this critical situation, and he asked for our support to help him in his stand against those who still opposed the position he felt he must take.

I said that two or three men in Missouri, whom I named, were back of all this trouble, and that they had stimulated a temporary, artificial interest in the minds of the Congressmen who had approached him. If an attempt was made to destroy the Survey, the Audubon Association could again engineer a fight for its defense, and we would let the public know why his Bureau had been attacked. I urged that we all stand by our guns.

The directors who were present had painful memories of the former congressional attempts to eliminate the Government's only bureau that was functioning in national bird-protection work. Therefore, they took the view that we should not attempt to force Dr. Nelson into limiting to February 1st the duck-season provision in the treaty, for the Survey must be maintained at any reasonable cost. Dr. Nelson had gone over my head by appealing to the Board and their action necessarily ended my agitation on the subject.

E. H. Forbush of Boston for years had been a most active anti-spring-shooting advocate. Upon learning that the Audubon Association would not further oppose Dr. Nelson's plan for changing the treaty, he at once filed his resignation as our New England representative, raised some money by solicitation from Dr. Hornaday and others, and employed Dr. George W. Field of Boston to go to Missouri and Illinois to find out just how strong was the opposition to the "February 1st" clause.

Dr. Nelson soon sent the treaty back to Canada, amended to permit spring shooting of wild-fowl. Then one day a message came requesting that I come to Washington at once. Upon arrival, he told me that Dr. Field's investigation had confirmed my opinion that the opposition from the Middle West was not important, and he wanted me to wire Dr. Hewitt and tell him to have the treaty changed again so there could be no shooting after February 1st.

"Why don't you wire him yourself," I asked in some bewilderment, "you are the government official handling these matters?"

He replied that Hewitt and I were close friends, that Hewitt was much put out with him for his former change of position, and that he thought I had better handle the matter. Within five minutes I had dispatched a telegram to Ottawa. This was on July 8, 1916. Dr. Hewitt's reply came from Banff. He had given up hope when the amended treaty came back from the Biological Survey so it had been signed and mailed to Washington before my wire reached him. And that is the story of why it is written in the treaty for the protection of migratory birds of Canada and the United States, that either country, at its pleasure, may permit the shooting of "ducks, geese and swans" as late in spring as March 10th. But, and this really is the important point, except in a few

Canadian Provinces, neither country operating under this treaty has permitted the killing of wild-fowl later than January 15th.

The difficulties encountered in the securing of the Weeks-McLean Migratory Bird Law and the Treaty which followed are examples of those that have arisen in attempts to accomplish virtually all national legislation intended to protect wild-life. There has always been the opposition of commercial interests and ever there have been the wiles of politicians to contend with. Usually, disagreements also have arisen among the proponents of these measures, which have not helped the cause. Always there have been those who have sought to draw attention to themselves by attacking those prominently active in conservation movements.

The Migratory Bird Treaty made by Great Britain and the United States was ratified in Washington, D. C., December 7, 1916, and was proclaimed the next day. It had taken hard fighting over a period of three years and eight months to bring this about. The Arkansas case that was to determine the constitutionality of the Weeks-McLean Law was now dropped by the Supreme Court, and the law itself was soon forgotten.

In order that a treaty may become operative, it is necessary for Congress to pass an Enabling Act, authorizing some Department of Government to see that its provisions are enforced. A fisheries treaty between Canada and the United States, ratified in 1908, has lain dormant ever since because Congress has not adopted an Enabling Act.

On January 13, 1917, Representative Flood and Senator Hitchcock both introduced enabling bills for the Bird Treaty. From then until March 4th, when Congress adjourned, I and others spent much time in Washington working with Senators and Congressmen. A special session of Congress was called in April and after a prodigious effort the Hitchcock Bill was passed on July 30th, but nearly a year

was to go by before we could get it through the House of
Representatives, although John Burnham and many others
labored constantly at the task. The Enabling Act became a
law upon receiving the signature of President Wilson on
July 3, 1918.

Thus, at last, the long campaign to get the Government to
assume protection of migratory birds was ended. The first
shot had been fired by George Shiras, III, on December 5,
1904, and victory came after thirteen years, five months and
two days. Thousands of people, in one way or another, had
been engaged in the endless series of contests in its behalf,
and many had rendered signal service at critical moments. If
ever an attempt is made to record the names of those who,
in the United States, played the most active and effective
parts in the long campaign, the list should be headed by
George Shiras, III, John B. Burnham and George P. McLean.

Chapter XVII

BATTLING FOR THE WILD-FOWL

THE INCENTIVE for shooting ducks and geese in wholesale numbers came abruptly to an end in 1918, when the sale of wild-fowl became illegal in the United States under the Migratory Bird Treaty Act. For the next two or three years much was heard of the increase of wild-fowl throughout the continent. The downward sweep in their numbers had been checked and an upward turn was apparent on the waters they were wont to frequent, since the devastating market-hunter was no longer abroad in the land. Conservative hunters looked forward to a continuation of their sport without apprehension, and thought with pleasure that their sons also would be able to shoot ducks when they became men. This feeling pervaded the country and expressions of thanksgiving were loud and cheerful.

However, another menace to the wild-fowl was rising like a dark cloud in the West. Many had seen and commented on it, but it was Dr. E. W. Nelson of the Biological Survey, who focused public thought on what was happening in regions where the bulk of the wild ducks breed. Thousands of sloughs, lakes and marshes were being drained to provide more lands for agricultural uses. Sixty million acres of more or less cultivable land had already been reclaimed and the nesting and feeding areas of many water-birds had thereby passed away. The whooping crane and the trumpeter swan had lost many of their breeding-grounds, and incidentally, meat- and feather-hunters had almost completed the extermination of these species in North America.

At a conservation convention in Ottawa, held February 18-19, 1919, Dr. Nelson made an address on this subject, which resulted in the launching of another national campaign for wild-fowl preservation. He urged that plans be devised for preserving numerous lakes, sloughs and marshes, such a program being necessary if the ducks and geese were to survive. Their nesting regions were disappearing, also duck food was growing scarce. Already it was reported "in some places wild-fowl are dying of starvation."

State and Federal authorities, as well as engineers and land speculators, were engaged in a wild orgy of ditch digging. In 1921 and 1922 attempts were made in Congress to pass bills providing for more than a billion dollars to be used for draining swamps and marshes to provide lands for rehabilitating World War veterans.

Dr. Nelson wanted the Canadian and the United States governments to acquire title to many lakes and marshlands, and to preserve them for birds, fish and fur-bearing mammals. He stated that prompt action was necessary since, in addition to drainage activities, the best of the remaining duck areas, especially in the United States, were rapidly being purchased by wealthy men for private shooting-clubs. Besides acquiring refuges, he wanted our Government to purchase some swamps and marshlands where the public was accustomed to hunt, and have these patrolled by wardens to enforce the hunting laws now being flagrantly violated. He suggested these places be called "public shooting-grounds."

To provide money to carry out these plans, a Federal hunting-license costing one dollar was proposed. This would be in addition to the state shooting-license which, by then, was generally required everywhere.

Mr. George A. Lawyer drew a bill to put Dr. Nelson's suggestions into effect. It was approved by many organizations interested in the preservation of bird life, the Audubon Association among others.

The American Game Protective Association, having so successfully led the legislative campaigns for the enactment of the Federal Migratory Bird Law, for the adoption of the treaty with Canada, and for the Migratory Bird Treaty Act, was, very naturally, asked by Dr. Nelson to sponsor this new undertaking. The bill was placed in the hands of its President, John B. Burnham, in January, 1921.

What was known as the "Public Shooting Grounds-Game Refuge Bill" was introduced in the Senate by Senator Harry S. New, on March 2, 1921, and three days later Representative Dan Anthony presented it in the House.

Its main provisions were three in number:

First, to establish a "Migratory Bird Refuge Commission," consisting of the Secretary of Agriculture, the Attorney-General, the Postmaster-General, two Senators and two members of the House of Representatives. This Commission was authorized to pass on proposed areas of land and water designed for refuges or public shooting-grounds and to establish the price which should be paid for them. Also, the Secretary of Agriculture was empowered to accept gifts of such useful lands and waters as might be offered to the Government. For many years, Senator Sheppard of Texas had vainly tried to secure a law authorizing the acceptance of such gifts from private individuals.

Second, to require a Federal hunting-license for shooting migratory birds, this to be purchased at post-offices. The form which it would take was left to the Postmaster-General and to the Secretary of Agriculture. Their Departments agreed to issue the license in the form of a stamp that could be affixed to a state hunting-license. Mr. Belmore Browne, a well-known nature artist, drew a design for the stamp which was acceptable to the authorities.

Third, to use 45 per cent of the money collected for the Federal hunting licenses in the purchase or rental of land- and water-areas and for their administration. Forty-five per cent was to go for enforcing the provisions of the two important Federal laws then in existence for wild-life protection, viz., the Lacey Act, and the Migratory Bird Treaty Act. The remaining 10 per cent was to cover cost of issuing licenses and other items.

As was to be expected, strong opposition was soon manifested. We would have thought that something was amiss if such had not been the case. I have never known an important bird-protection bill that was not bitterly fought. The opposition came from two sources, one composed of persons who maintained that as the American Game Protective Association had been organized and was maintained in large degree by the manufacturers of arms and ammunition, the bill it was sponsoring must be, of necessity, a thinly veiled plan to exterminate all the ducks and geese, and therefore must be defeated.

To support this claim they pointed to the "public shooting-grounds" feature of the bill, declaring that, if enacted, it would greatly increase "legalized slaughter of ducks" and hence increase the sale of ammunition. As a matter of fact, it would have the opposite effect because many marshes on which there had been little or no restraint in shooting would be taken over by the Government, and the laws strictly enforced by a special warden service. That Congress did not take the view that the public shooting-grounds feature of the bill was a matter to be condemned, was shown by its action when it voted money to acquire the great Bear River Marsh Reservation and the Upper Mississippi River Bird and Fish Refuge, both of which specifically called for public shooting-grounds. In these matters they were following a plan which in various states had proved to be beneficial to the wild game supply.

Most of those who opposed this provision were without experience in such conservation problems, and many had been misled by the propaganda of some who knew better but who nursed personal grudges against the chief sponsors of the bill.

I recall one story that the Audubon Association was receiving large gifts from the gun manufacturers in return for its influence in behalf of this bill; when, in fact, the officers and directors of the Association, as well as the membership generally, supported it warmly; and the Audubon Association subscribed liberally to the American Game Protective Association for its campaign expenses.

The second group of opponents to the bill was particularly dangerous because it was composed of men informed on all the points involved, and with influence potent in Congress. They were the state game officials in states bordering on the Great Plains and extending westward to the Pacific Ocean. In that region are situated many of the National Parks and enormous territories are covered by National Forests. Government agents were in charge of these properties. Then, too, there were many Federal men administrating the unpopular Volstead Act operating under the Eighteenth Amendment.

"There are more government agents, inspectors, rangers, and snoopers of various kind in my State than there are state employees," one Governor said to me, "and we do not want any more such men running about the country." "Increasing Federal domination," was a term of bitterness used with great frequency in the Bad Lands, the Rocky Mountains, and among the orange-groves of sunny California.

Western outdoor men liked the idea of bird refuges and public shooting-grounds, but many shied off from this bill in Congress. The members of the Western Association of State Game and Fish Commissioners, formed in 1919, began to fight it, and were a solid block of opposition. They felt that they could handle their own duck problems without the aid of Federal wardens. It was natural, therefore, that soon various Western Senators and Representatives in Washington, who had been supporting the measure, should begin to talk against it.

Mr. Will H. Dilg, President of the Izaak Walton League of America, first supported the bill and then joined its enemies, as did Dr. William T. Hornaday.

On August 20, 1925, matters between the warring elements came to a head at a convention of state and Provincial game commissioners and representatives of conservation organizations held in Denver. It was not convenient for me to attend, but J. B. Harkin, Commissioner of the National Parks of Canada, who was to preside, insisted that I should be there, since my personal relations with the contending groups were fairly good, and he hoped that I might play the rôle of peacemaker.

Never have I attended a convention where so many groups opposed one another as at this gathering held in the Capital City of Colorado. A gleaming spear was poised at every tepee entrance.

The first night in Denver many of the leaders assembled in my room for a conference, but soon adjourned to the more commodious quarters occupied by Ray Holland, editor of *Field and Stream*.

The Chairman of the Izaak Walton League's Board of Directors, George Selover of Minneapolis, was there. The League, which claimed a membership of 140,000, was split wide open on the matter of supporting the refuge bill. The directors favored it while Dilg and a large personal following were opposing it with great vigor. The directors had instructed Dilg not to attend the Denver meeting, but just the same he was there with a considerable band of supporters from Oklahoma and elsewhere. So satisfied was he that his ideas on the question were correct, that he would listen to no suggestions of a compromise, and that night flatly refused to come to the conference presided over by Mr. Harkin.

An outstanding figure in the room was David Madsen,

Game Commissioner for the State of Utah. He was the influential leader of the Western Association of State Game and Fish Commissioners. He said that, although he and his associates regarded the Game Refuge Bill as an important one, they could not support it because of certain objectionable features. He then stated that their hostility now was based not so much on the prospect of having more Federal officers in their states as it was on the idea of paying a dollar for a Federal hunting-license.

After some hours of discussion an agreement was reached and approved by all present. Mr. Madsen said that if, after serious efforts had been made to amend the bill in the way he urged, it should be found that this could not be done, he would support it as it now stood. His associates in the room joined in this promise. No understanding could be reached with Dilg and one or two other opposing elements; therefore, we went forward in our plans without them.

The next day, as Chairman of the Resolutions Committee, I presented for the approval of the convention our caucus plan to amend the bill by providing that a state representative should be on the Migratory Bird Refuge Commission in each state where it should operate; and further to arrange that the expenses for carrying out the provisions of the bill should be met either by direct appropriations of Congress or by the use of the existing excise tax on arms and ammunition.

The following resolution was at once adopted:

RESOLVED, That the action of the officers of the International Association of Game, Fish and Conservation Commissioners, in conference with the Officers of the Western Association of State Game Commissioners, in accepting in principle the amendments to the Federal Game Refuge Bill offered by Commissioner D. H. Madsen, of Utah, is hereby approved by this Convention:

AND BE IT FURTHER RESOLVED, That the Western Association of the State Game Commissioners, the International Association of

Game, Fish and Conservation Commissioners; the American Game Protective Association; the National Association of Audubon Societies and the Izaak Walton League, are requested each to appoint one member of a Committee of five for the preparation and the submission to Congress of the bill in accordance with this Resolution.

There were many expressions of pleasure that an agreement had been reached, so that all interested parties could work together. Mr. Dilg, catching the spirit of the moment, arose and shouted, "The hatchet is buried—buried so deep it can never be dug up again."

The Committee was appointed, met in the offices of the Audubon Association in New York, where it organized, and then proceeded to Washington. We labored assiduously with members of the House and the Senate Finance Committees, but every one said that Congress would not make any large appropriation if part of it was to be used for Federal warden service.

A few weeks later the Ways and Means Committee of the House granted us a hearing. Mr. Selover was ill; Mr. Madsen was in far-off Utah; Mr. Adams was busy; and Mr. Burnham was otherwise engaged, so, as Chairman of the Committee, I journeyed to Washington to tread the winepress alone before the Congressional Committee. I requested that the tax on arms and ammunition be allowed to stand, so that we could later ask the appropriations committees to provide that the $3,000,000 or more accruing from this source should be used to enforce the Federal game-laws and to purchase bird refuges and public shooting-grounds.

My talk was not received with any marks of enthusiasm, and upon leaving the room Representative Robert L. Doughton followed and told me that there was no hope for our plan since word had come from the White House that all the "nuisance taxes" created during the World War were to be repealed.

The Committee formed at Denver had attempted to do the work for which it had been appointed. It had failed, therefore it disbanded. The next year, on January 21, 1926, it was again called into existence by the National Conference on Out-door Recreation during its meeting in Washington, D. C. For two more years we struggled on in efforts to pass the bill.

Mr. David Madsen kept his word and supported the measure loyally. So did the other Western game commissioners, until something occurred in California that upset them again. This was a law adding another dollar on the cost of the state hunting license. This extra dollar was to be used by the California Game Commission to purchase state-owned wild-fowl refuges. Game Commissioners of other Western states saw in the adoption of such a plan a chance for them to get more money. They could easily use such an extra dollar or two in their work, but they could not expect their legislatures to grant this if an additional dollar for hunting was to be collected by the Government. Therefore, their support for the Federal license law faltered, then ceased, and the West again was in revolt. Thus the joy of the victory at Denver had turned to ashes.

Five years had elapsed since the first refuge bill had been brought before Congress. Each session of that body had seen it re-introduced, always with some changes. It had been passed by both Houses but not at the same session, so it had not yet become a law. Dr. Nelson, still seeing more and more marshlands drained, millions of ducks dying in polluted waters from some unexplained disease (now known to be botulism), annually disappointed because Congress continued to provide only enough funds for him to employ twenty-four wardens when he needed several hundred, opposed by various game commissioners, and constantly criticized and berated by a few noisy objectors who claimed that they were the true conservationists, still pinned his hope to this bill

as the only possibility of alleviating a situation daily growing more acute.

Senator Norbeck was handling the bill in 1928 as it lay
quiescent in the Senate, when one day I read in a Paris
paper that he had introduced a substitute bill calling for an
authorization of $7,875,000 to be used to purchase and main-
tain inviolate sanctuaries for migratory birds, and that the
bill had passed the Senate on April 18th. I at once cabled the
office of the Audubon Association to give it every support if
it came up in the House before my return.

Upon landing at New York, I learned that the American
Game Protective Association and other Eastern organizations were still backing the old bill.

An important gathering had been called to meet in Seattle
August 27-28, 1928. It was a combined gathering of the two
associations of game commissioners. Many officers of conservation organizations also would be present. Upon reaching
Seattle, I. T. Quinn of Alabama, President of the International Association of Game, Fish and Conservation Commissioners, said to me that the country was split wide open on
the subject of the two refuge bills.

"We are in for the biggest bear fight here you ever saw,"
he declared, "and you have been appointed Chairman of the
Resolutions Committee to handle the matter."

This was three years after the love feast in Denver, but
the hatchet had been dug up again despite Mr. Dilg's reas-
suring prophecy.

I at once decided on an unusual procedure, which I
asked Quinn to help me carry out. Therefore, the next morning when the convention opened, he announced that in the
evening the Resolutions Committee would hold a hearing on
the two conservation bills pending in Washington, and all
delegates were invited to be present and to take part in the
discussions.

They all came, as did many people from the city. I explained that the committee desired the opinions of those present as to just what kind of a resolution we should later bring to them on the subject of pending wild-life legislation in Congress. Lively debates followed but when adjournment came near midnight, unanimous votes had been taken on all the points discussed and every one had agreed to support the new Norbeck Bill, calling for the appropriations of funds to be used to establish and maintain inviolate sanctuaries. Every one seemed to be in a good humor; a fight on the convention floor had been averted, and we were all going to work together.

At the public session next day I presented the following:

BE IT RESOLVED, That the International Association of Game, Fish and Conservation Commissioners and the Western Association of State Game Commissioners representing the official state game departments in twenty-eight states which are here present and voting, do hereby jointly endorse in principle the provisions of the Norbeck Bill as approved by the United States Senate in April, 1928; and be it further resolved that to carry out the wishes of this joint convention in the matters recited above and to represent them and other organizations interested in wild bird and animal protection, and for the purpose of representing these several organizations in other Congressional efforts that may be attempted to further protection of our wild mammals and birds, there be and there is hereby created the "National Committee on Wild Life Legislation," consisting of eleven members to be selected as follows:

One to be appointed by each of the following organizations:
> International Association of Game, Fish and Conservation Commissioners,
> Western Association of State Game Commissioners,
> The American Forestry Association,
> American Game Protective Association,
> Izaak Walton League of America,
> National Association of Audubon Societies,

and that this Committee so created shall have power to add to its number five additional members selected at large throughout the United States.

The resolution was adopted by acclamation. Mr. G. H. Radebaugh of Illinois at once presented another from the floor:

I move you that a vote of thanks be extended to this Committee for its work in connection with the presenting to this convention of a resolution which, to my mind, is one of the most important contributions that this convention can make to the wild life of America. Certainly in this resolution they have presented to the United States one of the most important constructive programs that we could follow. I wish to congratulate them, and I make a motion that a vote of thanks be extended to them.

This was voted with hearty indications of approval.

On October 12, 1928, the National Committee on Wild-Life Legislation was officially organized in Washington, D. C., as follows: T. Gilbert Pearson, Chairman; Carlos Avery, President, American Game Protective Association, Vice-Chairman; Seth E. Gordon, Conservation Director, Izaak Walton League of America, Secretary; John C. Phillips, President, The American Wild-Fowlers, Treasurer; E. Lee LeCompte, of the International Association of Game, Fish and Conservation Commissioners; Roland G. Parvin, Director of the Western Association of State Game Commissioners; George D. Pratt, President, The American Forestry Association; Keith McCanse, Game and Fish Commissioner of Missouri; Gustavus D. Pope, of Detroit; I. T. Quinn, Game and Fish Commissioner of Alabama; and I. Zellerbach, President, California Fish and Game Commission.

Congress would meet in December for the "short term" which then still preceded the installation of the newly elected President on March 4th. Would it be possible to get the House of Representatives to take action during the less than ninety days it would actually hold sessions? If not, then the bill would automatically die with adjournment on March 3rd.

"You do not have more than one chance in a hundred of getting it passed in this short time," Dr. Nelson wrote me. With all of our conservation associations and with virtually every State Conservation Department behind us, we went to work. We had the usual noisy opposition, but it was ineffective. Dr. John C. Phillips, the Committee's Treasurer, worked for the sinews of war, to pay for circulars, postage and other necessary items. Mr. Seth Gordon, the Secretary, was young, resourceful and abounding in enthusiasm. The other members of the Committee were active in their separate spheres of influence.

The bill which had passed the Senate in April was in the hands of the House Committee on Agriculture of which Gilbert N. Haugen was the Chairman. It contained a clause requiring the Secretary of Agriculture to give the Federal bird sanctuaries, as established, to the states, if they so requested. It also provided that the Government must annually provide the states with money to maintain such sanctuaries. These features had to be eliminated or they would kill the bill in the House. Therefore, on December 6th a group of us called on Chairman Haugen and urged that this change be made in Committee. He asked the opinion of the Secretary of Agriculture, whose reply confirmed our contention, and the offending "Section 17" was stricken from the bill.

On December 10th I again appeared before the Committee by invitation. The next week, with Messrs. Avery, Gordon, and Pratt, I presented arguments to General Lord, head of the Budget Bureau, and urged that the administration consent to the authorization of the appropriations asked for. This request was granted nine days later. On January 21st I once more attended a meeting of the Agricultural Committee, this time with members of the Biological Survey. We were there to answer questions.

Nearly two months of our precious short period had passed

when, on January 24th, the Agricultural Committee reported
the amended bill favorably to the House, and Representative
August H. Andresen of Minnesota went into action in its
behalf.

This was the signal for which we had been waiting. Mr.
Gordon and I had been working day and night for many
weeks, lining up support over all the country. Other members of the National Committee had been getting the conservation societies and civic clubs of various kinds ready to
strike when the time came. Mrs. Katherine Tippetts, the
unusually effective Chairman of the Conservation Committee
of the General Federation of Women's Clubs, had explained
the situation to every state and local conservation committee
chairman in that great organization, and they all understood
what was expected of them when the precise moment for
action should arrive.

The day the bill was reported to the House, a few telegrams sent from the room Gordon and I occupied in the
Cosmos Club served to cut the props, and during the next
three weeks a flood of letters and telegrams from petitioners,
estimated to number from 200,000 to 300,000, deluged the
desks of the members of the lower House of Congress. On
February 9th the bill came up under special rule. Mr.
Andresen made a forceful presentation and it passed by a
vote of 219 to 0. Congressmen were willing to vote for expenditures from the national treasury as this would provide
money to be spent among their constituents, but a license
would have been a direct tax imposed on the men back home
whose votes they were loath to jeopardize.

A few days later Senator Norbeck suggested that he, Representative Andresen and I call on the President and see how
he felt about signing the bill. Mr. Coolidge listened to us and
said, "I feel inclined to sign it, but I don't know where the
money is to come from." His signature was affixed on February 18, 1929, and upon receiving the pen he had used, I

gave it, in the name of the National Committee on Wild-Life Legislation, to Chief Paul G. Redington for the Biological Survey.

Thus was passed the "Migratory Bird Conservation Act," which was an outgrowth of the old "Public Shooting Grounds Game Refuge Bill." It authorized appropriations of nearly $8,000,000 for the acquisition of feeding, nesting and resting areas for wild-fowl. It became a law just exactly ten years to the day from the date Dr. E. W. Nelson started the campaign for refuges in his address in Ottawa. It could never have passed Congress but for those long years of public education carried forward by many earnest men and women.

Following the then prevailing governmental custom, the Migratory Bird Conservation Act contained no item of appropriation to carry the law into effect. It did carry an "authorization" for $75,000 the first year, $200,000 the second year, $600,000 for the third year, and $1,000,000 a year for the succeeding seven years. Therefore, each of these annual appropriations would have to be secured by separate acts of Congress. Such aid as our National Committee could give was freely rendered, but the task was mostly a government departmental matter. After $275,000 had been appropriated, Congress became economical in its support for the birds, and the entire appropriations for acquiring sanctuaries the next five years amounted to only $1,225,050. With these sums the Biological Survey acquired something more than a million acres for water-fowl refuges.

During all these years the Federal game-warden force has been but slightly augmented. When, in 1931, our National Committee on Wild-Life Legislation was pleading with the Chief of the Bureau of Budget for $600,000 authorized that year for sanctuaries, we also made the strongest representations we could for $100,000 for additional Federal game-wardens—$25,000 was granted. At that point all increases for

Federal game-law enforcement ceased, despite the fact that a great "racket" in the bootlegging of wild-fowl had come into existence, that duck-hunters every year were increasing by tens of thousands, and that nesting and feeding areas for wild-fowl were daily diminishing. Nothing further occurred for the next three years.

By 1934 the duck situation had become appalling. The terrific drouth in the Western states and the prairie provinces had destroyed the great majority of the remaining breeding-places of our most common species, and shooting continued much as in former years. When it seemed that the end was near and the day rapidly approaching when the sable rangers of the clouds would drop down to fight over the bones of the last of the emaciated wild-fowl, amazing events suddenly began to happen.

On March 16, 1934, the Walcott-Kleburg Duck Stamp Bill became a Federal law, and that winter hunting-license stamps were bought to the amount of $635,344, 90 per cent of which was to be spent for bird sanctuaries as provided for under the Norbeck-Andresen Act of 1929.

I had been one of those fighting in the Federal Advisory Board for some years to stop the commercialization of ducks on the wing. I had studied the wild-fowl situation along our Atlantic Coast for a thousand miles, and visited some of the best shooting marshes in Arkansas, Louisiana, Tennessee and California, and had seen how the ducks were decreasing. At first hand I examined the "duck pens" of the Sangamon and Illinois river bottoms, where thousands of men every year paid for the privilege of shooting ducks on little private artificial ponds—ducks that were lured to their death by yellow corn and quacking decoys, and I constantly urged that such practices be terminated.

And then, in 1934, came Jay N. Darling, America's famous cartoonist, to the position of Chief of the Biological Survey, and things began to happen. In 1935 he induced the President to issue a proclamation prohibiting the use of bait and decoys. During his brief stay in office he also managed to wrangle more than fourteen and one-half millions of dollars out of various government relief agencies for the use of creating water areas for wild-fowl. How incredibly large these sums seemed to some of us who for years had worked our hearts out with little gain—who, much like the fishermen of Galilee, had toiled all the night and caught nothing!

But Mr. Darling has no delusions about the feeding- and nesting-grounds of the wild-fowl being assured. On May 28, 1936, he wrote me: "While approximately fifteen millions of dollars have been secured from all sources for restoration of drained wild-fowl water areas during the years 1935-'36, during the same time over *two hundred million* have been allocated by the Government *to drain more water areas!*"

Let him who is gifted in reading the secrets of the crystal ball tell us what the future holds for North America's wild-fowl!

And now let us record something of the doings of the Federal Advisory Board. Harking back to the Migratory Bird Treaty Act of 1918, discussed in the previous chapter, it may be recalled that the President was empowered to promulgate rules and regulations stipulating at what times and under what conditions migratory game-birds could be taken. The Secretary of Agriculture who had to enforce those regulations, would suggest to the President what rulings he should authorize. The Secretary did not personally draft these regulations; this was done in the office of the Bureau of Biological Survey. As a liaison group between the Government and the public, the plan was adopted of having an "Advisory Board" to the Secretary identical in nature to the one set up under the Weeks-McLean Migratory Bird Act five years before.

I was one of those asked to continue as a member of the recreated Board, and I believe I am the only one who has served the Government in such a capacity through all political administrations since the beginning of the first Advisory Board in 1913.

The Secretary would call us together once a year—rarely any oftener. We would go to Washington usually with little or no idea of what changes in the regulations we were supposed to consider. Dr. Nelson, Chief of the Biological Survey, would come before us and read the changes he thought it wise to make, and generally gave a second list of suggested changes to which he was either opposed or indifferent. Mr. Burnham, the Chairman, was always in close touch with Dr. Nelson, and together they discussed beforehand the business to be presented. Frequently there were complaints from Board members who thought that they should be furnished with agenda well before the date of the meeting, but the general policy of non-communication with the Committee members continued until Dr. Nelson's retirement under the Government's age law in 1929. However, the Board at times voted regulations of its own proposing.

Usually discussions at these meetings centered around such subjects as what shooting seasons should be allowed for ducks, snipe, rails or doves in this or that region. The states were grouped in zones each with its own shooting season; but often the states were themselves divided, sometimes in a very complicated manner. As an example, I will quote from the printed regulations, issued in September, 1928. The phraseology was continued in the regulations for several years. On pages 2 and 3, this pamphlet states that the open season for shooting wild-fowl shall be from October 16th to January 31st:

In that portion of New York known as Long Island and in New Jersey, New Mexico, Arizona and that portion of Texas lying west and north of a line beginning on the Rio Grande River directly west of the town of Del Rio, Texas; thence east to the town of Del Rio; thence easterly following the center of the

main track of the Southern Pacific Railroad through the towns
of Spofford, Uvalde, Hondo; thence to the point where the
Southern Pacific Railroad crosses the I. & G.N.R.R., at or near
San Antonio; thence following the center of the track of said
I. & G.N.R.R. in an easterly direction, to the point of the City
of Austin, where it joins Congress Avenue, near the I. & G.N.R.R.
depot; thence across said Congress Avenue to the center of the
main track of the H. & T.C.R.R. where said track joins said
Congress Avenue, at or near the H. & T.C.R.R. in an easterly
direction. . . .

And the description of the metes and bounds of this favored
section of Texas goes on for nine more full lines of fine type
without a single punctuation mark more formidable than a
semicolon.

At our Advisory Board meetings, hunters accompanied by
their Senators or Representatives would often appear and
demand that the regulations in their particular part of the
country should be modified to give them and their friends a
better chance to kill migratory game-birds. Almost never
did any outsider come to the Committee and ask for further
restrictions on killing. Still there were plenty of people who
found fault with our work and engaged in the popular
pastime of throwing brickbats at public officials. With great
frequency I have known Dr. Nelson, and after him Chief
Redington, and then Chief Darling, to be criticized bitterly
for rulings that were made when I knew positively that they
had done all that the politicians would let them do for the
birds.

One of the many troublesome problems with which we
had to deal was the regulation regarding the number of
wild-fowl that could legally be killed in a day.

The first Federal bag limit affecting migratory game-birds
was promulgated July 31, 1918. This placed the number of
wild ducks that it was permissible to shoot in a day at twenty-
five, although any state could adopt a smaller limit if it so
desired. It almost precipitated a civil war in some states where

no bag limit on ducks had ever been required under state law. The Biological Survey and its friends were bitterly assailed by many hunters. "Why deprive the honest, law-abiding sportsman in this way when you do not provide enough wardens to prosecute the great mass of game-hog pot-hunters?" they wanted to know. The Survey had to stand much pressure from Congressmen on this subject, and for the next few hunting seasons it was touch and go as to whether this regulation would not have to be liberalized or even abandoned.

In 1923 a man who was then a member of the Advisory Board demanded that the Board recommend to the Secretary of Agriculture that the bag limit be cut in half, and, at the same time, the shooting season should be reduced by one-half. Of the other eighteen members present, only one supported this suggestion. We knew that the politicians would not let the Secretary grant such a request, and that such advice on our part would greatly increase the bitter opposition against game-protective measures then pending in Congress.

Thus, the bag-limit law continued to stand as originally drawn. On December 9, 1926, Dr. Nelson, as Chief of the Biological Survey, called together the members of the Advisory Board and told them what he had recently found concerning conditions in the West. Millions of water-fowl were dying from a deadly duck disease, and the numbers of hunters were increasing rapidly. He thought the time had come to cut the daily bag-limit on ducks from twenty-five to fifteen.

The Board at once agreed to this reduction and so advised the Secretary of Agriculture. As soon as the action became known a flood of opposition poured into Washington and various and sundry Congressmen hurried over to see Secretary Jardine, with the result that when the next pamphlet of shooting regulations appeared, the "Bag Limits" paragraph contained the same old item, "Ducks (except wood duck and eider duck) —twenty-five in the aggregate."

The ducks continued to decrease, but it was not until four years later, that is, 1931, that another attempt was made by the Biological Survey to have the daily bag-limit on ducks reduced. For that season the number a man might take in a day was reduced from twenty-five to fifteen. But still the supply moved downward, and the Audubon Association on July 31, 1931, issued a call for a nation-wide moratorium for one year on the shooting of ducks and geese. The Government, fully informed of conditions but not feeling prepared to stop duck-hunting entirely, took a long step by reducing the shooting season to one month. This aroused intense resentment on the part of many hunters, but the Secretary of Agriculture stood his ground, and that season no one legally hunted wild-fowl more than thirty days.

Soon we were to have an example of political influence being exerted in high places. Certain hunters, determined that the short shooting season should not stand another year, went over the heads of the officials who were supposed to handle such matters and directed their steps to the door of the White House. As a result there was soon produced a "Proclamation," signed by Herbert Hoover on February 12, 1932, revoking the order for one month's shooting season and restoring the former hunting period of not less than three months. The preparation of this paper was carried out in the most quiet manner, but fortunately there was a leak, and by the merest margin of events the proclamation was not promulgated for reasons which I shall let someone else divulge. The order had been printed and was ready for distribution. It bore the label: "U.S. Government Printing Office: 1932. No. 1989." The name of "Herbert Hoover" appears in large letters, and the document also was countersigned by "Henry L. Stimson, Secretary of State."

This amazing document lies before me now. I doubt if

twenty men have ever seen it. At least it appears that these facts have never before been made public. It was a close call for the ducks.

Of late the shooting season allowed is of thirty days' duration, and the daily bag-limit is ten for ducks and four for geese and brant. No geese and brant may be shot in the Atlantic States, and at no place may the wood duck, ruddy, canvasback, redhead, bufflehead, Ross's goose, or swan be killed.

If one is inclined to condemn the Biological Survey and the Advisory Board because they were not more productive in effective efforts to preserve wild-fowl, it would be well to recall how very recently the general public has reached the point when it gives wide-spread support to such matters. Mr. William Brewster, although in his day regarded as a stalwart game-protector, resigned as a director of the National Association of Audubon Societies in 1912 because I was advocating the passage of a bill pending in the Massachusetts Legislature to stop the sale of game! In no country have the people ever exhibited a keen interest in wild-life protection until the supply of the wild life has become seriously threatened.

There have served on the Advisory Board through the years many able and well-informed men. Some of the names that stand out in memory are: Dr. George Bird Grinnell, Edward Howe Forbush, Marshall McLean, John C. Speaks, George Shiras, III, William L. Finley, S. B. Locke, Seth Gordon, Judge Lee Miles, who in 1932 succeeded Mr. Burnham as the Chairman, William C. Adams, Dr. John C. Phillips, I. T. Quinn, L. L. Dyche, Alva Clapp, E. Lee LeCompte, Jay N. Darling, and others, all of whom have rendered distinct and useful aid in various fields of wild-life conservation.

During the past twenty-three years I have often been asked whether the Federal Advisory Board has been able to perform any very substantial service for the birds. Despite the many handicaps under which it has functioned, I believe that its work has been very worth while. The majority of its members have upheld the Chief of the Survey in his recommendations for needed restrictions in hunting, and often it has served as a sedative for turbulent groups of gunners who chafed under the regulations that were promulgated. Most of the members have stood for what they believed to be best for safeguarding the wild-life supply.

In all the government work there has certainly been no more discouraging, nerve-racking, disagreeable and hopelessly unappreciated job than that of being Chief of the Biological Survey—ever since the day when the Survey was first called upon to act as the Government's agent in making and enforcing regulations dealing with the hunting of migratory birds.

It would appear that in Canada the duties of this nature have not been so harrowing, at least the popularity of Hoyes Lloyd, Supervisor of Wild Life Protection for the Dominion, seem never to suffer a reverse.

CHAPTER XVIII

HORSEBACK AND AFLOAT

THE THREE principal Bureaus of the United States Government dealing with wild birds and mammals are the Biological Survey, the Forest Service and the National Park Service, each with its friends and critics and official red tape.

The national wild-life societies generally give these Bureaus their active support. Among the larger ones have been the American Bison Society, American Forestry Association, American Game Protective Association, American Planning and Civic Association, American Wild-life Institute, Camp Fire Club of America, Izaak Walton League of America, National Association of Audubon Societies and the National Parks Association. Besides these, many hundreds of state and local groups have rendered useful coöperation.

The Audubon Association, for more than thirty years, has made available to the Government such services as it could render. Occasionally I have been called upon by governmental agencies to perform some service in connection with legislation, warden and sanctuary activities, or requested to help in matters requiring field expeditions. In both the National Park Service and the Biological Survey I have for some years held commissions as "official collaborator."

In March, 1931, the Senate Special Committee on Conservation of Wild-Life Resources planned to examine the Okefenokee Swamp in south Georgia to determine its availability as a government wild water-fowl reservation. Mr. Paul G. Redington and I were invited to be members of the party and give our opinions on what was found. The Chairman of this Committee was that staunch conservation leader Senator Frederic C. Walcott. Other members were Senators Peter R. Norbeck, Key D. Pittman, and Harry B. Hawes.

The Havana Special was stopped one morning at Folkston, Georgia, and a welcoming committee of local citizens took us to a restaurant for a "shad breakfast." I doubt if any of these Senators had ever before had his breakfast served in eight little individual dishes, all alike and resembling a canary's bath-tub.

"What is this?" Senator Norbeck asked me, tentatively sticking his fork into one of his small dishes containing white, soft, granular food.

"Grits," I said. "The dish most frequently served in Geogia."

"Grits?"

"Melt some butter in it while it's hot, and try it," I urged him.

He took a little, then some more. I saw in his face indications of great inner satisfaction.

"Here," I called to the waiter, "please bring some more grits for this gentleman."

At that moment, I have since felt, the senior Senator from South Dakota became one of my most devoted friends.

Together we all flew here and there over the great swamp with its wooded islands and open areas of grassy, lily-padded water. It was thought we would see herons, coots and ducks, but flying 125 miles an hour at an altitude of 1,000 feet the only living creatures we saw were two turkey buzzards.

From the eastern edge of the Okefenokee the St. Mary's River flows to the Atlantic, forming on its way the boundary line between Georgia and Florida. From its western side meanders the headwaters of the Suwannee that in time reaches the Gulf of Mexico. At Suwannee Lake on the edge of the swamp, perhaps two hundred people gathered from the surrounding country to give the Senators an old-fashioned picnic dinner spread on a long table under the trees.

I saw a tall son of the swamp-lands with a gray fox and induced him to sell it to me. After all had eaten to repletion, the company gathered into a semi-circle and I commented on the reasons for the Senators' visit; and in an apostrophe to the fox said, as I cut the rope from his neck, "Go, little friend, and tell the other foxes and the deer and the bear, and the wild birds, that some of us dream of a time, soon to come, when in all the Okefenokee country they and their young will be safe from hunting-dogs, traps and guns."

Some of the country people whispered their amazement at this strange man who paid five dollars for a fox and then let it loose; but the cameramen and the newspaper reporters understood the action.

In small duck boats the Committee crossed Chase Prairie and went into camp for a few days at D. L. Hebard's lodge on Floyd's Island. Under the guidance of John H. Hopkins, local manager for the swamp, we made trips to various flooded prairies and their wooded islands. It is a realm of primitive beauty.

To me the science of world finance had always seemed vague and not easy to understand. One night, standing before the fireplace, Senator Pittman made us a speech on silver, which was most lucid and extremely interesting. What subject is not enthralling when discussed by a master?

The Committee reported to the Senate, "This immense area is not of primary value for migratory bird refuge purposes. However, it is unique in many ways and would make attractive and valuable sanctuary for all forms of wild life indigenous to this region." The Okefenokee is a magnificent wilderness and in full agreement with Francis Harper who long has fought for its preservation, I profoundly hoped for its acquisition as a wild-life refuge, and was greatly pleased when in 1936 the Biological Survey secured title to 300,000 acres of the territory.

When, on March 14, 1931, our expedition to the Oke-fenokee was ended, I went with Mr. Redington to examine Blackbeard Island Bird Reservation. The Secretary of Agriculture had asked me to do this and thus be prepared to help defeat a movement in Congress designed to turn the island into a summer resort. Mr. Howard Coffin, the owner of near-by Sapelo Island, accompanied us on the long walk over Blackbeard, where our sufferings from hunger would have been even greater but for the discovery of an ample oyster-bed when the tide went out of the creek.

Some of my trips have been to the Western states.

The most talked-of group of deer in North America is the Kaibab herd inhabiting the Grand Canyon National Game Preserve in northern Arizona. These animals pass the summer on an 8,000-foot plateau, roughly eighteen by forty miles in extent. In 1906, Senator Reed Smoot of Utah secured the passage of a bill by Congress creating the Grand Canyon National Game Preserve, which was to be administered by the Government Forest Service. This action resulted in giving to the Arizona Cattle Company practically the exclusive right of grazing cattle in the Kaibab. No deer could now legally be killed in the region.

The Government's campaign to destroy all predators, as a protection to the domestic stock, also helped preserve the deer. During the next eighteen years the Preserve yielded the skins of 674 cougars, 3,000 coyotes, and many wildcats. Relieved from both human and natural destroyers, the deer flourished, and by 1920 had become so numerous that the Forest Service decided some of them must be removed as their food supply was much depleted. But a complication arose. The Grand Canyon National Park had been created in 1919, and more than one-fourth of the southern portion of the Kaibab had been included within its boundaries. Wandering deer seen on a morning in the Preserve might that afternoon be found in the Park.

Mr. Stephen T. Mather, Chief of the National Park Service, loved animals but was without wide practical experience in handling stock and appraising range conditions. Therefore, when the Forest Service began talking about killing some of the Kaibab deer, Mr. Mather said "No," and one of those inter-bureaucratic disagreements, which often occur in Washington, came to a head. This was the situation when, in 1924, Henry C. Wallace, United States Secretary of Agriculture, took a hand, and a committee of men not connected with any governmental agency was sent to study the problem and to make recommendations as to what should be done about the perplexing issues. The Committee consisted of Hayward Cutting of the Boone and Crockett Club, T. W. Tomlinson, representing the American National Livestock Breeders' Association, John B. Burnham, and the writer.

From Marysvale, Utah, I traveled southward over the semi-desert plains and ridges for about 160 miles, and on the evening of August 16th went into camp with my companions at the Big Springs ranger station under the western rim of the Kaibab Plateau. We had been joined by S. B. Locke, of the Forest Service, who was to guide us on our journeys. Also he would see that the cook and the rangers should do their part in keeping the Committee happy. Major E. A. Goldman of the Biological Survey and Richard T. Evans of the Geological Survey, both well acquainted with the region and its wild life, completed the party.

During the next ten days we worked, usually on horseback. Some days we covered twenty-five miles of forest. We traveled through Indian Hollow, Quaking Asp Canyon, the Big and Little Saddle regions, up Parishawampitts Canyon and out on Greenland Plateau. We studied the country from Bright Angel to Jacob's Lake, and from the Canyon rim looked over on Powell's Plateau and the Cockscombs. With our field-glasses we swept the Houserock Valley and North Canyon. All typical areas of the Preserve came under our observation. We studied the condition of the trees and shrubs upon which the deer depended for browse, and observed the physical condition of the deer.

The forage situation was appalling. The snowberry, the service-berry and the dwarf ceanothus had been vastly over-utilized. The twigs on the lower limbs of the locust and the aspen were eaten away as high as a buck could reach standing on his hind legs. The cliff rose was dead over large areas because of excessive use. There was no young growth of any kind as sprouts were bitten off by the deer almost as soon as they came above the ground. The smaller scrub oaks had been ridden down and all foliage including the terminal buds had been removed.

A few of the deer were killed for examination. They were pitifully poor and in their stomachs were needles of the fir which deer ordinarily do not eat in quantity unless driven to do so by threatened starvation. There was little grass in the Kaibab and where this was found there was scant evidence that it had been disturbed, for the mule deer primarily is a browser, rather than a grazer.

We counted more than one hundred deer a day as we rode through the forest. The outlines of their ribs were clearly discernible and this at a time of the year when the animals should have been fat and robust. Many of the does with fawns were in a most deplorable condition, and many young had died.

There are a few treeless glades in the Kaibab. On the largest of these there was at one time a cattleman's ranch. His brand was V. T., hence to-day this open area is known as "V. T. Park." Here in the evening many deer came to graze on the few weeds to be found and on the stunted clover hardly more than half an inch high. One evening I drove for about twenty miles along the road that in part traverses V. T. Park, and counted 1,028 deer.

On August 25, 1924, we gave a hearing at the Russ Hotel in V. T. Park. Mr. Mather came and brought some men who had ranged cattle on the Plateau for years. No local man would venture to estimate that there were less than 50,000 deer in the Kaibab. Our final estimates, based on our observations, were that the number certainly ran well above 25,000 or 30,000.

While staying here at the hotel I noticed feathers of small birds at various places about the yard, and soon came upon a cat eating a bird. An hour later I saw that cat spring upon a red-backed junco and carry it under the house. I was told that this was the only cat on the Preserve. However, one bird-eating cat is one too many in an 800,000-acre forest. With the consent of the owner I carried it up the wooded slope, and John Burnham with his rifle walked beside me.

Upon concluding its studies, the Committee recommended that the deer should be reduced at the earliest possible moment by removing 50 per cent of them. We suggested: (1) Build corrals and catch deer in the autumn as they drift from the Forest down to their winter range among the piñons and sell these for restocking at actual cost of capturing and shipping; (2) If not enough can be removed by this means, permit sportsmen to enter under government supervision and kill 15,000 deer, half of which must be does; and (3) As a last resort, send in government hunters to shoot at sight the first 15,000 deer encountered and deliver their hides to the Indian agencies. Also, we recommended that the cattle, even though they now numbered less than 5,000, should be further reduced.

The substance of our report was wired to Washington, and at once corrals were ordered built, but only eighteen deer entered them. Many killed themselves trying to escape.

One was shipped but died before it reached its destination —exit plan No. 1, at least for this season.

Sportsmen were then invited to enter under strict government supervision. They took away only 675 deer, there being no great rush to hunt these forlorn bags of bones as a sporting proposition.

Governor Hunt of Arizona arose in his wrath and sent game-wardens to arrest any hunters who brought deer out of the Kaibab. The United States sought, and after long delay secured, a court injunction which prevented the State from further molesting the Government's agents in the discharge of their duties in handling the Kaibab deer problem.

There was much excitement over the shooting of Kaibab deer, and our Committee took a beating from many quarters, for our "heartless" and "inhumane" recommendations. Mr. Mather and others appealed to the people of the county through the press.

Various propositions were brought forward for driving the deer to other feeding-grounds, although on three sides of the Plateau the inhospitable desert stretched for a great distance and on the fourth side was the Grand Canyon, thirty miles across and a mile deep, with the Colorado River roaring along at the bottom. Congressman Hayden of Arizona wanted an army to be ordered there for the job, but the War Department refused to send troops for such a purpose. On October 18, 1924, Governor Hunt wired the Secretary of Agriculture, and asked that permission be granted to drive several thousand deer from the Kaibab to forests on the south side of the canyon.

The message was relayed to John Burnham and to me and perhaps to other members of the Committee, and our recommendations were requested. Mr. Burnham and I replied that in our opinion the plan was thoroughly impracticable but advised that the Governor be given permission to make such an attempt.

On December 14, 1924, the first drive was attempted, about forty men taking part. Mr. Zane Grey, who it was reported contemplated writing a story based on the drive, stationed himself with some friends on one of the Cockscombs to see the deer assembled and driven by them. But the deer declined to take a part in the parade. They slipped by the horsemen or around the ends of the line. Two days later the big drive was undertaken by 125 men of whom 70 were Navajo Indians, but the deer easily eluded them and soon were foraging among the great pines as usual.

One question I have never heard answered. In case it were found possible to collect a thousand or more deer into a herd and then to drive them away, how were they to be kept together when night came? It was planned to take them to forests on the other side of the Grand Canyon. Evidently, too, the deer were expected to swim the turbulent Colorado River!

Had we over-estimated the depleted condition of the Kaibab range? Were the deer actually on the verge of starvation? Major E. A. Goldman found the answer when he visited the Kaibab the next spring. From a letter he wrote to me I quote: "Certainly the deer that perished on the Kaibab the past winter would run into thousands, and 10,000 to 15,000 may not be too high an estimate. Certainly 90 per cent of the fawns of the previous season, as well as large numbers of does, have disappeared."

The problem of this deer herd continued to trouble the public mind. Various people declined to believe there was any necessity for killing them. Surely, they contended, in a region as large as the Buckskin Mountain there is plenty of food for all the deer that are left.

For six more years the Battle of the Kaibab raged. On one side were the Forest Service officials and their supporters; on the other were certain kind-hearted people, some of whom liked to refer to themselves as "true conservationists."

Then the Government determined to have another committee study the problem on the ground. Between the time of the former committee's report and the end of 1930, 1,907 fawns and 745 adult deer had been captured, of which a total of 1,173 had been shipped for stocking purposes. During the same time, 11,641 deer had been killed by sportsmen under government permits, and government employees had shot 1,124. No one knows how many thousands died of starvation or were destroyed by predatory animals.

This new investigating Committee was a large one and included men of various viewpoints. We met at V. T. Park on June 8, 1931, to begin work.

On the Committee were George D. Pratt, President of the American Forestry Association; Mark Anderson of the Izaak Walton League of America; Dr. E. R. Hall, representing the American Society of Mammalogists; K. C. Kartchner of the Arizona Game and Fish Commission; J. M. Macfarlane of the American National Livestock Association; A. A. Nichol of the Arizona Game Protective Association; Paul G. Redington, and myself. With us also rode nineteen others, including experts in western outdoor-life problems.

Our travels extending over a period of several days led us here and there through the forest for six hundred and fifty miles. We visited every section and saw the condition of every type of forest growth. The range was, if possible, even more depleted than I had seen it on my former trip and the deer were far less numerous.

We recommended that there should be no increase of the few thousand live stock remaining in the Preserve; that efforts be continued to eliminate the wild horses; that all trapping and shooting of predatory animals at once be stopped, and that the reduction of the deer herd should be continued to a point that would give the range a chance to recover. As Chairman of the Committee, I at once transmitted our report to Washington.

After this was made public, opposition to the Forest Service's policies in the Kaibab lessened considerably. However, there were those who had been shouting "conservation" so long that they could not readily bring themselves to substitute for it the very practical and very useful phrase, "game management."

The Forest Service estimated the Kaibab deer herd in 1935 at 17,000, which was still too many to permit the range to recover to a point that would make it possible for even that number to live in happiness.

The tragedy of the Kaibab deer herd has been reenacted in other places. In Pennsylvania, for example, deer were allowed to increase over much of the State until by 1927 their browse had become greatly depleted. That year Vernon Bailey counted more than 1,000 deer that in four townships had died of starvation. The total for the entire State must have run into very large figures.

The next season the State Game Commission, now thoroughly alarmed, permitted the shooting of does which for some years had been protected. The official returns showed that 26,690 deer were killed. The tremendous cry raised against the shooting of does gave the authorities no end of trouble. I gladly joined with others in explaining to the public why such a course was necessary. Many animal-lovers as well as many game-killers need to be taught sane principles of wild-life preservation. The State continued its policy of permitting does to be shot, yet to-day Pennsylvania has one of the heaviest deer populations of any state in the Union.

A similar situation developed in the Pisgah Game Preserve of western North Carolina, created under an authorization by Congress, October 17, 1916. The deer so increased that in ten years the forest showed unmistakable evidence of being over-browsed. The Preserve was surrounded by private shooting territories which had the effect of preventing the deer from spreading out to other regions. In 1932 the Pisgah Game Preserve was opened for hunting under state regulations. Many people, including some members of the Audubon Association, were aghast to learn that I approved of the action which the Forest Service and the North Carolina Conservation Department felt it necessary to adopt. The annual shooting of deer in the Pisgah Game Preserve still continues in 1936.

Scores of similar situations exist to-day in our country. Some of them are very acute and there is a crying need for their solution. These apply not only to deer but also to antelope, buffalo and elk. During the ten years ending in 1935, big-game animals in the National Forests have increased at least 100 per cent.

The National Parks of the United States contain some of the finest exhibits of wild life to be found in our country, and the Audubon Association, therefore, has taken a deep interest in National Park problems which have included numerous attempts by commercial interests to exploit them for personal gain. Congressman Addison T. Smith, of Idaho, in February, 1920, introduced into the Lower House a bill to make a reservoir in the southwest corner of Yellowstone Park. Bechler Meadows was to become an artificial lake to provide water to irrigate ranches in Idaho.

About the same time, Senator Thomas J. Walsh was sponsoring a bill to provide for damming the Yellowstone River, which would make a reservoir of Yellowstone Lake. The water was to be used for irrigation in Montana. The defenders of the parks sprang to arms and a committee representing various organizations was formed to defeat these raids. I collected a war-chest of more than $6,000 for the Committee's use. After a hard campaign the bills were killed by means of circulars, newspaper publicity, lectures, hearings in Congress and interviews with scores of Senators and hundreds of Representatives.

The Yellowstone National Park, lying chiefly in north-western Wyoming, had been created by Congress in 1872. The principal regions it was designed to include were the Yellowstone Lake, Grand Canyon of the Yellowstone River, Mammoth Hot Springs, and the basins containing the world-famous geysers. It was marked off on a chart as a rectangular area approximately sixty-two by fifty-two miles in extent. There was nothing natural about the boundaries. They ran over the tops of mountains and crossed box canyons, which in some places rendered administration difficult. Yet for fifty-seven years these lines remained unaltered.

In 1925, a Coördinating Commission on National Parks and National Forests, appointed by President Coolidge's Cabinet Committee on Outdoor Recreation, made a survey of the boundary lines. It recommended several changes which, with two exceptions, were approved by Congress early in 1929. One of the Commission's proposals not acted upon was that for excluding from the Park the land inside a double loop of the Snake River. The other was designed to take from the Teton National Forest and include in the Park a region of 340 square miles covering the country about Thorofare Creek and the upper Yellowstone River.

About the time this subject was before Congress, Repre-sensative Smith's plan to seize the Bechler Meadows for a reservoir was revived. In consequence, a joint resolution of the Senate and the House was passed, February 28, 1929, authorizing and directing the President to appoint a Yel-lowstone National Park Boundary Commission to inspect the south, southeast, and southwest boundaries and report their findings and recommendations.

President Hoover named the following commissioners: E. E. Brownell, California; Arthur E. Morgan, Ohio; T. Gil-bert Pearson, New York; Charles H. Ramsdell, Minnesota; and Arthur Ringland, Washington, D. C. Mr. Ovid M. But-ler, Secretary of the American Forestry Association, went with us as a guest. The Commission assembled at Cody, Wyoming, on July 15th, and held a public hearing in the courthouse that night. The room was filled to standing capacity and the talk went on from 8 P.M. until about 1 A.M. The idea of transferring from the National Forest to the Park 217,000 acres met with almost unanimous disfavor. The one exception was Irving Larom, a widely known public-spirited citizen of Wyoming, and President of the Dude Ranchers' Association.

The local people wanted the privilege of continuing to furnish horses and guides to big-game hunters who had been going into the region. If the land should be included in the Park, all hunting would be at an end. A transfer of land to the Park also would render it impossible ever to assess such lands for taxes, and Wyoming wanted all the tax money it could get.

Two days after the Cody hearing, the Commission went into camp one evening at the lower end of the southeastern arm of Yellowstone Lake, and at an early hour the next morning we were in saddle. We explored the wonderful valley of the upper Yellowstone, with its beaver and Shiras moose; we climbed to the heights above the sources of Thorofare Creek where herds of elk watched us curiously. We visited upland meadows, some of them marvelous wildflower gardens where no cow or sheep had ever grazed. We saw bears and caught trout with ease. Regional Forester R. H. Rutledge took me to see two bald eagles about their nest at Bridger Lake, and at night we listened to the coyotes howl as the moon rose over Hawk's Rest Mountain.

We climbed to a spur of the Absaroka Range, where it sloped sharply to the meadows several thousand feet below, and from which we could see along the winding Yellowstone many moose feeding in beaver ponds. As we crossed Two Ocean Plateau I left the party for half an hour to follow the movements of a pipit with food in its beak. We camped on the Snake River and near my tepee a white-crowned sparrow had hidden its nest.

We traversed the Continental Divide and worked down into Jackson's Hole from Big Game Ridge, crossing Pacific Creek and following the migration route of the elk that in autumn trek that way. We passed by the mountains where Dr. O. J. Murie was studying the food of the elk, and later we saw where many of these animals starve in winter on the barren hills of Buffalo Creek and the Gros Ventre, and where others fatten on the hay harvested in pastures bought for them by the Izaak Walton League and the Biological Survey. At Moran we met and talked with Harold P. Fabian, who was buying many unprofitable ranches which on the east faced Jackson Lake and the magnificent mountains of the Teton Park. He was an agent for John D. Rockefeller, Jr., and when these lands after being cleared of old houses and unsightly sheds were offered to the Park Service, politicians in Wyoming cried out at the loss of taxes this acceptance would entail. They do not want Mr. Rockefeller to give these lands to the Government; they want to force him to keep title so taxes can be collected for the State of Wyoming, and thus far (January 1, 1937) they have had their wish.

We visited the Bechler Meadows in the southwest corner of the Park. Here were more moose and deer and ravens, and a pair of screaming sandhill cranes. At Jackson we held a hearing on the proposed changes in the Park boundaries and gave another at Ashland, Idaho, where we were told of the need of water which could be supplied if the Government could be induced to relinquish the Bechler for a reservoir.

Throughout our journeys we were accompanied by a group of splendid helpers. They were from the Park and Forest Services and the Wyoming Game Commission. Of invaluable assistance at all times was Horace M. Albright, former Superintendent of the Yellowstone Park and at that time Director of the National Park Service. His knowledge of the region was very great.

After three weeks we returned to Mammoth Hot Springs Hotel to consider our problems, many of which I shall not even attempt to mention. But we could not agree on our report. Differences of opinion had arisen among some of the members and we were all too tired out to compose them. Therefore, on August 5, 1929, we separated for a time and each man went his way.

Six months later, upon call of the Chairman, Dr. Brownell, the Commission met in Washington, D. C., and on February 3, 1930, gave another hearing. Governor Emerson, United States Senators Kendrick and Sullivan, and Representative Carter, all of Wyoming, together with twenty others, presented testimony either for or against extending the boundaries of the Park and giving up the Bechler basin to Idaho.

That night we met in my room at the Cosmos Club, hoping to reach an agreement, but after four hours of debate decided to adjourn until the next night. In the end we agreed on a course of action and our report prepared in final form by the Secretary, Arthur Ringland, was presented to President Hoover on March 6, 1930. He in turn submitted it to Congress on January 5, 1931. It fills a book of 184 pages and contains various maps and the reproductions of many photographs.

We recommended taking into the Yellowstone Park eighty-two square miles of the upper Yellowstone River country which includes meadows, mountains and Bridger Lake with its fascinating surroundings. We urged that the Snake River loop of forty square miles and the Bechler Meadows of twenty-seven square miles be retained in the Park. Incidentally, we pointed out to the people of Idaho a splendid site for a reservoir which our engineer had discovered on unappropriated public lands many miles from the coveted Bechler Meadows.

And now, in 1937, we are still waiting for Congress to act on our report.

The creation of a National Park in the Everglades of south Florida often had been suggested but nothing was ever done about it until December 12, 1928, when the Everglades National Park Association was organized in Miami, with Dr. David Fairchild, President, and Ernest F. Coe, Secretary. As a result of the campaign which was instituted, an Act was passed by Congress on March 1, 1929, directing the Secretary of Interior to investigate the desirability for establishing a park in the almost unknown wilderness of south Florida. The Secretary, Dr. Wilbur, thereupon appointed a committee to study the problem and its field work was carried on February 11-17, 1930. The personnel consisted of Horace M. Albright, Arno B. Cammerer and Roger W. Toll of the National Park Service staff; H. C. Bumpus, Harlan P. Kelsey and myself, official collaborators of the Park Service; and Ebert K. Burlew, Assistant to the Secretary of Interior.

In a blimp we flew across the Everglades from Miami to the Gulf, and circled back. We traversed the Tamiami Trail, then going to Lower Matacombe Key, went by boat along the Gulf Coast and up two watercourses leading from the interior. The entire party was deeply impressed with the many charms of this almost tropical country with its palms and abundant wild life. It was our verdict that the Everglades measured up fully to the exacting requirements for a National Park and Secretary Wilbur so reported to Congress.

Mrs. Ruth Bryan Owen, Representative in Congress from the eastern Florida district, introduced a bill in the House on May 14, 1930, providing for the establishment of an Everglades National Park at such time as the State of Florida should give land to the Government for that purpose. On

December 15th and 16th the House Committee on Public Lands gave a hearing on the bill and many of us appeared and presented testimony. The next day Senator Duncan U. Fletcher of Gainesville, Florida, offered to the Senate an identical measure. It was referred to the Committee on Public Lands and the members of this Committee concluded that it would be a good idea for them to go to Florida during the Christmas holidays and have a look at the territory. I was invited to be their guest and give them the benefit of such knowledge as I possessed regarding the region.

In the evening on December 26, 1930, the party left Washington. It consisted of Senators Nye, Norbeck, Walsh, of Montana, Ashurst, Glenn, and Oddie. Also there were Horace Albright and Arno B. Cammerer of the Park Service, and some others. I played bridge most of the next day on the train, my partner being Senator Walsh. He might have been classified as a conservative bidder and a deliberate player. Rarely did he make an unnecessary remark but about the middle of the afternoon, yielding perhaps to the gaiety about the table, he surprised us with an amusing story about an Irishman and a Jew.

That evening we were greeted at the station in Jacksonville by Mayor Alsop, his wife and a number of other people. During the wait of an hour or more we were driven about the city where the trees growing in many yards bore numerous electric lights indicative of the Christmas season. Returning to the train, we found our berths filled with flowers and oranges. The reception at Miami the next morning was equally gracious.

Various Senators were accompanied by their wives, and taking the party half at a time, I drove with them over the Tamiami Trail, pointing out turtles, snakes and numerous flocks of water-birds. Also, we made two trips over the Everglades in a blimp. We crossed the peninsula at a height of about 200 feet until we could see the waters of the Gulf.

Then I asked the pilot to raise to 2,000 feet to give the visitors a view of the Ten Thousand Islands and the intricate waterways that wound between them. The engaging and eminent agricultural explorer, Dr. David Fairchild, was with us always, being, in truth, the leader, and certainly the life, of the party.

One evening the Senators were the guests of the Committee-of-One-Hundred of Miami Beach. I was informed that Senator Nye and I were to make the speeches for the visiting party. Not expecting to attend any formal occasion I was not equipped with suitable attire, but our hotel host, Thomas J. Pancoast, and the irrepressible David Fairchild, had combed the city that day hoping to find in the wardrobe of some friend an evening suit which might in some measure fit my form. I have not quite forgiven these gentlemen for their merriment at my expense as they sought to play valet to me that evening.

We drove to Matacombe Key and in the house-boat *Friendship* proceeded to Cape Sable and then up the uninhabited west coast to Shark River. Here, in the evening, while three of us in a small boat rowed through a swampy region, great flocks of herons and ibises came in from the open glades to roost in the trees about us. I asked Senator Nye how many birds were in sight. Without hesitation he stated, "Two million."

"You exaggerate frightfully," reproved Senator Norbeck, "there are just exactly one million. I have counted them."

Returning to Washington, the Senate Committee reported the Everglades Park Bill, January 26, 1931. It passed the Senate and went to the House where the Owen Bill was pending.

These were busy days for the friends of this measure. Innumerable disappointments and delays occurred and many ridiculed the idea for which Ernest F. Coe was devoting his life. Some called the Everglades Park Bill a "Florida Grab"

—others dubbed the proposed park "A Snake Farm." Not until May 30, 1934, did Congress agree on an Act authorizing the acceptance of land for an Everglades National Park, and even then it contained a provision which read: "The United States shall not expend any public moneys for the administration, protection or development of the aforesaid park within a period of five years from the date of the approval of this Act."

Florida at once set to work to acquire title to private holdings in the southern Everglades but this has proved to be a slow process. On June 7, 1935, the State Legislature prohibited hunting within the 2,000-square-mile area of the proposed Everglades Park. In the meantime, wardens employed by the National Association of Audubon Societies continue to be about the only effective wild-life protective agencies of the region.

Pelicans have long been looked upon with suspicion. They eat fish; so do men. In the minds of many, therefore, the obvious course is kill the birds. A particular vicious war on brown pelicans broke out along the coast of our Gulf States in 1918, and many were killed. We were at war; food was said to be growing scarce and Herbert Hoover, as Federal Food Administrator, was urging people to eat more fish. The Honorable Jeremiah Hezikiah Williams, State Fish Commissioner of Florida, told a convention of food conservation people in Jacksonville that the depredations of the pelicans on the fish were terrific. He said that his investigations had revealed the fact that there were one million pelicans in Florida and that they ate $950,000 worth of fish every day. Mr. Williams went to the Food Administration in Washington and gave the same alarming information. Mr. Paden, the Food Administrator of Texas, stated it was reported that the pelicans of Texas ate more food fish in a day than the people of the State were able to catch in a year.

Many desired the Food Administration to kill the pelicans as a war measure.

Mr. Frederick C. Walcott, who was Mr. Hoover's right-hand man in many matters, asked several of us what we knew about the subject, and I went to Washington to talk the matter over with him. I had visited many brown pelican nesting-colonies and had made some notes regarding their food, but it was agreed that there might be much more to learn. Therefore, in June I visited all the breeding-colonies of pelicans situated between Rockford, Texas, and Cape Sable, Florida.

The pelicans were nesting on small isolated islands off the coast of Texas, Louisiana and Florida. Each of these states supplied me with a boat and crew.

There were many interesting experiences on this extended trip along our semi-tropical Gulf Coast. Trolling from the after-deck, I caught some sizable fish by using a man's white collar for bait. It was number 15½, and from the results I have no hesitancy in recommending it to other anglers who desire to fish for the larger-sized cravalle. In a Louisiana bay we found seine fishermen throwing away the mullets they caught and saving the gaff-topsail catfish. In Charlotte Harbor, Florida, exactly the reverse procedure was in operation. At one point a naturalist we had aboard killed several adult pelicans for his museum and we found their weight ranged from seven and one-half to eleven and one-half pounds. I estimated that at least 60,000 man-of-war birds were roosting on different islands, but the species has never been known to nest on the coast of the United States.

After counting the occupied nests on the islands of all the pelican states of the Gulf and multiplying this by two, we added 30 per cent for non-breeding birds, and reached a total of 65,000. The combined figures I had received before leaving Washington indicated that there were 5,000,000 of these voracious destroyers of America's food supply!

Both young and adult pelicans readily regurgitate their food when one comes among them. Thus on the nesting islands barrels of fish were presented for our inspection, many of which were in such perfect condition that not a scale had been disturbed. From south Texas to Tampa Bay every fish we collected was a Gulf manhaden, an oily fish never used for human consumption. From St. Petersburg to Man-o'-war Bush in the lower keys we collected 3,428 fish that we watched pelicans disgorge. Only twenty-eight were food fish. They were mullet, pig fish, pin fish and cravalle. We found not a single trout, mackerel, pompano or other highly valued food fish.

Post-cards containing a pelican's picture are popular at Florida coast resorts and a good deal of money is made by their sale—perhaps even more than the value of the food fish destroyed in summer by the living pelicans that flop and sail about the bays of that charming state. The Federal Food Administration, I am glad to record, took no steps to destroy the brown pelican.

My last cruise of this trip ended at Long Key. Just at night the yacht *Seafoam* came to anchor two hundred yards from the dock and within one minute a horde of mosquitoes covered us like a smothering blanket. With all possible speed the Captain rowed me to the dock and turned again for the yacht. In the gloom I saw a man leaving at our approach. I called to him but he did not stop. Feeling sure that he was a Negro workman, I said, "Don't you run away, I've got a warrant for you."

"I ain't done nothin' much," he answered, and stopped.

"What you doing here anyway?" I asked.

"Nothin' harmful," he declared. "Just waitin' around for the train from Key West. I hopes to ketch me a ride up to Homestead."

"So do I," I told him, wiping scores of mosquitoes from my face and the backs of my hands.

"Get these two bags and wait on me until the train comes and I'll see if I can find you a little piece of money."

"Yas, Sir," he said, and picking up the bags we started along a trail of sand through the palmettoes.

"Where you want me to carry you, white folks?" he asked.

"Up to the hotel," I told him.

"Dar ain't nary hotel here," he said in surprise at my ignorance.

"Then take me to that famous fishing camp. Maybe they will let me in."

"Nobody ain't dar," he advised. "Dem white gentmen is all shut up and gone back 'mong the Yankees."

"Then take me to a boarding-house, a saloon or a livery-stable—any place where I can get away from these mosquitoes."

He stopped and set down the bags.

"Boss, dar hainten nobody on dis island septin de man what runs de post-office and his old woman."

"Lead me to them," I implored.

A few hundred feet farther on we came to the track of the Florida East Coast Railway. A light was visible through the door of a small house. I stepped upon the porch, wondering if I could get that screen door open before the mosquitoes had finished me. It was locked. A man was sitting in an elbow chair reading a paper, and a woman sat near. They looked up at the sound of my steps.

"I have just landed from a boat," I told him. "May I sit with you until the train comes?"

"Am sorry," he said, in a tone clearly designed to be kindly and disarming, "but we make it a rule never to take in strangers."

"Well, can't you do something for me; give me some rags to burn, or a lantern, so I can see how to find some other house?"

"We have no rags," he said. "I'll bring the lantern out to

flag the train when I hear it coming." As he spoke he arose and closed the inner door.

"Jim," I asked, "what in the world are we going to do?"

"Just set around on the cross-ties, I reckon, and bust all de mosquitoes we kin 'til railroad comes," he grinned.

I could see the dim outline of a small hut. It had a thatched roof and was open at one end. We found some coconuts, and smashing these with a pole on the cross-ties, carried the husks inside the shelter and built a fire. I sat on the sand and my helper used my coat as a fan to drive the smoke over me. Courage began to return for I felt sure he would not desert me—as long as I kept an eye on him. When the husks burned low he pounded out some more.

He told me that he had been working on a ditch over at Cape Sable but got a worm in his neck and was trying to get where he could see a doctor. Ten o'clock came and then eleven. The train was due, and my neck, face and hands were completely smeared with my own blood.

"Are you a married man?" I asked.

"No, Sir," he declared with great emphasis. "Wonst I did study about gittin' married but the gal's old woman lammed me over de haid with her washing club and I don't keer much about woman no more."

Twelve o'clock, one o'clock—it is amazing what suffering a human being can endure.

"Do mosquitoes bother you much?" I asked.

"Sometimes dey does when dey gits bad," he admitted.

Two o'clock, two-thirty, and then the tardy train arrived.

At a sportsmen's dinner in New York that autumn an enthusiastic sail-fish angler asked me, "Have you ever been to Long Key?"

"Yes," I told him, "I spent six months there one night last June."

CHAPTER XIX

ATTEMPTS AT REGIMENTATION

IN the United States there have been many attempts to form nation-wide wild-life protective organizations. Here and there a standard has been raised aloft with the hope that local and state organizations, as well as large numbers of individuals, not only would flock to it but would support permanently the new group of national crusaders in its efforts to save "the remnants of America's wild life" and restore species to their pristine abundance. Many such efforts quickly failed. The duration of the life of others, which for a time seemed firmly established, has depended largely on the energy and ability of a few leaders to raise money for maintaining them. Some movements endured long enough to attract wide attention. Some are operating to-day and in the future others undoubtedly will come into existence. Without exception, the larger enterprises have accomplished much good for the cause they served, and even the more ephemeral ones usually have aroused more or less public interest in conserving the out-of-doors resources.

The first of what may be called the quasi-permanent national nature-protective organizations depending for financial support on the aid of lesser groups and on individual membership fees and contribution was "The League of American Sportsmen." It was launched at a gathering held in New York City, January 18, 1898, under the leadership of G. O. Shields, who it was said had shot nearly every kind of game in North America. As reported at the time, this meeting was "attended by one hundred and forty thoroughly representative sportsmen" from seventeen states. To quote Shields, "The League was organized for the purpose of protecting game and game-fish, the song, insectivorous and other interesting birds not classed as game-birds. Its prime object is to enforce game-laws where such exist and to secure and enforce such laws which are not now existent. It aims to promote good-fellowship among good sportsmen, foster a love for nature, encourage propagation of game and game-fish, restock game fields and public waters; to oppose excess killing and the sale of game and fish; and work for reasonable bags and gun-license laws."

Mr. Shields was the editor and publisher of the periodical *Recreation*, which at this date had been appearing for four years. He was attracting much attention by his fight to regulate the amount of game that one man might kill. At that time "bag limits" were few and far between in the states of the Union. In the twenty-fourth issue of his magazine, which was the one for June, 1896, he had said: "The man who boasts of taking 100 or 200 trout or bass in a day is written down as a 'fish hog.' A man who tells of killing 100 or 200 quail in a single trip is written down as a 'game hog,' and so shall it ever be in this office."

He launched into a campaign of abuse of hunters whom he regarded as being guilty of too much killing, and advertised (July, 1896): "Any man who may be reported to *Recreation* as having slaughtered either fish or game will get roasted no matter who he may be"—and most certainly he made good his threat.

From the Americus (Ga.) *Recorder* he quotes: "Jarret Wilson and Boyce Adams take first prize for killing blackbirds recently and sending to town a bunch of 900 of the songsters, the result of one day's hunt. The birds entirely filled the body of the buggy."

Shields comments: "Wilson and Adams are unquestionably game hogs of the Southern razorback variety." He explains that the birds were what generally are known in the market as "reed-birds" and in the North are called "bobolinks."

Two men hunting in West Casco, Maine, for a week were reported as killing 142 pickerel, 107 black bass, 5 snakes, 260 brook trout, 250 perch, 60 hornpouts, 36 gray squirrels, 6 woodcocks, 7 black ducks, 5 blue jays, 2 crows, 2 polecats, 1 mink and 2 coons. Shields thought if this were true these men would be "entitled to wear one champion hog collar by turns."

W. W. Storcer of Mt. Sterling, Kentucky, is quoted as stating that he and John Curry bagged, in Tennessee, 120 quail in a day. The editor remarks: "I pity the dogs that were forced to associate with such miserable swine as these. If they were 'grand field dogs,' as Storcer says, they should belong to gentlemen."

He called Ray L. Markel of Massillon, Ohio, "a local game hog" for killing 175 quail in one day.

A writer in *Recreation* tells of a four-day hunt with a friend in the Wind River country, during which they caught 37 trout and shot 24 grouse, 8 antelope, 3 deer and 9 elk. Shields printed his letter and asked the man whether he was trying to make a record to boast of, or trying to exterminate the game. "On the face of this story it looks as though you and S. R. C. are entitled to a corner in the pig pen."

A party of five sportsmen in Utah killed 1,493 wild-fowl in a two days' hunt. They were chastized.

Three California men, killing from 35 to 48 ducks each, were called "vermin."

A Kentuckian caught 60 fish in one hour. Shields tells him, "Instead of boasting of your shameful work, you should have gone and hid yourself in the Ohio River swamps until the mosquitoes could have had time to suck the bad blood out of you."

A photograph was reproduced in *Recreation,* showing an immense number of game-fish strung to poles and ropes.

Behind the fish stood six men. The article accompanying it is entitled, "Another Minnesota Herd." In a caption beneath it we read: "Hog No. 1, W. H. Pringle of East Grand Forks, Minnesota, cashier of a bank there." The name of every man in the group is given, and all are supplied with numbers in the "Hog Pen."

In the January, 1902, issue, there is reproduced a photograph of a man said to be Herbert Gardiner of Colorado Springs, He is dressed in hunting costume, has a gun in his hands, and is standing by a large number of game birds and animals. The man who sent it urged Shields to write Mr. Gardiner and ask if he killed all those birds and animals. Shields said: "I did write the big hog and asked him if the report was correct, but he evidently smelled something besides his own filth and declined to answer."

In 1901 there was a "fish war" on at Lake Winnebago, Wisconsin. Commenting on it, Shields said: "The State should employ, as deputy wardens, a few expert long-range riflemen, give them high-powered smokeless rifles and plenty of cartridges. The sooner the Winnebago fish poachers are sent to the bone-yard, the better."

Six slaughter pictures of ducks, deer and fish were shown. Accompanying them was a poem entitled, "The Grunt of the Game Hog."

A reproduction of a photograph revealed nearly 100 fish. The legend runs, "Caught in one day in the waters of St. Clair River, Michigan, by H. Lee Borden of Chicago, owner of the famous steam yacht *Penelope*." Shields says: "Any reader of *Recreation* can tell you about the length of Mr. Borden's bristles after looking at the record of his butchery."

Shields quotes from the Los Angeles (Calif.) *Times* an account of a duck-hunt by Admiral Kirkland of the Mare Island Naval Station, his son and three others. They bagged 246 ducks. He said: "There should be a law to reduce a naval officer to the ranks for such an exhibition of swinishness as this and to compel him to scrub decks for the next three months."

In July, 1901, *Recreation* reports a picture published in a San Diego paper showing 200 ducks hanging on a rack and bearing the caption, "Result of a forenoon's sport of Major General Nelson A. Miles, U. S. Army." The General wrote Shields that the statement was not exactly correct, but that he was a member of the party of nine that in four hours killed 450 ducks—an average of 50 ducks each. Shields, in an open letter, says: "You have disgraced yourself, and the fact that the notorious Babcock and his fellow swine preserve a lake and make butchers of themselves is no reason why you should have descended to their level. It will be many a year before the people will forget this unsportsmanlike act of yours."

Mr. Shields continued to give people numbers in the "Hog Pen." In the magazine for November, 1903, under the caption, "Yanked out of Paradise," he reproduced a picture of three men and two women with a great string of black bass. An accompanying letter explains that over 300 were caught by three men in one day. The five people shown in the picture are given numbers in the "Fish Hog Pen" from 904 to 908.

This policy of abuse and vituperation had three logical results: first, for a time the circulation of the magazine grew by leaps and bounds; second, the terms "game hogs" and "bag limits" became well known in the homes and clubs of hunters and fishermen; and third, there rapidly developed a large class of men who profoundly disliked Shields and all his works. Many approved of this campaign by the President of the League of American Sportsmen, and its membership grew rapidly.

I have mentioned only a few of the many vials of wrath that Shields poured out in the pages of *Recreation* during the period from June, 1896, to February, 1905, but these serve to emphasize what was happening to our fish and game a comparatively few years ago, for the men whom Shields was denouncing were acting entirely within their legal rights. The League of American Sportsmen was fighting for a great issue, which was to establish legal daily "bag limits" in the taking of wild life.

In January, 1904, I received from Mr. Shields an invitation to attend the Seventh Annual Convention of the League, which shortly was to be held in Columbus, Ohio. I was busy with my biology classes and was devoting every spare moment to developing the State Audubon Society and organizing the State Game Warden force, but I accepted the invitation and went to Columbus, thirty-three years ago last February, where I attended my first national convention of sportsmen and game-protectors. More than one hundred people were present at the business sessions, and at the banquet, at which I was a speaker, two hundred were seated, including the Governor of Ohio and the Mayor of Columbus. Resolutions were passed urging the prohibition of the spring shooting of all game, laws to prohibit aliens from hunting, and other subjects regarded as highly important at that time.

Dr. T. S. Palmer, W. F. Scott of Montana and I assembled all the state game officials present and revived the National Association of State Game and Fish Wardens which had been started by Scott two years before, but had not been continued. From that date it has been an active organization. It holds annual conventions and has been long known as the International Association of Game, Fish and Conservation Commissioners.

At Columbus, Shields reported that the League then had 9,815 members, 48 state divisions, and 188 volunteer wardens, who the past year had been responsible for 600 convictions for violation of the game laws. He was very enthusiastic about the League and what it had done, so much so, in fact, that in an editorial in *Recreation* for April that year he said: "The problem of saving the wild animals and birds of this country is well nigh solved. The laws of many states are practically perfect, and those that still need amending will be made good in the near future. It remains now only to stop, absolutely and at all times, the sale of game in a few Eastern states, such as New York, Pennsylvania and Massachusetts. When this shall be done, we may confidently expect to see game increase rapidly everywhere."

Mr. Shields drafted and sponsored many proposed legislative measures for game protection. One of his most notable undertakings was a campaign begun in January, 1904, against the use of auto-loading shot-guns, but he did not live to see their use abolished. Other agencies, however, continued the agitation against these deadly weapons. For many years the only legal restrictions on their use in North America were state laws in New Jersey and Pennsylvania, and in some of the Canadian provinces. In Canada a Federal regulation issued May 11, 1920, prohibited their employment in hunting migratory game-birds and the use of all magazine shot-guns for the same purpose, if carrying more than three cartridges, was debarred in the United States by Presidential proclamation February 2, 1935.

Some time after the Columbus meeting I received a telegram from Charles Francis of New York, saying that he was on his way to see me. Upon arrival he told me that the Francis Press printed *Recreation,* that the magazine had a large income from subscriptions and advertisements, but that Shields was very unbusinesslike and owed him heavily. Mr. Francis had been urging him for a long time to get a business manager who would be given full authority in handling the finances of the publication. Shields had always turned a deaf ear until a few days before, when he had signed an agreement that he would consent to this plan if I could be secured to take the job. Mr. Francis offered me a salary of more than three times that which I was receiving and promised to double the amount within a year.

I told him that I was flattered by the offer, but thought it unwise for me to accept the proposition. He insisted, saying, among other things, that the position would give me an opportunity to be in the very midst of the most active forces working for game protection, and that a young man of my tastes and interests could not afford to decline such an opening. I then said frankly that Shields and I were temperamentally unsuited to work together.

Not long after this, the Francis Press assigned part of its claim to a man who then petitioned to have Shields adjudicated a bankrupt and the petition was granted. The last number of *Recreation* published by Shields was for February, 1905. When the March issue appeared, under new management, Dan Beard was the editor. It contained the following editorial declaration: "Our Future Policy. Exit the Game Hog. We hope to leave the Game Hog to wallow in his own mire, with good officials to watch him so that his snout may be kept from appearing in this magazine. We think that the valuable space heretofore occupied by him can be put to better purpose. (Signed) William E. Annis, Publisher."

The history of *Recreation* from this time was fraught with many changes. It had various editors, and its name was changed frequently. For a time it was *Outdoor World and Recreation,* then *Recreation and Outdoor World.* In 1915 it went back to the old name, *Recreation,* only to be changed to *Outer's Recreation,* and then to *Outer's Book and Recreation.* In 1927 it was combined with *Outdoor Life,* and thus, after a more or less tempestuous life of thirty-three years, it ceased to exist.

After losing *Recreation,* Shields started another publication in March, 1905. He named it *Shields' Magazine.* It did not prove to be a profitable venture and was discontinued with the number for August, 1912. The League Membership largely had fallen away. It no longer was a novelty and other subjects were bidding for the attention of the average American citizen. Sportsmen seemed to lose their interest in its work. In a published account of the League convention held in Buffalo in 1906, Shields stated:

"Not a single Buffalo member attended the meeting, and no attention whatever was paid to the visiting delegates by any citizen of that mossback town. Hereafter the men who attended the convention will know what it means when they hear any one speak of having been 'Buffaloed.'"

I believe the final meeting of the League of American Sportsmen was the one held in Lawton, Oklahoma, October 12, and 13, 1908.

Mr. Shields was getting old and had become somewhat embittered by his misfortunes. He lectured now and then in Western Chautauqua courses and did some writing, but Fortune seemed to desert him. The last time I saw this remarkable man was October 5, 1918. I met him on Broadway. He was dressed in a G. A. R. uniform and was selling war stamps. The next day he wrote me the following letter: "I hereby present to your Society my twenty bound volumes of *Recreation,* my five volumes of indexes thereto, and my twelve volumes of *Shields' Magazine,* to be delivered to your Society after my death, and I shall arrange with my executor to notify when and where to call for them. Yours truly, G. O. Shields." The Audubon Association never received the books.

For a long time he lived in a small flat in the East Bronx, New York City. He was very lonely and said that his friends were few. During the last years of his life his chief support came from Ernest Thompson Seton. To Mr. Seton he gave his set of *Recreation* and *Shields' Magazine.* There was little else he could do for the friend who had stood by him so loyally in his time of greatest need. He died in New York in November, 1925, at the age of seventy-nine, and no one ever revived the League of American Sportsmen.

Although unknown to most of the present generation, the name "Colonel G. O. Shields" was upon the lips of every American sportsman thirty years ago. To him, more than to any other man, is due the credit of arousing public sentiment against the excessive killing of game, which was a necessary prelude to the adoption of our bag-limit laws. He was a forceful warrior whose lusty shouts rallied many spears to his support. In battle he fought with a bludgeon rather than with a rapier.

President Theodore Roosevelt called the State and Territorial Governors to the White House in May, 1908, and had a serious talk with them about the wasteful manner in which coal, forests and other natural resources were being handled. They agreed to support him in doing something about it, so on June 8th he appointed a National Conservation Commission of forty-nine members, of which Gifford Pinchot, Government Forester, was named as Chairman. The Commission was asked to assemble data and report on the country's resources of water, forests, lands and minerals. It was understood that wild life also was included under three of these headings. Numerous societies, institutions, bureaus and other agencies were invited to furnish information of value. Matters moved rapidly and the first week in December delegates from all over the country came to Washington for a Joint Conservation Conference.

A new and broad undertaking was being started with governmental backing, and it had been launched by a popular President. Enthusiasm ran high. Dr. T. S. Palmer and I were on hand to look out for the interests of the Audubon Society movement. A printed report of the proceedings stated that here was given "the first inventory of the natural resources of the United States ever made."

An outgrowth of this gathering was a permanent organization known as the National Conservation Association. Offices were opened in Washington, with Thomas R. Shipp, Executive Secretary, in charge. The Association was to sponsor conservation legislation in Congress and stimulate conservation generally throughout the country. Also, it was planned that an annual Conservation Congress should be held where reports of progress would be given and plans matured for future activities.

Attracted by the name and the prominence of its leaders, almost every conceivable kind of commercial and eleemosynary organization sought to become attached to it and clamored for the recognition which it felt was its due. Looking over the long list of those whose aid was accepted, one finds the names of groups interested in lumber products, land taxation, improvements of river navigation, political and social science, agricultural colleges and experimental stations, chemistry, electricity, bird protection, mining, medicine, newspaper publications, automobiles, cotton and fire insurance.

State conservation associations began rapidly to be formed and thoughout the land the word "conservation" was heard everywhere. August 26-28, 1909, the Washington State organization was host, in Seattle, to the First Congress of the National Conservation Association. I prepared for Mr. Pinchot a report on bird preservation, but I think it was not read at Seattle. However, among the thirty-nine papers presented was an address by the Audubon Association's Western representative, William L. Finley, his subject being "Conservation through the Aid of Birds and Animals."

The Second Congress convened in St. Paul the next year. Large audiences were present, 15,000 people being attracted in part by the appearances of President Taft and ex-President Theodore Roosevelt. Messrs. Frank M. Chapman and Radcliffe Dugmore gave illustrated addresses on natural history subjects. These men, together with W. W. Grant and myself, constituted the Audubon delegation. I was on the Resolutions Committee and secured action, pledging the support of the Congress to the bill for Federal control of migratory birds, then pending in the United States Congress.

In February, 1910, Secretary Shipp brought out the first issue of the Conservation Association's magazine, *American Conservation,* which continued to appear until 1913, when it was combined with *American Forests.*

The Third National Convention was held in Kansas City, Missouri, September 25-27, 1911. Interest was great and the attendance was large. Mr. William Jennings Bryan was the notable attraction. Subjects dealing with the conservation of water, forests, soil, phosphate rock, good roads, health and a flood of other subjects were discussed at length. William P. Wharton and Dr. George W. Field were there for the Audubon Association, and both of them presented the claims of wild-life protection, as did also W. E. Coffin of the Camp Fire Club of America. However, in the 319 printed pages of the report of this convention, the entire space devoted to reporting the wild-life protection addresses covered just three pages in the "Supplementary Proceedings." Mr. Wharton, being a member of the resolutions committee, saw to it that the claims of wild life were placed on record.

We were disappointed in the lack of interest exhibited in birds and mammals at these Congresses. There was only a little handful of us in those days who took part in wild-life meetings away from our home states, and the Audubon Association was the only sizable group in America devoting its entire energies to bird and mammal preservation. Contending with us for recognition at these meetings were many who had pet theories of government, and others who were representatives of large business interests. They were always on hand and exhibited amazing ability in securing assignments for the best places on the programs. After all, the fortunes of wild birds and wild mammals did not loom overly large in the public mind and many considered such subjects as of slight importance.

Some of us determined that more attention should be devoted to wild life at the Congress to be held in Indianapolis, October 1-4, 1912, and Secretary Shipp assigned me to a place on the program for the first afternoon. For some days before the meeting the press dispatches from Indianapolis carried news of our coming, and quoted various things I would say about the needs for bird preservation. The Indiana Nature Study Society and the State Game and Fish Commission busied themselves with local people to see that I had a good audience.

Fully a thousand people greeted us that afternoon, and William Haskell, Dr. Hornaday and I took up the time of the session. I exhibited numerous colored slides made from photographs taken on bird reservations and urged the great need of bird preserves throughout the country. Our hearers may not have enjoyed all this talking about bird protection, but at least they exhibited a kindly patience.

The Conservation Congress held in Washington, in 1913, was chiefly notable for the unprecedented fight that took place over water-power. The Pinchot forces won, but so much bitter feeling was engendered that the meetings never again were of the size and importance of those that had gone before. The last night of this Congress I gave an illustrated address in the grand ballroom of the New Willard Hotel.

The National Conservation Association continued for another ten years and then went out of existence. Thomas R. Shipp ceased to be the Secretary in 1912, and Harry Slattery served in this arduous capacity until 1918, when he became the organization's counsel. I asked each of these men to tell me what he thought had been the value of this government-sponsored effort for conservation. Mr. Shipp replied: "The most important work done by the Association and the Congress was the awakening of the people of the United States to a realization of the importance of our natural resources and the urgent need for conserving them. Until they took up this work, there had been no coördinated plan for the conservation and use of natural resources. The practical effect of the work done was revealed in the formation of thirty-six state organizations and in work, policy and plans for conservation through governmental bureaus."

Mr. Slattery said: "This Association played a large part in starting the movement for conservation of our natural resources and for putting a stop to the continuance of the ruinous and devastating methods then in practice and now recognized universally as being of great detriment to the Nation."

In this movement Gifford Pinchot was the leading spirit and its chief inspiration, as President Theodore Roosevelt heartily testified. One lasting impression left on the public mind was the word "conservation," with which the speeches of Mr. Pinchot rang throughout the land. It was not until this organization came into existence that one heard such terms as "Conservation of Forests," "Conservation of Wild Life," or "Bird Conservation."

To-day the word "conservation" is in wide use and is applied virtually to any effort having to do with preserving mineral, vegetable or animal resources. "Conservation" societies are everywhere. Great numbers of local, state and national organizations have "conservation" committees. In virtually every community one may hear some man or woman spoken of as a "good conservationist" or as a "poor conservationist." In 1908 political departments of state engaged in enforcing game and fish laws were in general referred to as "State Game Commissions." As a result of the popularity of Pinchot's magic word, on July 12, 1911, New York State dropped the term "Forest, Fish and Game Commission" and adopted "Department of Conservation." Louisiana followed suit the next year when, in July, 1912, it abandoned "Board of Commissioners for the Protection of Birds, Game and Fish" for the more brief and inclusive title, "Conservation

Commission." Others followed until by 1936 the states using the name "conservation" in the titles of their game departments also included Illinois, Indiana, Iowa, Maryland, Massachusetts, Michigan, Minnesota, North Carolina, West Virginia and Wisconsin.

During the fifteen years of the life of the National Conservation Association, the Audubon Society workers took every advantage of the growing public interest to push the cause of bird and mammal protection. The American Game Association and the Izaak Walton League, both of which had come into existence during this period, also were advocating the claims of the wild creatures of the forests and the fish of the streams. Federal and state park and forestry interests had received much impetus and the State Game Departments had grown in strength and power. When it ceased to function in 1923, a hundred people were talking about preserving natural resources for every one that even mentioned the subject before President Theodore Roosevelt issued his first call for conservation activities in 1908.

It took money to operate this organization, and it was getting harder all the time to collect the amounts that were needed. Finally, it was decided with some relief that a good job had been accomplished and that the conservation organizations should now each go forward with its own momentum.

However, there were men interested in the out-of-doors who thought that organizations dealing with recreation problems should in some way be reassembled under the prestige of government leadership. Among those of this opinion were Charles Sheldon, a prominent naturalist and sportsman of Washington, and Colonel Theodore Roosevelt, Assistant Secretary of the Navy. They interested President Calvin Coolidge in the idea and he appointed a Cabinet Committee of John W. Weeks, Secretary of War; Henry C. Wallace, Secretary of Agriculture; James J. Davis, Secretary of Labor; Hubert

Work, Secretary of the Interior; Herbert Hoover, Secretary of Commerce; and Theodore Roosevelt, to consider the subject and to call a meeting of organizations interested in various phases of outdoor recreation.

Many of us were delighted. However, true to the history of conservation undertakings, the motives of President Coolidge and other leaders were at once questioned. The story was circulated that this was but another of the various public conferences which it was said the Administration was holding in order to distract attention from the Teapot-Dome scandal that was bringing so much criticism on the Republican Party. On May 22, 1924, there assembled at the National Museum in Washington, 309 delegates representing 128 groups of people, and there was then organized the National Conference on Outdoor Recreation.

President Coolidge briefly greeted the Conference, and Theodore Roosevelt, Jr., whom the President had appointed "Executive Chairman," followed with a ringing speech outlining the needs for coördinating and advancing the work of conservation activities. That wild-life protectionists had come into their own in the matter of national recognition was manifest that afternoon when, among the nine speakers, there appeared Dr. Frank M. Chapman, Will H. Dilg, Dr. C. C. Adams, Dr. W. T. Hornaday, W. C. Adams and Dr. Henry B. Ward.

My illustrated address with what was designed to be an alarming title, "The American Plan of Game Protection is Tottering," occupied the time of the evening session on the second day. I stoutly contended that a large and profitable supply of upland game-birds could not be produced and maintained in our country unless it could be made to the benefit of the individual landowner, to conserve and care for them.

All sessions of the Convention were well attended by the general public. It was a busy time, as each group present sought to gain friends for its undertakings. Much of the work of planning for the coördination of future activities was performed by nineteen committees. I was Chairman of the Committee on Birds and from our report of some 1,500 words, came the resolutions on bird protection adopted by the Conference.

When, after three strenuous days, we separated, there was much talk of how all future efforts in wild-life protection by allied interests would be carried on in harmony, and the wild birds and mammals would greatly profit thereby.

Six months after the Conference, its Advisory Council convened in the American Red Cross Building in Washington, with delegates present from eighty-four of the participating organizations. Mr. Chauncy J. Hamlin presided. Mr. Herbert Hoover made the opening address. He said in part: "The semi-official or unofficial activities relating to the forms of social welfare in which outdoor recreation is important, are carried on by a large number of organizations of national, state, or lesser scope, each specializing in and aggressively emphasizing certain restricted phases of what is really one common problem.... They need simplification, to use a term in department parlance, and they need a little standardization, and above all they need a definition of the social objective to which they are directed."

He explained: "The desirability of coördinating these various forces and resources so that they will result in a planwise and harmonious movement toward a single social objective, with duplication and confusion held to the irreducible minimum, had long been evident to the leaders of thought in fields of outdoor recreation, and this conference was called for the purpose of a solution, and it is that work on which you are engaged."

Other speakers followed. These included Dr. George Bird Grinnell, the veteran worker for birds, big game, and national parks. Besides Dr. Grinnell and myself, two other directors of the Audubon Association, Dr. T. S. Palmer and William P. Wharton, took part in the proceedings.

The organization was much in need of funds with which to function and I was asked to serve as Chairman of a Committee on Finance. When the Council adopted our report which asked that all affiliated groups should contribute what they could, I made some remarks and pledged $250 from the Audubon Association. I had previously indulged in some earnest private talks that now bore fruit as various delegates one after the other arose and announced subscriptions. With this beginning sufficient funds were provided to carry on the work of the Conference for the coming year.

The Second National Conference on Outdoor Recreation met in Washington, D. C., for two days, January 20-21, 1926. One evening program was devoted to the consideration of wild-life problems. As Chairman of the Resolutions Committee I presented and secured the adoption of a resolution approving of the "Migratory Bird Refuge and Marshland Conservation Bill," then pending in Congress, and one favoring a wide program of nature study. Objections were made to our report. One delegate thought the Committee remiss in not calling for better protection of city property against fire, and others were critical because we had nothing to say about the conservation of human life. One supporter of this thought declared, "There are two 'camps' here, the conservation camp and that which should look out for human interests." There were so many interruptions it took more than half an hour to consider our eight resolutions. Mr. Hamlin gave a good demonstration of how an experienced chairman may diplomatically handle one difficult situation after another. The report of this, the second and last Conference on Outdoor Recreation, is a 175-page pamphlet issued as Senate Document No. 117 of the 69th Congress.

The organization continued to function for two years more. It was liquidated upon the publication of Senate Document No. 158 of the 70th Congress epitomizing the results of major fact-finding surveys and projects undertaken under the auspices of the Conference. This report, transmitted by Chairman Hamlin to Secretary of War Davis, Chairman of the President's Committee on Outdoor Recreation, was designed to give a perspective of the general field of outdoor recreation and of some of the initial approaches which were considered as fundamental to the establishment of a national policy. In this respect the Conference made a valuable contribution, for the material it brought together has been of definite service in shaping present-day conservation policies.

Despite the heroic efforts of Chairman Hamlin and the hard-working Executive Secretary, Arthur Ringland, the further objective of the Conference to effect coördination failed because the participating organizations could not be held together to work for a common end. Few reformers very long enjoy carrying spears in the ranks, but many are eager to wear braid and flash a sword. Furthermore, most local leaders find it more pleasing to use such money as they are able to collect for furthering their own undertakings than to send it away to some national headquarters. The only phase of the entire undertaking of the National Conference on Outdoor Recreation still alive is the Committee on the Conservation of the Jackson Hole Elk, our latest meeting of which was held in Washington in February, 1936.

Twelve reports of various kinds published during the years 1924 to 1928 inclusive, and containing in the aggregate 1210 printed pages, record the story of this third effort, which, even with the help of governmental backing, sought vainly to regiment the conservation forces of our country into one coordinating body. Its span of life had been just four years.

On September 27, 1911, three years after the League of American Sportsmen held its final meeting in Oklahoma, and while the third Congress of the National Conservation Association was in session in St. Louis, there was organized in New York the American Game Protective and Propagation Association. Elsewhere I have spoken of the circumstances under which it came into existence.

The officers of this new wild-life organization were John B. Burnham, President; William S. Haskell, Vice-President, Treasurer and Counsel; and George M. Fayles, Secretary. There was a board of twelve directors, all of whom were representatives of various fire-arms and munition companies which had formed and were largely to finance the new movement. There were also listed forty "Honorary and Associate Members," beginning with the names of ex-President Theodore Rosoevelt, Henry L. Stimson, United States Secretary of State; Henry S. Graves, United States Forester; and Dr. Henry van Dyke. There were six ornithologists in this grouping—John Burroughs, George Bird Grinnell, C. Hart Merriam, William Brewster, A. K. Fisher and John E. Thayer. Among other outdoor men appeared the names of Charles Hallock, Dwight W. Huntington, Casper Whitney, W. B. Mershon, John H. Wallace, William C. Adams, and John W. Titcomb.

The Constitution stated that the objects of the organization are "To preserve and propagate game and fish" and to work for laws to accomplish these undertakings. Also, that it would "coöperate with and assist the proper authorities, regularly organized societies, clubs and individuals, in enforcing the laws for the protection and propagation of game and fish." It planned to establish preserves for propagating game, "to buy and sell game and fish and eggs of game-birds, as permitted by law, for purposes of the corporation."

One of the tenets for which the Association stood was the continuation of "free shooting" in this country. In a booklet issued at this time its President stated: "This country stands to-day at the parting of the ways in the matter of field sports. It faces to-day the question of whether free shooting shall continue or whether the European system of preserves and posted lands is to become universal." Also, "It [the Association] believes that the average citizen and the poor man should have their opportunity." And again, "It believes that no game, bought or raised by the use of hunters' license fees, should be put out for stocking lands which may be posted against public shooting, and it believes that a proviso should be added in the laws of the states which are propagating game that no land shall ever be posted which has been stocked freely by the state."

During the next two years the Association published eight small pamphlets or bulletins and on November 1, 1913, appeared the first number of a quarterly illustrated *Bulletin,* nine by twelve inches in size. In July, 1925, the title was changed to *American Game,* under which name it continued to appear until the issue for September-October, 1935, when under a new management it became *American Wildlife.*

In 1913 the name of the Association was shortened by omitting the words "and Propagation" so that the title read "The American Game Protective Association." In 1931 the word "Protective" also was dropped.

The large work of this organization in national and state legislation, in game propagation, game-law enforcement and other useful fields, is well recorded in its periodicals, a complete series of which is preserved in the library of the National Association of Audubon Societies, and, undoubtedly, in many other places.

Among its many activities especially should be noted the American Game Conference, organized by E. A. Quarles, Vice-President of the Association, in New York City, March 1, 1915. Such gatherings continued annually until 1935. The attendance grew rapidly and for many years these conferences have been the largest meetings of sportsmen, game breeders and conservationists generally, that have come together in this country. For example, in 1935 more than eight hundred delegates attended the Twenty-first Annual Conference held

January 21-23. The report of the proceedings forms a volume of 424 pages.

No active organization can long survive without funds to pay expenses. The League of American Sportsmen had failed because of lack of public support to keep it going. The American Game Association in the beginning had the pledged support of fire-arms and powder manufacturers to the extent of about $25,000 a year for at least five years. It was hoped by many that the sportsmen of the country would so rally to the corporation that in time it would be unnecessary to accept money from commercial sources. Such support, however, never was given in sufficient volume to relieve the organization of the necessity of accepting what its critics called "tainted money." The Association did not publish annual reports and consequently statements of its income and expenses were not in this way given to the public.

President Burnham worked hard to accumulate support from sportsmen and their clubs. He has written me: "From the very start of the organization back in 1911, we worked for both individual memberships and club affiliations. At one time we had thirty-five state organizations affiliated with our national organization, and I should say also more than two hundred clubs of less than state-wide coverage."

These efforts were continued by Carlos Avery who became President upon Mr. Burnham's retirement April 19, 1928, and by Seth Gordon who assumed this post on January 1, 1931, following Mr. Avery's death, October 5, 1930.

Of recent years it has been often stated that eight or nine million men in the United States enjoy shooting game as recreation. From these, the leaders of the American Game Association expected substantial and continuous support, but this hope was not realized, and when the contributions of the manufacturers lessened perceptibly the activities of the Association were terminated on August 20, 1935.

With a single exception, all notable attempts in the

United States to create nation-wide wild-life protective organizations, financed by membership contributions have had their bases either in New York City or Washington, D. C. The one exception has been the Izaak Walton League of America seated in Chicago.

Fifty-four sportsmen sat down together for luncheon in the Chicago Athletic Club on January 14, 1922, to talk about improving the country's supply of wild game and fish—especially fish. One of the group, Will H. Dilg, an advertising agent, read a speech that for forensic argument must have been unusually stimulating for, from that hour, the Izaak Walton League dates its birth. The League adopted as its slogan, "Restore to posterity the outdoor America of our ancestors."

At this time, fourteen years had elapsed since the League of American Sportsmen had held its last convention; the National Conservation Association was on the point of closing its doors; the American Game Protective Association was eleven years of age; the National Association of Audubon Societies was just celebrating its seventeenth birthday; and more than two years were to pass before the National Conference on Outdoor Recreation was to spread its sails to the uncertain winds of public support.

On March 1, 1922, the League opened an office in Chicago. Mr. Dilg threw himself into the undertakings of the new organization with great fire and energy. He became a modern Peter the Hermit, preaching to the people of the Middle West the gospel of wild-life restoration. Agents were employed on a commission basis to enroll members and collect their fees. Chapters sprang up everywhere. State Divisions were formed and soon were holding annual meetings.

Before long, delegates were being dispatched to the National Conventions, usually held in Chicago. These were largely attended, the delegates being seated around standards bearing the name of the states they represented. The press of the country rang with accounts of these assemblages and the resolutions that emanated from them.

But the Izaak Walton League was not all talk, by any means. For a time its greatest strength was in that portion of the country lying between the Alleghenies and the Rocky Mountains. This interior region had lost a greater proportion of its forests and wild-life than had any other part of the United States. Numberless streams had become polluted and opportunities for angling were growing scarcer. There had been comparatively few game-protective societies that were effectively functioning in these states, and the public mind was ripe for the message so dramatically delivered by Dilg.

Sportsmen flocked to his standard by tens of thousands. These men were in earnest and hundreds of projects were soon under way. Here a fish pond was provided; there a dam was built; yonder a band of League members with the ardor of vigilantes were apprehending and prosecuting game-law violators or reporting law-breakers to the state game-wardens. Game-breeding farms were started and pheasant eggs were distributed to farmers. Picnics were planned where speeches on conservation were given. Conservation talks were delivered in a thousand school-rooms. Hundreds of League members worked with hoe and pick and shovel in building fish or wild-fowl resorts. War on stream pollution was declared and waged in nearly every state in the Union and before Congress. Waltonians appeared in state legislative halls and demanded better game-laws. They pledged candidates for Congress to vote and to work for conservation bills. They became a force to be reckoned with in a hundred Congressional districts, and Congressmen seized opportunities to insert in the Congressional Record evidences of their good-will for the League, and then sent copies of these to their constituents.

In December, 1923, Dilg, with others, drafted a bill providing for a Federal wild-fowl and fish refuge among the islands and marshlands along a 300-mile stretch of the Mississippi River.

The Upper Mississippi River Wild Life and Fish Refuge Bill was introduced in the House on December 20, 1923, and on February 11th, following, the Agricultural Committee of the House gave a hearing on its provisions at which I represented the Audubon Association.

Dilg had taken a suite of rooms in the New Willard Hotel in Washington to direct the fight in Congress for the 300,000-acre land purchase contemplated by the framers of the bill. He had a staff of assistants, he had many callers, his messengers constantly came and went. He conducted his campaign on an expensive scale heretofore unknown in conservation circles. On June 7, 1924, the bill, under the leadership of Senator McCormick and Representative Hawes, became a law, and Dilg's name swept the country from coast to coast. Wherever two or more sportsmen met, Dilg and the Izaak Walton League were discussed.

Naturally, Dilg was elated with this initial success in an important legislative measure. In the July number of the League's magazine, his leading editorial bore the caption, "Victory," and the first sentence read: "Our League now stands at the top of the world!" And again: "The battle is over and the right of the Izaak Walton League of America to National Jurisdiction goes unchallenged." He did not mention, however, that the $1,500,000 appropriation asked for had not yet been provided. Nor did he speak of the necessity of getting the consent of the Legislatures of Minnesota, Wisconsin, Iowa and Illinois, before the Government could acquire title to lands in these states.

It may be here mentioned that for the fiscal year 1926, Congress provided $400,000 toward carrying out this Act; and a second appropriation of $892,338 was made for expenditures, beginning July 1, 1936. Approximately 140,000 acres of land and water are to-day under Federal jurisdiction within the boundaries of the Refuge, most of it, but not all, having been acquired by purchase.

In the autumn of 1924, Dilg was deep in an undertaking to raise $40,000 to purchase 2,000 acres of hay lands for the starving Jackson Hole Elk herd. The plan was largely successful and in 1927 the League deeded its Wyoming land acquisitions to the Government. Another victory came about this time, when the League was chiefly responsible in preventing the spoliation of the wilderness character of the Superior National Forest in northern Minnesota. Then there was the campaign to purchase and restore Horicon Marsh in Wisconsin, for which purpose the Wisconsin Legislature later appropriated $260,000.

Mr. Will H. Dilg, of whom few conservationists had ever heard, leaped into national prominence almost over night. He had been very successful and if you had any doubt on that point he was quite willing to set you straight. He was thoroughly convinced that the League was the only effective conservation organization that ever had been formed. He despised the American Game Association and wholly ignored the Audubon Association. In conversation he liked to dismiss any reference to them with the offhand remark that they would soon be tails to his kite. He stated that within a year or two it would not be necessary for him to go to Washington to get bills passed for the League, as all that would be needed would be for him to write a letter to Congress and the desired law would be enacted.

Frequently I came in contact with Dilg and always was impressed with the peculiarities of his temperament. I had a feeling that he might do or say something unusual at any moment. One morning in September, 1925, I left the train at Williamsport, Pennsylvania, with Gifford Pinchot, and together we proceeded to a near-by hotel. We had come to speak at a dinner given in connection with the meeting called to form a State Division of the Izaak Walton League. While waiting in the hotel lobby for Pinchot to come downstairs, Dilg came up and asked me if I expected to address the League. I replied that I had been invited for that purpose. Instantly he left. A little later a League member came in and said: "We are having quite a time with Dilg. He doesn't want you and Pinchot to speak here."

"Well, just let me sit and listen to him and the rest of you," I said. "It won't break my heart not to speak."

"Not much," he said, and turned away.

After a little time Dilg again appeared. "The Convention is in session," he said, "come along."

When we entered the hall he took me by the arm and as we went up the center aisle he held out an imperious hand and the proceedings stopped. Then in a friendly, eulogistic manner he presented me to the audience, but that night after I had spoken at the banquet he passed me without a word.

Trouble had been brewing in the National League for some time. Its financial affairs were not satisfactory. At the annual meeting in Chicago, April 10, 1926, a new President was elected. In less than a year Will H. Dilg died in Washington, D. C., on March 27, 1927.

This leader possessed an unusual ability to fire men and women with enthusiasm for conservation work. During a period of only four years he had founded and built up the largest and most dynamic force of unselfish workers for conservation that this, or any other country has ever seen.

Mr. George E. Scott of Chicago has been of great assistance to the League. He gave and solicited some $50,000 in its early days and in 1928 incorporated the Izaak Walton League Foundation that collected $218,000 to advance its work.

Among its leaders there have been many strong men. One was Charles W. Folds who succeeded Dilg as President in

April, 1926. Mr. Folds was followed in the presidency successively by J. M. Dickerson, Dr. Henry Baldwin Ward, George Edgar Vincent, Dr. Preston Bradley, and in 1935 by Judge George W. Wood, of Waterloo, Iowa. Splendid men though they are, none has ever been the equal of Dilg as a campaigner. His enthusiasm was missed, but even two years after his retirement the League reported 3,000 local Chapters distributed throughout forty-three states, and a membership of 100,000.

Still a year later, April, 1929, when I was a banquet speaker at the League's Annual Convention in the great ballroom of what was advertised as "the largest hotel in the world," the room was filled with as enthusiastic an audience as I have ever seen. The *esprit de corps* of the League was splendid.

The *Izaak Walton League Monthly* was started in August, 1922, and after missing two issues terminated with the number for August, 1923. *Outdoor America* appeared the next month, and continued until the April-May number for 1933. Much of the time it ran from eighty to ninety pages, contained many articles by well-known outdoor writers and was well supported by advertisers. In July, 1933, it was replaced by a smaller periodical, *The National Waltonian* which, in November, 1935, in turn gave way to the revived *Outdoor America*.

Seth Gordon came to the League in 1927. As Extension Director, he traveled over the country meeting sportsmen and helping branches of the League with their problems. Also, he edited a department in the League's magazine. In January, 1931, he left to become President of the American Game Association.

S. B. Locke, a graduate of the Yale Forestry School and for many years a naturalist with the United States Forestry Service, became the League's Conservation Director in November, 1931. With him has since largely rested the responsibility of handling its executive details and editing its publications.

In the Izaak Walton League of America there is opportunity for building on a broad and non-commercial basis a tremendous institution of incalculable value to the country.

In October, 1933, a train of events began which, in a little more than two years, led to the launching of a new movement, the General Wildlife Federation.

Thomas H. Beck, President and Editorial Director of *Collier's Weekly*, and Chairman of the State Board of Fisheries and Game of Connecticut, thinking that of all the money being spent by the Government to bring back prosperity some of it might well be used for the restoration of wild life, went to President Franklin D. Roosevelt and urged that a substantial sum be allocated for the establishment of inviolate nesting areas for wild water-fowl and upland game-birds. Later, when the administration ear-marked $25,000,000 for purchasing farm lands of low agricultural value, Henry A. Wallace, the Secretary of Agriculture, sent for Mr. Beck and said it was the wish of the President and of himself that he accept the chairmanship of a committee of three to formulate a national program of wild-life restoration along the lines of Beck's former suggestions. The assumption was that perhaps a large share of the money to be used in purchasing sub-marginal farm lands could be spent for lands that would be useful for water-fowl, upland game-bird, non-game bird and mammal refuges.

January 3, 1934, Mr. Beck assumed this task. Associated with him on the Committee were J. N. Darling of Iowa and Aldo Leopold of Wisconsin. A diagram in the Committee's printed report indicated a proposed plan similar in character to others which in the past had been suggested by various Presidents and organizations, namely that all wild-life matters handled by different Government Bureaus and agencies be combined under the authority of a single Federal official who, in this case, it was suggested should bear the title, Restoration Commissioner. The report also called for $25,000,000 to be expended for land acquisitions, and for a similar amount to be allocated from the Public Works Administration and the Civil Works Administration monies for the payment of workers to be engaged for improvement operations on these wild-life refuge lands as chosen. The President seemed to think favorably of the report but its recommendations were never put into operation.

Secretary Wallace on March 1, 1934, appointed J. N. Darling, his friend and neighbor in Des Moines, to the post of Chief of the Bureau of Biological Survey. Mr. Darling, popular cartoonist and experienced duck-hunter, had long been fighting with voice, pen and brush against excessive killing of wild-fowl, and this new official position gave him an arena to exercise his dynamic energies and convincing personality in behalf of needed hunting restrictions, some of which he was to secure ere long. Then, too, he managed to get hold of eight million dollars of government money and used it to establish wild-fowl refuges as provided for in the Migratory Bird Conservation Act, back in 1929. A little later he secured more money, making in all $14,500,000 available to expend on the Government's refuge program. Also he induced certain fire-arm and ammunition manufacturers to agree to provide $30,000 annually for a term of five years which, with like appropriations from State Game Departments and land grant colleges, would be used to conduct researches and give courses in game management and restoration in nine states to be selected.

Another current of influence which now came into operation was the American Wildlife Institute, which was organized in New York City on August 14, 1935, by sportsmen, conservationists, and representatives of various automobile, ammunition, and other commercial agencies that supply equipment for outdoor activities. Thomas H. Beck became the President, and served until February, 1936, Frederic C. Walcott then taking this position. Henry P. Davis has been the very active and resourceful Secretary.

Within a week this new organization took over the staff, equipment, files, and membership of the American Game Association, which the same day ceased to function as an active agency. The charter of the Institute provided that it "shall be a permanent, central organization, national in scope, to promote and assist in the coördination of the wild-life conservation of the Western Hemisphere."

The Institute immediately pointed its program toward three goals: starting a wild-life research and demonstration program concerning wild-life restoration; a mobilization of wild-life forces and the welding of them into one strong channel of influence; and the dramatization of the seriousness of the wild-life situation.

Through coöperation with the Biological Survey, the state game and fish departments, and the land-grant colleges, nine research and demonstration units are put into operation, on a five-year basis, in the following institutions: Alabama Polytechnic Institute, Connecticut State College, Iowa State College, University of Maine, Ohio State University, Oregon State Agricultural College, A. & M. College of Texas, Utah State Agricultural College, and the Virginia Polytechnic Institute. These units at once began working on varied programs designed to be of local and regional value.

Mr. Darling and Mr. Beck suggested to President Roosevelt that he call an outdoor conference, and invite all individuals and groups interested in wild-life preservation, whether their interest was from a commercial standpoint or otherwise.

The North American Wild Life Conference, therefore, convened in Washington, D. C., February 3, 1936, and its sessions lasted for five days. Some twelve hundred people were registered. Representatives were present from every state and also from Canada and Mexico. Mr. F. A. Silcox, Chief of the Forest Service, presided. Ira N. Gabrielson, Chief of the Biological Survey since Mr. Darling's retirement on November 15, 1935, was Chairman of the Program Committee which provided a long list of speakers, including Secretaries Ickes and Wallace of the President's Cabinet.

Mr. Darling in an inspirational address effectively welded the opinion of all groups on the main point under consideration, which was that of forming an international federation of wild-life conservation. It was hoped that the activities of all existing conservation groups in Canada, Mexico and the United States could be coördinated and thus greatly increase their effectiveness. It was planned for them to function by the "registration of mass opposition" to unwise legislation, in "demanding wild-life representation on state and Federal resource and planning agencies," and in other ways.

A temporary organization known as the General Wildlife Federation was formed on February 5th. It will come into permanent being when state federations are formed and the general plan has been ratified by a majority of these state groups.

Mr. Darling was chosen President with unanimous and enthusiastic expressions of approval. Mr. Frederic C. Walcott of Connecticut, I. T. Quinn of Alabama, and Dr. William L. Finley of Oregon, were elected Vice-Presidents.

The plan of organization contemplates including all groups interested in matters pertaining to wild life. On the Suggested Organization Chart, which was widely distributed, there is indicated on an outline map of South Dakota how this may be done. In each county twelve groups, or twelve series of groups, indicated as follows: Sportsmen's Groups, Chambers of Commerce, Girl Scouts, Bird Clubs, 4-H Clubs, Women's Clubs, Farm Groups, Garden Clubs, Future Farmers of America, Schools, Boy Scouts, and Civic Clubs are to be organized into a county federation. From four to ten contiguous counties, when thus organized, are to combine to make a district organization, and the twelve district groups in the State, in turn, will have a state headquarters. The states of the nation are to be formed into thirteen regional groups, each with a "regional director." The regional directors will keep in close touch with the headquarters of the proposed General Wildlife Federation in Washington, D. C. By December, 1936, thirty-five state organizations of the Wildlife Federation had been created, although none of them included all the groups of people it was hoped còuld be interested.

The Washington gathering was financed chiefly by the American Wildlife Institute, which it is expected will also sponsor the Second Conference called to meet in St. Louis the first week of March, 1937.

In addition to the wild-life protective organizations that have depended on nation-wide financial support, there are others interested chiefly in game breeding whose money has come from comparatively small groups of supporters. Their leaders had become convinced that restrictive legislation on hunting would never secure the continuance of a wild game supply in the country. What was needed, they thought, was for emphasis to be laid on producing more game, artificially and otherwise; and the way to encourage game production was to permit the sale of game produced by industry under state license and supervision.

One of the first active advocates of this doctrine was Dwight W. Huntington. He became editor of the *Amateur Sportsman* in 1908. Many men at first opposed his teachings, fearing that these would lead to the re-opening of the sale of wild game. His first law to encourage game breeding was passed by the New York Legislature in 1911. In 1912 he organized the Game Conservation Society, which at once founded the magazine, *Game Breeder,* and he became its editor, serving in this capacity until 1925, when he was succeeded by his son, John C. Huntington.

Turning now for a moment to another group of men, we find them in 1927 organizing The American Wild Fowlers. They saw the game growing scarcer, realized that extremely little government money was available for enforcing wildfowl protective laws, and, as active sportsmen, they felt that future possibilities for hunting were being jeopardized by active radical sentiment that wanted to stop all hunting. They proposed to champion the cause of the upright law-abiding sportsman in these matters. Dr. John C. Phillips became the President, and Nash Buckingham the Secretary. No list of financial supporters was made public.

Mr. John C. Huntington, representing the Game Conservation Society, spent some time in 1929 with Joseph P. Knapp of Knotts Island, North Carolina, and under his supervision 3,000 ducks were artificially bred that spring. Mr. Knapp became impressed with Mr. Huntington's ideas and ability, and secured his services when, on October 1, 1931, he and some friends incorporated a foundation known as More Game Birds in America. To it were turned over the records, files, and debts of The American Wild Fowlers. Mr. Arthur L. Foran was elected President, and was generally in attendance at all important conservation gatherings until his retirement in 1935.

More Game Birds continued the work of securing the passage of state laws to encourage game breeding. They succeeded in many states, and by July 1, 1936, nearly 7,000 game farms had come into operation.

The influence of More Game Birds has been pronounced in encouraging people to raise game birds for liberation and in fact-finding campaigns regarding the breeding range and numbers of various species. The organization maintains offices at 500 Fifth Avenue, New York City. Lists of its contributors are not published.

Chapter XX

CAMPAIGNING ABROAD

TAKING ADVANTAGE of the peace and quiet in the office on holidays, I long spent them all, with the exception of Christmas Day, working at my desk. Armistice Day, 1921, I heard a tap on my door. Dr. and Mrs. A. Burdet of Overveen, Holland, whom I had recently met in Philadelphia, were calling, hoping that by chance they might find some one there who would let them see where we worked.

Dr. Burdet was President of the *Nederlandsche Vereeniging tot Bescherming van Vogels,* and was one of the most prominent photographers of birds of Europe. It was a delight to hear him talk and we had much in common to discuss. He urged me to come to Holland to see what was being done there to protect birds, and extracted from me a halfway promise to pay him an extended visit the next spring. Before leaving he handed me a check for life membership in the Audubon Association.

That evening I told Mrs. Pearson of our pleasant meeting and of his invitation. She said, "Of course, you must go to Europe. It is your business to learn all you can about bird preservation everywhere." The Board of Directors seemed to be of the same mind, and on April 5, 1922, passed a resolution authorizing the President "to visit such countries in Europe this season as he deems advisable in the interests of wild-life protection."

From the deck of the *Savoie,* kittiwakes were the first European birds I saw, and the black-headed and herring gulls were clustered about the ship when, on the evening of May 14th, we came to anchor off the cliffs of Le Havre. Susceptible as always to the charms of a new environment, my excitement allowed me little sleep that night.

From the train windows next morning on the way to Paris I saw goldfinches, jackdaws and rooks in the fields of Normandy. The blackbird, which has since been my favorite of all European birds, I discovered in Paris singing among the horse-chestnuts of the Champs-Élysées. At the office of the Société Nationale d' Acclimatation de France, at that time on Avenue Saint Germain, I met many people interested in birds. One night I spoke at a meeting of the French League for the Protection of Birds, my remarks being interpreted by Jean Delacour, President of the Society and the leading ornithologist of France. Before leaving the country I acquired a slight acquaintance with a number of French birds—a hoopoe on a broken gun-carriage near Soissons, a pair of kestrels in the shattered towers of the Cathedral of Rheims, skylarks towering in the fields of Chamery, and house sparrows feeding their young in a shell-splintered tree beside the desolate Chemin des Dames.

I was delightfully entertained by Jean Delacour at his elegant and modernly appointed Château de Clères. On the extensive grounds, with their great variety of native and exotic trees, and their ponds and watercourse, were many hundreds of birds ranging from humming-birds to rheas. Some were in spacious flying cages, but many ducks, geese, cranes and flamingoes shared the ample grounds with antelope, kangaroos, cavies and deer.

"How much land do you have here?" I asked my host.

"About two hundred hectares," he replied.

"Hectares. What is the size of a hectare compared to an acre?"

"An acre?" He looked at me in surprise. "What is an acre?"

Consulting a dictionary, I learned that a hectare has about two and a half times the area of an acre. He learned that an acre is about one-fifth the size of a hectare.

One day he took me to see the beautiful Collège de Normandie, a private school for boys in the department of Seine Inferieure.

"We have three American boys here now," a teacher told me.

"Where from?" I asked.

"One from New York and two from the Argentine," was her reply.

Mr. Delacour told me that on account of the expense only wealthy Frenchmen sent their boys to this school. But when I inquired of the headmaster the necessary costs for a student, I discovered that these were much less than in similar schools at home, and that with the rate of exchange so favorable to the American dollar my family could live in France and the children attend the best schools at less expense than in New York. I wanted my children spared the handicap I was experiencing of being able to speak only one language so I arranged to send my sons Gilbert, Jr., and William the next year to Collège de Normandie, and Mrs. Pearson and our daughter Elizabeth, to Tours.

Seldom have I passed a more interesting period than the days I was the guest of Dr. and Mrs. Burdet in Holland. They have a magnificent home and a great estate where every known device is employed to attract and protect wild birds. Dr. Burdet owns also a great area of sand-dune country near the sea, where he does much of his bird photography. Here he showed me nests of the lapwing, curlew, oyster-catcher and the stone curlew. He pointed to the tracks of wheatears at the mouth of a rabbit burrow in which a pair had hidden their nest. It seemed odd to see ducks flying about among these barren dunes, but some were there—the strikingly colored sheld ducks.

The Burdets took me to the Naardermeer sanctuary lying between Amsterdam and the German frontier, with its breeding-colony of white spoonbills and their neghbors, the purple herons. We went to the Island of Texel, lying between the mouth of the Zuider Zee and the waters of the North Sea. Four interesting bird colonies were visited on this island so graphically described in the Introduction of *The Americanization of Edward Bok.*

I met various people in Holland who were devoting their attention to bird protection. One of these was J. Drijver of Santpoort, and another was that premier of all bird-protectors in Europe, Dr. Peter G. Van Tienhoven, whose success in the establishment of nature preserves has exceeded that of any other living man. Another bird student whom I met was Dr. Jac. P. Thijsse, a German by birth and training, now serving as a college professor in Holland. It was he who had devised the plan for placing perches on the lighthouse tower of Terschelling which proved so successful in saving bewildered birds on foggy nights that others had been erected not only in Holland, but in Germany and England. He told me much about bird-protection work in Germany of which I knew but little. But when he said that Germany was the leading nation in bird preservation, I bristled slightly and asked, "What about America?"

"I don't know anything about such matters in America," he replied in a tone which I interpreted to mean that, in the unlikely event that America did do anything about bird protection, the fact was of small consequence. He showed me a nightjar sitting on its two eggs and we separated, but as I shall mention later, that remark of the distinguished German zoölogist set moving a train of thought that has been responsible for many of my subsequent actions, which, I believe, have been not without value.

Leaving Holland, I crossed the Channel to England, where being inexperienced in counting English currency, my first taxi-man in London said, "I beg your pardon, sir, you over-paid me by half a bob, sir."

"He is not like the cabmen on Broadway," I thought, as I pocketed the change.

He had taken me to the home of Mr. and Mrs. Reginald McKenna on Smith Square, where I was to be a guest for the next few weeks. Mrs. McKenna had been very active in working for the passage in Parliament of the recently en-acted anti-plumage law, and we had exchanged many letters.

The morning after my arrival, Mrs. McKenna said, "Rep-resentatives of the press will be here in a few minutes to interview you."

I felt a little panicky. My mind was full of a plan that I had been evolving since encountering Dr. Thijsse, but the slightest mention of it at this time might easily prove fatal to my hopes. What was I to say to them? Soon I was called downstairs. Eight or ten men rose to their feet with pencils poised.

"What is the object of your visit to England at this time?" the leader asked.

"I have never heard a nightingale sing and I have come to England hoping to hear one," I told him with as much self-control as possible. Pencils scribbled rapidly.

"What do you think of the dole as administered by the English Government?" was the next question.

I swallowed hard. "I should prefer to mention that subject only in a written statement which I have not yet had time to prepare," I declared. And then suddenly, "I shall have to ask to be excused now in order to keep a pressing engage-ment," and thus made my escape.

The fact that I was the guest of one of the world's greatest bankers, the man who as Chancellor of the Exchequer had borrowed billions for the Allies during the Great War, and who, before that, as First Lord of the Admiralty, had been chiefly responsible for the building of many of England's largest war-ships—this, it seemed, automatically stamped me as a man whose opinions on governmental affairs were worth giving to the world.

The story that I had come three thousand miles from across the Western Ocean to hear a nightingale sing was published throughout England and was cabled to the United States. At least two dozen letters soon arrived, kindly inviting me to visit in the country and listen at night to the world-famous songsters in the gardens.

Lord Edward Grey planned a two-day field-trip that I might make the acquaintance of various English birds. With us in the cars were Lady Glenconner, Mrs. Reginald McKenna and H. J. Massingham. The trip took us south into Surrey. We paused by a bank to watch a colony of sand martins, and descended into the Devil's Punch Bowl to hear the song of the grasshopper warbler. In an abandoned field we sought for, and listened to the strains of the rare Dartford warbler which was inhabiting a heavy growth of prickly gorse that, true to Cowper's description, "decks itself with ornaments of gold."

We went to Selborne and saw the house where Gilbert White had lived, the church in which he preached, and his gravestone near by. I took a photograph of the large memorial window which in its colored glass was said to depict fifty of the birds referred to in his *Natural History of Selborne*.

In the garden of Munstead House, the home of Sir Herbert and Lady Jekyll, near Godalming, I sat with Lord Edward until after ten o'clock hoping to hear the nightingale, then discouraged we went into the house. I was on the point of retiring when the butler tapped on my door and said, "Lord Grey asks that you raise your back window for a nightingale in the garden is now singing in great power." I rushed to the casement and throwing up the window listened for many minutes to the musical, measured notes of great sweetness and variety that floated to my ears. At later times and in various countries I have heard the song of this bird, and often have thought of the truthfulness in Shakespeare's statement:

> The nightingale, if it should sing by day,
> When every goose is cackling, would be thought
> No better a musician than the wren. . . .

As a matter of fact, the nightingale does sing by day, but its song easily may be overlooked among the chorus of bird notes that fill the air.

We visited Lord Grey's fishing camp on the Itchen River where he often sought seclusion during the trying days of the World War when, as England's Foreign Secretary, his harassing duties were almost more than a man could bear.

One day as we were having tea under a great oak by the side of a little pond, Lord Grey remarked that Tennyson had often come here to be alone and to write. Then he pointed to an old stone wall a hundred yards or more away and said that at one time Tennyson walked over there and found a flower that inspired him to write that exquisite poem which begins, "Flower in the crannied wall". . . .

My host told much of the habits and distribution of the birds of the country-side. As we crossed a little foot-bridge, I asked him in what kind of situation the gray wagtail made its nest. He dropped the end of his cane to a grass-covered shelf at the side of the stream and said that a site like this was often chosen. To my amazement I saw a nest and four eggs of a gray wagtail within three inches of the end of his cane. He had not seen it for his eye-sight was becoming much impaired. Later, at Fallodon, his home in Northumberland, even with his field-glasses he was unable to determine with accuracy whether a duck some forty feet away was an European widgeon or a pochard.

I was much impressed with the great numbers of birds to

be seen and heard in the gardens and along the hedge-rows of England.

A few days after returning from our field trip to Surrey, Lady Glenconner and Lord Grey were married on June 4, 1922.

Mrs. McKenna was a wonderful hostess and made my stay in England of great interest and value. Knowing of my deep interest in bird sanctuaries she took me with Mr. and Mrs. Massingham to the Farne Islands where guillemots nest and puffins sit about their burrows; where shags and cormorants come, and the brooding eider ducks let the keeper stroke their backs. She drove with me to London's bird sanctuaries in Hyde Park, Richmond Park and Kensington Gardens. She showed me English robins, tree pipits and a nesting-colony of common herons, and she sent me to the bird sanctuary of the Selborne Society. She arranged with Dr. Sydney H. Long, of Norwich, to take me to Stalham Broad to hear the bitterns boom, and to watch the common snipe as, in its period of dalliance, it swept "lambing" through the sky.

I was much pleased to find that the name "Norwich" is pronounced "Norige" and was the place which, according to a rhyme of childhood, was sought by "a man in the moon" who "came down too soon."

One Sunday the Norwich Walking and Reading Club took me for a stroll of perhaps fifteen miles, which permitted me to add various birds to my English list. In a mere on Thorp Heath, a pair of Canada Geese appeared with four young. I learned that the species had been introduced into England a long time ago, and was breeding in a wild state in various places. One of the men that day said to me, "Yankees are pretty good traders, but we think that we rather got the better of you when we traded you the house sparrow and the starling for the wood duck and the Canada goose."

In the local paper the next day I was quoted as saying that what in England are called "meres" in America would be known as "ponds" and the comment was added, "This is but another example of the paucity of the English language as employed by Americans."

In Mrs. McKenna's home I was to meet many interesting people, Lord William Percy, for example, and Radcliff Dugmore and Lady Scott, whose husband had lost his life at the South Pole. One day, to my great joy, Mrs. McKenna announced that W. H. Hudson had accepted her invitation to dine that evening, but in the afternoon a telephone call announced that he had been taken ill and would be unable to be with us. His illness proved fatal and some weeks later, on August 18th, he passed away. I feel sure that his books, including *Far Away and Long Ago*, will stand as a far more effective memorial to this interesting man than will the atrocious stone panel of Epstein, depicting "Rima," the heroine of *Green Mansions*, which in 1925 was unveiled in Hyde Park.

One night I talked with Mrs. McKenna about the bill pending in the United States Congress to prohibit vessels from discharging oil overboard in territorial waters, and about a similar bill for Great Britain then being considered by the House of Lords. The Royal Society for the Protection of Birds and the National Audubon Association were especially interested in these proposed measures, which, if enacted, should do much to save sea bird life.

The next morning she read to me an article from the London *Times*, stating that the day before the bill had been up in the House of Lords on second reading and that discussion had been postponed for some future time. She thought this was simply a move to defeat the measure and feared it might be the end of the oil pollution bill, as Lord Bearsted, who was actively opposing it, was particularly influential. When I asked if there was not some one who had sufficient influence to get Bearsted to let the bill go on, she said "Wait a minute," and left the room.

In a short time she returned. "I have just been telephoning," she beamed. "It is all arranged for you and Stanley Baldwin to spend the week-end together at Godalming. That will be your chance to tell him all about the need for passing the oil bill. If any one can move that bill it is Stanley Baldwin."

Sunday morning at Munstead House, I came down to the breakfast room, accepted a kidney and a cup of coffee from the butler, reached for my pipe and went into the garden. It was not very long before I saw Mr. Baldwin emerge from the house, lighting his briarwood. I had him to myself for at least an hour.

On June 14th the Oil in Navigable Waters Bill was again brought up in the House of Lords, and the London *Times* the next day stated editorially: "Lord Bearsted in the end withdrew his opposition," and "The bill passed the second reading."

The editorial also referred to my being in London and said, "not only the bird-protection societies which he represents, but other important interests, are supporting a similar appeal in the United States, and he hopes that national action here and in his own country will speedily be followed by international action"—which was a summation of my talk with Stanley Baldwin.

The Oil in Navigable Waters Bill passed the House of Lords and the Commons and soon received the Royal Assent. It went into force January 1, 1923. My small effort probably had little or nothing to do with its passage but it was a pleasure to be able to testify in its behalf.

The Oil Pollution Act became a law in the United States on June 7, 1924.

Just here it may be remarked that while these and similar restrictions adopted in some other countries have had beneficial effects, oil on the high seas continues to be very harmful, as much of it is washed ashore. In an effort to secure an international treaty to put an end to this menace, there assembled in Washington, June 8-17, 1926, at the invitation of President Coolidge, an International Conference on Oil Pollution. Fourteen countries were represented. It was planned that all countries should agree to prohibit the discharge of mineral oils on the seas within fifty nautical miles of the shore, and that "special provisions for encouraging vessels and shipping interests to install 'oil separators' on vessels and in harbors for the dual purpose of conserving oil and aquatic resources," should be included. The plan failed as several countries refused to be signatory to the Draft Convention, although some steamship lines adopted these recommendations. In 1934 the British Government asked the League of Nations to bring about some such international understanding, but up to January, 1937, nothing of great importance has taken place.

Mr. Baldwin, Mrs. McKenna and I called to see A. Thorburn, a Scottish bird-artist of great distinction. He exhibited to us several dozen of his magnificent colored drawings. When I remarked that on the walls of the Audubon Association office we displayed various drawings of birds by Fuertes and Horsfall, he said he had not heard of these gentlemen, but offered to sell me one of his own original drawings, about the size of a post-card, for fifty guineas! After tea with the family, at which I had my initial adventure with a Scottish scone, we went to the garden to watch two bullfinches feeding their young—then started homeward across the fields.

"Would you care to meet Bernard Shaw?" Mrs. McKenna asked me one day.

I thought the experience might be interesting and the next night sat with the famous playwright on the rostrum of Queens Hall before two thousand people interested in humane education. Mr. Shaw first devoted his attention to the "Ruling classes of England," which he said send their children to the Public Schools, "so-called because the public is excluded from them." He declared that the chief lessons these sons of rich men are taught are to handle their whiskey like gentlemen and to torture little foxes by chasing them across the country. Soon he had the audience shouting with delight. Then, with his matchless powers, he held up to ridicule the struggles of a poor boy trying to get an education so that he can enjoy a better position than his father ever held. It was an amazing performance.

I had long looked forward to meeting personally the leaders of the Royal Society for the Protection of Birds of whose splendid work I had been reading in *Bird Notes and News* during the past nineteen years. The opportunity came on June 9th, when I had the privilege of being the Society's guest of honor at the Zoological Gardens in Regent's Park. Here I met the Earl Buxton, Sir Montague Sharpe, K.C., Mr. and Mrs. Frank E. Lemon, Mead-Waldo, W. P. Pycraft, the Dutchess of Somerset, Lady Sharpe, Lady Lockyer, Lady Rolleston, Dr. Chalmers Mitchell, Hon. Mrs. Dewitt, Dr. Dewitt, and many others.

After tea in the new pavilion, I spoke in the Lecture Hall. This kindly greeting by Europe's best-known society for bird protection was most stimulating and I came away with a heart brimming with happiness for having been associated with those who had long been fighting for the preservation of British birds.

About this time, also, I was the guest speaker at a dinner of the Ornithological Club of the British Ornithologists' Union, and my association with William L. Sclater, Percy Lowe and other prominent English ornithologists began.

I now felt that the time had come to attempt the plan of which I had been thinking ever since my conversation with the esteemed German professor in Holland. He did not know anything about bird protection in America and probably neither did any of his co-workers in Germany or the Netherlands. And how many people in the United States or Canada knew what the Germans or the Dutch or the Japanese were doing to save their birds; or what methods they were employing in their undertakings? In every country possibly some plans were in operation which with modifications could be adopted by others to advantage if they but knew of them. I had already decided to attempt to get Holland's system of lighthouse racks accepted in America.

Surely there was much that we could learn from each other. Why not effect an international organization which, among other things, would further stimulate interest in bird protection by the interchange of publications and by occasional conventions where representatives of different countries could meet in council? Also there were a number of problems that were distinctly international in their bearing, such as oil pollution on the high seas, and the export and import of birds or their feathers.

Lord Edward Grey said he thought that the plan was a good one and would gladly lend it his support. I therefore invited a few people interested in bird protection to meet with me in London at the home of Mrs. Reginald McKenna on June 20, 1922.

There were present: Viscount Grey of Fallodon, K.G., the Earl Buxton G.C.M.G., Frank E. Lemon, Dr. Percy Lowe, William L. Sclater, H. J. Massingham, and Mrs. Reginald McKenna, all of England; Dr. Peter G. Van Tienhoven and Dr. A. Burdet of Holland; Jean Delacour of France, and myself.

In my presentation, I laid stress on the fact that if the preservation of wild birds was one half as important as some of us thought, then the task of defending them should not be left entirely to a few comparatively small bird-protection societies. That in Great Britain, for instance, the work of the Royal Society for the Protection of Birds should be augmented by the very active coöperation of certain other groups who until the present time, I understood, had done next to nothing in behalf of the interests of the living bird. Some of those which I suggested should lend a hand were the British Ornithologists' Union, the Zoological Society of London, and the Scottish Zoological Society. Why not form a British National Section of a proposed International Committee for Bird Preservation that would include these and other similar groups, and follow the same method in as many other countries as we could interest? After free discussion by all present the following resolution presented by Lord Grey was adopted:

"We who are present at this meeting under the presidency of T. Gilbert Pearson, unanimously agree that for the purpose of coördinating and encouraging the preservation of birds, it is desirable that an International Committee should be constituted and that steps should be taken to have such a Committee formed by asking societies in different countries interested in the preservation of birds to nominate members to form such a Committee."

Plans were at once put into operation for the preparation of a Declaration of Principles and a set of by-laws to govern our activities. At the conclusion of this meeting I felt that my work in Europe was done for the present.

While returning to New York on the steamship *Homeric* I was asked to address the passengers one evening in the saloon. Some new memberships in the Audubon Association resulted.

In the correspondence awaiting me in the office I found a clipping from an Idaho paper giving a cable dispatch from London, announcing that at Godalming, in Surrey, I at last had heard the song of the nightingale.

Nine months passed and I found myself again leaving the United States, this time for the Bahama Islands to visit the haunts of the American flamingo, the world's largest bird of brilliant plumage.

Many years before, when the Directors of the Audubon Association held their first meeting, we adopted a resolution appealing "to the Governor and the Assembly of the Bahamas to give to the birds of these islands such legal protection as would insure their preservation." This was January 30, 1905. Before the year passed a Bahaman Wild Birds' Protection Act went into effect. It provided for closed seasons on hunting game-birds, prohibited all killing of song and insectivorous birds and empowered the Governor to establish bird reserves from time to time throughout the various islands.

Seventeen years later, Dr. L. C. Sanford of Connecticut went to the Bahamas to collect birds. His guide and companion on Andros Island was E. W. Forsyth, who told him of the extensive killing of flamingoes for food and urged him to try to induce the Governor to create a sanctuary to protect the large breeding-colony which had been brought to public attention by C. J. Maynard in 1884, and extensively studied by Dr. Frank M. Chapman in 1902 and 1904. Dr. Sanford responded to this appeal with the result that on May 15, 1922, Sir Harry Cordeaux, Governor of the Bahamas, issued a proclamation establishing a flamingo sanctuary covering some five hundred square miles of the south end of Andros Island. The government provided for the services of two wardens; but two patrol boats were needed and the Audubon Association was glad to give the money to supply this want.

It now seemed expedient, therefore, to make the acquaintance of Commissioner Forsyth and to gather first-hand information regarding the flamingo colony. Hence, in March, 1923, accompanied by George Innes Hartley, I left Nassau in a small sea-going yacht, and the next day we waded ashore on Andros where, in a beautiful coconut-grove, Mr. Forsyth's residence was situated. The vessel on which we had arrived departed at once for New Providence.

The island, some sixty miles in length by twenty in width, had a human population of eight white people and perhaps seven thousand Negroes.

All night after our arrival men worked, calking the bottom of a sloop which was the only boat now available for our use. Next morning, with Commissioner Forsyth in command, we sailed southward many miles and went ashore in a little indentation of the coast. It was a long journey Mr. Forsyth led us over jagged coral-rock beds and up the shallow "swash," where much of the time we were obliged to pull the skiffs in which we had expected to ride. To our keen disappointment the great colony of flamingoes had not yet arrived from their winter wanderings. Only one bird was seen. It was asleep and I think I could have taken it in my arms if the sound of Mr. Hartley's eager advance through the shallow water had not awakened it. Nests of the previous year were present in great numbers, for the coral marl of which they were made becomes very hard when exposed to the sun and they keep their form long after the birds have ceased to use them.

We found much to claim our attention on Andros. Grove-billed anis, or "Jew birds," in small companies sat solemnly on the tops of bushes; and the members of a reddish egret colony were found to be about equally divided between the white and blue phases of plumage. By far our most interesting experience was the association with Commissioner Forsyth, a man of erudition and of charming personality, who conscientiously and effectively was governing this stray bit of the great British Empire set in a lonely sapphire sea. Hurricanes often have decimated this flamingo colony, but of late it has been prospering and Mr. Forsyth reported that in the summer of 1935 more than 2,000 young were brought to maturity from the 3,000 nests that were constructed.

By May, having recovered from a fever contracted in the Bahamas, I again sailed for Europe, where I hoped further to organize the International Committee. The New York Bird and Tree Club asked me to take a few thousand dollars they had collected, and use it in planting fruit trees for some of the people of France whose gardens had been destroyed in the great bombardments.

Finding my young sons just beginning a week's vacation, I took them with me to Verdun and then worked eastward along the battle-front through the Argonne and Champagne sectors until we reached the shattered town of Château-Thierry. Here I arranged for planting an extensive orchard near the place where the American soldiers first went prominently into action during the World War.

With Mrs. Pearson I attended the sessions of the Congrès International pour la Protection de la Nature Sites et Monuments Naturels, in Paris, May 31-June 3, 1923, where her knowledge of French was invaluable in giving me a better idea of what was going on. The afternoon I spoke there were many new faces in the audience.

"These are not scientists who have come to hear you," Mr. Delacour said, "they are the milliners of Paris."

Despite their expressed objections, my resolution for discouraging the traffic in the plumage of egrets and birds-of-paradise went on record.

Proceeding now to Switzerland, I met the ornithologist Alfred Richard, and some of his friends in Neuchâtel. A Swiss Section of the International Committee resulted.

While crossing Austria I was in a country of inflated currency, and for my luncheon on the train the bill came to 36,500 krone, which a few years before would have been the equal of $7,300. I gave the waiter a one-dollar bill and received a handful of paper money as change. In Vienna it cost 7,000 krone extra to have butter served with my meal.

In Budapest I was welcomed by Titus Csorgey and Dr.

Jacob Schenk of the Royal Hungarian Ornithological Institute, and other naturalists. A National Section of our
International Committee has since been in operation.

With Dr. Schenk I traveled southward to Kisbalaton, and
in the great marsh I helped him "ring" various young spoonbills and black ibises. Here I saw the squacco heron, a little
white and yellow egret-like bird. There was also a small
colony of large white egrets of which Dr. Schenk was most
solicitous. The marsh was on the estate of the Grand Duke
Festetics Tassilo. After our work with the birds, the boatmen brought us ashore where Szabo György, the manager,
and his brother were waiting. Four men in a wagon arrived,
one with five dead birds that I took to be young jackdaws.
On a table placed in the shade of a tree a luncheon was
spread, consisting of a great bowl of fried chicken, a roast
leg of lamb, generously seasoned with garlic, a very large
round loaf of dark bread, quantities of small cakes and two
kinds of wine.

I do not know what language György used. Dr. Schenk
spoke German and a limited amount of English. On the
table beside him was a bilingual dictionary. Our conversations were interesting if not voluminous.

In the name of the Audubon Association I was happy to
contribute sufficient funds for Dr. Schenk to keep two guards
on Kisbalaton, and two on another bird preserve, for a period
of three months. The salary to be paid each man was three
dollars a month, a sum to them quite satisfactory. We went
to Fenék Farm near Lake Balaton, where I counted thirty-
one occupied nests of white storks in the trees of a five-acre
grove. Here magpies and gray-headed crows were common.

Dr Schenk was anxious to start a bird-protection society.
He said that during the previous year there had not been
one conviction for violation of the bird-laws in all Hungary.

Going on to Italy, where I had not a single friend nor
acquaintance, I sought out the veteran ornithologist, Dr.

Sassi, whose home was in Florence. My interpreter was an exiled Russian nobleman. Then I went to see Count Arrigoni Degli Oddi. I found him in his palace at Padua, where his great rooms were beautifully furnished with marble carvings of Conova and other priceless works of art. On the wall of his study a framed card bore the legend, "Red Letter Days in Duck Hunting." Then followed a series of dates with the number of ducks he had killed on each occasion. Many of these recorded more than 200, and one especially fortunate day he had taken 662. Between the years 1877 and 1921, he had shot and retrieved 51,303 wild ducks. It was evident the Italians were not taking care of the wild-fowl any better than were the people of North Carolina and Illinois.

The Count showed me a book given him some years before by a visiting American, Dr. Louis B. Bishop. It was *Birds of Connecticut*, by Sage and Bishop. I talked to him about the desirability of forming an Italian Section of our Committee for Bird Preservation. For a time he was not very responsive. At length he said, "We will go to Bologna and see Ghigi."

As we walked through the gate at the railway station he exhibited a little gold badge, and with a bow the guard admitted us to the train without tickets.

In the University of Bologna I found Professor Alessandro Ghigi equally reluctant about undertaking my suggested movement for bird preservation. In the end he decided that the plan might be worth trying. Together we all spent a pleasant afternoon at his palace outside the city. In my schooldays I had read of the Leaning Tower of Pisa, and had supposed that it was only one in the world, but in Bologna I found another.

In Rue Romano, Naples, many dead birds were offered for sale. Some of the prices in terms of American money were: thrushes and skylarks, four cents; small sandpipers, eight cents; bitterns and black ibises, twenty cents; and ducks, eight to twenty-four cents. I visited bookshops in Naples,

Rome, Venice, and Florence. Not one of them could produce a book for identifying birds, but all had publications for sale which explained the most effective methods of capturing them. I was handed one book on netting birds that had been printed in 1684.

One day in Rome, after two operators had worked for an hour over the city's five telephone systems, during which they had exclaimed *pronto* several hundred times as they vainly tried to make a connection for me with the Chigi Palace at Ariccia, I gave up the attempt, and going to my room wrote a letter to His Holiness the Pope, expressing the hope that he might urge the people of Italy to stop killing song birds for food. The letter perhaps did not reach the Pontiff.

Back in London the McKennas again received me into their home and provided another period of wonderful entertainment. One day the ample salon was filled with various gentlemen of the peerage, their ladies and others. They had come by invitation to meet me and to hear me speak. Naturally I discussed the need of world-wide bird preservation and exhibited motion-pictures I had brought across the sea.

With Mr. and Mrs. Massingham, Mrs. McKenna took me to Edinburgh and down to the mouth of the Firth of Forth, where two days in succession we made journeys to the famous Bass Rock Sanctuary with its colony of 8,000 breeding gannets, known of old as solan geese. This was long supposed to be the only place in the world where the gannet bred, and this fact is memorialized in the scientific name of the bird, *Móris bassána*.

On the island were underground chambers of an ancient prison and from a book of local history I learned that Robert Gillespie, who was a paternal ancestor of Mrs. Pearson, had been imprisoned in one of its cells for fifteen years. He had been accused and convicted of the crime of preaching the Presbyterian doctrine.

One day we went to Westminster Abbey to attend the memorial exercises of my fellow North Carolinian, Walter Hines Page, whom I had long known and admired. The tablet that day unveiled to the memory of this American who was Ambassador to England during the World War, bore the inscription: "He was England's friend in her time of sorest need."

Mr. Hugh Gladstone had accepted the Chairmanship of the British Section of the International Committee and I visited him on the family estate, "Capenoch," in Dumfrieshire, Scotland. There were many grouse on the estate and he told me that there had been good shooting there for several hundred years. He explained that the "grouse disease" that sometimes greatly reduced the birds was caused by an over-increase of parasites always present in the birds, but which became unduly numerous when, due to drought and over-stocking, there were not enough young leaves of heather to keep the birds in normal physical condition.

One day I asked Mr. Gladstone if there ever had been such a person as Annie Laurie.

"Oh, yes," he said, "but we call the name Lory."

He told me that the present Laird of Maxwelton, Sir Claude Laurie, was his intimate friend and half an hour later we were on the "bonnie braes" of Maxwelton. Hanging in the living-room was the painting of a lovely girl—she was Annie Laurie. I told Mr. Gladstone that I would rather possess that picture than to own the Mona Lisa. We drove five miles to the Ferguson estate, "Craigdarrach," where Annie Laurie lived and reared her children. Here I saw her wedding stone set in the wall of the house, and read the wedding contract in her own handwriting. Mr. Gladstone told me that about the year 1700 a young man, William Douglas of Fingland, wrote a song about Annie Laurie and soon went away to the wars, but upon his return found that his adored one was wedded to another. Perhaps sixty years later, a writer while gathering Scottish folk songs, heard an old woman sing "Annie Laurie" and published the words, which about 1835 were changed to the form in which we know it to-day. Here are the words of the song as it is said to have been written by the young lover 237 years ago:

> Maxwelton's banks are bonnie
> Where early fa's the dew,
> Where I and Annie Laurie
> Made up the promise true;
> Made up the promise true,
> And never forget will I,
> And for bonnie Annie Laurie,
> I'd lay down my head and die.
>
> She's backet like a peacock,
> She's breasted like a swan,
> She's jimp about the middle,
> Her waist you weel may spän;
> Her waist you weel may spän,
> And she has a rolling eye,
> And for bonnie Annie Laurie,
> I'd lay down my head and die.

During this stay in England I again had various conferences with our co-workers, and learned more of Britain's bird-protection problems.

The next spring a call came to visit Panama and help plan laws for wild-life preservation. This pleased me very much. What bird student has not thrilled at the thought of wandering in tropical jungles and making the acquaintance of some of their brilliant avian denizens?

A joint invitation had reached me from a committee appointed by Governor Jay J. Morrow of the Panama Canal Zone, and a committee from the Panama Rotary Club. Better protection should be accorded the birds both in the Canal Zone and in the Panamanian Republic, they said. Would I not come and give them the benefit of such advice as I could offer? Mr. G. Lister Carlisle, Jr., of New York City, generously offered to pay my expenses, and soon from a rolling deck on the Caribbean I was lifting my eyes to the Southern Cross.

A few days later I was in the wilderness as a guest of Captain E. T. Brown. Fascinating days and nights were spent along the Bayano and Pacora rivers that empty their waters into the Pacific well down the coast below Panama City. Crocodiles, small lizards and iguanas were plentiful. Birds were everywhere in abundance. Green parrots in great flocks, always separated into pairs, passed over the forests continually in the evening. A companion shot one, and its mate flew back and forth overhead until night, its calls never ceasing. There were land rails and flocks of the great purplish-black ani, nineteen inches in length. Jacanas fed on the shingly beaches of the rivers instead of running over lily-pads, as pictures often show them. Guans shrieked and revealed their presence when they heard us tramping through the leaves. Woodhewers cheeped like young turkeys; little black manakins with red caps and ridiculously short tails made sounds as if they were striking pebbles together. Cormorants went up the rivers in endless streams. Toucans were everywhere, and I saw natives shooting them for food. I visited some of the jungle villages with their thatched huts, where domesticated black-bellied tree ducks fed with the chickens. Through an interpreter I learned something of the people's attitude toward wild life.

Back in Panama City, brown pelicans haunted the harbor and stole fish from the fishing boats at the docks. Black vultures and man-of-war birds perched together on flat roofs overlooking the bay, and streams of little parrakeets flew over the town. Great frigate birds with inflated red gular sacs as large as oranges decorated trees on the islands in Panama Bay. The whole country was amazingly rich in bird life, and yet throughout the 500 miles of the length of Panama there was not one law to protect them in any possible way.

One morning Mrs. Samuel D. Sturgis took me to the markets in Panama City as the stall-keepers were sweeping out the bodies of dozens of brightly colored birds that had died during the night. She purchased a number of the surviving prisoners but when we liberated them on her lawn in Balboa Heights we found, to our surprise and to our sorrow, that their wings had been clipped and they could not fly away to the forest.

Aigrettes and paradise plumes were displayed in the shops of Panama City and I saw United States naval officers purchasing them. The Pacific Fleet was about to sail for California, and I was told by the captain of a cruiser that the baggage of naval officers is never examined for smuggled goods.

I gave illustrated lectures in the club-houses of Balboa and Colon and also spoke in the high school building of Balboa. The well-known local naturalist, Dr. James Zetek, took me to the Tropical Research Laboratory on Barro Colorado Island in Lake Gatun.

At the request of Dr. Belisario Porras, President of the Panama Republic, I prepared and submitted to him my recommendations calling for restrictions on bird killing, but chiefly in the four Departments adjoining the Canal Zone where Americans were wont to shoot almost any creature they found.

In the Panama Canal Zone I found the open season for shooting the native ducks—chiefly the muscovy, or "pato-real" and the black-bellied tree duck or "wichity"—covered the period when they were breeding. I called attention to the error and it was rectified.

So generous had been the gift of Mr. Carlisle that I found upon leaving Panama I should be able to gratify my earnest desire to visit a region reported to contain breeding flamingos on the north shore of Cuba.

Upon landing in Havana I found trouble in the wind. A rebellion had broken out in the territory through which I would be forced to pass. No dispatches had been received from the eastern part of the island in two days. Troops were being rushed to the troubled region. The train I expected to take was to be blown up that night in Santa Clara Province. These were some of the disquieting stories that filled the lobbies of the hotels and of the American Club. Uncertain as to what I should do, I went to the railway station. Very few civilians were traveling but armed soldiers were crowding into the train. I decided to go with them. Therefore, at 9 P.M. on May 1, 1924, I boarded the Expreso Limitado.

In my *dormitorio* I had a good night's rest and the next forenoon I arrived at Moron. Here I discovered that although a launch and men had been provided for me, there was a shortage of gasoline, as such shipments had been terminated. Despair seemed imminent, when suddenly a supply of eighty gallons was discovered. I bought the lot for eighty cents a gallon. On the way to the canal where the launch was lying, we were pursued by taxi-drivers who shouted offers of one dollar a gallon for the precious fluid.

The launch which had been engaged was about thirty feet in length and covered with a light canopy. There were no cabin, bunks, tables or chairs. The entire equipment consisted of a small skiff, a charcoal cooking bucket, and three or four cooking utensils. For seats we could use the boxes containing our cans of gasoline. Our food consisted almost wholly of canned goods I purchased in Moron, the most of which I found it impossible to eat. A man in the United States who sold such canned filth could be sent to jail for the rest of his life. My crew consisted of a Cuban captain whom I was told was the *patrón,* a Cuban assistant and a young American interpreter who tried to cheer me about the food by saying that I would have a splendid dinner that night at the headquarters of the Turiguano Development Company.

Seldom, if ever, have I seen larger mangroves than those constituting the submerged forest through which we passed before reaching the open waters of the bay. It would have been a pleasant cruise that day but for the combination of nausea and hunger that grew in intensity as the afternoon wore on.

At sunset we reached the dock at Isle Turiguano, where I saw a house on a hill perhaps a mile away. Here lived E. J. Barker, Manager of the Development Company. It was he who had written me of the flamingos on his island, had arranged for the launch, and had sent the interpreter to Moron to assist me. There was no car or other vehicle of any kind to meet us at the landing, although my guide assured me that Mr. Barker was anticipating my arrival and would expect me for dinner. I brushed up a little, donning fresh linen and putting on a new gray suit.

The young American said we would not follow the road but would take a path which would bring us more quickly to the house. He moved away with great assurance and trustingly I followed. The path was not very plain and before long we were among bushes. Very quickly the darkness came. We lost the trail and soon were merged in a thicket that in places was impenetrable. I had no idea as to what direction lay the house or the boat. Fire had burned through this region recently and the branches and twigs marked our hands, faces and clothing with the soot and charcoal with which they were covered. I was scratched with briars, fell into holes and became exhausted; but so tenacious of life is man I would not give up, although the thought crossed my mind that the time might come when hunger would cause us to draw lots as to which should eat the other. However, the guide exhibited his intimate familiarity with the country by ultimately leading into a clearing and, according to my notes of the next day, at 9:40 P.M., reeking with perspiration and marked like a zebra, I staggered up to the door and knocked.

We were ushered into a room where three immaculately attired gentlemen, one of whom was a very formal Englishman, gazed at us in astonishment. I asked which was Mr. Barker, introduced myself, explained why I had appeared in this condition, and apologized for being late to dinner. So surprised was he at the unholy spectacle before him that the word "dinner" appeared not to sink into his consciousness. After talking about flamingos for half an hour, during which time the Englishman said nothing but occasionally cast horrified glances in my direction, I asked Barker if there was some one with a car who could take me back to the boat. He seemed suddenly to sense the possibility that there was a human being inside the soiled apparition before him and his humane instincts leaped to the surface. I must not think of going to the boat, I must spend the night with him. I had a bath and a good bed, but I had no food.

In the morning Barker greeted me with a smile. My hands and face were more presentable and my hair was combed, but my gray suit looked like something I might have picked up on the beach.

"The flamingos are waiting for you," he said.

From the veranda he pointed to a distant line of scarlet. As he watched it separated into elongated reddish dots—the birds arose and in a long line broadly followed the curve of the island until they came to rest in a shallow lagoon. After breakfast we followed them and as we watched from behind a mangrove bush we estimated their number at about seven hundred. Perhaps one-fifth of them were in the white immature plumage.

Mr. Barker kindly loaned me a canvas cot and we began

a search for the flamingo breeding-colony. For three days we visited various places where the *patrón* said they had colonized in past years. Often we waded half a mile or more to get ashore and we walked and waded many miles over the marl flats. We visited sections of Turiguano, Cayo Coco, and a number of smaller islands. No occupied nesting-place was found, but nests of former years were seen in three places. The *patrón* took me to a site on Cayo Coco, from which he and his crew had taken 1,500 young birds two years before. In his schooner they had been removed to the mainland, herded through the streets like domestic geese, and sold for food. The old nests of the birds here occupied a strip of shoal from 75 to 150 feet wide and about a hundred yards in length.

We visited three or four breeding-colonies of other waterbirds, including snowy egrets, white ibis and man-of-war birds. Reddish egrets were fairly common and one flock of more than eighty roseate spoonbills were noted. We saw great white herons, egrets, caracaras, ospreys, willets, black-necked stilts and a few limpkins. At a cormorant colony the Cubans with their oars struck a number of young from their nests. These were skinned and the pot on the charcoal bucket soon boiled and bubbled merrily. The odor was most offensive, penetrating and far-reaching. The stench filled the atmosphere and drifted to leeward. I have little doubt but that it arose until it swirled and moaned about the portals of heaven.

Flamingos were seen in many places, singly or in small flocks, sometimes flying, but usually feeding on the shoals. Counting the flock at Turiguano at 700, the entire number noted was 1,805. One evening the *patrón* caught one with a broken wing.

"He says it will make him a fine feast to-morrow night," the interpreter explained.

The next morning when I awoke my first thought was of

that handsome bird which I had seen tightly bound and
thrust into a box. The three men lay sleeping on the floor.
I released the bird from its cramped position, cut the rope
that was wrapped about it and trimmed off the dangling
portion of the wing. Then with strips of my pocket handkerchief I bandaged the wound as best I could, the bird, meanwhile, making no effort to escape. At first it could not stand
and when at length it attempted to do so it pitched forward
and with its beak resting on the floor, stood tripod-fashion
for a time. When finally it assumed a normal attitude it
uttered a low musical "ha-honk" and began to preen its
feathers. The *patrón* stirred and I slipped it back into the
box.

After breakfast I took a seat in the stern of the skiff and
on my lap rested the flamingo hidden from sight by my
raincoat. I told the *patrón* I wanted to go to an island a
mile distant. He had a way of standing in the prow while
he poled across the shallows which meant that his back was
toward me most of the time, hence when I slipped the bird
overboard he did not see the action. As I looked back I saw
it fall forward. For perhaps a second its head seemed to rest
on bottom, then it straightened and began wading toward
some other flamingos feeding at a distance. What the *patrón*
said when he found that he had been deprived of his bird
for supper was one of the many things which the interpreter
thought it unnecessary to relate to me.

Despite the simpleness of my outfit, the daily expense was
considerable and I insisted on long days of work hoping to
cover all the flamingo territory on the coast of Camaguey
Province. This course proved to be an unwise one. The
morning I said we would go to Cayo Romano, the principal
remaining island I had planned to visit, I expressed surprise
at the direction in which the boat was headed. The interpreter said, "We are not going to Cayo Romano, we are
returning to Moron."

"What does this mean?" I demanded.

He grinned. "The *patrón* says you work him too hard, he is tired and is going home."

The next day in the Seville Hotel in Havana, I met Barker and we planned together what had best be attempted for saving the flamingos of Camaguey. I sought the aid of our American Ambassador, General Enoch H. Crowder. Sometime before this, a Decree was issued in Cuba for the protection of non-game birds of the island. However, few people knew of this fact, and broadly speaking, no one paid any attention to the statute. I offered for the Audubon Association to print cloth warning notices of the law if the Cuban authorities would post them along the north coast. But the Secretary of Agriculture under whose authority this would have to be done was not in position to act just then, as his brother seemed to be mixed up in the little rebellion then stirring the island.

I was unable to make any progress but Barker, who became deeply interested in these birds, continued his efforts and nine years later, July 28, 1933, President Machado signed a Decree creating a flamingo sanctuary covering the northern coast and all of the adjacent islands of the Province of Camaguey.

This was followed by two other Decrees; one on April 3, 1936, prohibiting the exportation of flamingos and certain other birds for a period of twenty years; another, on June 1, 1936, extending the flamingo sanctuary over the entire northern and southern coastal territories of the Provinces of Camaguey and Santa Clara.

Occasionally a few flamingos visit the shallow waters of south Florida but none has been known to breed in the state. Within the race-track of the Miami Jockey Club, at Hialeah, two hundred or more have been kept of late, and they have built a few nests—in fact, thirty-four were constructed in 1936. That year, May 24th, an egg was laid, and on June 2nd another appeared. They did not hatch but they established the record of being the first eggs of this great scarlet bird known to have been laid within the boundaries of the United States.

CHAPTER XXI

PROBLEMS IN EUROPE

OTTO HERMAN, prominent Hungarian ornithologist, was born June 27, 1835, and died December 27, 1914. He was largely responsible for establishing the Royal Hungarian Central Bureau of Ornithology and in 1894 founded, and through twenty large volumes edited *Aquila*, the official Magyar Ornithological Journal. In 1907 he issued at Budapest a 241-page book entitled *The International Convention for the Protection of Birds*, which contains the most complete information available about the early efforts to protect birds by means of a treaty.

The first undertaking of this nature was in Germany about 1868, when the farmers and foresters held their 26th General Assembly. They urged the Austrian and Hungarian Foreign Minister to persuade his Governments to join other States in a treaty for the protection of animals of value to agriculture and forestry. Consent was given, if the call were "restricted to the protection of birds useful to agriculture." Negotiations were carried on until 1872 when the Swiss Federal Council proposed an International Commission to draft the agreement. Then dissension arose as to the kind of agreement which should be drawn and the movement collapsed.

The next year there was held in Vienna an International Agricultural Congress. At the suggestion of Dr. Tschudi, an Austrian delegate, the Imperial Austrian Government was "requested to secure the protection of birds useful to agriculture by means of treaties." After three years of diplomatic correspondence a protocol for a consideration of the subject was issued to several countries. France and Switzerland agreed to the idea of getting together to see what could be done about the matter, but Germany, Belgium, Holland, Spain and Greece would not agree to send delegates even to talk it over, and thus Failure No. 2 went on record in 1876.

Eight years later, in 1884, an International Ornithological Congress was held in Vienna. Many wanted birds protected but quickly found themselves in disagreement as to which were the worthy species, so a Permanent International Ornithological Committee was formed to work out this debatable point. But soon the Chairman and the Secretary developed a war of their own and the Committee never had a meeting.

The Hungarians, under the leadership of Otto Herman, called the Second Ornithological Congress in Budapest in 1891. Many prominent ornithologists were present. Papers were read on bird protection—or the lack of it—in many countries. The Congress requested the Austrian and Hungarian Ministers of Agriculture to bring about an international convention for the protection of birds useful to agriculture. There the matter rested until the 1895 Conference for Bird Protection which took place in Paris.

The French Government now suggested that all interested countries agree to ten clauses regarding methods of capturing or killing birds, caging birds, etc. Three lists or schedules of birds were to be recognized. These were Useful Birds, Winged Game and Noxious Birds. After long discussions a modification of these proposals was tentatively accepted by the delegates of fourteen countries which, however, did not include Great Britain, Holland and Russia. Italy, a short time later, declined to take further part. Soon Switzerland wanted modifications and so did Sweden. Then Austria desired special privileges, and again the whole scheme blew up.

Five years passed and in 1900 the Third International Ornithological Congress met in Paris. The Paris feather merchants and milliners appeared in force to fight for their right to sell the feathers of birds, and things slowed down. Somebody's suggestion that the Governments of Europe be asked to study the food habits of wild birds to ascertain which were beneficial and which were noxious, was adopted. Then every one packed his bag and went home.

However, matters at last were taking shape, and at an official Congress of delegates in Paris on March 10, 1902, an international Convention was signed "for the protection of birds useful to agriculture." The document bore the signatures of the representatives of "His Majesty the Emperor of Austria, King of Bohemia, etc., and Apostolic King of Hungary, in the name of His Highness Prince Liechtenstein as well; His Majesty the German Emperor, King of Prussia, in the name of the German Empire; His Majesty the King of the Belgians; His Majesty the King of Spain, and, in his name, Her Majesty the Queen-Regent of the Kingdom; the President of the French Republic; His Majesty the King of the Hellenes; His Royal Highness the Grand Duke of Luxemburg; His Highness the Prince of Monaco; His Majesty the King of Portugal and Algarbia; His Majesty the King of Sweden and Norway, in the name of Sweden; and the Federal Council of Switzerland."

The document consisted of sixteen Articles and two appended "Schedules." In these we find that it is forbidden at any time "to steal nests and eggs, to take or destroy nestlings," and it is prohibited to sell or purchase such articles. These prohibitions, it was explained, do "not concern nests built by birds in dwelling-houses, or any kind of buildings, on the same or in the interior of courtyards, which may be destroyed by owners, occupiers or any person authorized by the same." Also the restrictions did not apply in the case of the eggs of lapwings and gulls. The wholesale capture of birds was discouraged by forbidding the "construction and employment of traps, cages, nets, nooses, lime-twigs" or other similar instruments. "In case the high contracting parties should not be in a position to enforce the prohibitions" against nets, traps, etc., they "may mitigate the severity of the said prohibitions."

By Article 5, "it shall be forbidden, from March 1 to September 15 of each year to take or kill" the useful birds enumerated in Schedule 1; or to permit the import, delivery, or transport of said birds during this period; although the season prescribed can be modified in the countries of Northern Europe.

Licenses may be issued "to the owners of vineyards, orchards, and gardens, of nurseries, afforested ground or cornfields . . . for the shooting of birds whose presence is harmful and causes real damage."

Provision is made for scientific collecting and "for the taking, sale and keeping of birds intended to be kept in cages." "Winged game" raised on preserves is not included in the provision of the Convention, and such birds on other territory may be taken only with fire-arms and during the hunting season prescribed by law.

In Article 9, we read: "Each of the contracting parties may grant exemption from the enactments of the present Convention,

"1. In the case of birds, the shooting and destruction of which, as noxious to the interests of shooting sport and fishing, is permitted by the Parliament of the respective country;

"2. In the case of birds branded as noxious to the agriculture of the country by the Parliament of the respective State."

The high contracting parties were expected to take steps to have their laws brought into harmony with the provisions of the Convention.

Then followed two schedules. One lists useful birds which should be protected under the Treaty. In part these include eight kinds of owls, all woodpeckers, the common roller, bee-eater, hoopoe, swifts, nightjar, nightingale, wheatear and various warblers, wrens, titmice, flycatchers, swallows, wagtails, pipits, starlings, and white and black storks—about 149 species in all.

Schedule 2 names the noxious birds which were not to be protected. In this is included the bearded vulture, osprey, all kinds of eagles and kites, the goshawk, sparrow-hawk, harriers, and all falcons, except the kestrel. The eagle owl is not accorded protection, neither is the raven, magpie, common jay nor bittern. Condemned also are the gray, purple, and night-herons, the pelican, cormorants, smews, and grebes.

Various insect-eating species were not mentioned in either schedule, as, for example, the golden oriole and the various thrushes. Perhaps the oriole was an oversight but we may assume that the omission of thrushes was intentional, so widely are these birds used for food. It may be noted that under Article 5 birds listed as valuable to agriculture temporarily were not accorded any protection during five and one-half months each year, but it was expected that Governments later would make more restrictive regulations.

The Treaty became operative on December 12, 1905. Thirty-seven years had passed since the German foresters and farmers in 1868 first launched the movement for a treaty to protect European birds. Other countries joined the movement, and by January, 1936, the Treaty was in effect in the following thirteen countries: Austria, Belgium, France, Germany, Greece, Holland, Hungary, Luxemburg, Monaco, Portugal, Spain, Sweden and Switzerland.

Treaties are never satisfactory to every one concerned, and certainly this one has been no exception to the rule. Many leaders in European bird protection feel that it does not go far enough and there have been various attempts to have it revised, or a new treaty adopted. Switzerland, Hungary, Germany, Great Britain, Finland and the Scandinavian countries have been especially outspoken on the subject.

An International Congress for the Study and the Protection of Birds was held in Luxemburg, April 13-16, 1925. I attended this gathering for the purpose of furthering my acquaintance with European bird-protectors and learning all I could about their various problems. One day my daughter Elizabeth served as interpreter during a conversation I had with a gentleman whom I understood to be the State Forester of Belgium. His Government had sent him to Luxemburg to ask me to correct a statement I had published in an American magazine, in which I quoted a Belgian as saying that 6,000,000 small birds were annually netted or trapped in that country. He said it was forbidden to catch small birds unless a netter had a permit, and that from the number of permits the Government had issued the past year it was believed that not more than 3,000,000 birds had been taken legally, and he doubted if more than 1,000,000 had been killed illegally. Would I please correct the erroneous statement that had been made. I assured him that I would do so and I am here fulfilling my promise.

According to his figures it would mean that in Belgium, in 1924, there were captured and used either for caging or for food an average of 500 birds for every square mile of country. Belgium is one of the countries that signed the Paris Treaty for the "protection of birds useful to agriculture." One of the many subjects discussed at the Luxemburg meeting was that of revising the Treaty. A committee was appointed to consider the matter.

During the last session of that Congress, representatives of the Grand Duchess entered and bestowed three decorations. La Marquise de Pierre of Belgium and Jean Delacour each was made a *chevalier,* and to me was given the rank of Officer of the Order of the Oaken Crown. I was told that when attending formal functions in the Principality of Luxemburg, in respect to Her Highness it was expected that I should wear the medal that was given to me with a certificate of the decoration.

At Luxemburg the members of the International Committee had held two conferences. The resolutions we prepared were adopted by the Congress.

In addition to the ornithologists gathered in Luxemburg, I met many other nature-lovers during that trip to Europe. We were the guests of Prince and Princess Francesco Chigi at their fascinating Castle Fusano, near the Mediterranean coast a few miles south of the mouth of the Tiber. The interior walls and ceilings are decorated with paintings placed there before Columbus sailed from Palos. Port-holes formerly of use in repelling Barbary pirates are still available should occasion arise. Two soldiers of stone yet stand guard on the parapets, although moss has gathered on their arms and helmets. The estate covers 4,500 acres, the shooting being chiefly boar, deer, hare, woodcock, pigeon and quail.

We walked in the forest and watched great kites sailing overhead. We tramped among the dunes by the sea, where in the stunted trees were many small birds; we visited the adjoining King's game preserve of 16,000 acres where for the first time I saw wild boars and herds of sambur. As on other occasions, my language difficulty was ever present, but Elizabeth served as interpreter, for which purpose she had accompanied me from over sea. She and the Princess must have become very weary of so much talk about birds and bird protection, but I was having a wonderful time learning about these subjects and making notes of what I was told the Prince was saying.

One day they took us to the ancient Chigi palace at Ariccia where the Prince keeps his collection of mounted birds and bird-skins. He showed me a specimen of a North American bird taken in Italy and beamed with pleasure at my surprise and exclamation—"*Junco hyemalis!*"

We visited the estate where the Princess lived as a girl, but by this time out of long-delayed consideration for the others I had stopped asking questions. In fact, the only thing I learned here was that the firewood which I saw being cut on the estate was sold by the pound.

In Budapest we had long conferences with Titus Csorgey and Jacob Schenk. Then there were the never-to-be-forgotten visits with Dr. Lehn Schioler in Copenhagen, whose great book on the birds of Denmark was nearing completion, and with that very distinguished scientist, Dr. Einar Lonnberg in Stockholm; and in Prague, with Dr. Cavro and Dr. Prochazka. In Oslo we met Dr. Hj. Broch, who was to become Chairman of the Norwegian Section of the International Committee for Bird Preservation when the Section was formed. We talked bird protection with Dr. Brinkmann and Dr. Johnsen in the museum in Bergen, and with Poulsson and Arentz of the Stavanger Museum. In Stavanger I addressed a gathering of the Anglo-Norse Society.

On the steamer going from Norway down to New Castle we traveled with the oceanographer and whale expert, Dr. Johan Hjort, who told us much of his work. I had read that he was "tagging" whales and when I remarked that it must be a man-size job to board whales and put rings on their ankles, he explained that he marked whales with a barbed disk which was shot into them. The wound, he said, was slight and the barb kept the disk in place permanently.

In Harrod's store in London, great numbers of black grouse, wild ducks, partridges, hazel hens, ptarmigans, and quail were for sale on May 1, 1925. In the Cecil Hotel, boiled lapwings' eggs cost thirty cents each. The scales in the lobby registered my weight as "12 stone, 5."

It was decided at Luxemburg that the International Committee should hold a Congress of its own in Switzerland in 1927, but two extended hospital experiences prevented me from taking part in such a plan, and it was not until May 21-22, 1928, that we came together in Geneva. Delegates and guests were present from seventeen countries as follows: Austria 1, Belgium 2, Bulgaria 1, Czechoslovakia 3, Denmark

1, France 5, Germany 8, Great Britain 2, Holland 3, Hungary 3, Italy 3, Japan 1, New Zealand 1, Norway 1, Sweden 1, Switzerland 17 and the United States 4.

In my address at the opening of the Congress, I spoke of man's destructiveness to the birds throughout the world, and enlarged on this under four heads: viz., upland game-birds; ducks, geese and shore-birds; insect-eating and weed-seed-eating species; and birds killed for their plumage.

Official representatives from the League of Nations and from the Institut International d'Agriculture of Rome took part in the much-discussed question as to whether the Committee should request the League of Nations or the Institute of Rome to assume the task of attempting to secure a revision of the Paris Treaty of 1902. After debating the matter stoutly nearly all one day, the delegates by large majority voted that they preferred the subject should be handled by the League. Decidedly my wisest act of Geneva was in getting Jean Delacour, linguist and diplomat, to preside at that heated discussion. I knew this question was coming up at Geneva, and with Mrs. Pearson had visited the offices of the International Agricultural Institute in Rome to talk about it with the gentleman in charge. He was too busily engaged to see us, we were informed. Possibly some one suggested that he had made a mistake, for a few days later I received his apology and a representative of the Institute came to our meeting in Geneva.

It was quite a task arranging for this Congress and looking after numerous details, including a dinner for more than eighty people. Many little occurrences enlivened the occasion, two or three of which I may mention.

Sir Eric Drummond, Secretary-General of the League of Nations, appointed Major A. Buxton to assist me and to serve as "observer" for the League at our sessions. Major Buxton was most helpful in a number of ways. One of his practical aids was to supply a professional interpreter. He said that as presiding officer it was my business to see to it that every one in the room understood all the speeches and that the interpreter sitting beside me would translate into any language I desired any talk that might be made. The first session had not proceeded far when a lady delegate arose and began speaking in a language which I supposed was either French or Flemish. When after a few minutes she paused a moment, I said to Gulloux, the interpreter, in a voice loud enough to be heard by the eighty or ninety people present:

"Please translate into English."

He turned to me in amazement.

"The lady is speaking English," he announced in an even tone.

When a married man makes a *faux pas,* it is instinctive for the miserable creature to look quickly at his wife hoping for signs of forgiveness. I saw Mrs. Pearson, with downcast eyes, sink lower in her chair, and felt sure that Prince and Princess Paul Murat, who sat beside her, were making royal efforts to suppress their amusement.

There was a delegate present from Italy named Borghesani who lauded Mussolini for establishing two great sanctuaries for wild animals. Mr. Leonard Hawksley, who knew Italy as do few Englishmen, at once stated that those sanctuaries had been created years before any one ever heard of Mussolini. Later, to Mr. Hawksley and to me the Italian stated: "When we are away from Italy we must at all times speak strongly for the Fascisti."

Before the sessions began I received a letter from the Chairman of the Austrian National Section of our International Committee, Dr. Eduard Melkus of Vienna, who said that his Government had informed him that it had been approached by the milliner merchants of Austria, asking that he be instructed to perform no act at Geneva which would help place the Congress on record in a way harmful to the millinery trade in birds' feathers. He also warned me that the

AN INTERNATIONAL CONFERENCE FOR BIRD PROTECTION

Delegates from seventeen nations gathered at Geneva, Switzerland, for the fourth meeting of the International Committee for Bird Protection, May 21-22, 1928.

milliners of France and Germany were approaching their Governments on the subject. I was glad to be put on guard but confidently felt the matter could be satisfactorily handled when the time came—and it was.

I shall here record some resolutions which were adopted at Geneva, as they give an idea of the scope of the subjects which were uppermost in the minds of the delegates gathered from Europe, America and Asia. Various representatives present had been sent by their Governments and would be expected to make reports upon their return. Hence, in addition to a number of general resolutions, the following were adopted:

RECOMMENDED FOR OFFICIAL ACTION

1. That a Conference of Government delegates should be summoned either under the auspices of the League of Nations, the International Agricultural Institute at Rome, or in any other way considered appropriate, with full powers to sign an international convention embodying the following provisions:

That to protect migratory birds during the period of their spring migration and while engaged in rearing their young, all shooting, trapping, or other destruction of birds, together with their sale or exposure for sale, shall cease not later than March 1st, in Europe, Asia and North America, and not later than September 1st in countries in the southern hemisphere, and that such prohibition shall continue until the opening of the shooting season in the autumn. In countries north of 53° latitude north, moderate spring shooting of some species might be allowed through government license for about twenty days on account of their different climatic conditions.

2. As an aid towards the attainment of such an international agreement the Conference respectfully invites the International Agricultural Institute at Rome to publish a short report containing a summary of the information in its possession on the value of birds to agriculture.

3. That, as recommended by the preliminary conference of experts from thirteen countries held at Washington in 1926, a conference of government delegates should be summoned for the

purpose of drawing up an international convention on oil pollution of navigable waters, and that it take into consideration the great loss of birds from this cause.

The Conference asks its Chairman to request the Secretary-General of the League of Nations to call the attention of the Council of the League to the recommendations for official action Nos. 1 and 3.

Furthermore, be it resolved that the Chairman of each National Section of this Committee shall be asked at once to communicate with his government and urge that favorable action be taken on the subject of these official recommendations.

Following this Congress there was much publicity in the press throughout Europe regarding our appeal to the League of Nations. We had active friends in the Secretariat and we approached delegates to the League in many countries who pledged their support of the plans we presented, but nothing tangible has yet resulted from these efforts.

Correspondence in connection with the International Committee had been increasing and at Geneva it was decided that acting under Article 3 of the By-laws, the Chairman should appoint a European Secretary. I thereupon named Dr. J. M. Derscheid, of the International Office for the Protection of Nature in Brussels, for this position.

The next gathering of the International Committee took place at Amsterdam, June 2-7, 1930, in connection with the Seventh International Ornithological Congress. Delegates were present from sixteen of our National Sections, and many other visiting ornithologists attended the meetings to hear papers that were presented. The resolutions adopted by the Ornithological Congress were prepared by our Committee. These included a Declaration that "the principle of bounties on the destruction of birds of prey is economically unsound" and it was urged "that the practice be abandoned in all countries where such conditions obtain," that laws requiring the installation of oil separators on oil-driven or oil-burning vessels be enacted by the Governments of nineteen maritime countries, which were named; that all countries of Europe and North Africa were urged to prohibit the import, export or transit of migratory quail; and that countries of Southern Europe adopt laws to protect egrets.

In my address I laid stress on the agencies of destruction that in many forms mankind has let loose upon the wild bird life of the world. I concluded with the statement:

The preservation of wild life is not the problem of any one country alone, it is an intricate international problem. Treaties covering migratory birds of North and South Americas, others dealing with the bird life of Europe and Africa, or the whole of Asia should some day be written large by the law-makers in these countries.

I love the cardinal and the mocking-bird of my own homeland, but the snipe diving through the air over the Norfolk Broads, the ruffs dancing by the road on Texel, the white spoonbills in their reedy home in the Kisbalaton, the mot-mot eternally swaying its tail in the jungles of Panama—all appeal to me as strongly as do the birds that enthralled me in the days of childhood.

The wild bird makes its appeal in all lands, and all may enjoy it. The deaf may watch its flight and rejoice in its brilliant plumage. The blind are uplifted by its music.

We are engaged in a work of inestimable value to mankind. The agencies of destruction are terrific. With united and harmonious efforts much may be accomplished. May we at all times work with the utmost harmony in teaching to others in the world the value of wild bird life, which it is to-day our high privilege to enjoy.

A matter of much importance was the Committee's action in appointing a group to "approach the International Office for the Protection of Nature in Brussels to work out a survey of the present status of bird protection in all European countries." This resulted in the publication, in 1933, of an extensive volume entitled, *Synoptic Summary of Principal Legislative Measures Concerning Bird Protection in Europe and Northern Africa.* Thus, for the first time, there was made available in one language the facts regarding the seasons when birds are protected in a large number of countries.

At various conferences in Europe I have pled for laws throughout the world prohibiting the sale for food of all game-birds not raised in shooting estates, but in this call I have not been supported by even one European delegate.

The Fifth Meeting of the International Committee convened at Oxford University, England, July 5, 1934, at the time of the Eighth Ornithological Congress. The session was well attended. Interesting talks and papers were presented, explaining the advancement of the bird-protection movement. Again the subject of the feather traffic, the pollution of the seas by oil, the need for bird sanctuaries, the evils of indiscriminate slaughter of birds-of-prey, the netting of small birds, the drainage of marshes and the shipment of quail from Africa were brought home to the audience. And again I pounded away on the danger of continuing to permit the sale of wild game, saying, in part: "Various species of wild life are rapidly being swept from the earth because they are subject to constant and increasing slaughter for commercial purposes. When a price is put on the head of any kind of wild bird or mammal that species is placed at once in grave potential danger."

Before leaving England many of the delegates of the Ornithological Congress journeyed in *char-à-bancs* to the coast of Wales, where as guests of the British Admiralty we embarked on two torpedo-boat destroyers and spent a wonderful day visiting the bird islands of Skokholm, Skomer, and Grassholm. To me the most interesting sights were the thousands of Manx shearwaters gathered in Broad Sound as the evening closed down, and the amazing spectacle of 9,000 gannets covering the sloping side of the Isle of Grassholm.

One of the deeply interested ornithologists on this trip was ex-King Ferdinand of Bulgaria. He asked me various questions about the International Committee for Bird Preservation and expressed the hope that, using his name if I desired, I should write to his son, King Boris, and suggest that Bulgaria form a National Section of our Committee. I did so, but without results.

The most recent meeting of our International Committee was held in Brussels, June 11 and 13, 1935. Many of the questions for discussion dealt with European problems and Mr. Delacour presided during much of the two sessions. The matter claiming the greatest attention was the question of a new bird treaty to take the place of the Paris Treaty. This subject had been brought forward by the ornithologists of Sweden, Denmark and Finland. This same question claimed much attention of the Permanent Commission for Migratory Birds of the Conseil International de la Chasse, which was meeting in Brussels about the same time. I attended its sessions as a member of the Commission and as the delegated official representative of the State Department of the United States Government.

This International Hunting Council of sportsmen was founded in 1930. Its work is directed by Maxime Ducrocq and ably assisted by the Secretary, Count W. d'Adix, both of Paris. These gentlemen give virtually all their time and tens of thousands of francs annually to the development of the work for game preservation. In 1935 the Council's membership extended throughout fifty-seven countries and enrolled among its active supporters the Presidents of eighteen Republics.

Another group workng on international lines is the International Office for the Protection of Nature, at Brussels, which was established in 1928. One of the organizations associated with this undertaking is the American Committee for International Wild Life Protection, organized in 1930 with Dr. John C. Phillips, President, and Harold J. Coolidge, Jr., of Cambridge, Massachusetts, the very active Secretary. This Committee is mainly sponsored by leading American natural history museums and zoölogical societies, and was founded largely through the efforts of the Boone and Crockett Club of New York City. It concerns itself with efforts to preserve threatened species particularly of larger mammals in various parts of the world outside the United States. Already it has performed splendid work and has published several valuable pamphlets.

The International Committee for Bird Preservation has a very simple organization. It is in no sense a society whose officers or executive committee in any way control the actions of the representatives of numerous scientific and conservation societies and institutions composing its membership. It is a federation of completely independent units which in their Declaration of Principles have unanimously declared their desire to stimulate a more adequate protection for wild birds throughout the world. Its gatherings are open forums for its members.

Since the inception of the Committee in 1922, bird-protective laws have been passed in many countries. These have not been the result of direct efforts by the International Committee but in many cases their enactment has been largely due to the efforts of members of this Committee working through their own local channels of activity.

The killing of wild birds goes forward with little restraint over much of the earth's surface. The heaviest slaughter is in the Christian countries or is carried on by natives in more uncivilized regions under the stimulus of Europeans and Americans. In Mohammedan countries bird persecution is comparatively light. In England, Germany, Holland, Switzerland and other Northern European countries, birds are widely appreciated and the public interest in their preservation is a great factor in their favor.

We have all heard much of the killing of small birds for food in the south of Europe. In Italy I have seen many blinded birds kept in small cages to serve as decoys to lure other birds to the guns, nets or limed-twigs, where capture and death awaits them. In northern Italy some 1800 elaborate bird-catching devices called *roccoli* are known to exist. Usually these are operated by owners of large estates, for the *roccolo* is a rich man's device. However, restrictions on bird-killing are growing, and a gradually awakening public is beginning seriously to fight the custom of the wholesale trapping of birds that has gone on continually at least since the days of the Cæsars.

The quail of Europe migrate to Africa in the autumn and return in the spring. While in Africa, great numbers are netted either for consumption in the country or for shipment abroad. For example, in the year 1933, 542,000 quail were shipped by rail northward into lower Egypt. Of these 440,450 live birds were shipped from the port of Alexandria. In Italy, France and England their throats were cut and they were sold in the markets, while another hundred thousand were disposed of in the markets of Egypt. This figure does not include an unknown number of birds killed and consumed locally in Egypt.

In 1934 Belgium issued 9,776 licenses to net birds for food or for caging. Conditions are bad for the birds also in Greece, Yugoslavia, southern France and Spain.

But before an American waxes too self-righteous and rises to condemn the practices of some other countries, he might, with propriety, pause and ask in which country and by what people were the passenger pigeon, Labrador duck and heath hen obliterated from the earth. Who was it that all but exterminated the terns and the egrets of a continent for the money their feathers would bring? In what continent have the wild ducks been reduced to their lowest level in history?

In Florida, ibises, spoonbills and young great blue herons are still illegally killed and eaten for food. In Louisiana night herons furnish the "gros bec" dinners enjoyed along many a moss-draped bayou. A few months ago in Arkansas

I talked with fishermen who, in conversation, quite casually referred to their custom of using the flesh of little blue herons, pileated woodpeckers, cardinals and thrushes for baiting their cat-fish hooks. By the roadside in Utah I one day counted the bodies of seven Swainson's hawks that had been shot by passing motorists as the birds, perched on telephone poles or fence posts, sat watching for ground squirrels that are the daily plague of the ranchman.

It is a rather amazing fact that many otherwise well-informed people are ignorant of the game-laws. For example, note the following quoted from the *Evening Star* of Washington, D. C.:

Aboard President's special train en route to Superior, Wisc., August 25, 1928.—President Coolidge to-day, for the first time since the days of his youth in the hills of Vermont, shot and killed a living thing. It was a large crane, caught by him in the act of spearing a trout in the water where he was fishing. He brought the bird down with the second shot of a .38-caliber automatic revolver which he borrowed from Walter Ferguson, one of the Secret Service men in the canoe with him at the time.

This bird referred to as a "crane" was a great blue heron protected by Federal law under the Migratory Bird Treaty Act.

Again, from the New York *Herald Tribune* of December 22, 1936:

Willis Van Devanter, Associate Justice of the United States Supreme Court, was disclosed to-day as a violator of a Federal law. Justice Van Devanter, a member of the Supreme Court since 1911, was hunting with the Rev. Ze Barney Phillips, rector of the Church of the Epiphany in Washington and Chaplain of the U. S. Senate, at the Deep Hole Point Club at Occoquan, Va., when the infraction was discovered. The two men were in a duck blind. A Federal game warden approached and courteously requested their licenses for inspection. The minister's card was correct, but a glance at Justice Van Devanter's permit revealed

they had come in great numbers and brought their wives, their grandmothers and their neighbors.

Large audiences I have always found stimulating, for numbers seem automatically to add enthusiasm. I have formed certain theories about public speaking. For example, one must capture the interest of his hearers within the first two minutes or he may lose them, and then it is serious business to get again their close attention. When during the course of an address a speaker sees the slightest movement among his hearers, he should quickly reach in his bag of tricks and give them a story or a quip or a quirk of some kind, for inattention easily spreads. Finally, it is my strong opinion that, if possible, one should stop when the interest is strongest. I have seen many a man mistake polite attention for intense interest, and talk too long. Better send them away saying, "I do wish he had spoken longer," than have them declaring, "The last half-hour I became a little weary."

One night I was the speaker at the dinner of the annual gathering of the Wild Life League of West Virginia. Before being introduced there was presented for a five-minute talk a guide from the mountains called Rimfire Hemrick. He was a tall, picturesque mountaineer. He began: "When I got here this evening some of these here gentlemen said to me, said they, 'Rimfire, do you ever git lost up in them thar mountains?' 'No,' I told them, 'I've been bothered right smart for two or three days now and agin about gittin' back to my cabin, but I ain't never been lost yit, no sir-ee!'" His speech was a great success.

They may have had trouble getting a speaker for their dinner the next year, for they wired asking me to come again. As I wound through the mountains in a day coach I was introduced by the conductor to the only other passenger, a woman of his acquaintance. She told me her name, her husband's business, and asked for my name, where I was from and where I was going. Upon learning my destination she said that the year before she had attended the dinner of the Wild Life League, and beamingly declared that it was the most interesting entertainment she had ever experienced. She enlarged at great length on the intelligence and oratorical abilities of Rimfire Hemrick. At length I inquired, "Was there any other speaker?"

"Yes," she answered without enthusiasm, "a man made a talk about birds but it was not so good. He talked too long. But I do wish you could have been there and heard Rimfire."

Once after I had spoken to a ship's company in Alaskan waters, two Canadian ladies approached me. Evidently they had never been in the deep South. With sweet seriousness one of them exclaimed: "Oh, I did enjoy your stories so much. I just now said to my friend here, 'That gentleman's Negro talk was so perfect I really expect he has just a little bit of Negro blood in his veins.'"

My long-established rule not to murder defenseless women saved her life.

Through the years the Audubon Association has employed various lecturers to tour the country and speak in schools and before other groups. Among these have been Herbert K. Job, who in 1919 inaugurated and for two years conducted our summer school at Amston, Connecticut; Edward Howe Forbush, William L. Finley, Alden H. Hadley, Winthrop Packard, James Henry Rice, Miss Helen Pratt, M. B. Davis, Bertram Bruestle, Mrs. H. U. Goode, Miss Etta Wilson, Sidney R. Esten, Miss Frances Hurd, Dr. Eugene Swope, Miss Mary Sage, Mrs. Mary E. Wingo, Dr. Henry Oldys, Miss Mary T. Moore, E. V. Visart, S. E. Perkins, III, and J. P. Jensen.

Scores of times we have lent slides and motion-pictures to other speakers to help stimulate local interest.

We have published a very large amount of literature on the habits and values of birds. By the close of 1934 we had distributed 270,000,000 pages of such printed information and more than 53,600,000 copies of colored pictures of birds reproduced from drawings made for us by Brooks, Fuertes, Horsfall, Sawyer and Brasher.

The basis of much of our educational work has been the unique and highly successful undertaking with the organization of children's bird-study clubs. With the $5,000 contributed by Mrs. Russell Sage in 1910 for work in the South, we started the experiment of interesting teachers in forming Junior Audubon Clubs among their pupils. The plan was to furnish each child with a bird-button and a set of Educational Leaflets accompanied with colored plates of birds and outline drawings of these pictures to be filled in with crayons or with water-color paints. Each teacher directing a club received free a subscription to *Bird-Lore*. Each pupil was asked to pay a fee of ten cents on the theory that it would cover one-half of the total cost of handling this work.

The first school year we formed 533 children's clubs with a total enrolment of 10,595 members. Mr. William P. Wharton became interested and was responsible for our receiving a check for $5,000 so that we might introduce the junior work in other states. He said the money had been given by some one whose name he was not privileged to reveal. With this additional assistance the total junior enrolment the next year was 29,369.

Mrs. Sage's contributions continued annually until her death seven years later. The gifts of our unknown benefactor increased each year, until in 1915, it reached the magnificent sum of $20,000. The same amount was provided each succeeding year until 1922, when the donor presented the Association with $200,000 for an endowment. Even since that time, the annual gifts from this source have been very substantial ones. By solicitation we have secured numerous other gifts for the work with the chidren. Some years these have totalled as much as $10,000.

For several years the annual junior enrolment ran to more than a quarter of a million. In 1930 it was 385,845. By October 10, 1934, bird-clubs for children had been organized and operated to the number of 148,917, with a total paid-enrolment of 5,079,559 members.

Many teachers hesitated to organize Junior Audubon Clubs because they knew so little about birds. Clearly, therefore, we should help teachers to receive instruction in bird-study and a good place to reach them was at their summer schools. Early in 1915 I asked permission of the Board to develop some work of this character; then, raising special funds, began seeking for bird-lecturers and for summer-school superintendents who would accept their services.

We engaged for that season Dr. C. Hart Merriam to give a lecture course at the University of California, in Berkeley; A. A. Saunders to teach a bird-study class at the University of Montana; and Dr. H. F. Perkins to teach a six weeks' course at the University of Vermont. Mr. Ludlow Griscom offered two courses, each of six weeks, at the University of Virginia, and Dr. Eugene Swope delivered lectures and conducted field-trips at the State Summer School of South Carolina. Professor R. J. H. DeLoach and Professor C. F. Hodge for two weeks lectured and handled the field work at the University of Georgia, and Dr. G. Clyde Fisher was our representative for a month's course at the University of Florida. I also gave lectures that summer at several places, including the South Carolina State College and the Universities of Vermont, Virginia, Georgia, and Florida. We continued these summer-school courses for five years, and many speakers represented us in twelve or fifteen states.

With the junior members we have held photographic, birdhouse building and essay contests. One year they built and erected 75,000 bird-boxes. The children fed the birds in winter and often put out Christmas trees for them. The Junior Audubon Club work proved successful from the be-

LITERATURE
FOR CHILDREN'S
BIRD CLUBS

Part of one day's shipment
of bird pictures and leaflets
from the office of the National Association of Audubon Societies in 1930.

ginning and the identical plans of operation still remained unchanged after the continuous tests and experiences of twenty-six years.

We have long kept on file the names of available speakers on ornithology, and often have been able to help them secure engagements. We have never permitted any one to pay the Association for recommending his bird-boxes or other merchandise.

To acquaint people with bird-protective laws we have issued many editions of cloth warning notices, which have been placed on display in every state in the Union. In 1914 we issued an illustrated book, *Alaskan Bird-Life,* 10,000 copies of which were given free to the people of that Territory. In 1928, 10,000 sets of twenty bird pictures with descriptive text, and also an eight-page leaflet on the *Value of Alaskan Birds,* were distributed among the population of Alaska. Our educational efforts have been so numerous and so varied it would require an entire chapter to discuss them adequately.

One very difficult problem with which we have long wrestled has been that of securing laws to protect useful hawks and owls, and of educating the public to realize that most of the species of raptores usually are beneficial to man's interests. The fight for these birds began in 1893 with the publication of the book, *Hawks and Owls of the United States,* by Dr. A. K. Fisher. It was issued by the United States Department of Agriculture and in its pages were set forth most of the data then available on the economic value of these species.

Since those days the Audubon Society workers have struggled in Legislatures, and by means of the press, the rostrum, and the radio, to induce people to believe that hawks and owls as a class are well worth preserving. Many references to this work are recorded in *Bird-Lore,* including my extensive trip in Alaska in behalf of the bald eagle in 1927, our eagle bill in Congress in 1930 that was passed by the Senate but not by the House, and many successful undertakings for hawk protection in State Legislatures of the land. The preparation of the book *Hawks of North America,* written by Dr. John B. May under my direction and illustrated by Major Allan Brooks, was completed for the press during my administration.

For the past twenty years and more, laws intended to protect useful hawks and owls have existed in most of the states, but farmers, sportsmen, and others shoot most hawks when opportunity offers. Rarely is any one arrested for killing a protected hawk and often states have paid bounties on any kind of hawk that may be shot.

In the spring of 1934, accompanied by my son T. Gilbert Pearson, Jr., I visited thirty-two of the large quail preserves in North Carolina and South Carolina. Pole-traps to catch birds-of-prey were in operation on many of these estates. Such traps usually catch any bird that lights on them. From the jaws of one on a South Carolina preserve, Gilbert took an unfortunate chuck-will's-widow!

In 1930 a Golf Club Bird Sanctuary Committee was appointed, consisting of Dr. Arthur A. Allen, Bruce Barton, Dr. Frank M. Chapman, Robert T. ("Bobby") Jones, Jr., Grantland Rice, Eugene S. Wilson and the writer.

Dr. Allen was engaged for a year to give half his time to this work. He organized as bird sanctuaries the grounds of a number of golf-clubs, and prepared and widely distributed a bulletin of sixty-four pages, containing 136 illustrations, giving instructions on how to attract and care for wild birds. Also, he made the Association's film entitled "Putting the Bird Into Birdies."

The expense of this undertaking, amounting to nearly $10,000, was borne by Thomas Cochran of New York City, at whose suggestion the enterprise was undertaken.

Of later years numerous other agencies have become active in educational work for wild-life protection. Note, for example, the articles on birds and mammals in the *National Geographic Magazine* and the *Nature Magazine*. Then there have been the Cornell leaflets and the work of various large museums and colleges. The publications of the National Parks Association, founded by Robert Sterling Yard, in 1919, have aided wild-life conservation. The Federation of the Bird Clubs of New England, under the leadership of Laurence B. Fletcher and Charles B. Floyd, has sold to the people of New England the idea of bird reservations.

Another important feature of the Association's work has been the protection of water-bird colonies. I personally sought out most of the islands where sea-birds breed along 3,500 miles of coast from northern Nova Scotia to the Mexican border, and in nearly all that territory our wardens have operated. Also, we have at times maintained guards in Oregon, in the Great Lakes region and at many points inland from North Carolina to Louisiana. We acquired by lease, purchase, or gift: Old Man Island, Maine (1905), Bird Island, Orange Lake, Florida (1910), Buzzard's Island, South Carolina (1913), Green Island, Texas (1921), and Little Duck Island, Maine (1934).

We have been forced to decline many proffered gifts of forest and swamp lands for bird sanctuaries because of our financial inability to guard them properly.

The wide coastal marshes of Louisiana have long been famous as a winter refuge for wild ducks and geese. Senator George P. McLean and I went to some of these marshes in Vermillion Parish in December, 1915, as the guests of M. L. Alexander, State Game Commissioner. Again, in May, 1916, I was through much of this country at the time when Mrs. Russell Sage and the Rockefeller Foundation offered the Association two tracts of marshland totaling 163,000 acres, if we could finance their maintenance as bird sanctuaries.

When Paul J. Rainey, renowned big-game hunter and photographer, died September 18, 1923, my mind reverted to a wild-fowl shooting preserve that he and E. A. McIlhenny owned in this region. Learning that Mr. Rainey's sister, Mrs. Grace Rainey Rogers, was heir to his estate, I suggested to her that she present this territory to the Audubon Association with an endowment for its upkeep, and we would preserve it as a sanctuary especially for the wild ducks and geese resorting in the region. The thought appealed to her and she tried to buy Mr. McIlhenny's one-third ownership, but he declined to sell. The property, therefore, was divided and Mrs. Rogers deeded to us the 26,161 acres she received as her two-thirds interest. Our contract with her was signed June 18, 1924. She provided for guarding the sanctuary until 1927 when, as originally planned, she gave the Association a special endowment to cover taxes and help in the upkeep. This amounted to $156,786.

The number of wild-fowl spending the winter in the region was very great although market-hunters and sportsmen had been laying heavy tribute to them for many years. An unusually competent superintendent, Richard Gordon, was soon in charge. One permanent assistant, with others at times, was employed to guard and patrol the property on which we have continually made improvements. In winter hundreds of bushels of rice have been fed to keep the ducks on the sanctuary as much as possible. Two near-by game preserves baited their shooting blinds and thus competed with us for the duck population.

The Rainey Sanctuary is in the center of the winter range of the blue goose, from 20,000 to 40,000 of which are often seen on our property, always accompanied with a few lesser snow geese. Muskrats, minks and raccoons abound, and in common with the adjoining state wild-life refuge and those purchased by Mrs. Russell Sage and the Rockefeller Foundation, we deemed it necessary to keep these undesirable tenants in check, as authorized by Mrs. Rogers in her deed of gift.

A person without practical experience in such matters would be amazed at the numbers of these animals to be found in the lowlands of Louisiana. Using the most humane traps available, which at the same time were effective, there were taken during the short legal trapping season of the next eleven years, 3,683 mink, 3,024 raccoon, and 267,792 muskrats. To exterminate them was, of course, impossible, but surely enough were destroyed to furnish some relief to the birds that came to us. The furs were sold and the income greatly aided in developing the sanctuary. Also, by this means the Rainey Sanctuary Endowment Fund received additions that raised it to $200,000.

Some people voiced their objections to the Audubon Association's permitting the trapping of muskrats that destroyed goose food and tunneled holes in the levees, and the taking of mink and raccoons that prey upon the wild life. The Directors, therefore, engaged Dr. Robert K. Enders, the zoölogist, to study the situation and advise whether our course was wise. The examinations were made in December, 1933. His studies convinced him that control measures were highly desirable, and the Board accepted his report as conclusive.

Among the many visitors to the Rainey Sanctuary have been various distinguished naturalists. In our comfortable headquarters may be found a library of useful bird-books. Among them is a pamphlet telling of the establishment of the sanctuary and giving a list of 142 species of birds that had been found within its boundaries. On January 21, 1935, the Board of Directors voted to discontinue all control efforts of wild animals on the Rainey Sanctuary; however the removal of injurious species is encouraged on some of the other bird reservations operated by the Association.

For many years we lent a hand here and there to help reëstablish the American bison whose teeming millions had all but vanished. However, the agencies mainly responsible for saving it from extermination have been the American Bison Society, of which Edmond Seamore is the leading spirit, certain departments of the Canadian and United States Governments, and a handful of public-spirited individuals.

In 1905 only about 970 bison were left. In 1933 a census revealed their number to be 21,701. To-day there are more than we know what to do with. Every year of late the United States Biological Survey and the National Park Service have been inviting people to take surplus bison off their hands. In Canada from time to time it has been found necessary, in order to keep the buffalo herds within the grazing capacity of their range, to reduce their numbers. During the sixteen years ending in January, 1936, Canadian bison to the number of 12,257 were destroyed under the direction of government agents. At the present time the bison seems to be in no more danger of extermination than is the deer, coyote, or English sparrow. "Save the Buffalo" is a cry no longer heard in the land.

It is generally believed that formerly prong-horned antelope were as numerous on the Western plains as were their great shaggy neighbors. However, they were not slaughtered wholesale as were the bison for their hides and tongues, but prospectors, Indians, sheep-herders, and other riders of the range, pursued them for food, even after all the Western states had passed laws to protect them. Of recent years government, state and private enterprise have stayed the killers' hands and the fleet and the beautiful creature is again increasing in numbers.

In 1923 I had a talk with Dr. E. W. Nelson about the antelope situation, and we agreed on a joint course of action. I wrote to many men and asked if they would attend a conference on the subject; and Nelson agreed to have a census made of the existing antelope population. The result was a well-attended meeting in Washington on December 14th, at which Dr. Nelson reported that 22,000 antelope were living in small scattered bands in sixteen Western states. It was decided that all present would support the Audubon Association in an attempt to establish a Federal antelope preserve on the public domain in Lake County, Oregon. The American Bison Society had tried the same plan a few years before, but hostile local sentiment in Oregon had defeated the undertaking. Recently ranchers of the region had agreed to support such a measure, and as guests of the Audubon Association two of their leaders had been brought to the Washington meeting.

We, therefore, felt hopeful of success, but as it turned out, the Oregon State Game Commission and the owners of the nomadic sheep herds that enjoyed free grazing on the public domain, were able to defeat our plan. Several years later the State of Oregon became aroused and established a guardianship for these animals that has caused their numbers to show an encouraging increase.

In the summer of 1927, while riding the semi-desert wilds of Nevada with E. R. Sans of Reno, he told me of the Last Chance Ranch in the northwest corner of the State, which still contained many antelope. However, the owners were wanting to sell and there was grave danger that the ranch would pass into the hands of sheep-men. "And this will mean the end of these antelope," Mr. Sans said grimly. He told me that he had tried desperately to get various people and societies to buy the ranch for an antelope sanctuary but had been turned away by all parties.

That autumn, by consent of the other directors of the Audubon Association, I acquired possession of this property of 380 acres on December 24, 1927, taking it over on a five-year option to purchase for $7,500. The area was reported to contain the only permanent springs in a territory of one hundred square miles, and he who controls the water in a thirsty land is master of the desert roundabout. Early in September of the next year, Mr. Sans took me from Reno 200 miles over roads that in places were thrillingly precarious and just at night we reached a small four-room stone house which was the one dwelling of the Last Chance Ranch. Coyotes howled, horned owls hooted, but we were soon asleep.

The next morning before sunrise Sans awoke me. "Look out of the window," he said.

Eighty feet away at the spring were three antelope and five mule deer. When I opened the door they fled up the hill through the sage-brush. At a two-strand barbed-wire fence the antelope dropped to the ground and, without a pause, shot under the wire. The deer, of course, sailed over the top like meadow-larks. That day we visited our four springs. In the flats and on the sage-brush slopes I counted 130 antelope and many sage hens.

Some time later in New York I wrote Kermit Roosevelt, Secretary of the Boone and Crockett Club, that I wanted to talk with him about the antelope in Washoe County, Nevada. Over the luncheon-table I showed to him, George D. Pratt and Childs Frick photographs of the region I had visited and told them of the marvelous antelope sanctuary which the Audubon Association was creating. There were six additional holdings of unfenced privately owned sage-brush hills and dales that we should possess. It was well known that the Boone and Crockett Club, founded by Theodore Roosevelt in December, 1887, was interested in the protection of game animals, and I asked whether among its 175 members there were not those who might like to contribute to the success of our undertaking. My hearers were interested and soon Childs Frick became Chairman of a special committee to consider my proposition.

On November 9, 1928, I wrote Mr. Frick expressing the hope that his club would coöperate with the Audubon Association in helping to raise $20,000 to insure the project, and mentioning that the area might be called the Charles Sheldon Memorial Sanctuary. The late Mr. Sheldon had been a prominent member of the Boone and Crockett Club and a director of the Audubon Association.

The next spring Mr. Sans joined me in Washington and we paid a visit to the Public Land Office. This resulted in an Executive Order by President Hoover, dated June 20, 1929, by which certain public lands in Nevada, covering an area of 30,720 acres, were "temporarily withdrawn from settlement." It was within this boundary that the Last Chance Ranch and certain other privately owned lands were situated.

Soon after this, Mr. Frick advised me that the Boone and Crockett Club members would guarantee half of the $20,000 which I estimated would be the cost of completing the sanctuary for antelope. I then authorized Mr. Sans to begin purchasing for the Audubon Association the remaining private holdings we desired, and turned my attention to the task of raising the rest of the money needed to complete the project.

On January 26, 1931, the area that had been withdrawn from entry was, by a second Executive Order, declared to be the Charles Sheldon Wild Life Refuge.

For four and one-half years the Audubon Association maintained strict warden service over the territory at an additional cost of $7,190, and on October 13th, 1932, we gave to the Biological Survey our Nevada lands consisting of 2,375 acres, as a present from the National Association of Audubon Societies and the Boone and Crockett Club.

The Biological Survey has developed the sanctuary by building adequate headquarters, improving the springs and surrounding the entire property with a wire fence, which keeps out wandering cattle and horses, but permits the passage of antelope. No shooting has been reported. Coyotes, naturally, continue their depredations. Mr. Ernest J. Greenwalt, who has been the warden on the refuge since the early days of the Association's ownership, reported in 1930 fifty-five antelope killed by these predators. The sage-grouse are sorely persecuted for both by day and by night four-footed and winged enemies come for their cess.

Despite the losses from natural causes, the wild life of the sanctuary is in flourishing condition. Three thousand prong-horned antelope at some time of the year occupy the territory.

In compliance with the advice of the Biological Survey, President Roosevelt on December 21, 1936, greatly extended the sanctuary so that it now includes approximately 573,000 acres, and this covers not only the summer but also the winter range of the Sheldon antelope herd.

In January, 1936, Ira N. Gabrielson, Chief of the Survey, advised me that there were not less than 60,000 antelope in the United States, which is three times the number reported by Nelson thirteen years before.

Of our big-game animals, deer alone exist in large numbers to-day. It seems safe to assume that there are some tens of millions of the three species—white-tail, mule, and Columbia black-tail.

Black bear are common in some places but in most of the United States they have vanished along with blanket Indians and wolves. There are reported to be 50,000 in the National Forests, 2,000 in our National Parks, and, of course, there are many others in the swamps and mountains of our broad country. Grizzlies are few and are becoming scarcer, although Montana, due in large part to the protection afforded by the Yellowstone Park, claims about 800.

We read in a report of F. A. Silcox, Chief of the United States Forest Service, that in 1935 there were some 18,511 mountain-goats and 12,924 big-horn sheep in our National Forests. The sheep, at least, appear to be decreasing. Mr. George M. Wright of the National Park Service, in February, 1936, advised me that two of the parks contained a total of 1,217 mountain-goats and that big-horns to the number of 805 are living in six of the parks.

Of elk there appear to be enough to insure the continuation of the species and in some places surplus animals are hunted every autumn. Moose are gone from the greater portion of their former range in the United States but there are still some thousands of them, especially in Minnesota, Montana and Wyoming.

The above figures do not include any of the big-game animals in Alaska, Canada or Mexico.

The Audubon Association is much interested in the welfare of these important mammals and at different times has been able to perform notable service in their behalf.

No man in American political life during the past fifty years more stimulated the minds of his countrymen than did Theodore Roosevelt. When he passed away on January 6, 1919, the emotions of the nation were deeply stirred. Soon several Roosevelt memorials were started. The first one was launched by the Audubon Association.

On the morning of January 23, 1919, I met with the Executive Committee of the Audubon Association and suggested that we establish a memorial to Mr. Roosevelt in the form of a bird-fountain, as he had always entertained a deep interest in ornithology and at the time of his death was President of the Long Island Bird Club that encouraged people to care for birds. My suggestion was adopted and together we prepared a list of those to serve with me on a committee to issue a call for funds. We invited Howard H. Taft, John Burroughs, Henry Fairfield Osborn, Gifford Pinchot, Ernest Thompson Seton and twenty-eight others, all of whom accepted, and before the effort was finished more than $16,000 had been collected.

For a time we were at a loss for a fitting location for our memorial. On October 18, 1923, W. Emlen Roosevelt, cousin of Colonel Roosevelt, deeded to the Association eleven and one-half acres of land, surrounding on three sides the little Young's Memorial Cemetery at Oyster Bay, Long Island, N. Y., where Theodore Roosevelt lies buried. Dr. Eugene Swope of Cincinnati was asked to take charge of developing the area as a Roosevelt Memorial Bird Sanctuary, and he began his residence at Oyster Bay, January 1, 1924. The association leased a house adjoining the property and here Dr. and Mrs. Swope have made their home.

The land given to us had been the dumping-ground for many of Oyster Bay's tin cans, baby carriages, bed springs and old automobiles. Poison ivy densely covered acres of ground and thick masses of these troublesome vines had grown upward and enveloped more than 1,200 of the trees. In these forbidding surroundings, Dr. Swope began his work and gradually the area developed into a bower of beauty. This settled our problem as to a suitable situation for the fountain and on May 26, 1927, it was unveiled. In the audience were Mrs. Roosevelt and many friends and admirers of the late President. Several were from a distance, including Mrs. Elizabeth Marmon who had come from her home in Indianapolis to be present.

During the ceremony, Dr. Swope told of the development and usefulness of the sanctuary. Dr. Chapman spoke on "Roosevelt, the Bird-Lover," and George K. Cherrie told of his trip with Roosevelt on the River of Doubt. In my talk as representative of the donors of the fountain, I stated that it was thought most fitting for the Association

... to erect some tangible memorial to the great friend of the cause which we espouse. ... The plan has materialized in the form of a bird-fountain, cast in bronze, standing here at the entrance of the Roosevelt Bird Sanctuary, which this Association owns and hopes to maintain for all time as a place consecrated to the happiness of wild birds and as an object lesson to those who would learn the practical means of attracting birds about their homes. We hope ever to keep the birds singing over the grave of Theodore Roosevelt whose great spirit looks down upon us from the brow of yon near-by hill.

The gifts of more than two thousand of our members and friends made possible the erection of this fountain executed by Bessie Potter Vonnoh.

The Roosevelt Sanctuary has been one of the Association's very successful projects. Approximately 30,000 people annually enter the Court of the Fountain. Every year hundreds of earnest visitors are conducted through the sanctuary by Dr. Swope, who points out to them the extensive plantings of berry-producing shrubs and the many devices in operation for attracting and protecting the birds. The house occupied by the Swopes, together with the plot of ground surrounding it, at my solicitation were added to the Sanctuary by gift from the Trustees of the Young's Memorial Cemetery in the spring of 1934.

Perhaps because the Audubon Association has been the most outstanding wild-life organization in securing continuous public support, and for the further reason that it had long lived within its means, I have been asked many questions about its business affairs, some of which I shall mention briefly.

When it was founded, provision was made for a Board of thirty Directors. In 1908 the number was reduced to eleven, and in 1933 it was raised to fifteen. The following named men and women have served as Directors for the time indicated after each name:

DIRECTORS OF THE AUDUBON ASSOCIATION

Horace M. Albright, 1933–
Joel A. Allen, 1905–1921
Harold E. Anthony, 1935–
H. P. Attwater, 1905–1909
John H. Baker, 1933–1934
Roger N. Baldwin, 1934–

E. H. Baynes, 1915–1920
W. J. Blakely, 1905–1909
Frank Bond, 1905–1910
William Brewster, 1905–1912
Herman C. Bumpus, 1905–1911
S. T. Carter, Jr., 1905–1906

Frank M. Chapman, 1905–
Jay N. Darling, 1936–
Mrs. E. B. Davenport, 1905–
1909
Ruthven Deane, 1905–1909
William Dutcher, 1905–1920
Jonathan Dwight, 1908–1929
Guy Emerson, 1936–
Isaac N. Field, 1905–
William L. Finley, 1905–1908
William H. Fisher, 1905–1909
W. W. Grant, 1910–1911
George Bird Grinnell, 1905–
1931
Alphonso Hodgman, 1905–
1907
Ralph Hoffmann, 1905–1908
Carlton D. Howe, 1907–1909
Dryden Kuser, 1920–1935
Mrs. C. Grant LaFarge, 1905–
1909
Aldo Leopold, 1935–
F. A. Lucas, 1907–1929
Mrs. Kingsmill Marrs, 1905–
1908
Heloise Meyer, 1920–1936
Frank M. Miller, 1905–1908

Robert C. Murphy, 1921–
J. J. Murray, 1934–
A. H. Norton, 1905–1908
Frank R. Oastler, 1928–1936
Theodore S. Palmer, 1905–
1936
George Panitz, 1905–1907
T. Gilbert Pearson, 1905–1934
John C. Phillips, 1936–
Kermit Roosevelt, 1934–
George B. Sears, 1905–1909
Charles Sheldon, 1912–1915
Witmer Stone, 1905–1908
Abbott H. Thayer, 1905–1908
John E. Thayer, 1905–1909
Mrs. E. M. Townsend, 1934–
1935
Mrs. Carll Tucker, 1930–
W. Scott Way, 1905–1909
Fay Welch, 1936–
Alexander Wetmore, 1929–
1935
William P. Wharton, 1915–
R. W. William, Jr., 1905–1908
Mrs. Mabel O. Wright, 1905–
1928
Mrs. Robert C. Wright, 1936–

The first Chief Clerk employed in the office in 1905 was B. S. Bowdish. He was followed by Ernest Ingersoll, and later by Walter McMahon, who was killed in France during the World War. Mr. John Holman was with us for some time, and Alden H. Hadley came to the office in February, 1926. Mr. Ernest G. Holt was Director of Sanctuaries in 1932 and 1933. He was followed in this position by Robert P. Allen, who had been with the Association since 1930. Mr. Irving Benjamin, able bookkeeper and accountant, has had charge of the office business details since 1922. Many other men and women as clerks in various capacities during the years of my chief responsibility bore much of the burden of the daily office-routine.

The Audubon Association has never worked on the theory that it should be financed by state organizations, which in turn should draw their support from local chapters. Our business connection with other Audubon groups has been of the simplest nature. Until recently state and local organizations were received to membership by paying the same fee as does an individual. The largest enrolment of affiliated groups was in 1921. That year they numbered 154, of which 23 were State Audubon Societies. At times some of the affiliated groups have made gifts to the national work, and often the Association has financially aided them in their efforts.

During the first thirty years of the Association's history the total number of people and organizations enrolled as sustaining members with an annual fee of five dollars, approximated 25,450. Constantly there were losses from death, resignation, delinquency, and sometimes by transference to the life-membership class. On an average a sustaining membership lasted about four and one-half years. The highest paid-up enrolment of annual sustaining members during any one year was 8,303 in 1930.

When the Audubon Association was incorporated, *Bird-Lore* was selected as its organ. Dr. Frank M. Chapman, the owner and the editor, agreed to provide space for our articles and reports, and to furnish subscriptions for our members at cost of production.

Members sometimes complained because our notes on bird-protection matters were printed in small type in the back of the magazine, and never displayed prominently in larger type in the main body of the publication, but our arrangement with Dr. Chapman rendered this course necessary. I approached him on the subject of buying *Bird-Lore* for the Association and changing its policy so that articles on conservation might be more conspicuously presented, but he did not care to sell the publication and felt also that *Bird-Lore,* as it stood, was performing an important function in encouraging people to study birds, which, of course, was quite true.

One day in 1915, needing some data I had seen in an outdoor magazine, I sent a messenger to the New York City Public Library to copy the notes for me. He returned with the statement that the magazine was not available, and further reported that *Outing* was the only current outdoor magazine in the library that was anything like complete. Various inquiries soon convinced me that at no place was an effort being made to accumulate and preserve such publications. As much of the history of game protection is to be found in these magazines, I became impressed with the idea that the building of a library on wild-life conservation was a duty which the Audubon Association owed to the students of to-day and those of the years to come.

I brought from my home all the outdoor magazines, reports of State Game Departments, leaflets of State Audubon Societies and most of my ornithological journals that I had been saving for years. By correspondence and by visits to old bookstores and elsewhere, I began the accumulation of much additional historic material on wild-life matters. The policy of binding these into volumes and placing them on our shelves has since been continued.

In our library one may find one of the two known complete sets of the *American Field* since its founding in 1876. Also there is here every number of *Forest and Stream* printed during its lifetime, which ran from 1873 to 1930. This magazine contains hundreds of ornithological notes published before the *Auk* was established. Particularly proud am I of an almost complete set of the magazines, circulars, announcements and miscellaneous papers issued by the State and local Audubon Societies since that name came into existence in 1886. Every publication issued by the Biological Survey during its history has carefully been collected, and until the more recent issues, these have been bound in book form.

This gives only a slight suggestion of what the Association's library consists to-day. For several years students have been visiting the offices of the Association to study this historic material, and their numbers are increasing annually.

Frequently to the Board of Directors and at times to the membership of the Association, I spoke of the need of a building to serve as a home for the Association. Some of the Directors examined several residences in the West Seventies, thinking it might be wise to invest a portion of our endowment funds in buying and renovating one of them. However, the idea was discarded for a house only twenty-five feet in width was considered unsuitable for our purposes. At length in December, 1922, at my request, the Board authorized a call for subscriptions with which to acquire suitable headquarters. In telling of the kind of building for which we were asking money, our announcement explained the need for an adequate fireproof structure to house our large and rapidly growing library of conservation and natural history, space to exhibit bird paintings and photographs, a museum of conservation, apparatus for attracting birds, an assembly-hall, and more office space and storeroom facilities.

We began mailing these appeals in January, 1923, and by the 1st of March had received 173 gifts totaling $2,925. We kept working on the problem year after year. I was much encouraged by the fact that one gentleman indicated a willingness to duplicate the fund when it should reach $100,000, but when this mark was passed in 1930 our generous friend was no longer living. By October 10, 1934, subscriptions to the number of 21,572 had been made to the building fund. And now after the passage of fourteen years since we began this effort my dream is not yet realized, although every year the fund grows a little larger. Sometimes as I see in the mirror the reflection of my graying hair, I wonder if I shall live long enough to enter the portals of the "Temple of Conservation" of which I have so long dreamed.

The amount of work that a public-spirited organization is capable of performing is usually dependent to a large degree upon its financial strength. Many a well-intended effort fails from lack of money. I felt that it was of prime importance to build an Endowment Fund of sufficient size to insure the Association's permanency, and with this idea the other members of the Board were in entire accord. There were three ways we might hope to accumulate an endowment—by gifts, by bequests, and by life-membership fees. We appointed a finance committee, but it brought in no money. Our field-agents, as a rule, said that they were not able to raise funds and usually, I think, shrank from such a disagreeable undertaking. My duty in the matter was clear; I must raise the money myself.

For the endowments we received some gifts, but not many. The two outstanding ones were the contributions of Mrs. Grace Rainey Rogers, and an unknown benefactor to whom I have already made reference. I spoke to many people about bequeathing money to the Association and some of the legacies we have already received came from those who promised to act on the suggestion. Until the close of the fiscal year in 1934, the Association had been a beneficiary under fifty-five wills to the total amount of $731,632.

From life-membership fees of $100 each, $290,100 were collected and added to the endowment during my administration. When I became the executive officer in October, 1910, our Endowment Funds amounted to $350,845. Unexpended funds for specific purposes were $4,590. There was a deficit of $7,780 in the general working-fund account.

During the first year of my financial responsibility, we paid off our deficit. During the twenty-four years that I was the executive officer we never closed a fiscal year with a deficit in any of our various working funds, but instead always showed a surplus. At the time of my retirement from the Presidency in the autumn in 1934, the certified accountants attested that our Endowments amounted to $1,514,527. In addition to this the Building Fund stood at $133,769. Also, there was $20,000 "reserved for contingencies" and a cash surplus of $21,136 for starting the next year's current expenses. The total cash income (without duplications) of the National Association from the date of its founding in January, 1905, to October 10, 1934, was $5,058,790.

Some societies devote a large part of their resources to officers' salaries. I knew one national wild-life organization that expended more than 65 per cent of its income in this way. The Audubon Association's record is that only one officer has ever been paid for his services and his total remuneration during a period of thirty years averaged slightly over 5 per cent of the organization's income.

The years between 1911 and 1934, crowded with duties, were rich with delightful experiences. It was during this period that the most of my modest writings were produced— *The Bird Study Book, Tales from Birdland,* parts of some other books, and many magazine articles, bulletins, reports, leaflets and circulars, on hawk protection, depredations of cats, the need of being conservative and broadminded in our work, and numerous other subjects. *The Birds of North Carolina,* prepared in collaboration with Messrs. H. H. and C. S. Brimley, was ready for the press in 1913. A few days before it was to be distributed fire swept the establishment of the State Printer in Raleigh and the book was destroyed. Only a galley proof and the blocks for the twenty-four color-plates were preserved. New illustrations to the number of 275 were drawn and the work of resetting the text was begun, but further delay prevented its publication until 1919.

I have formed many pleasant connections and have been associated continually with men whose interest in the preservation of our country's wild life has been most encouraging. One group particularly stimulating to me is the Conservation Committee of the Camp Fire Club of America, of which I have long been a member. Since 1909 it has worked on numerous projects, including many legislative activities. At its monthly dinners, presided over by William B. Greeley, the current problems of conservation are discussed in detail. Various members at personal expense make long journeys in order personally to study problems in the field.

One of the latest angles to the wild-life preservation movement has arisen largely from the teachings of Aldo Leopold and Herbert L. Stoddard who so forcefully have been proclaiming the gospel of game management by the restoration of attractive environment both for swamp and upland species. The possibilities for useful efforts in this direction are almost limitless.

In the autumn of 1934 I retired from the executive duties of the National Association of Audubon Societies and became its President Emeritus. Mr. Kermit Roosevelt was chosen President and John H. Baker became Executive Director. Younger men have taken on the duties of guiding the destinies of the Audubon Association, which will be called on to help solve those problems of wild-life preservation that shall arise with the passing years.

The past year and more my time and thought have been given to the work of the International Committee for Bird Preservation. It is most desirable that those countries which have been neglectful of their wild life should be given the benefits of some of the lessons which we in North America have learned, often to our great sorrow. Furthermore, the interests in Canada and the United States are considerably at stake. Recently I have found from a study of the laws in other American countries that in virtually all of these countries to the south of us, our birds that migrate there in winter are without legal protection. Thus, in various regions many of our song-birds, more than twenty kinds of ducks, and forty-one species of our shore-birds may be shot at will after they have migrated beyond our southern borders.

In June, 1936, for the eighth time in succession, my associates in five continents honored me with the election for a two-year period as Chairman of the International Committee for Bird Preservation. Our Committee in December, 1936, consisted of 219 members, representing 138 leading scientific and wild-life conservation organizations, that compose the National Sections in the following twenty-seven nations: Argentina, Australia, Austria, Belgium, Bulgaria, Canada, Czechoslovakia, Denmark, Ecuador, Finland, France, Germany, Great Britain, Hungary, Italy, Japan, Mexico, Netherlands, New Zealand, Norway, Poland, Rumania, Sweden, Switzerland, Union of South Africa, United States, Yugoslavia.

The work of the Committee in continental Europe is handled largely by Leon Lippens, Secretary, and his assistant, Dr. Tordis Graim, of the International Office for the Protection of Nature, in Brussels. They have the constant coöperation of Jean Delacour of France and of Dr. P. G. Van Tienhoven of The Netherlands. The past year that office has been very active in sounding public sentiment in European countries on the advisability of adopting a new European international treaty for bird protection, to include North Africa, as proposed in 1935 by the delegates of the Scandinavian nations.

The Committee's efforts in the countries of the British Empire are conducted from the London Zoölogical Gardens in Regent's Park by Miss Phyllis Barclay-Smith, Sub-secretary, with the active backing of Dr. Percy Lowe, eminent ornithologist of the British Museum. The past year they have been much occupied with the extensive task of making a survey to determine the extent of the present wild-fowl supply in Western Europe, and have been urging the delegates to the League of Nations to adopt methods to prevent oil pollution on the high seas.

The preservation of the bird life of any nation is not merely a domestic problem, but is one that affects the interests of many countries between which there should exist active coöperation in this vast and important undertaking.

Since the days of my childhood in the piney woods of Florida, great changes have come over the public mind in our country regarding its duty to the wild birds and mammals. I feel that I am one of the most fortunate of men to have been able to follow closely the halting—and at times perhaps the stumbling—steps of a people which in time have brought them to a point of vantage where many of the natural beauties of earth are more clearly discernible. With equal pleasure I am to-day eagerly watching the signs of similar developments in countries widely scattered throughout the earth.

It was probably because of my efforts rather than from any special accomplishment that in 1924 I was recalled to the University of North Carolina, where from the hands of its President, Dr. Harry W. Chase, I received the degree of Doctor of Laws conferred by my Alma Mater.

And now let us gratefully recall our debt to the hosts of unnamed men and women whose moral and financial support have made possible many of the accomplishments for wild-life preservation, some of which are recorded in these pages.

INDEX

Acklen, Colonel J. H., tests migratory bird-law, 280

Adams, Dr. C. C., speaks in Washington, 351

Adams, William C., on Legislative Committee, 296; on Federal Advisory Board, 310; address in Washington, 351

Akeley, Carl, meeting with, 38

Alaska, bird books and cards, 427

Albright, Horace M., a valuable aid, 326; in Everglades, 328; with Senate Committee, 329; Audubon Society, Director, 439

Allen, Arthur A., works with golf clubs, 428

Allen, Joel A., first meeting with, 71; works for bird protection, 258; officer of Audubon Association, 209; Director, 439

Allen, Robert, on Maine coast, 231; Director of Sanctuaries, 440

American Bison Society, 312; when founded, 133; Edward Seamore, President, 432

American Forestry Association, 312

American Game Protective Association, 234, 345-357

American Ornithologists' Union, Committee on Bird Protection, 73, 216-217

American Planning and Civic Association, 312

American Wild Fowlers, organizing of, 369

Andresen, August H., sponsors sanctuary bill, 302

Antelope, protection of, 432; number in 1923, 433; failure to protect in Oregon, 433; preserve in Nevada, 433-436; number in 1936, 436

Anthony, Harold E., Director of the Audubon Association, 439

Arbib case, 268-270

Archer, Florida, Pearson family's arrival, 1

Arrigoni Degli Oddi, Count, guest of, in Padua and Bologna, 388

Attwater, H. P., Director of the Audubon Association, 439

Audubon Bill, passage of in South Carolina, 149

Audubon Law of North Carolina, passage of, 87

Audubon Society, opposed by Currituck hunters, 122-123; agreements with milliners, 259

Audubon Societies, National Committee formed, 214; see also National Association of Audubon Societies

Audubon Societies founded, first one, 127; Georgia, 141; Louisiana, 220; Missouri, 146; North Carolina, 67; New York, 209; South Carolina, 137

Aunt Ann, lends Pearson money, 59

Aunt Celie, 8

Aycock, Governor Charles B., message of, 78

Bag limits on ducks, 307-309

Baker, John H., Director of Audubon Association, 439; Executive Director, 446

Baldwin, Roger N., Director of the Audubon Association, 439

Baldwin, Stanley, oil polution, 379; visits A. Thorburn with Pearson, 380

Barclay-Smith, Phyllis, sub-secretary, International Committee, 447

Barker, E. J., and the Cuban flamingoes, 95-396, 399

Bauknight, Charles, 4

Richard, Alfred, of Neuchatel, Switzerland, 386
Ridgway, Robert, meeting with in Washington, 35
Ringland, Arthur, and Yellowstone Park Boundary Commission, 324, 327
Roberson, Westcott, sponsors Audubon Bill in North Carolina, 76, 79, 86
Roberts, Thomas S., meeting with, 71; sportsman and bird protector, 215
Robin, campaign for protection of, 201-203
Rockefeller, John D., and Jr., purchases of at Jackson Lake, 326
Rockefeller Foundation, offers Louisiana lands, 429
Roosevelt, Franklin Delano, letter from, 223
Roosevelt, Kermit, consults with, 434; elected Audubon Association President, 446
Roosevelt, President Theodore, signs bill, 243; creates 51 bird reservations, 257; calls first Conservation conference, 345
Roosevelt, Theodore, Jr., Assistant Secretary of Navy, 350
Roosevelt Sanctuary, 437-439
Root, Elihu, suggests bird treaty, 276
Royal Society for Protection of Birds, 272, 378
Rutledge, R. H., regional forester, 325

Sage, John H., meeting with, 71
Sage, Mrs. Russell, donation for robin protection, 201; for children's work, 203; offers Marsh Island, Louisiana, 429
Sans, E. R., works for antelope sanctuary, 433-435
Saunders, A. A., teaches bird-study, 426
Sawyer, E. J., paints robin picture, 201

Schauver, H. C., his case goes to Supreme Court, 280-281
Schenk, Jacob, of Budapest, 387; visits Kisbalaton, 387, 408
Schioler, Lehn, in Copenhagen, 408
Schlemmer, Max, great feather dealer, 250-252
Sclater, William L., at Ornithological Club dinner, 381; at Mrs. McKenna's, 382
Scott, George E., patron of Walton League, 362
Scott, Lady, in London, 378
Selover, George, Chairman of Izaak Walton League's Board, 294; illness of, 296
Senate Committee on Conservation of Wild-Life Resources, F. C. Walcott, Chairman, 312
Seton, Ernest T., aids Shields, 344
Sharpe, Sir Montague, 381
Sharpless, Isaac, at Haverford, 58
Shaw, George Bernard, speech in Queens Hall, 380-381
Shea, James, handles New York plumage bill, 182; belief of, 191; shows skylark head, 193
Sheldon, Charles, prominent sportsman, 350
Sheldon Antelope Sanctuary, 433-436
Shields, Colonel G., meeting with in New York, 129; edits Recreation, 337; President of League of American Sportsmen, 336-344; lectures, 344; death of, 344; credit due to, 345
Shields' Magazine, 344
Shipp, T. R., Secretary of National Conservation Association, 346; editor, 347; gives assistance, 348; opinion of, 348
Shiras, George, III, his bill in Congress, 275; his brief, 279; credit due to, 288
Shore-birds, slaughter of, 52
Skeele, Mrs. H. B., arranges lecture, 139
Slattery, Harry, Secretary of National Conservation Association, 348; his opinion of Association's value, 349

(1)

H 1107